The Asian American Movement

In the series

Asian American History and Culture,

edited by Sucheng Chan

WILLIAM WEI

The Asian American Movement

 Temple University Press / Philadelphia

Temple University Press, Philadelphia 19122
Copyright © 1993 by Temple University. All rights reserved
Published 1993
Printed in the United States of America

The paper used in this publication meets the minimum requirements of American
National Standard for Information Sciences—Permanence of Paper for Printed Library
Materials, ANSI z39.48-1984 ∞

Library of Congress Cataloging-in-Publication Data
Wei, William, 1948–
    The Asian American movement / William Wei.
      p.   cm.—(Asian American history and culture series)
    Includes index.
    ISBN 1-56639-049-4 (alk. paper)
    1. Asian Americans—Politics and government.   2. Asian Americans—Social
conditions.   I. Series.
E184.06w44   1993
305.895′073—dc20   92-29438

To my daughter, Leslie Ann

Contents

Preface

"What are *you* going to do for the Movement?" an Asian American sister of the Maoist persuasion wanted to know. "I am going to write a history of the Movement" was my spontaneous reply. Clearly, I had erred in her eyes, for she looked at me with disbelief and disappointment. I suspect that she expected an Asian American brother who had participated in some of the same political struggles to express an interest in working on one of the many social issues being discussed at the Midwest Asian American conference we were attending at the University of Wisconsin, Madison, in that fall of 1974. I suppose the "politically correct" thing to do would have been to fall back on some appropriate saying, such as "serve the people." But I did not. Instead, I had, without fully realizing it, committed myself to writing a history of the Asian American Movement. This book is a fulfillment of that commitment.

The decision to begin this book came after I gave a guest lecture on the Asian American Movement in Russ Endo's sociology class on Asian American communities at the University of Colorado, Boulder, in fall 1984. Russ and I went to the Student Union to drink some coffee and reminisce about our student activist days at the University of Washington, Seattle, and the University of Michigan, Ann Arbor. In the course of the discussion, I mentioned that someday I intended to write a book-length history of the Asian American Movement. Russ said that he had considered writing a similar work. I suggested that we write it together. The time was right; over fifteen years had passed, providing the historical perspective necessary for such a scholarly study.

Unfortunately, my friend and colleague Russ Endo experienced personal problems. His troubles were such that he was unable to do much work on the book and eventually was forced to drop out of the project altogether. This left me with sole responsibility for doing most of the research and writing all the chapters.

From the beginning, I made several decisions that shaped the study. Los Angeles, San Francisco, and New York City were selected as the principal research sites, because they were the places with the most Movement activity and were cities that could be reached on my limited resources. From these three locations I was able to take side trips to such places as Sacramento, Washing-

ix

ton, D.C., and Boston. I thought about doing research in Hawaii, since some of the early activists were originally from there, and as Franklin Ng later reminded me at the Ninth National Association for Asian American Studies Conference in San Jose, much of the early materials used in Asian American Studies dealt with the islands and their diverse Asian American population. Besides, any excuse to visit such a beautiful place was worth considering. But I concluded that the Asian American Movement in Hawaii was, in many respects, unique from that of the mainland and deserved a book of its own.

In terms of the scope of the study, I decided that it should begin with the late 1960s and end in the present, which turned out to be, more or less, fall 1991. Even today, Asian American activists are emphasizing the need for a pan-Asian consciousness and an inter-Asian coalition to attain the basic goals of racial equality, social justice, and political empowerment. Originally, I had planned to pay equal attention to all the ethnic groups and social classes that made up Asian America. But in the course of my research it became evident that though in principle the Movement embraced all Asian ethnic groups and crossed socioeconomic lines, in practice it was a social movement dominated mainly by middle-class, second- and third-generation Chinese and Japanese Americans.

While Filipino and Korean American activists were present from the start of the Asian American Movement, they were not as visible as their Chinese American and Japanese American comrades, because it was not until the 1970s that their numbers increased through immigration. Understandably, recent Asian immigrants and refugees have been preoccupied with economic survival and social adjustment. Those who have been politically active have been involved in "homeland" issues, such as the corrupt Marcos regime in the Philippines, the legacy of a divided Korea, the establishment of communist regimes in Southeast Asia, and the religious divisions in South Asia, with little time for and interest in the Asian American Movement. But that is changing. As they produce a second generation, more and more of them are becoming involved in the Asian American Movement. Consequently, one of the important issues today is whether Chinese Americans and Japanese Americans are willing and able to share power with the leaders emerging from the other Asian American communities.

Perhaps my most significant decision was to base this study on materials generated by the Asian American Movement itself and on interviews of individuals who had participated in it. Because I wanted the research to be a dynamic process, interviewees cited in the text or notes were sent a draft for comment. It was a time-consuming and paper-intensive process, but a worthwhile one, for many of them sent back critical comments and important information. I presume that those who declined to respond thought the reconstruction and explanation of events were satisfactory. It should be noted that a few interviewees asked to be anonymous, lest they offend erstwhile comrades, and some demanded that any reference to their comments be expunged because they disagreed with my interpretation of the Asian American Movement. All such requests were honored.

This work has taken far longer than I had originally planned; however, in spite of some unexpected problems and changed circumstances, I decided to carry on because of my firm conviction that the Asian American Movement is a significant but overlooked part of our history. It was one of the ethnic-consciousness movements that emerged during the 1960s and became integral to the ongoing movement to change the United States from a predominantly monocultural society into an authentic multicultural one. As such, it is part and parcel of the struggle to attain the ideal of an American cultural democracy.

Acknowledgments

I am grateful to Sucheng Chan, the general editor of this series, and Judy Yung, my closest friend and colleague, for carefully reading the entire manuscript and offering incisive criticism and copious comments. Being the first-rate scholars that they are, both of them raised significant questions, helping me think through many of my ideas. Thanks also go to Janet Francendese, Joan Vidal, and the rest of the editorial staff of Temple University Press for taking the manuscript in hand and turning it into this book; and to Bob Hsiang, Connie Hwang, and Corky Lee, visual interpreters of the Asian American experience, for the use of their photographs.

I also wish to thank my University of Colorado colleagues Lee Chambers-Schiller, David L. Gross, Robert D. Schulzinger, and Thomas Zeiler for the conversations that we had on the social movements of the 1960s; Gladys Bloedow, Kellie Matthews-Simmons, Pat Murphy, and Betty Jo Thorson for furnishing the kind of staff support that makes scholarship possible in the academy; and Nancy Mann for editorial assistance.

Financial support for this work was afforded by the Rockefeller Foundation, and the University of Colorado's Council for Research and Creative Work, IMPART program, and the Committee on University Scholarly Publications. Research support was rendered by the Asian American libraries at the Berkeley and Los Angeles campuses of the University of California, and the Federal Bureau of Investigation, which supplied documents requested through the Freedom of Information Act. Needless to say, the comments and conclusions in this study are my own, and not necessarily those of the above-mentioned institutions.

Chapter 3 is a revision and expansion of a paper presented at the University of California Forum on Asian American Women, Berkeley, 5–7 June 1987. Chapter 5 is a revision and expansion of Russell Endo and William Wei, "On the Development of Asian American Studies Programs," in *Reflections on Shattered Windows: Promises and Prospects for Asian American Studies*, ed. Gary Y. Okihiro et al. (Pullman: Washington State University Press, 1988), pp. 5–15.

Without the cooperation and assistance of a great number of people, research for this study would have been impossible. I owe a debt of gratitude to Dale Minami and Diane Yen-mei Wong, Harlan Himel and Barbara Takei, Yuri and Bill Kochiyama, Feelie Lee and Alan Grinnell, Tony Marshall, Fred Dow, David Monkawa, and Dean Toji for extending the hospitality of their homes during my field trips. I am also indebted to the following individuals for sharing with me their personal experiences in the Asian American Movement or providing me with materials about it:

Kevin Acebo	Thomas Chinn	Neal T. Gotanda
Chris Aihara	Helen Choi	Philip Kan Gotanda
Marilyn Alquizola	Chris Chow	Kwang-woo Han
Richard Aoki	Peter Chow	Eric Hayashi
Shoshana Arai	Curtis Choy	Pat Hayashi
Nancy K. Araki	Judy Chu	Shotaro Hayashigatani
Susan Asai	Anni Chung	Phil Hays
Daniel Begonia	Chuong Hoang Chung	Harlan Himel
Amado Y. Cabezas	Malcolm Collier	Alex Hing
Jeff Chan	Dorothy Cordova	Ray Hing
Sucheng Chan	Henry Der	Lane Hirabayashi
Susan Chan	Arthur Dong	Irene Hirano
Yuen Ying Chan	Fred Dow	Fred Wei-Han Ho
William Chandler	Russ Endo	Sasha Hohri
Barbara Chang	Pat Eng	Becky Hom
Madeline Chang	Yen Le Espiritu	Nancy Hom
Phyllis Chang	Angie Fa	Patricia H. Horikawa
Tisa Chang	Chrys Fa	Bob Hsiang
Wilson Chen	Marian C. Fay	Thomas Hsieh
Lucie Cheng	Colleen Fong	Mary Li Hsu
Fay Chew	Norman Fong	Floyd Huen
Fay Chiang	Michael Friedly	Jackie Huey
"Charlie" Chin	Isao Fujimoto	Chris Huie
Frank Chin	Margaret Fung	Connie Hwang
Gordon Chin	Warren T. Furutani	David Hwang
Kenny Chin	Lillian Galedo	Yuji Ichioka
Laura Chin	Marguerite Gee	Kazu I. Iijima
Rocky Chin	Mutya Gener	Momoko Iko
Frank Ching	Daniel Gonzales	Denise Imura

Georgette Imura
Lloyd Inui
Caryl Ito
Karen Ito
Bruce Iwasaki
Miya Iwataki
George Kagiwada
Gary Kawaguchi
Akemi Kikumura
Elaine Kim
Eugene Kim
Oaksook Kim
Tom Kim
Yoon Hee Kim
Aichi Kochiyama
Bill Kochiyama
Yuri Kochiyama
Doris W. Koo
Loretta Kruger
Norbert Kumagai
June Kuramoto
Stewart Kwoh
Him Mark Lai
Chuck Lee
Corky Lee
Feelie Lee
Louis Hop Lee
M.B. Lee
Mae Lee
Margi Lee
Pat Lee
Robert Lee
Virgo Lee
Russell Leong
Peter Leung
Ginger Lew
Genny Lim

Susie Ling
Mini Liu
Robert Liu
Ted Liu
Juanita Tamayo Lott
Ray Lou
Miriam Louie
Pat Luce
Harold Lui
John Lum
Linda L. Lum
Mary Lum
Stanford M. Lyman
Linda Mabalot
Nobu McCarthy
Wayne Maeda
Diane Mark
Fay Chew Matsuda
Minako Maykovich
Dale Minami
Norman Y. Mineta
Nobuko Miyamoto
David Monkawa
Jeff Mori
Sandy Mori
Mike Murase
May Nai
Robert A. Nakamura
Don Nakanishi
Roy Nakano
Penny Nakatsu
Joyce Nako
Phil Tajitsu Nash
Irene Natividad
Franklin Ng
Mae Ngai
Viet Nguyen

Alan Nishio
Anne Okahara
Marian Okamura
Gary Y. Okihiro
Jim Okutsu
Glenn Omatsu
Michael A. Omi
Kenneth Ong
Priscilla Ouchida
David Oyama
Gin Y. Pang
Linda Y. Peng
Wei Chi Poon
Jean Quan
Katie Quan
Sarah Reyes-Gibbs
Carlton Sagara
Peggy Saika
Dale Shimasaki
Yoichi Shimatsu
Young Shin
R. A. Shiomi
Jane Singh
Herbert Sue
Andrew I. Sun
Betty Lee Sung
Brenda Paik Sunoo
Judy Tachibana
Dana Y. Takagi
Jerrold Takahashi
Ronald T. Takaki
David K. Takashima
Barbara Takei
Shih-ying Tan
Julie Tang
John Kuo Wei Tchen
Shiree Teng

Dean Toji

Casi Tolentino

Maeley L. Tom

Chris Tomine

Te-kong Tong

Pauline W. Tsui

Mayumi Tsutakawa

Kathy Owyang Turner

Karen Umemoto

Eileen Voon

Yori Wada

L. Ling-chi Wang

Nora C. Wang

Colin Watanabe

Mike Watanabe

Penny F. Willgerodt

Lyle ("Butch") Wing

Alan Wong

Charles Pei Wong

Diane Yen-Mei Wong

Eddie Wong

Eleanor S. S. Wong

Elena B. Wong

Germaine Q. Wong

Joyce Wong

Sau-ling Wong

Emily Woo

George K. Woo

Merle Woo

Parker Woo

Odoric Wou

Robin Wu

Robin C. C. Wu

Vivian Wu

Karen Yamamoto

Tohru Yamanaka

Qris Yamashita

Alan Yee

Harold Yee

James Yee

Monona Yin

Jean Yip

Steve Yip

Teddy Yoshikami

Evelyn Yoshimura

Liz Young

Eleanor Yung

Judy Yung

The Asian American Movement

Introduction

Each group of Asians in America has had a long history of fighting for equality and justice, using its members' common cultural heritage and ethnic identity as the basis for collective action. Chinese, Filipino, Korean, and Japanese have all mobilized their compatriots by appealing to shared values and customs, in a common language. On this basis they have engaged in labor struggles, initiated litigation in the U.S. courts, participated in "homeland" politics, and shared other activities to defend their interests. But the small size of each Asian ethnic group limited its effectiveness. Not until the civil rights movement of the 1960s exposed the pervasive problem of racism in U.S. society and raised questions about exactly how democratic the nation's political system in fact was did members of the various Asian ethnic groups begin to think of themselves, and to act politically together, as Asian Americans. Thus was the Asian American Movement born.

Among the last of the "ethnic-consciousness movements," the Asian American Movement has been essentially a middle-class reform movement for racial equality, social justice, and political empowerment in a culturally pluralist America. It has functioned as an inter-Asian coalition that embraces the entire spectrum of Asian ethnic groups, acknowledging their common experiences in American society and calling for a higher level of solidarity among the groups. Central to its existence has been a new sociopolitical entity called the Asian American, for although the coalition reflects its members' diversity as Chinese Americans, Filipino Americans, Korean Americans, Japanese Americans, and other kinds of Asian Americans, it also affirms their unity with other Americans. The concept *Asian American* implies that there can be a communal consciousness and a unique culture that is neither Asian nor American, but Asian American. In defining their own identity and culture, Asian Americans bring together previously isolated and ineffective struggles against the oppression of Asian communities into a coherent pan-Asian movement for social change.

The Movement, as it was popularly called, began in the late 1960s and was primarily the result of the convergence of two historical developments: the emergence of a generation of college-age Asian Americans and the public protests surrounding the Vietnam War. The first wave of Asian immigration produced few Asian American children, for exclusion laws effectively limited the ability of most Asian immigrants to establish families in the United States.[1] Those who were able to do so found it difficult to provide their offspring with an adequate education because in many places the children were forced to attend segregated schools or the parents had to establish their own schools.[2] But the eventual elimination of discriminatory laws and the baby boom of Asian American children in the United States during the immediate post–World War II period eventually resulted in a significant number of college-age Asian Americans by the 1960s. In 1970, 107,366 Asian Americans were enrolled in colleges and universities.[3] Of that group, 83 percent were Chinese Americans and Japanese Americans. Except for a few activists from the working class, these Asian American college students made up the majority of Movement activists and were the Movement's main driving force.

These Asian American activists reached adolescence during one of the most difficult periods in U.S. history. The murders of President John F. Kennedy in 1963 and his brother Robert F. Kennedy and Dr. Martin Luther King, Jr., in 1968 sent the nation into a state of shock. Following Dr. King's death, riots exploded in urban ghettos across the land. All the while, the U.S. military was sinking deeper and deeper into the quagmire of the Vietnam War. Moved by a mixture of moralism and idealism, Asian Americans participated in the civil rights, New Left, women's liberation, antiwar, and other movements organized to change the country. But it was mainly the antiwar movement that brought them together psychologically and politically, making them aware of their "Asianness," their membership in a pan-Asian community, and the need for an Asian American Movement (see Chapter 1).[4]

In the beginning, Asian Americans participated in the antiwar movement as individual protestors; later, they joined "Asian contingents" of major demonstrations and Asian American antiwar coalitions that were founded across the country. They began in earnest to organize across Asian ethnic lines to oppose the war. To a certain extent, the formation of these Asian American antiwar coalitions was fortuitous, since the college-bound Asian Americans began arriving on campuses in large numbers just as the black liberation movement and the New Left student movement dovetailed in opposition to the Vietnam War. As antiwar activists, Asian Americans contributed a unique perspective that emphasized the racial underpinnings of the conflict overseas and linked it to the oppressive conditions in their communities. But they soon became estranged from the antiwar movement, which treated them as "token" members and ignored the issues and concerns they raised, making them realize the need for their own movement for social change.

Even though the Movement has been an integral part of the Third World[5] effort to establish an equitable society in the United States, it has remained socially invisible. *Lau* v. *Nichols*, a 1974 landmark case involving non-English-speaking Chinese students who filed a successful suit against the San Francisco Board of Education for failing to provide equal educational opportunities for all students, mandated bilingual–bicultural education in the United States, yet Asian Americans are rarely acknowledged for taking this major legal step toward defending the rights of limited-English-speaking students and for "recognizing the pluralistic nature of our society."[6] More recently, one of the five key Supreme Court cases that "limited the rights of plaintiffs in job discrimination cases and stirred public outrage that eventually moved Congress to pass the . . . [1991] Civil Rights Act"[7] involved Asian Americans, but that too has hardly been noticed. In *Wards Cove* v. *Atonio*, the mainly Filipino American workforce filed suit against an Alaskan cannery for engaging in discriminatory employment practices that one U.S. Supreme Court justice characterized as bearing an "unsettling resemblance to aspects of a *plantation economy*."[8] Yet, a provision of the 1991 Civil Rights Act excluded the two thousand Wards Cove cannery workers from any changes under the legislation, shielding the employers from liability for unfair employment practices. The Northern California Asian Pacific American Labor Alliance has begun a broad campaign to support legislation to repeal this provision.

The nature of the Movement was one reason for its lack of visibility. It lacked a nationally known leader, such as Dr. Martin Luther King, Jr., was for the civil rights movement, Malcolm X for the Black Power movement, Rodolfo "Corky" Gonzales for the Chicano movement, or Russell Means for the American Indian movement. The Movement had charismatic leaders, to be sure, but they were usually prominent only within a local area or particular Asian ethnic group. The diversity of the Asian American population made it difficult for people to rally around a single figure. The Movement also lacked an ideology or even a plan of action to attract and unite a following. The groups that sought to develop such an agenda and plan, especially Maoist groups, failed to capture the popular imagination. The Asian American Movement's invisibility was also a result of its small size. As a result of discriminatory immigration policies and antimiscegenation laws, the Asian American population was only 878,000 in 1960 and 1,369,000 in 1970—less than 1 percent of the total U.S. population.[9] Within such a small population, the proportion of Asian American activists was actually quite large.[10]

The obscurity of the Asian American Movement is also related to the dichotomous nature of race relations in the United States. Traditionally, the question of race has been addressed and understood mainly as a black and white issue, even though the United States has four major racial minorities with similar histories of oppression. Understandably, African Americans have received the most attention because of the widespread public awareness of their history of exploitation as slaves, their large proportion in the American population, and their long and visible struggle to achieve equality. Because their large numbers seem to threaten the dominant society, a concern that can be traced back to pre–Civil War days when the southern population lived in constant fear of a slave insurrection, African American issues have been taken more seriously than those of other minorities. Asian Americans, in contrast, have been ignored because of their small numbers and little-known history of labor exploitation and resistance to oppression. Having finally disarmed the imagined threat of the so-called Yellow Peril with a series of Chinese exclusion laws, the "barred zone" clause of the 1917 Immigration Act, and the 1924 Immigration Act, all of which excluded Asian laborers from the United States, European Americans expected that the Asians among them would eventually disappear. Furthermore, even though many Asian Americans have had forebears in this country for several generations, they are still perceived as foreigners, physically and culturally, whose issues and concerns are therefore irrelevant to the rest of society. Contradictorily, they are also perceived as the country's "model minority," that is, the one group to have successfully integrated into American society despite seemingly insurmountable racial barriers. Presumably, they have been able to accomplish this because of cultural values that were similar to those of European Americans.

Given the absence of national leaders, the lack of a set of specific aims, the small number of participants, and the common assumption that U.S. race relations involve mainly blacks and whites, it is reasonable to ask whether the Asian American Movement can be called a social movement, that is, an effort by "unconventional groups that have varying degrees of formal organization . . . to produce or prevent radical or reformist type of change." [11] I would argue that it can. As this study shows, Asian Americans, a group that has historically stood outside the institutionalized framework of American society, addressed significant social issues, participated in a plethora of political activities, and started numerous organizations in order to change the country into an authentic ethnically pluralist one. Though their organizational formats varied, the ultimate goal of all these groups was the same: to gain greater equality for Asian Americans. Moreover, in the early years of the Movement, when many Asian Americans participated in antiwar activities, their protests were national in scope.

One consequence of its invisibility is that the Asian American Movement has been overlooked in the literature on social movements.[12] Asian American activists have received short shrift even in works that mention significant events in which they have played a major role. A case in point is Stewart Burns's *Social Movements of the 1960s: Searching for Democracy*, which omits any mention of Asian Americans in the Third World strike at San Francisco State College: "Fighting institutional racism, black and Chicano students at San Francisco State, backed by white radicals, sustained the longest student strike ever, punctuated by police battles almost daily." [13] David Caute, in *The Year of the Barricades: A Journey through 1968*, does somewhat better and makes this single reference to Asian Americans: "At this stage the radical specter at San Francisco State was expanded by a new force, the Third World Liberation Front (TWLF), composed of Orientals and Latinos." [14]

Nevertheless, recent books on Asian American history are starting to consider certain aspects of the Movement. Sucheng Chan, in *Asian Americans: An Interpretative History*, discusses recent political activism; and Diane Mei Lin Mark and Ginger Chih, in *A Place Called Chinese America*, depict social changes in the Chinese American community.[15] But others continue to ignore the Asian American Movement. According to L. Ling-chi Wang, Ronald Takaki's *Strangers from a Different Shore* and Roger Daniels's *Asian America: Chinese and Japanese Since 1850* are flawed by their failure to include the Movement.[16] He notes with dismay Takaki's "silence on the historic emergence of 'Asian America' in the late 1960s and early 1970s," especially since the "genesis of the Asian American movement is the turning point in our history in this country." [17] Takaki, however, argues that he implicitly deals with the Movement when he talks about some of the outstanding issues and concerns of the post–World War II era: "Actually my book does analyze and highlight the movement for justice for Vincent Chin and also the movement for redress and reparations. The final chapter is entitled, 'Breaking Silences,' as a tribute to contemporary Asian American movements." [18]

Aside from books, a number of essays focus explicitly on the Movement. [19] Two early essays published in the alternative Asian American press include Amy Uyematsu, "The Emergence of Yellow Power in America," and Paul Wong, "The Emergence of the Asian-American Movement." [20] Uyematsu's article first appeared in the October 1969 issue of *Gidra*, an Asian American underground newspaper, and was later reprinted in *Roots: An Asian American Reader*. In it she discusses the reasons for the emergence of the Movement, its relationship to the Black Power movement, and its relevance to Asian Americans. Besides explaining its existence, she seeks to encourage Asian Americans to participate in it. Those doing so must challenge two common assumptions: "first, that the Asian Americans are completely powerless in the United States; and second . . . that Asian Americans have already obtained 'economic' equality." [21] Uyematsu concludes that "the use of yellow power is valid, for Asian Americans do have definite economic and social problems which must be improved." [22]

Wong's article appeared in the fall 1972 issue of *Bridge* magazine. He too discusses the origins of the Movement, focusing on salient features and internal contradictions. Wong acknowledges the influence of other social movements but also attributes its emergence to certain external factors, such as the country's "imperialist foreign policy" and the resistance of Asian nations to that policy. Moreover, he asserts that in contrast to the white radical and other racial-minority movements, the Asian American Movement is the only one that is an integral part of the "Asian peoples' struggle for liberation" with strong ties to Asian nations. That is debatable. Except for the fact that its participants were of Asian ancestry, there is little evidence to support the assertion that the Movement had ties with Asian nations. In any case, both Uyematsu and Wong provide useful overviews of the Movement in its formative years.

There are also two essays about aspects of the Movement that were published in professional journals: Ron Tanaka, "Culture, Communication and the Asian Movement in Perspective," and Richard J. Jensen and Cara J. Abeyta, "The Minority in the Middle: Asian-American Dissent in the 1960s and 1970s." Tanaka tries to develop a model for "self-determination in communications," with particular emphasis on the Japanese American community. Tentatively concluding that the Asian American Movement is an "intermediary stage in the integration of Sansei into a larger American conceptual framework," he implies that the Movement, like Japanese Americans, will probably disappear into the wider society.[23] While the statistics on outmarriage suggest that Japanese Americans may very well become an extinct ethnic group,[24] this is hardly true for other Asian Americans, nor does Tanaka take into consideration interracial marriage among particular ethnic groups within the Asian American community.

Jensen and Abeyta examine the rhetoric of the Asian American Movement to propose a "refinement of theories on social movements through the addition of a pre-inception stage to current theories."[25] They argue that because the Movement was unable to transform the self-image of some members of the community, it remained in an embryonic phase of development and a localized phenomenon. As this study argues, however, the Asian American Movement was and is a national phenomenon, following the geographic contours of the Asian American population, and has created a viable Asian American consciousness, especially among young people. There have been nationwide campaigns to defend the civil rights of Asian American victims such as Chol Soo Lee, imprisoned for a murder he did not commit, and Vincent Chin, murdered by two unemployed autoworkers who mistook him for a Japanese, as well as national mobilization around significant Asian American community issues such as immigration policies and media stereotypes.

Finally, in 1989, on the twentieth anniversary of the San Francisco State College strike, *Amerasia* published an issue celebrating the Asian American Movement. Its centerpiece is Karen Umemoto, " 'On Strike!' San Francisco State College Strike, 1968–69: The Role of Asian American Students." In addition, there is a potpourri of essays on various aspects of the Movement, especially the relationship between the campuses and the communities, and a variety of answers to the question "What have we learned from the 60s and 70s?" by people who participated in the Movement. The volume was intended to be a salute to past Asian American activists and, presumably, to inspire future ones. But, it did not contain a history of the Asian American Movement, though the editors noted that one was sorely needed.

This book aims to fill that gap. I present a social history of the Asian American Movement from the late 1960s to the beginning of the 1990s and argue that the Movement was and is an effort to realize the ideal of a culturally pluralist society. From its inception, the United States has been made up of many ethnic groups, each with its own world of symbols and standards, and the country still aspires to develop a society where these groups live in cooperation and harmony. In fact, tolerance is touted by many Americans as one of its national virtues and is manifest in its national motto, E Pluribus Unum (Out of Many, One). Americans consider it consistent to express a strong ethnic *and* national identity. But this ideal has been an elusive and contradictory one, especially for racial-minority groups, in American history, with its stories of contention and conflict. Yet the past has taught Asian Americans and other ethnic groups the paradoxical lesson that in order to be an integral part of American society and to interact with others on equal terms, they must first become an autonomous and empowered people. Only in so doing can they become real members of the nation; otherwise, they face a bleak future of continued marginalization.

For Asian Americans and other people of color, equality has been difficult to attain because they have had to cope with one of the most oppressive systems of racial prejudice and class domination that has ever existed in any democratic country, the ideals expressed in the American creed notwithstanding. They have been excluded from the nation's economic and political life. In discriminating against them in the workplace, the dominant society has made a hypocrisy of the belief that America is the "land of opportunity," which has always been central to its national ideology; in denying them political participation and legislative representation, the nation has made a mockery of its democratic ideals. In spite of these disadvantages, racial minorities have had the will and resources to organize themselves to advance their own interests, as the achievements of the civil rights era testify. Though there has been a backlash in recent years—efforts to undermine the Civil Rights Commission and dilute affirmative action programs come to mind—American society, for the most part, has accepted the legitimacy of these interests and has grudgingly accommodated them. But constant vigilance by racial minorities is necessary to protect their interests. People of color have had to point out repeatedly that racial subordination is inconsistent with the nation's cherished value of equality and to demand that the government serve all its citizens. For Asian Americans, the Movement has been the primary vehicle for advocating their rights in an ethnically pluralist America.

As this study shows, the Movement has sought to change the existing power relations between Asian Americans and European Americans, and the racial presuppositions that undergird them. Since few people willingly relinquish power, the Movement, through organized opposition, has become one way of wresting it from the dominant group. The Movement has also challenged the prevailing perception that Asians in America are members of an exotic and inferior race, which historically has been a social construction to justify the subordination of Asian Americans and the power and privilege of European Americans. Those in control see opposition as a threat to the nation's well-being (erroneously equated with their own) and the liberalization of society (believed to be at their expense) as undermining its foundations. In reality, the persistent pursuit of racial justice and the successful reduction of racial inequalities have validated American democracy and its ideals, helping to transform this nation into a truly multicultural society.

As a social history, this work locates the beginnings of Asian American political activism and its coalescence into the Asian American Movement, highlights the salient aspects of the Movement's development, and assesses its significance in Asian American history. While the Third World strike at San Francisco State College in November 1968 was a defining moment in its history, the Movement did not begin there and then diffuse throughout the nation, as is commonly assumed. During the late 1960s, Asian American activists on other campuses and communities also responded to the significant issues and concerns of the period, quite independently of what occurred at San Francisco State. Gradually, these activists recognized that they belonged to a racial minority subordinated by and separated from the dominant society by race-based policies and practices, rejected their previous efforts at assimilating into that society, and reaffirmed their right to an autonomous ethnic identity in a culturally pluralist society.

A major aspect of this book is an evaluation of the Movement's effort to develop a unique but cohesive ethnic identity. Asian Americans attributed their individual and group powerlessness, in part, to the dominant society's control over and manipulation of their identity and culture. Conversely, they believed that a prerequisite for attaining power was the development of an identity and culture they could call their own. Political activists sought to eliminate stereotypes that degraded Asian Americans, impugned their dignity as people, and influenced the way they were treated in society and even the way they perceived themselves. Demanding, instead, portrayals that reflected their individuality and humanity, Asian Americans have unearthed authentic historical information and created positive images to replace the dehumanizing stereotypes. Whether the existing ethnic culture gives adequate support to an Asian

American identity remains a matter of considerable controversy within the Movement.

Equal attention is given in this study to the Movement's attempt to institutionalize itself by founding counterinstitutions on campuses and in communities. Activists set up Asian American Studies courses and programs in colleges and universities, as well as community-based organizations in Asian ethnic enclaves. They wanted curricula to discuss the experiences and contributions of Asians to America; to determine the various economic and political forces that brought them to these shores but moved them to the margins of mainstream society; and to examine their race, class, and gender relationships to European Americans. They wanted the revised curriculum to benefit the Asian American community. At the same time, activists founded agencies that provided human services and scarce resources as well as addressed significant issues and concerns in the community. But assessments of these academic studies and community organizations have often depended on whether one has a reformist or revolutionary perspective on the Movement.

One of the themes that runs through this study is the rivalry among political activists for the hearts and minds of Asian Americans. Though they espouse many different political philosophies, activists can be classified as either reformers or revolutionaries. Acting on their awareness of themselves as Asian Americans, reformers established community-based organizations as a source of countervailing power that would increase Asian Americans' influence on the wider society and advance their interests more effectively. Revolutionaries, in contrast, were committed to scrapping the current social order altogethe., considering it irredeemably corrupt. They believed that Asian Americans could be empowered only through the overthrow of the capitalist system, which was, in their eyes, inherently racist. For this purpose, they established Maoist sects. But by the middle of the 1970s, instead of working toward the revolution, they lapsed into sectarianism, vying for power in the radical community and fighting each other over the "correct political line," while their rivals, the reformers, were learning to function effectively within the American political system.

What follows is the story of the Movement and the significant role it has played in the Asian American quest for a meaningful place in this ethnically pluralist nation. That story properly begins with the emergence of Asian American activism in the Asian ethnic communities and college campuses of the United States during the late 1960s.

1 Origins of the Movement

I looked in the mirror,
And I saw me.
And I didn't want to be
Any other way.
Then I looked around,
And I saw you.
And it was the first time I knew
Who we really are.
—"Something about Me Today"
  A Grain of Sand music album

During the late 1960s, Asian American political activism began spontaneously in different places, at different times, and with different perspectives. On the West Coast, it began when community activists focused attention on the wretched conditions of San Francisco's Chinatown and campus activists protested the absence of their historical experiences in college and university curricula. From these demonstrations came a plethora of community-based organizations providing much needed social services to the Asian ethnic communities and campus organizations offering vehicles for Asian American student activists throughout the western seaboard to participate in protest politics. On the East Coast, political activism began quietly in New York when two *nisei* women lamented the absence of a Japanese American community and the steady erosion of a Japanese American identity among their children. It was based mainly in New York City and its leaders developed an early enthusiasm for radical ideologies. In the Midwest, political activism began when Asian American college students came together for mutual support and collective action. Many of them eventually left college to go to an Asian ethnic community, usually on one of the coasts, in search of their roots.

The West Coast: "Beyond the Chinatown Youth Problems"

As with other social movements of the 1960s, the Asian American Movement owes a debt of gratitude to the civil rights movement for exposing the gap between the country's image of itself and reality: Instead of a land of equality where a person could achieve success through individual effort, the United States was criticized as a land of inequality where racial discrimination degraded African Americans, relegating them to second-class status. Raising the issue of race forced the nation to examine its concept of democracy and the inferior place it reserved for African Americans and other people of color. In the vanguard were southern blacks, America's "wretched of the earth," living in an oppressive milieu undergirded by organized terror. With a courage and determination that they did not know they possessed, they confronted authority and fought tradition: Rosa Parks was arrested in December 1955 for refusing to leave a seat reserved for whites on a bus in Montgomery, Alabama; David Richmond, Franklin McCain, Ezell Blair, and Joseph McNeil, four freshmen from the then all-black North Carolina Agricultural and Technical College, sat at the Greensboro Woolworth store's white-only lunch counter and asked for service in February 1960; Medgar E. Evers, National Association for the Advancement of Colored People (NAACP) leader in Mississippi, was murdered by racists in June 1963; and there were many others.[1] Their moral example moved people of every hue to support the civil rights movement. And that movement was triumphant: The U.S. Supreme Court's momentous decision in *Brown* v. *Board of Education* (1954) concluded that public school segregation was inherently unequal and denied African Americans equal protection under the Constitution; the 1964 Civil Rights Act and the 1965 Voting Rights Act prohibited discrimination in voting, education, employment, and public facilities and gave the federal government the power to enforce desegregation by denying federal funds to segregated schools and programs; the 1968 Civil Rights Act barred racial discrimination in the sale or rental of housing.

Asian Americans, too, crossed the color line to embrace the ideals of the civil rights movement. Out of a sense of moral outrage, they participated in the effort to eliminate discrimination and segregation of blacks from the rest of society. But in working to attain legal rights for African Americans, they came to realize that the struggle for social justice in America was more than an African American and European American issue; it involved other people of color. In a rude awakening, Asian Americans became acutely aware that they had more in common with African Americans than with European Americans, that racial injustice had been visited on them as well. As individuals, they too had experienced prejudice and discrimination; as a group, they too had been victims of institutionalized racism and had been excluded from mainstream society. They became aware that the discrimination they suffered was more than the work of individual bigots who should know better; it was in fact an intrinsic feature of American society. This new awareness generated not only ambivalence about their own identity but also disillusionment with a society that failed to live up to its principles of equality and justice for all. While they had started out identifying with liberal European Americans trying to help oppressed African Americans integrate society, they ended up empathizing with African Americans and saw the need to achieve racial equality for Asian Americans.

Inspired by the civil rights movement's breach of racial barriers, community activists tried to reform the condition of their own communities. On the West Coast, one of their earliest efforts was to get the San Francisco city government to address the concerns of Chinatown. Activists held a series of forums at the Commodore Stockton Auditorium and Portsmouth Square to focus public attention on the community's problems. Of these meetings, the most significant was an all-day "informational convocation" for Bay Area Chinese American students held on 17 August 1968 at the Cumberland Presbyterian Church by the Intercollegiate Chinese for Social Action.[2] It was designed to educate people about Chinatown's socioeconomic ills, such as poor housing and health, unemployment, "negative" education, and the fact "that her poor, 80 per cent of the population, needed help."[3] At the end of the day there was a protest march down Grant Avenue, Chinatown's main street. L. Ling-chi Wang, a graduate student in Near East linguistics at the University of California, Berkeley, and a community activist who was working for the Chinatown Youth Council at the time, recalled:

> It was quite a political event in Chinatown. Those of us who were
> involved in it were very nervous of possible violence. Although our
> intentions were peaceful, we did not know whether the Chinatown

establishment considered us a threat or not. But it turned out to be very peaceful, although we were denounced by the Chinese Six Companies. For the first time problems were articulated beyond the Chinatown youth problems which were publicly aired before.[4]

It was these "youth problems" that made the public aware that something was amiss in Chinatown. An increasing birthrate among Chinese Americans, and the influx of immigrants after the country's discriminatory immigration laws were changed in 1965, swelled the ranks of young people dissatisfied with the patently unpleasant, unproductive, and unpromising life of the ghetto. Caught between the "American Dream" and their inability to attain it, many of them gravitated toward gangsterism and threw in their lot with groups like the Wah Ching (literally, "Chinese youth"), the largest street gang in Chinatown.

A few youngsters joined Leway (a contraction of "legitimate ways"), a local self-help group begun by some American-born Chinese street youth whose pool hall was about to be closed.[5] In an effort to preserve their "hangout," one of the few recreational facilities in Chinatown, they came up with the idea of a nonprofit youth agency. So in May 1967 they established Leway to manage the pool hall and a soda fountain, the profits from which would be used to fund programs that would serve the needs of local youth. As it turned out, the monies were used for legal assistance and rent instead. As one former member recalled, operating the facility was an effort at cooperative capitalism, purer than that practiced by most corporations because Leway eschewed government assistance in any form. As a matter of principle, the group refused to apply for federal funds because its leaders believed that the existing antipoverty monies available to youth groups were being used to coopt them.

In its own inimitable fashion, Leway sought to rehabilitate erstwhile juvenile delinquents and combat the social causes of their delinquency. As Leway president Denny Lai put it, "Most of us cats are misfits, outcasts with a rap sheet. What we're trying to do is to keep the hoods off the streets, give them something to do instead of raising hell."[6] Besides providing a haven, Leway tried to find its members jobs and get them admitted to college, and it offered draft counseling as well. But a number of factors conspired to close Leway down. It was never able to build on its initial support from the community, which began to blame Leway members as well as other youths for the increasing violence in Chinatown. Nor was it able to establish a working relationship with the police, whose continuous surveillance and harassment, more than anything else, forced Leway to shut its doors in the summer of 1969.

Meanwhile, Asian American student activists were addressing the adverse conditions at San Francisco State College and at the University of California, Berkeley. Their source of inspiration here was different. They were influenced more by the militant Black Power movement than the pacifist civil rights movement. They were particularly impressed with the Black Panther party, which had been founded in nearby Oakland in 1966. The Panthers traced all oppressed people's problems, foreign and domestic, to American imperialism, an idea that was gaining currency in the New Left student movement around the same time. In general, radicals began placing the problem of Third World people in the political context of U.S. imperialism and thought it imperative that people of color and progressive European Americans join together in what they believed was a movement for their common liberation.

"Shut it down!" was the rallying cry of Asian Americans and other students of color who participated in the Third World strikes at San Francisco State College (6 November 1968 to 27 March 1969) and the University of California, Berkeley (19 January 1969 to 14 March 1969). As part of the Third World Liberation Front (TWLF), they went on strike to achieve self-determination for themselves and their communities and to eradicate individual and institutional racism. Their immediate goal was the establishment of autonomous Ethnic Studies programs for the racial-minority groups in the TWLF, programs in which the students would control both the faculty and the curriculum. It was an educational goal rooted in cultural nationalism.

Ethnic Studies was to be open to all students of color who wanted a higher education. Its central purpose was to imbue them with the knowledge, understanding, and commitment needed to solve the problems of their communities. It would increase the diversity of the student body and faculty at San Francisco State and the University of California, Berkeley, making them more representative of the society they served and less exclusively European American. It was deemed necessary because conventional educational institutions offered a curriculum that was said to be irrelevant to the experiences of people of color. University courses, the strikers claimed, suppressed the social and political consciousness of students of color by denying or distorting their historical experience and by promoting a Eurocentric ideology that denigrated other cultures.

These Third World strikes were the labor pains that gave birth to Ethnic Studies programs on the two campuses as well as others across the nation. Ethnic Studies programs at San Francisco State and the University of California, Berkeley, failed to meet completely the demands of the students but nevertheless represented partial victories. The strike at San Francisco State was more effective than the one at Berkeley. At State, the strikers were able to shut down the campus three times and win the support of the American Federation of Teachers, which struck for several weeks in solidarity with the students. At Berkeley, the strikers were unable to close the campus.

One study argues that the difference between the San Francisco State and University of California, Berkeley, strikes essentially reflected the class character of the two campuses.[7] San Francisco State was a working-class commuter school with students from the inner city, while Berkeley was an elite school with students from all over the nation. The strikers at State were more willing to employ militant confrontational tactics and had greater faculty and community support, which was indispensable in the protracted struggle against the college administration. The strikers at Berkeley were isolated from fellow students and the community. Nor did they get much sympathy from the faculty, who felt that the style and substance of their scholarship were being impugned, and who, as a professional elite, lacked the trade union consciousness of their colleagues at State.

Community support was of critical importance to the Asian American students. A former member of San Francisco State's Asian American Political Alliance recalled that some community leaders, such as Clifford Uyeda, long-time Japanese American Citizens League (JACL) member and national president from 1978 to 1980, opposed the actions of the students. Ever since World War II, when conservative JACL leaders cooperated with the authorities by convincing fellow Japanese Americans to go quietly into the concentration camps, the JACL had advocated that "Japanese must 'prove' themselves as Americans by solidly integrating with the larger society."[8] But other *nisei* (second-generation Japanese Americans), people like Yori Wada, Edison Uno, and Ray Okamura, supported the students.[9] A former member of the Intercollegiate Chinese for Social Action recalled that the more conservative Chinatown leaders initially denounced the students as violent radicals, but later gave their support when they realized that the strike was to enable their children to attend San Francisco State.[10]

The Asian American contingent of the TWLF at State consisted of the Inter-collegiate Chinese for Social Action (ICSA), Philippine-American College Endeavor (PACE), and the Asian American Political Alliance (AAPA). Both ICSA and PACE were Asian ethnic organizations, that is, they represented a particular Asian group, with ties to Chinatown and Manilatown, respectively. Their commitment to improving their communities through the existing educational system in general and State in particular shaped their social and political agenda. While AAPA shared ICSA and PACE's desire to provide community services, its main interest was in the then novel idea of creating a pan-Asian identity, that is, a collective identity that encompassed all Asian ethnic groups in America.

Of these three groups, ICSA was the most prominent.[11] Established in November 1967 to work for social change, ICSA was a refreshing change from the social clubs of years past, which had spent their time preparing for the annual party for Chinese students in Bay Area colleges. It attracted the more socially concerned and politically aware students, most of whom were from relatively well-off families that had managed to escape from the ghetto to the suburbs. Later, its ranks were augmented by students directly from the ghetto, many of whom were recruited through a special admissions program. According to Stanford Lyman, one of the significant though unintended effects of the recruitment of students from Chinatown was to compel the organization to reconsider "the whole relationship of college to community and eventually to reevaluat[e] their priorities of education and service." [12]

Through the innovative Community Internship Program, San Francisco State students volunteered to work for some of Chinatown's social service agencies, such as the War on Poverty office; they also set up their own project to teach English to immigrant youth. At the suggestion of George Woo, who had been working with Chinatown youth, ICSA then requested funds from the college's Associated Student Government to set up community programs of its own. Under the leadership of Mason Wong, ICSA established a youth center in Chinatown and served as its direct link to the Chinese American community.

During the Third World strike, the youth center housed the Free University of Chinatown Kids, Unincorporated, which attempted to teach local youth about the history of Chinese in America and in the process to politicize them.[13] But neither a political organization nor a revolutionary ideology emerged from it because its focus was on the oppression of the Chinatown community, rather than racism as a larger social phenomenon. More than anything else, it served as a drop-in facility for youth, many of whom belonged to the Wah Ching, an informal grouping of rebellious immigrant youth from Hong Kong who, like their American-born peers in Leway, were under- or unemployed and excluded from the wider society, but had the additional burden of being illiterate in English. Wah Ching's leader was Stan Wong, who later joined San Francisco State College's Asian American Political Alliance, and its spokesman was George Woo. The Wah Ching sought help from various city agencies and the Six Companies, the umbrella organization that traditionally represented the Chinatown community, but to little avail. Eventually, it fragmented into factions, some of which were absorbed by Chinatown associations that used them as "looksee" men (i.e., sentries) for illegal operations.

Initially, ICSA was reluctant to join the Third World Liberation Front because its members thought that belonging to the coalition might jeopardize their programs. They were also uneasy about the militancy of the Black Student Union, which was allied with TWLF. ICSA's vacillation about joining TWLF threatened to rend the organization asunder. With the support of an insurgent faction within the organization and Leway, Mason Wong convinced ICSA to ally itself with the other students of color. In late spring 1968, Mason Wong was elected chair; soon after, the group officially joined the TWLF. In retrospect, Wong noted that the group eventually decided that "not to be involved was to be out of touch." [14] By the following fall, at the height of the Third World strike, ICSA boasted a membership of about a hundred students, though far fewer actively participated in the strike.

Some of the most active Asian American student leaders in TWLF were from Philippine-American College Endeavor (PACE). PACE was organized principally by Pat Salavar, who served as campus coordinator, and Ron Quidachay, an early leader of the TWLF. Like ICSA, PACE had a strong community orientation and was actively working with youth from low-income families. Its major service program was to recruit and tutor Filipino American college applicants. Its political goal was to organize disaffected Filipino American students to oppose racism and "internal colonialism"; leaders like Salavar also hoped that it would stimulate the development of a "revolutionary consciousness" among the students.[15] But most Filipino American students were uninterested in PACE's political perspective.[16] PACE participated in TWLF mainly to ensure that the proposed School of Ethnic Studies would teach Filipino American culture, language, and history. Of primary importance to PACE members would be the educational and socioeconomic plight of Filipino Americans.

Histories of the State strike make only passing reference to the Asian American Political Alliance (AAPA), yet AAPA members were among the most militant of the Asian Americans involved in TWLF, with proportionally more of them involved in strike activities than either ICSA or PACE members.[17] AAPA's relative newness and the amorphousness of its purpose contributed to its lack of prominence, but the main reason was the visibility and credibility of ICSA and PACE leaders such as Ron Quidachay, the chairman of TWLF the year before the strike, and George Woo of ICSA, who represented all the Asian American students in negotiations with other minority groups in the coalition and with the college administration. A former AAPA member humorously recalled that Woo had the respect of friends and foes alike because he seemed to embody every negative stereotype that they ever had about Asians.[18] He appeared to be the quintessential "inscrutable Oriental" with hidden powers ready to be unleashed on unsuspecting opponents, an incarnation of Genghis Khan. AAPA, in contrast, was led by Penny Nakatsu, an intelligent and strong person whose gender placed her at a decided disadvantage in dealing with Third World student leaders and European American college administrators, all of whom were men.

Penny Nakatsu and two other Japanese American women started the San Francisco State AAPA in the summer of 1968.[19] They had met at a Berkeley AAPA meeting and agreed that their school needed a similar group. An informal group of middle-class students with continuing but attenuated ties to the Asian American community, the State AAPA consisted mainly of Japanese Americans. This led Stanford M. Lyman to conclude that "although it had its leftward leaning and radical members, AAPA at San Francisco State College came to be more a Japanese-American group and less an outlet for radical expression."[20] Unlike the Chinese and Filipino Americans, who had their own ethnic organizations on campus, the Japanese Americans had only AAPA. But AAPA's main attraction to its members was its emphasis on pan-Asianism.

Even though AAPA was in the midst of defining its ideology and setting up its organization when it joined the strike, it was clear from the beginning that this group was committed to an Asian American community. Alienated from an Asian culture with which they had little contact and an American culture that excluded them, its members developed an interest in unifying Chinese,

Filipino, Japanese, Korean, and other Asian Americans instead of committing themselves to the well-being of a specific Asian American community like Chinatown. That was probably why AAPA disappeared after the Third World strike at San Francisco State; its members devoted their energies to Ethnic Studies or the Equal Opportunity Program, both of which gave them a chance to realize an Asian American community that had previously existed only as an abstraction.

AAPA's initial agenda called for consciousness-raising sessions dealing with Asian American identity as a prelude to political action. Its focus on action was the reason that the group attracted people with previous involvement in social movements. They were anticipating a major political action at State as the campus remained tense after the previous spring's sit-in to protest cutbacks in the Equal Opportunity Program and the termination of one of its minority faculty, Juan Martinez. The stage was set for the Third World strike in the fall semester.

Probably more than any other single event, the Third World strike at San Francisco State symbolized the potential of Asian American activism. On the basis of a shared identity and history, the students coalesced into an inter-Asian coalition that in turn became a part of a still larger student-of-color coalition. Together, they challenged school authorities and acquired the power necessary to change their educational institution so that it reflected more accurately America's ethnic pluralist society. Doing so was an empowering experience, one that convinced many Asian American activists that they could collectively change themselves and their communities through direct action. But, as a later chapter discusses, the next major challenge was to ensure that the changes at State and at other campuses, and in the Asian ethnic communities lasted.

As political as State's AAPA was, it was considered less radical[21] than Berkeley's AAPA, which had its beginnings in the Peace and Freedom party, a coalition of antiwar activists and Black Panthers promoting third-party candidates. On the basis of the party's mailing list, Yuji Ichioka called together an Asian Caucus to discuss issues of mutual concern. His appeal to all Asian Americans, rather than to members of a single ethnic group like the Chinese or Filipinos or Japanese, reflected a recognition of their similar history in America and an appreciation of strength through numbers. From this caucus came the Berkeley Asian American Political Alliance, the first of many AAPAs that sprang up around the country.

In the beginning, the Berkeley AAPA consisted of about ten members. Later, these ten contacted Bay Area students and community workers they thought might be interested in a political, rather than social, organization. The first members were a diverse group. Richard Aoki, one of the leaders of the Third World strike at Berkeley, recalled that AAPA included people of various political persuasions, from liberal to anarchistic (though there were no conservatives) and represented "the best, most highly conscious, most politically developed members out of these social clubs that Asians tend to join when they go to college." [22] These students "made a strong recruitment drive in the community drawing in ex-farm workers, ex-detainees of the concentration camp from the Japanese American community, progressive elements from the Chinese [American] community, and a large anti-Marcos grouping from the Filipino [American] community." [23] Their general purpose was to bring about the kind of social and political change in America that would result in self-determination for people of color. For that reason, while preparing to teach an experimental course at Berkeley on the Asian American experience, they participated in the campaign to free Huey P. Newton, co-founder of the Black Panther party who had been convicted of voluntary manslaughter. The course would be a way of educating Asian Americans about themselves, a prerequisite for determining their own lives and asserting their own identity.

AAPA held meetings to address issues and concerns that were pertinent to Asian Americans. According to George Woo, it was at the second meeting that Larry Jack Wong first brought up the internment of the Japanese Americans, saying, "Hey you're Japanese. Why don't you people protest about the concentration camps?" [24] Woo noted that a long discussion ensued and, ever the gadfly, he said, "Hell, the way things are going now, they might do that to us. So you're not doing this just for the Japanese, but for all other people. I'll handle it different, I'll take a few of them with me." [25] Wong and Woo had touched upon a taboo topic, one that older Japanese Americans had sought to forget. After that tragedy was revealed to *sansei* (third-generation Japanese Americans) participating in the Asian American Movement, the internment during World War II became *the* issue among Japanese American activists and, for many of them, the sole reason for being involved politically.

In spite of their successes at Berkeley, some AAPA members became increasingly disenchanted with campus politics. Feeling also some guilt about being in college while other Asian Americans lived lives of quiet desperation in the ghetto, they decided in December 1969 to return to the community. They moved into the basement of the United Filipino Hall in the International Hotel; but, except for a vague yearning to return to their roots, the Berkeley AAPA students were uncertain about what to do there. Initially, they maintained an informal office that provided reading materials from Asia, especially China, and on the weekends showed movies to local residents. During the two months following their arrival, they analyzed the abysmal conditions of the community and concluded that it and other Third World communities in the United States were nothing more than internal colonies exploited for their manpower, "insulted constantly, and brutalized by the forces of law and order." [26] In the course of this brief period of study, some of them decided to formalize their presence by establishing, in March 1970, the Asian Community Center (ACC).

Officially, the ACC was a collective guided by a steering committee, but because of the high degree of camaraderie decisions were made through mutual consultation and consensus. [27] According to ACC leader Steve Yip, initially the organization consisted mainly of second-generation Chinese Americans; later, its ranks were augmented by pro–People's Republic of China (PRC) Chinese students from overseas whom it had protected against local thugs hired by the Kuomintang (KMT; Nationalist party). [28] It envisioned itself as an "idea" around which the Asian community could rally and unite. That idea was a common Asian American identity rooted in a past history of oppression and a present struggle for liberation. In this it was heavily influenced by Maoism, particularly the belief that once ideas are grasped by the masses, they turn into a material force that changes society and the world. But the members were shrewd enough to realize that before the idea could be grasped by the working people in the community, the group needed to attract their attention. This it did by providing community services.

Among its activities, the ACC's Free Film Program was one of the most popular. Initially intended as entertainment for local residents, the program evolved into what was mainly a pro-PRC film series, interspersed with political movies about liberation struggles all over the world and in the United States. But the films attracted viewers interested not so much in communism as in learning about their homeland and how it was faring, information that was scarce in Cold War America, especially in KMT-influenced Chinatowns. Needless to say, this more than anything else antagonized the KMT and its clients, the Chinese Six Companies. [29]

The interest in movies about the PRC was not just a San Francisco China-town phenomenon. Whenever films about the mainland were shown in the United States, Chinese and Chinese Americans turned out in large numbers to see them. In Ann Arbor, Michigan, the organizers of China Week were as-tounded when hundreds of people attended the film showings. It seemed as if the entire Chinese American population in Michigan had come to see *The East Is Red*, a tedious propaganda film about the Chinese Communist Revolution. I Wor Kuen, a militant group in New York City, had a similar experience when it showed the film on three consecutive nights in a vacant-lot playground in Chinatown. Such were the emotional ties that Chinese Americans had to their former homeland and their craving for information about it.

Among the filmgoers were Chinese students from Hong Kong, Taiwan, and overseas Chinese communities. Alienated from their home countries and, in the case of those from Taiwan and Hong Kong, dissatisfied with dependence on the United States and England, they identified with the People's Repub-lic of China, the homeland that their parents or grandparents had left during the Chinese diaspora. While democratic nations (and the Soviet Union after 1960) considered China a pariah, overseas Chinese students admired it as an increasingly powerful nation that commanded respect in Asia and in the world. Many of them abandoned their studies to join pro-PRC groups, especially those working for the normalization of relations with the United States.

ACC's main political action was its participation in the struggle to save the International Hotel from destruction. The I-Hotel, as it was known, was what remained of Manilatown, a once thriving community that had covered ten city blocks between Chinatown and the nearby financial district and served as a debarkation point for Filipino laborers. It was one of the few low-income dwellings in the area, housing mainly elderly Filipino and Chinese bachelors, victims of California's anti-miscegenation laws. It came to represent the right of senior citizens and others to decent low-cost housing in their own commu-nities. In December 1968, the hotel owners tried to evict the tenants to build a parking lot in its place.

The Filipino and Chinese communities were unwilling or unable to take a stand against eviction; but for many young Filipinos in search of their ethnic identity and cultural place, the I-Hotel symbolized the history of the *manongs*— aging Filipino immigrants, the generation of their fathers.[30] They went to defend the hotel and their cultural legacy. They were joined by Asian American students from Berkeley, Davis, Stockton, Sacramento, San Jose, and as far away as Fresno. Saving the I-Hotel was the first issue that brought large numbers of Asian American students into the community. Students organized demonstrations, tried to rehabilitate the building to meet city codes, and negotiated with the owners and the city in a futile effort to save the hotel. Meanwhile, renovated storefronts on the ground floor were sublet to programs that sought to serve the community: the Kearny Street Workshop, Jackson Street Gallery, Asian Community Center, Chinese Progressive Association, Chinatown Youth Council, and Everybody's Bookstore. The students were aided by Berkeley's newly founded Asian American Studies program, which provided university transportation to ferry students from the campus to the hotel several times a day and even used university money to pay the first year's rent. Floyd Huen, who was in charge of the program at Berkeley, recalled paying the rent with student fees and rationalizing it as returning resources to the community.[31]

Unfortunately, the campaign to protect the I-Hotel became mired in factionalism, the worst antagonism being between the Asian Community Center (ACC) and the International Hotel Tenants Association (IHTA). The IHTA, representing the interests of the elderly residents, focused on immediate steps to safeguard the hotel and was willing to work with the mayor's office and employ legal strategies to achieve its goals. But the ACC considered this a class struggle between the rich and poor, for which building a mass support base was a political prerequisite. ACC members thought that negotiating with the mayor was useless, since he and other public officials would accede to their demands only if they applied constant community pressure. Each group thus accused the other of undermining the struggle to save the hotel.

On the night that the I-Hotel fell, hundreds of demonstrators linked arms to prevent the police from carrying out the eviction order. In spite of this valiant effort, the building was finally torn down in 1977, leaving a huge hole in the ground and an unresolved issue. After all these years, the community and the city are still negotiating about what will be built in its place.

**The East Coast: "The Center
of the . . . Power Structure"**

Asian American activism is commonly seen as an exclusively West Coast phenomenon because of its intensity and breadth there. In a letter published in *Gidra* (November 1969), Don Nakanishi, a member of the Asian American

Political Alliance at Yale University, noted that Asian Americans on the West Coast seemed to believe that their few compatriots on the East Coast were all "bananas," that is, Asian American Uncle Toms.[32] Referring to the large population and the existence of radical political organizations on the East Coast, he pointed out that the east was "the center of mass communications, the power structure, and the major capitalistic undertakings" and that any actions that eastern political groups took would have greater national impact in the long run.[33]

Among the groups that Nakanishi mentioned were the Asian American Political Alliance at Yale and at Columbia. Indirectly influenced by the Berkeley AAPA (they had "heard about this group on the West Coast, and it sounded good"),[34] East Coast AAPA members identified with the antiwar and black liberation movements rather than the conservative social clubs at their schools. In September 1969, the Columbia AAPA sent two of its members to Berkeley for an Asian American Studies conference. It was an inspiring visit that renewed their efforts to organize students on their own campus, though a sustained and systematic drive for an Asian American Studies program never materialized. Instead, some of them began to be involved in Asian Americans for Action, an anti-imperialist and intergenerational organization.

One of the first pan-Asian organizations on the East Coast,[35] Asian Americans for Action, or Triple A, was founded by Kazu Iijima and Minn Matsuda, two *nisei* women with an extraordinary history of fighting for social justice. In 1968, on one of those beautiful fall days that mask the grimness of New York City, they got together on a park bench to eat lunch and to talk. Among other things, they expressed admiration for the Black Power movement, with its emphasis on ethnic identity and pride, and concern about their college-age children, who were losing their cultural identity. What was needed, Ijima and Matsuda decided, was a Japanese American community and cultural organization that their children and other young adults could belong to. But Chris Iijima, Kazu's son, convinced them that only a pan-Asian organization was viable.[36] The thought of bringing together diverse Asian Americans was a new and exciting idea, as it proved to be elsewhere in the nation. Only after Triple A was established did they learn of Asian American political activism on the West Coast.

Iijima and Matsuda proceeded to contact both mature and young people they knew or had heard about. Only a few, like Yuri Kochiyama, an activist in the Japanese American community, responded. Much to their disappointment, other progressive individuals of their own generation, including those who had been active in the antifascist Japanese American Committee for Democracy, were uninterested in participating in an Asian American organization. Some had become complacent or concerned with their careers, others were still feeling the aftereffects of the McCarthy period, and most were wary of working with young people. At the antiwar demonstrations they attended regularly, Iijima and Matsuda approached every Asian they saw and got his or her name and address. Kazu Iijima recalls with a certain amount of mirth that at the time these young people must have thought that they were "crazy little old ladies." [37] From these encounters, they compiled a long list of names.

On 6 April 1969 Iijima and Matsuda held their first meeting, which drew about eighteen people. Most participants were Chinese American college students from Columbia University and the City College of New York. Ijima and Matsuda expected that the students would want to focus on cultural and identity issues, but much to their surprise and delight, the young people, most of whom had participated in the Black Power movement, Students for a Democratic Society (SDS), or other New Left student organizations, also wanted to address political issues. They agreed that their purpose would be to establish a political voice for the Asian American community and serve as a means for collective action; hence the name Asian Americans for Action. Their primary political concern was opposing the Vietnam War.[38] They called for the immediate withdrawal of all U.S. and allied troops from South Vietnam, upheld the Vietnamese struggle for self-determination, and acknowledged the National Liberation Front as the military and political representative of the people. Naturally, those who were uncomfortable with Triple A's political dimension dropped out quickly. Those who stayed did so because they had finally found a group that they could identify with racially and relate to politically. Among their Asian "brothers and sisters" they felt a level of comfort that they never felt as members of European American or even African American organizations.

Unlike most other antiwar groups, Triple A placed the Vietnam War in the larger context of imperialism and racism.[39] According to its analysis, the war was being fought to obtain resources from and to promote business in Asia and was part of a "Pacific Rim" strategy that placed the defense of American interests in the nations surrounding the Pacific Ocean above the rights of the people in those nations. From Triple A's perspective, American foreign policy was controlled by a military–industrial complex that greedily sought profits at the expense of other countries, especially vulnerable Third World nations like those in Southeast Asia. Victims of American neoimperialism thus had a common interest in resisting America's designs on Asia. Emphasizing the racial aspects of American foreign policy in general and in the Vietnam War, the Triple A reasoned that, because American government leaders considered Asians biologically and culturally inferior, an Asian nation had been invaded to satisfy the United States's insatiable search for resources. Moreover, this racial bias served to justify the American military's brutality toward the Vietnamese people and mirrored the racial animosity directed against Asian Americans and other people of color in the United States. Conversely, any setbacks experienced in Asia resulted in an increase in hostility toward Asian Americans.

As part of its anti-imperialist activities, Triple A took the lead in opposing the United States–Japan Security Treaty. It published *Ampo Funsai* (literally, Smash the Treaty), which indicted both countries as imperialist partners in Asia, and in November 1969, on the occasion of Prime Minister Eisaku Sato's visit to the United States, Triple A organized a rally against the treaty. About three hundred people went to Washington, D.C., where they put on street theater that featured a cloth dragon bearing a cardboard head resembling a malevolent imperialist Uncle Sam and a tail labeled Sato. The group marched to the Japanese embassy and tried to present a petition to the prime minister. Twenty of the demonstrators allowed themselves to be arrested. As a media event, the demonstration was a success: Not only did it receive front-page coverage in the *Washington Post* and *Washington Star*, but it was reported by journalists from Japan as well.

But all was not well with Triple A as it struggled with external subversion and internal dissension. A takeover was attempted by the Progressive Labor party (PL), a Maoist faction that had splintered from the Communist party, U.S.A., over the Sino-Soviet dispute, attacking the revisionist policies of the Soviet Union and identifying with the People's Republic of China. Its disciplined cadre lived a puritanical lifestyle (among other things, they eschewed rock music to avoid offending "the workers") and were committed to creating a dictatorship of the proletariat in the United States. PL espoused revolution, talked of violence, and studiously cultivated college students as part of its so-called worker–student alliance. It had already successfully absorbed the Students for a Democratic Society and tried this tactic during the Third World strike at San Francisco State. Leroy Goodwin, a Black Student Union Central Committee member, described the PL as "professional at meeting disruptions, coup de tai [*sic*] (overthrown) manufacturers," who were always trying to "show why the people should transfer their allegiance from the present organization to PL." [40]

Several PL members, including Jerry Tung, who later went on to establish the Communist Workers party, tried to insinuate themselves into Triple A for the purpose of recruiting new members and influencing its policies, a ploy used by many Marxist–Leninist organizations of the period. They waged an incessant ideological struggle at Triple A meetings, trying to direct discussions and packing meetings whenever there was a vote on some important social or political issue. But their political philosophy, which held that nationalism in any form was reactionary and racism was a social aberration rather than an intrinsic part of the American social fabric, was fundamentally at odds with Triple A and other ethnic-based organizations. Their ideology and methods were intolerable to the rest of the members, and eventually they were expelled from the group.

The internal dissension was less manageable. One interpretation is that "ultraleft" elements in Triple A (as well as in Columbia AAPA) polarized the organization. [41] In one camp were the older members (mostly Japanese Americans) who advocated working on the "anti-imperialist international front"; in the other were younger members (mostly Chinese Americans) interested in working in New York's Chinatown. [42] The latter employed "wrecking tactics," [43] accusing those unwilling to organize in Chinatown of being insufficiently political. Another interpretation is that the split was mainly a matter of style. On the basis of their past experience, older members viewed the issues in a larger international context and wanted to tone down the rhetoric in order to obtain the support of as many people as possible. But the younger ones would have none of such moderation, preferring the rhetoric and style of SDS and militant African Americans. An older member analyzed the problem this way:

> For the young people this was the first time that they had the opportu-
> nity of taking a political thing and doing it on their own so that rhetoric
> and everything was part of the catharsis. They had to get it off their
> chests. . . . Before they were always a part of larger white or black
> groups. And this was the first time that we were taking responsibility for
> our own way of demonstrating, our own slogans, our own everything.
> So the tendency was to be very rhetorical, very militant, very up front. [44]

In hindsight, a younger member concluded that such behavior was simply a matter of political immaturity on the part of his peers. [45]

In all probability the conflict was a manifestation of the generation gap that was talked about so much during the 1960s. It was natural for young people to lash out against authority figures. After all, it was an era when the young distrusted anyone over thirty. These generational conflicts resulted in bitterness, name-calling, and finally the departure of practically all the young people, most of whom later went on to establish I Wor Kuen, a Maoist sect based in New York's Chinatown.

Those remaining in Triple A felt dejected, abandoned, and weary. They considered simply ending the organization but were convinced by Pat Sumi, who had just returned from visits to North Vietnam and North Korea, to carry on. In spite of its reduced size, Triple A continued to be active in the New York area. One of its major initiatives was a plan for an Asian community center, an effort that quickly expanded beyond Triple A and became the main focus of activity among Japanese Americans in the city.[46] The Ad Hoc Committee for an Asian Center, chaired by Bill Kochiyama, had ambitious plans, including a day-care center and a multilingual informational hot line. On 10 December 1972 the United Asian Communities Center opened its doors. The Center became a hub of Asian American social and political activities in New York City but eventually was forced to close because of inadequate financing. The acrimonious relations within the Asian American Movement during the mid-1970s made it impossible to launch a fund-raising campaign to save the Center.

The latter half of the 1970s was a difficult period for the Asian American Movement. Unity provided by the antiwar movement ended with the end of American intervention in Southeast Asia in 1975, while radical Asian American organizations, particularly Marxist–Leninist ones, engaged in bitter and violent rivalries. Many groups experienced significant changes, including Triple A. In 1976 it changed its name to the Union of Activists and moved away from being an exclusively Asian American group concerned with ethnic issues to one that embraced all progressive people involved in multinational class struggle. It managed to continue its activities to the end of the decade, when it decided to dissolve itself after its members began to have a falling out over the issue of Soviet socialist imperialism.

The Midwest: "This 'Vast Banana Wasteland' "

While East Coast Asian American activists felt misunderstood by those on the West Coast, the ones in the Midwest felt ignored by both. As the Rice Paper Collective of the Madison Asian Union put it, "Our invisibility is so total that

Asian Americans are not thought to exist in this 'vast banana wasteland.' " [47] Except for those living and laboring in such places as Chicago's Chinatown, most midwestern Asian Americans had disappeared into suburbia. Without a physical community to relate to, midwestern Asian Americans found it difficult to start and sustain an ethnic-consciousness movement. Accordingly, Asian American activism started later in the region and Asian American groups had a harder time recruiting and retaining members. In order to overcome the geographic and spiritual isolation they felt, midwestern activists regularly visited one another as well as activists on the coasts.

These problems notwithstanding, during the 1970s there was significant Asian American activism in the Midwest, enough to warrant organizing two Midwestern Asian American Conferences in Chicago (12–14 April 1974) and Madison (26–29 September 1974), and a Midwest Regional Conference on Asian American Mental Health (Chicago, May 1974).[48] Most of the Asian American groups in the region were campus groups whose central concern was personal identity.[49] The Minneapolis Asian American Alliance (organized in 1971) spent its first year holding "rap sessions" on Asian American identity and awareness, for example.[50] The purpose of the University of Illinois Asian American Alliance (also organized in 1971) was to "create a new sense of awareness and identity, to derive some sense of belonging, and to provide a deeper and broader understanding of our Asian heritage." [51] The Oberlin Asian-American Alliance (organized in 1972) designed an entire program around the issue of identity.[52] Not surprisingly, the Second Midwestern Asian American Conference (Madison, 1974) was organized around the question "What's beyond identity?"

One of the centers of significant Asian American activism was the University of Michigan at Ann Arbor, home of three successive groups: the Ann Arbor Asian Political Alliance, Yisho Yigung, and East Wind.[53] The Ann Arbor APA was born during China Week, a series of events focusing on the People's Republic of China, held on campus in spring 1971. China Week was sponsored by the University of Michigan's chapter of the Committee of Concerned Asian Scholars, a group of radical Asian Studies students and scholars, and Armed Revolutionary Media, a media collective that had emerged from the 1969 Woodstock music festival. While each had its own reasons for organizing this event, both groups agreed that one of the legacies of the Cold War was an American public ignorant about China, which was still considered an outlaw nation. So China Week was organized to inform the people.

During one of the events, Louis Tsen of the Detroit Asian Political Alliance, a study group headed by Grace Lee Boggs, asked that Asian Americans get together afterward to discuss the possibility of organizing a group on the Ann Arbor campus. Two dozen people remained to do so and engaged in what can be characterized as a large consciousness-raising session. It was obvious that participants were interested in a support group. A few who had been involved in social movements wanted a more political orientation; but apparently this demand alienated some people, so only a handful of Asian American students went on to establish the Ann Arbor APA.

The political issue that preoccupied Ann Arbor APA members and most other Asian American student activists on college campuses was ending the Vietnam War. Like other Asian Americans opposed to the war, APA members believed that it was a conflict with racial overtones. They noted that "as Asian-Americans we have a particular perspective from which to view this war and are in a position to contribute to the struggle for peace." [54] During the Peace Treaty Conference at Ann Arbor, APA held a caucus to unite all Asian Americans against the war in Indochina. Later, a few of them formed one of the many "affinity groups" that went to the 1971 May Day Tribe demonstrations in Washington, D.C. to try to stop the federal bureaucracy from conducting "business as usual" while Americans *and* Asians were dying overseas. But the Ann Arbor APA's antiwar activities proved to be secondary to its role as a support group for Asian Americans who had become alienated from American society.

Ostensibly, Ann Arbor APA was interested in bringing together Asian Americans who identified with their Asian brethren in Vietnam and who had experienced discrimination in America. In actuality, only two individuals seemed really interested in an Asian American perspective on the war; the rest were preoccupied with personal issues such as male chauvinism and homophobia (one gay member had been expelled for his sexual orientation from SDS, which condemned it as a bourgeois aberration). [55] In emulation of the Chinese in the PRC, Ann Arbor APA devoted some of its meetings to mutual criticism and self-criticism about these concerns, which were to be recurring issues for Asian American radicals in the Midwest. [56] But it was only in the middle and late 1980s that the topic of human sexuality became important in the Asian American community in general.

During 1972, the dominant interest in a support network became manifest when the group changed its name to Yisho Yigung, combining Japanese and

Chinese terms to mean "One Life Together." The new name expressed members' solidarity as Asian Americans and their intention to become a "family"; it also reflected the involvement of more Japanese Americans. Yisho Yigung's main activity was frequent, informal, social meetings. In keeping with the spirit of collectivity, it had no leaders and no ideology. Such formlessness made it difficult for the group to act politically. Still, it continued to maintain a political direction and engaged in antiwar activities. In the fall of 1971, with the assistance of some Vietnam veterans who opposed the war, it staged a piece of "guerrilla theater" depicting war atrocities. Yisho Yigung members played Vietnamese civilians. The performance was considered provocative enough to be featured in the *Michigan Daily*. In the spring semester, Yisho Yigung offered "The Asian American Experience" through Michigan's experimental courses program. One member recalled the class as a series of "rap sessions" in which the students, most of whom were Asian Americans, were divided into small groups and discussed the anti-Asian movement in America and the issue of identity (i.e., their personal ambivalence about being Asian Americans)—in short, an extension of Yisho Yigung meetings.

Paradoxically, Yisho Yigung's emphasis on interpersonal relations eventually weakened the group. People began to resent having their lives scrutinized minutely. They thought it unreasonable to be considered insufficiently militant or Asian American when there was no consensus on what constituted militancy and Asian Americanness. The criticism and self-criticism sessions degenerated into the persecution of some members for personal character flaws, real or imagined. By spring 1972, its members embittered, the group more or less disbanded. The debacle made it difficult to start another Asian American organization. Most former members still on campus were reluctant to get involved with an Asian American group again and preferred to concentrate on their studies or other things that had been neglected during the past year, though some of them would occasionally participate in activities sponsored by East Wind.

East Wind, founded in fall 1972, attracted a new generation of Asian American students, most of whom were enthusiastic and energetic underclassmen. Its name came from Mao Tse-tung's famous speech at the Moscow Meeting of Communist and Workers' Parties (18 November 1957): "The East Wind is prevailing over the West Wind . . . the forces of socialism have become overwhelmingly superior to the forces of imperialism." [57] The name was selected because it sounded Asian American and came from Mao, who was widely respected as the leader of a revolutionary society, rather than because it represented a commitment to communism. Most members had only a nodding acquaintance with Marxism–Leninism or the thoughts of Mao Tse-tung. Only one was knowledgeable about Mao and the Chinese revolution, and he considered himself a left liberal.

In the beginning, two graduate students, one of whom had been involved in the founding of the Ann Arbor APA, provided some guidance to East Wind, but they consciously adopted an older brother attitude rather than assume the role of leaders. They recognized that the major problem with campus organizations was the periodic leadership vacuum that occurred whenever students graduated or left school for other reasons and that to achieve continuity, the organization must train future leaders. They made it a point to involve younger members in the decision-making process and let them be responsible for organizing events. There was ample opportunity for East Wind members to be in charge, since authority was a matter of involvement and respect rather than the result of a formal system of governance.

Most East Wind members had little experience with past Ann Arbor groups and could start fresh. Though in the beginning two former Yisho Yigung members tried unsuccessfully to inveigle East Wind into becoming a support group in the Yisho Yigung mode, both eventually dropped out in disappointment. Instead, East Wind became mainly a service and education organization. It was much more energetic than either the Ann Arbor APA or Yisho Yigung in encouraging students to join the group. It sponsored *chiaotzu* (steamed dumpling) dinners to attract students, organized an Asian American Awareness Week, and conducted an Asian American orientation program to reach large numbers of students early in the semester. Besides acquainting them with the organization, it also introduced them to Asian American history. Educating Asian Americans about their own history and culture was an important aspect of East Wind.

Because most students were from middle-class families that lived in isolated suburban midwestern communities where they were often the only Asian Americans around, they found it difficult to relate to the changing socioeconomic conditions of Asian ethnic communities elsewhere in the nation. For that reason, East Wind members thought it essential to focus on identity and to teach history as prerequisites for developing a commitment to the Asian American community. In fall 1973, they taught "The Asian American Experience" course through the Course Mart program.[58] Except for the title, this course had no connection to the one organized by Yisho Yigung. Much more rigorous and modeled on conventional courses taught at Michigan, it consisted principally of prepared lectures, followed by discussions and examinations. But it was offered on a pass/fail basis, used guest speakers for subjects with which the staff was unfamiliar (e.g., the internment of Japanese Americans during World War II), and allowed innovative class projects in lieu of papers.

East Wind stressed that "the history of Asian Americans is similar to that of the other visible minorities. Because we share a common past and future, it is imperative that we join hands with other U.S. minority people for the eventual liberation of us all." [59] Working closely with other students of color on campus, East Wind played a key role in organizing the Third World Solidarity Conference (22 February 1974), which featured Angela Davis, Clyde Bellacourt, Ramsey Muniz, and Pat Sumi as speakers.[60] Sumi, an Asian American activist from San Francisco State College, spoke with quiet conviction, although substantively she was as militant as Angela Davis, endorsing political revolution and advocating socialism as the only solution to the problem of racism in America. The unity achieved among the minority groups during this conference would be the basis for the Third World Coalition Council (TWCC), which led a sit-in at the university administration building a year later.

In February 1975, frustrated with the university's failure to fulfill its promises to the Black Action movement five years earlier and its unwillingness to meet the needs of other minorities, nearly three hundred students of color and European American students took over the central administration building for three days.[61] At the start there were the predictable banner headlines—"Minorities Occupy Ad. Bldg.; Vow to Remain Until Demands Are Met"—and talk of a return to the radical 1960s. The demonstration had a superficial similarity to the Third World strikes at San Francisco State and Berkeley, but it lacked the organization, unity, and violence of those earlier events. As a *Michigan Daily* headline succinctly said, "Sit-in '75: Ain't the Old Days." [62] For people at Michigan, it was mild in comparison to the Black Action movement (BAM) strike of 1970. As one administrator noted, "The mood was entirely different—the hostility, the vehemence, I can't describe it. The tenor of this was totally different." [63]

The TWCC made numerous demands, several of which merely reiterated or extended requests already granted during the Black Action movement strike of 1970, such as a minimum 10 percent African American student enrollment. One of its most widely supported and long-standing demands was for an Asian

American advocate.[64] An editorial in the *Michigan Daily* captured the sentiment of the supporters:

> Neglect of the Asian-American community's needs is standard policy of the Administration. Advocates represent the voice of the minorities, and only they can provide the direct link to the Administration that the Asian-American students here need for response to their problems in academic, counseling, and financial affairs. At this point, East Wind . . . has carried the burden of unofficial representative of Asian-Americans on campus. . . . In retrospect, the general attitude of the Administration is one of "legal" recognition and tokenism in meeting the individual and unique needs of Asian-American students.[65]

The struggle for an advocate reflected East Wind's concern for parity with other minority groups, for recognition as a Third World group, and for institutionalizing its presence on campus. It had recognized that relying on students, even so-called perpetual students, placed Asian American activism on campus at risk.

None of TWCC's demands were met outright; the university would agree only to negotiate with the students.[66] As for an Asian American advocate, the university continued its practice of tokenism. Initially, it set up a ten-hour per week work-study position. Later, since it planned to phase out the advocacy program (and thus rid itself of some of the key people involved in TWCC), the university agreed to hire an Asian American representative, rather than an advocate. To add insult to injury, the person eventually hired was the students' second choice, presumably because she would be more pliable. As one of East Wind's negotiators had predicted, "the only thing we can probably expect is an Asian face in the administration." [67]

By spring 1976, the East Wind founders had left Ann Arbor. Although they left behind a viable organization, it was different from the one they had started: less interested in politics and more interested in culture. In an article aptly titled "Asian Group's Activism Cools: East Wind Refocuses," an East Wind member was quoted as saying, "A 'friendlier, less politically-oriented' leadership has taken control as the last of the East Wind's original leaders . . . left the community. . . . Folk singing, poetry readings and social functions, now carry importance equal to political activities under the new seven-person steering committee or 'core group.' " [68] It was a sign of the changing times.

Like other activists in the Midwest who identified with the broader Asian

American community but were frustrated with organizing on campuses that had comparatively few Asian American students or in isolated communities that had apathetic residents, East Wind leaders eventually left to participate in political struggles elsewhere, usually on the West and East Coasts. A few of them went to nearby Chicago to work at the New Youth Center (NYC) in Chinatown. NYC was founded in fall 1971 by a group of Chinese American and overseas Chinese students who had organized English- and Chinese-language classes the previous spring.[69] Apparently, its name was taken from *Hsin ch'ing nien* (New Youth), the most influential intellectual journal of the May Fourth Movement (1915–1923) in China. Originally a liberal publication that served as a forum for the translation, discussion, and dissemination of new artistic forms and social values, by 1920 the journal had been radically transformed into a Chinese Communist political organ.

The NYC experienced a similar fate. While it began as a liberal community-based organization, it ended up being controlled by Workers Viewpoint Organization, a Marxist–Leninist group. The Federal Bureau of Investigation regarded its activities as sufficiently suspect to order its Chicago field office to ascertain whether the NYC was "affiliated with the American Communist Workers Movement or any other basic revolutionary organization."[70] The Chicago office opined that the NYC was a "front organization strictly focusing on community services in order to gain wide acceptance before it becomes more openly pro-mainland,"[71] though it offered no evidence other than its support for the local U.S.–China Friendship Association, a pro-Maoist group.

The NYC organizers enlisted the support of young Asian Americans attending midwestern colleges and Chicago Chinatown youth. In addition to providing a variety of community services, it had a political agenda:

> The New Youth Center's major purpose is to serve the Chinese-American community . . . thru its participation in the Chinese people's fight for democratic rights in the U.S. Democratic rights are the basic rights of people to decent housing and jobs, to adequate food, clothing, education, and health care, and to the liberties of free speech and belief as guaranteed in the U.S. Constitution. All people in America, whether white, Black, or Asian, are entitled to these basic democratic rights.[72]

As an advocate of democratic rights for Chinese Americans, the NYC engaged in a number of "fights." For example, in 1974, it tried to convince the Pekin (Illinois) High School basketball team to change its name from "Chinks" to something else. NYC members and other Asian Americans traveled to Pekin to make a presentation to the school and urge the student council to hold a referendum on the question. They noted that the school mascot, Mr. Bamboo, who welcomed fans wearing a silk gown and cap, and sporting a drooping mustache and queue, degraded Chinese Americans.[73] Two history teachers at the school remarked that the teach-in represented the first lesson on the problem of racial prejudice in America that their students had ever had. While the teach-in convinced many students that their sports teams' nickname perpetuated negative stereotypes, it was unable to persuade enough of them to change the name. Its success was limited to the development of a "new social sensitivity" among the students. In 1982, the school administration finally decided that the name was indeed derogatory to Chinese Americans and, in spite of student opposition, changed it to the Dragons. Older Pekin High School alumni, however, continue to refer to themselves as "Chinks."

NYC also struggled to establish a much needed day-care facility for working mothers in Chinatown. While it was able to overcome what it referred to as the "feudal mentality" of Chinese women and to mobilize them to support the drive for a day-care center, it was unable to gain the cooperation of the Chinese Consolidated Benevolent Association (CCBA).[74] The CCBA offered several spurious reasons for its unwillingness to cooperate: the lack of federal monies (though there were sources like the Model Cities program), the lack of a suitable site (though there were several potential ones available), the possibility of racial tensions (a real but minimal concern), the need to place the program for a day-care center under the guidance of "influential people" (presumably themselves) rather than continue it as a community effort, and finally, the alleged lack of a real need for a day-care facility, since the Chinatown women could care for the children themselves if they simply stopped playing so much Mah-Jongg. Actually, the CCBA was mainly concerned about risking a loss of power over the Chinatown community. CCBA's unwillingness to cooperate with the NYC resulted in a further erosion of its credibility as the ruling body in Chicago's Chinatown.

The Emergence of the Movement

As Asian American activists emerged throughout the country to engage politically in a variety of campus and community concerns, the transcendent issue for them as well as for other political activists was the Vietnam War. The United

States intervened in South Vietnam as part of its post–World War II strategy of containing communism, which, with the "loss of China," seemed to be spreading rapidly throughout the Third World. Ironically, the antiwar movement it engendered would end the Cold War consensus against communism as increasing numbers of people questioned how democratic the United States was in suppressing a national liberation movement and reappraised Marxism–Leninism in the light of what many considered American imperialism in Indochina. With the passage of the Gulf of Tonkin Resolution (7 August 1964), President Lyndon B. Johnson committed the United States to war in Southeast Asia and authorized the drafting of college students the following year. As U.S. military involvement escalated, so did the opposition to it. On 24 February 1965, the United States began operation "Rolling Thunder," the bombing of North Vietnam, and on 8 March 1965, two U.S. Marine Corps battalions arrived in South Vietnam to protect the Da Nang air base; by the end of the year American troop strength had reached nearly 200,000. Liberals, with roots in the old peace movement, joined student radicals to organize an antiwar coalition. On 24 March 1965 the first "teach-in" was held at the University of Michigan at Ann Arbor; by the end of the year, the antiwar movement began using "direct tactics" to try to disrupt the war effort.[75]

The Vietnam War and the opposition to it unified Asian Americans psychologically and politically. The war catalyzed the development of an Asian American identity, mainly because it reawakened the sociomilitary phenomenon known as "gookism."[76] "Gooks," a pan-racial epithet first used during the Philippine–American War (1899–1902) to refer to Filipino "natives who had no mixture of European 'blood'—a particularly despised (or pitied) category which imperialists freely predicted would die out as 'progress' occurred."[77] Historically, the appellation has been applied to Haitians, Nicaraguans, Costa Ricans, and other people of color, but since the Korean War it has been used mainly by U.S. soldiers to denigrate Asian people.[78] It implied that they were something less than human and could be dispatched with few qualms. It was used in the Vietnam War to prepare soldiers psychologically to maim and kill Southeast Asians, according to some Asian American veterans. During the Winter Soldier investigations into U.S. war crimes, Scott Shimabukaro, Third Marine Division, testified that "military men have the attitude that a gook is a gook. . . . Once they get into the military, they go through this brainwashing about the Asian people being subhuman—all the Asian people—I don't mean just the South Vietnamese. . . . All Asian people.[79] "Gookism" made no distinction between the Vietnamese, Laotians, and Cambodians (among other Asians) encountered overseas and Asian Americans at home just as no distinction had been made between Japanese and Japanese Americans during World War II. The term was even used to refer to Asian Americans serving in the U.S. military. As far as European American soldiers were concerned, Asians and Asian Americans not only looked alike but were one and the same. Mike Nakayama, First Marine Division, noted that he was called "Ho Chi Minh . . . Jap and gook" and that returning servicemen referred to Asian Americans as "gooks."[80] As a result of their military training and their brutalization by the war, therefore, American soldiers developed a deadly disdain for all persons of Asian ancestry. As far as they were concerned, "The only good gook is a dead gook."[81]

Asian American activists, in response, opposed the war as unjust *and* racist. They considered the derogatory designation "gook" a graphic illustration of the connection between racial oppression and the Vietnam War, raising disturbing questions about the nation's commitment to democratic ideals. Some of them argued that Americans were waging a "genocidal" conflict against Asian people considered to be biologically and culturally inferior, an assumption that was traceable historically to nineteenth-century imperialism in Asia, and believed that racial hatred was the underlying reason for the numerous atrocities committed overseas. In this they were implicitly supported by Al Hubbard, executive secretary of the Vietnam Veterans Against the War, who observed that "most 'war crimes' are committed by people who feel they have some kind of permission for what they do—even to the point of feeling righteous— and who commonly regard their victims as less than human. Dehumanization provided the means of tolerating mass destruction or genocide."[82] Among the many crimes committed in Vietnam, the most infamous was the My Lai massacre. On 16 March 1968, 105 soldiers of Charlie Company, Eleventh Brigade, Americal Division, rounded up and killed 347 men, women, and children in the Vietnamese hamlet of My Lai.[83] At the trial of Lieutenant William Calley, who was in charge, reference was made to the "Mere Gook Rule," a tacit military policy that condoned the slaughter of Vietnamese civilians.[84] But the soldiers who did the deed were not the only ones responsible. As Hubbard noted, "It is hypocritical self-righteousness to condemn the soldiers at My Lai without condemning those who set the criminal policy of free-fire zones, strategic hamlets, saturation bombing, etcetera, from which My Lai was the inevitable result."[85]

In emphasizing the racial underpinnings of the Vietnam War Asian Ameri-

cans were addressing an issue usually ignored by antiwar activists. They replaced slogans like "Give peace a chance" and "Bring the G.I.s home" with
"Stop killing our Asian brothers and sisters" and "Asian lives are not cheap
and Asians must say so now!" But they were roundly rebuffed by fellow antiwar dissidents, who regarded the issue of race as divisive and distracting.
Asian Americans became increasingly disillusioned with the white-dominated
antiwar movement, just as feminists were becoming dissatisfied with the movement's refusal to recognize that American soldiers were raping Asian *women*.

Though Asian Americans continued to support the antiwar movement, they
did so on their own terms. That often meant forming separate groups in the
major demonstrations that were erupting across the country, such as when several hundred Asian Americans (80 percent of whom were students and youths,
equally divided between Chinese and Japanese) marched as a separate contingent in the November 1969 antiwar demonstration in San Francisco or when
Asian Americans decided to march apart from the main body of protestors because the coordinating committee of the April 1971 antiwar demonstration in
Washington, D.C., was unwilling to adopt a statement against racism.[86] Sometimes it meant engaging in provocative actions, such as when one group of
Asian American activists seized the speakers' platform at an April 1971 antiwar rally at San Francisco's Golden Gate Park in order to "read a statement
supporting the Vietnamese peoples struggle against U.S. aggression, and denouncing . . . [the antiwar organizers'] disregard for Asian people."[87] In order
to make their presence felt in the broader antiwar movement, Asian American
activists organized their own antiwar coalitions, such as the Bay Area Asian
Coalition Against the War, Los Angeles Asian Coalition, Sacramento Asian
Coalition Against the War, East Coast Ad Hoc Committee of Asians Against
the War in Vietnam, and Asian-American Veterans Against the War.[88]

The antiwar movement was most effective during the Johnson administration (1963–1969) because it divided the Democratic party. In 1968, after the
Tet offensive resulted in the brief capture of cities and towns, political leaders
realized that the United States was not winning the war and gradually reduced
American forces and turned over the ground war to South Vietnamese forces.
Except for massive demonstrations during fall 1969 and spring 1971, the antiwar movement gradually lost steam during the Nixon administration (1969–
1974) as the "Vietnamization" of the war resulted in fewer American casualties
but greater Vietnamese ones, raising suspicions that the antiwar movement was
chiefly concerned about the well-being of Americans who might be sent to

fight and die overseas, rather than about the Vietnamese people. But for many Asian American antiwar activists, the fate of the Vietnamese became equally important as they increasingly identified with other Asians. Some of the more extreme elements even called for the National Liberation Front of South Vietnam to be victorious, chanting such slogans as "Ho Chi Minh! Madame Binh! NLF is gonna win!" After the Paris Peace Accords (27 January 1973), the antiwar movement essentially changed from protests to vigilance to ensure that the agreement was implemented.

For many Asian Americans, the antiwar movement was their first engagement in political protest. Indeed, the antiwar movement became the main means of politically engaging Asian Americans, especially students and youth, who made up the majority of the protestors. As antiwar activists, they overcame ethnic differences and geographic limitations in a common struggle to stop the war. In the process of traveling to other parts of the country to work against the war, they met other Asian Americans with whom they shared similar concerns and perspectives. Involvement in the antiwar movement convinced many campus and community activists that if they were ever to have a voice in this country, they would have to work together as a people—an Asian American people. In bringing Asian American activists together to participate in a common cause that transcended college campuses and Asian ethnic communities, the antiwar movement helped transform previously isolated instances of political activism into a social movement that was national in scope—the Asian American Movement.

Although the antiwar movement politicized a generation of Asian Americans, the Black Power movement moved them toward the goals of racial equality, social justice, and political empowerment. The Black Power movement emerged from the left wing of the civil rights movement, rejecting its integrationist ideology and assimilationist approach.[89] Instead, Black Power adherents advocated "community control," that is, local control of economic, political, social, and cultural institutions in African American communities. African American urban ghettos in America, they argued, were "internal colonies" that paralleled African colonies, while the Black Power movement paralleled the national liberation movements in Africa. In this "internal colonialism" paradigm, both were legacies of nineteenth-century imperialism that had divided the Third World into colonies exploited by a capitalist-dominated world economy.

Asian American activists too drew parallels between their communities

(Chinatown, Little Tokyo, Manilatown, etc.) and colonies (such as the Philippines, whose long history of foreign domination began with Spain and ended with the United States).[90] They argued that Asian American workers were politically subjugated and economically exploited for their labor. And they further drew parallels between their incipient Asian American Movement and the national liberation movements in Asia, particularly in Vietnam and China. They readily identified with Asians struggling to free themselves from Western colonizers, especially American imperialists. At the Berkeley "Yellow Identity" conference, which is discussed in Chapter 2, Isao Fujimoto cited "extensive evidence to shatter the myth of assimilation and to prove how the racist, colonialist majority exploited the minorities."[91] Although scholars have found the "internal colony" paradigm wanting as an analytical tool, Asian American activists at the time appreciated it, for it placed racial conflicts within an international context. The concept synthesized the disparate elements of racism—economic exploitation, political powerlessness, geographic ghettoization, cultural contempt—into an intelligible system of oppression. Moreover, it implicitly called for internal resistance to that oppression.

The Black Power movement, which had cultural nationalism as one of its central features, was therefore a natural model to emulate. By emphasizing racial pride and African American culture, the Black Power movement inspired Asian Americans, especially middle-class college students, to assert themselves as a people of color.[92] As an ethnic-consciousness movement, the Black Power movement made Asian Americans realize that they too had been defined by European American attitudes and dominated by an Eurocentric culture. They had to rethink who they were and re-create their own cultural identity, forging distinct Asian ethnic group identities into a pan-Asian one. The foundation for this unique identity was their experience as Asians in America—a common history of oppression and resistance that would serve as the basis for a "bold culture, unashamed and true to itself."[93]

For Asian Americans, the antiwar movement crystallized their understanding of racial discrimination against Asians in America and convinced them that an inter-Asian coalition was an effective way of opposing it. By couching the criticism of the Vietnam War in racial terms, they raised people's consciousness about the problems that Asians in America had and the need to solve them. The Black Power movement focused their attention on the needs of Asian ethnic communities and the potential power of a pan-Asian identity and culture.

Activists would transcend Asian ethnic divisions and coalesce into a pan-Asian social movement based on racial consciousness and radical politics. Learning that it was necessary to act collectively in a European American society, they became a band of brothers and sisters with the basic goal of individual and group empowerment, the very pursuit of which affirmed their right to be part of the American pluralist system of democracy. They participated in national campaigns demanding justice for individual Asian Americans and national mobilizations around such important community concerns as bilingual/bicultural education, immigration reform, and redress and reparations for Japanese Americans incarcerated during World War II. In the process, they would erode the existing power structure in Asian ethnic communities and redefine their relationship to the wider society.

An integral part of pan-Asianism was an Asian American identity and culture. Seeking to reclaim a common past and working for a common future, historians, writers, artists, and performers worked to define who an Asian American was. As Amy Uyematsu noted in her well-known essay "The Emergence of Yellow Power in America," the underlying motivation for activism was concern over personal identity, all the rhetoric about politics notwithstanding. Asian Americans realized that in trying to be assimilated "Americans" they had rejected Asian culture and accepted the values and attitudes of European American people, and even tried to look like them.

> They have rejected their physical heritages, resulting in extreme self-hatred. Yellow people share with the blacks the desire to look white. Just as blacks wish to be light-complected with thin lips and unkinky hair, "yellows" want to be tall with long legs and large eyes. The self-hatred is also evident in the yellow male's obsession with unobtainable white women, and in the yellow female's attempt to gain male approval by aping white beauty standards. Yellow females have their own "conking" techniques—they use "peroxide, foam rubber, and scotch tape to give them light hair, large breasts, and double-lidded eyes.[94]

Such pathetic efforts were all for nought: European Americans still considered them foreigners, relegating them to the margins of society. Being neither European American nor African American, Asian Americans were left with a disquieting question, "Who am I?" To find an answer, many people participated in the Asian American Movement.

2

Who Am I?

Creating an Asian American

Identity and Culture

> If the Asian American is to live in a
> very complex America and an even
> more complex world, and if he is to be
> able to assert his own humanity in
> these spheres, he must know his own
> cultural history as an Asian American.
> —An Asian American student (1968)

Where are you *really* from? Often asked of Asian Americans, this question implies that they are strangers in the land, as European Americans seldom accept an American locality as an answer. The question haunted many of those who participated in the Movement, especially young middle-class Asian Americans who were twice alienated from American society. As with other members of their generation, they were suffering from the spiritual malaise that came with life in what young people in the 1960s and 1970s regarded as a culturally sterile and one-dimensional society dominated by complex and corrupt institutions that sought to "coopt" them.[1] In the eyes of these disaffected youths, none was more powerful and perverse than the U.S. government, which was pursuing what many young people perceived as a misguided foreign policy in Southeast Asia and conscripting them into the U.S. military to enforce it. They began to question anything that was beyond their personal control. In addition, young Asian Americans were hurting from the effects of racial prejudice. They reluctantly acknowledged that though they felt like Americans, behaved like Americans, and shared the prevailing cultural values and norms, the majority of their fellow countrymen treated them, including those born and raised in the United States, as unwelcome foreigners. Excluded by mainstream society, they were *in* American culture, but not *of* it.

On the heels of this realization came a disillusionment the depth of which revealed how thoroughly Asian Americans had embraced the nation's ideals, especially the principle of equality and the dignity of common people. They believed, as generations of American schoolchildren have been taught, that they enjoyed an inalienable right to "life, liberty and the pursuit of happiness"— only to discover that the U.S. Constitution applied only to white Americans. Quite understandably, they felt that their country had deceived them and had betrayed its commitment to racial equality and social justice, feelings that moved them toward radicalism. Having tried to assimilate into mainstream culture, only to be rejected as "unassimilable sojourners," they sought alternatives. Instead of seeking to be integrated into the institutions and processes of the wider society, many of them realized that a more attainable aim was to make a place for themselves in America's ethnic pluralist society through the development of a unique ethnic identity and counterculture. The Movement gave them an unprecedented means of developing a pan-Asian consciousness, changing them from Asian ethnics into Asian Americans.

Yellow Identity

An early effort to develop an Asian American identity and culture was the "Asian American Experience in America—Yellow Identity" conference held on 11 January 1969 at the University of California, Berkeley. An estimated nine hundred Asian Americans, mainly Chinese and Japanese Americans from the West Coast, participated in this extraordinary event to learn about "Asian-American history and destiny, and the need to express Asian American solidarity in a predominantly white society."[2] If nothing else, the "active participation and vocal spontaneous exchanges throughout the day unmistakably exploded the myth of 'mellow yellow.' "[3] But what began as a first-of-a-kind educational forum turned into an unexpected political convention when student panelists and "some out-spoken students from S.F. State College quickly shifted the subject-matter of the Conference to the struggle at State College" and took over the conference.[4] They tried to get the conferees to adopt a resolution supporting the Third World strike at San Francisco State. Meanwhile, the three groups (Nisei Students Club, Chinese Students Club, and Chinese Students Association) that had sponsored the conference publicly dissociated themselves from any resolutions that might be adopted. Though the conference ended in political disarray, it did make Asian Americans realize that it would take more than a single event to achieve ethnic solidarity. Indeed, it eventually took myriad meetings by small groups of Asian Americans across the country to develop a collective consciousness.

Asian Americans soon began to gather together in consciousness-raising groups to address the issue of identity. During the many meetings they attended, Asian Americans experienced a catharsis, releasing years of pent-up negative feelings about themselves and dissipating inner tensions and anxieties. They helped each other expose and deconstruct unconscious cultural assumptions. A tragicomic discovery was how some of them had tried so futilely and frustratingly to transform themselves physically into European Americans. Amy Tan, the well-known novelist, recalled that as a youngster she had placed a clothes pin on her nose, presumably to make it more like the aquiline noses of her European American friends.[5] Edward Iwata, one of the new generation of Asian American journalists, confessed to having had an "eye and nose job" in an ill-advised attempt to make himself look more European American; afterward, he realized that it was "psychic surgery, an act of mutilation, a symbolic suicide."[6]

Many Asian Americans concluded that they felt confused (and inferior) about who they were because society had forced the dominant culture on them and prevented them from forming an identity they could call their own. Without a self-defined identity, they realized, they were vulnerable psychologically and politically. They therefore consciously set out to develop "a new identity by integrating [their] past experiences with [their] present conditions" and to raise "group esteem and pride, for it [was] only through collective action that society's perception of the Asian-American [could] be efficiently altered."[7] The Movement became the means of accomplishing this.

Asian American activists agreed that cultural domination played a central role in shaping their individual identities and that the absence of an autonomous culture contributed to their powerlessness as a people. They felt estranged from things Asian because they had seen Asian life through the prism of a Eurocentric culture.[8] And what they had seen they had despised: Asian cultures' emphasis on the tyranny of the group over the individual, the agrarian stagnation and material backwardness of Asian societies, and the existence of polygamy and the oppression of women. American culture, in contrast, was esteemed for its emphasis on individual freedom, commercial enterprise, material advancement, and monogamy.

Before the 1960s, most people assumed that Asian Americans were beneficiaries of both American and Asian cultures—the best of two worlds.[9] Nevertheless, Asian American cultural activists such as Frank Chin have pointed to the dual heritage as a racist concept.[10] They have argued that the dominant society has convinced itself that through some unexplained and probably inexplicable process Asian Americans have maintained their cultural integrity as Asians, thus developing a dual personality that can be analytically separated into Asian and American components. This false notion has been used to explain the Asian Americans' seeming inability to assimilate into American society, rationalizing the injustices visited on them and placing the blame on the victims' shoulders.

Asian American activists rejected the concept of a dual heritage that artificially divided their identity into abstract Asian and American halves. Instead, they acknowledged a distinct Asian American identity that had evolved over the years, based on the experiences of Asians in America. It was in the crucible of "Asian America" that their individual and group identities were shaped and had integrity. But what *was* Asian America? Except for an emotional affinity, they were uncertain about its characteristics. Before they could define it with any precision, Asian Americans had to refute societal stereotypes that had degraded them; reclaim their history, which had been relegated to the periphery of American historiography; and reconstruct a culture that reflected their experiences. Then and only then could they begin bringing Asians in America together and giving them a sense of who they were.

Refuting Stereotypes

Solving the problem of stereotypes was and still is a major concern in the Movement. Historically, racial stereotypes reflected the country's antagonism towards Asian immigrants and Asian countries.[11] Before the passage of the Immigration Act of 1924, which effectively ended the immigration of all Asian groups to the United States, anti-Asian hostility reflected an unwarranted fear of the economic competition of Asian workers and the threat of "racial mongrelization" through miscegenation. It was obviously a manifestation of nativism, which held that Asians were unassimilable aliens. In actuality, nativists actively discouraged Asians from assimilating into society and supported laws that prevented them from ever becoming citizens of the country.[12] The corollary to the image of Asian Americans as perpetual foreigners in the land was that only European Americans could become "authentic" Americans. In the 1930s, anti-Asian animus arose from anxieties over the military threat (and in more recent years, the economic competition) posed by various Asian nations, especially Japan. In both eras, Asians were perceived as a Yellow Peril that threatened Western civilization in general and the United States in particular. The Yellow Peril was a myth to justify imperialism in Asia and anti-Asian policies and practices in the United States.[13]

Basically, racial stereotypes have portrayed Asians as a "special" species—as subhumans, inhumans, even superhumans, but rarely as humans. These unidimensional caricatures convey implicit messages about the peculiar genetic makeup and cultural values of Asians. As subhumans, they presumably have a low regard for human life, notably their own. In war movies, soldiers (Chinese, Japanese, Korean, Vietnamese, regardless of which side they are on) display utter disregard for life by attacking in human waves (and in the process dying in droves) or committing suicide to atone for some egregious human mistake. As inhumans, Asian arch-villains totally lacking in compassion seek to control the world, particularly its women. In the pulp novels of Sax Rohmer, the quintessential fiend was Fu Manchu, "whose lust was only exceeded by his sadism." [14] As superhuman, they are geniuses who possessed the hoary wisdom of the East, or masters of some arcane science or art form, which could be perverted for evil purposes. Charlie Chan, the Chinese detective who never quite mastered the English language, was pure intellect housed in a bovine body; Bruce Lee, the kung-fu master, was a one-man wave of death and destruction; neither was quite human.

Asians and Asian Americans have been considered fundamentally different from European Americans, who are of an indeterminate ethnicity and the standard against which people of color are measured and found wanting. The latter have been invariably perceived as innately inferior because of biology or culture, even in the case of superhuman Asians, whose exaggerated attributes are narrowly focused and are achieved at the expense of other qualities so that they are incomplete as human beings. A recent variation is the insidious "model minority" stereotype, which suggests that Asian Americans are more adept than other people of color at "making it" in mainstream society. Like other stereotypes, it serves a particular social purpose—in this case, to make invidious comparisons with other people of color, blaming them, rather than the economic and sociopolitical barriers in American society, for their problems.

Stereotypes are learned at an early age and disseminated through children's books and the elementary school curriculum. Whatever information about Asian Americans they include is usually distorted and misleading.[15] Instead of conveying accurate knowledge about Asian Americans, books and curricula more often than not promote misconceptions about them. According to the Asian American Children's Book Project, which had been organized by the Council on Interracial Books for Children, an examination of sixty-six children's books published between 1945 and 1975 revealed that, with one or perhaps two exceptions, they were, "racist, sexist, and elitist."[16] The eleven Asian American reviewers in the project concluded that "a succinct definition of the image presented would be: Asian Americans are foreigners who all look alike and choose to live together in quaint communities in the midst of large cities and cling to 'outworn,' alien customs" and criticized the books for failing "to depict Asian American culture as distinct from Asian culture or some 'Oriental' stereotype of it, or on the other hand, as distinct from the culture of white America."[17]

Strengthening the stereotypes promoted in children's books and school curricula are images derived from what Carlos E. Cortés calls the "societal curriculum," that is, the "massive, ongoing, informal curriculum of family, peer groups, neighborhoods, mass media, and other socializing forces that 'educate' us throughout our lives."[18] Over the years, such popular Western cultural classics as Gilbert and Sullivan's *The Mikado*, a comic opera written in 1885 reflecting Western domination and exploitation of Asian societies, promoted "racial stereotypes by accentuating 'Oriental' despotism and submissiveness; confusing China and Japan; using nonsensical racist names (such as Nanki-poo, Yum-yum, Pooh-bah, Pish-tush, and Peep-bo), 'nigger,' and other racial epithets; exaggerating preoccupations with suicide and death; and using racist caricatures of Japanese music."[19]

Another, less obvious, part of the societal curriculum are comic books, several million of which are circulated among children (and many adults). They constitute a convenient means of conveying stereotypes to a popular audience, leaving unforgettable and unfavorable images of Asians in the reader's psyche. According to Michio Kaku, a physicist and member of Asian Americans for a Fair Media, these stereotypes fall into specific "syndromes": Fu Manchu, Kemosabe, Confucius Say, Banzai, and Dragon Lady.[20] In general, Asian men are portrayed as "retarded, sadistic, or bucktoothed," and Asian women are reduced to "exotic" sex objects, with a penchant for European American men.

Whether negative or positive, stereotypes are essentially false images that obscure the complexity and diversity that is an inherent feature of Asian Americans as well as other people. The majority of the stereotypes apply to Asian nationals, rather than Asian Americans, but because most Americans are unable or unwilling to distinguish one from the other, they have been readily transferred to Asian Americans. Since there are so few Asian Americans, most of whom live in major urban areas such as New York, San Francisco, and Los Angeles, the probability of having the kind of interracial interaction that would correct these misconceptions is slight.

Among social scientists the question of whether stereotypes have a deleterious effect on people is an open one; among Asian Americans it is generally believed that they have had a profound psychic impact on them. Asian Americans have long known that stereotypes are detrimental: demeaning their dignity by denying them individuality, undermining their identity by limiting their self-expression and self-development, engendering ambivalent feelings by instilling self-hatred. For a generation of Asian Americans, Ronald Tanaka's poem "I Hate My Wife for Her Flat Yellow Face" (1969), captured the anguish of self-contempt stemming from humiliating self-images:

> I hate my wife for her flat yellow face
> and her fat cucumber legs, but mostly
> for her lack of elegance and lack of
> intelligence compared to judith gluck.[21]

More recently, Asian Americans have argued that stereotypes constitute a form of "psychological violence" that leads to physical violence against them, especially during periods of tension between the United States and Asian nations.[22]

Out of such ambivalence came a desire to emulate European Americans, who are considered physically, morally, and sexually superior. For certain cultural nationalists, Asian Americans who tried to become European American were "conditioned to accept and live in a state of euphemized self-contempt. This self-contempt itself is nothing more than the subject's acceptance of white standards of objectivity, beauty, behavior, and achievement as being morally absolute, and his acknowledgement that, because he is not white, he can never fully measure up to white standards." [23]

Ever since the inception of the Movement, Asian American activists have challenged these stereotypes. One of the earliest organized efforts was Asian Americans for a Fair Media, which evolved into the Asian American Journalists Association. In 1972, there was a community effort to denounce an International Ladies Garment Workers Union (ILGWU) advertisement that was appearing on New York City subways. Asking a loaded question, "Has your job been exported to Japan?" the ad implicitly blamed its members' problems on Japanese nationals and, by extension, everyone who looked Asian. (Paradoxically, many ILGWU members were Asian Americans!) It was all too reminiscent of the nineteenth-century practice of using Asian Americans as scapegoats for the country's economic woes. After Asian Americans for Action organized a coalition of concerned people of color and European Americans to demonstrate in front of ILGWU headquarters, many participants felt that "a permanent body should be set up to coordinate protests against racism in the media"; hence the founding of Asian Americans for a Fair Media (AAFM).[24]

AAFM developed a broad-based strategy for combating stereotypes. In New York City, it organized a task force to gather examples in the media, which were then displayed on the bulletin boards of various community groups. This effort heightened Asian Americans' awareness of the magnitude of the problem, encouraging them to protest offensive advertisements and demand retractions or "equal time" on radio and television programs. AAFM also tried to ally itself with other people of color around the country concerned about racial bias in the media. Finally, it tried to educate European Americans about the deleterious effect that stereotypes had on Asian Americans. Among other things, it disseminated a handbook containing illustrations and commentary on the Asian American stereotypes permeating the media.[25] Through this educational device, the organization hoped to convey its conviction that racial images had "an explosive psychological force that warps human relationships and wreaks havoc on one's personal dignity." [26]

Since the days of AAFM, there have been other efforts to eliminate demeaning and debilitating stereotypes. One that was national in scope was the

"C.A.N. Charlie Chan" campaign. In 1980, the Coalition of Asians to Nix Charlie Chan organized to protest the production of *Charlie Chan and the Curse of the Dragon Queen*, which starred Peter Ustinov and Lee Grant parodying Asians. As *Bridge* explained, "Charlie Chan represents the most derogatory stereotype of Chinese, and in general, Asian America. To perpetuate such an inglorious and outdated myth in the 1980s is unwise, odious, and insulting." [27] Chan, supposed to be a well-educated immigrant with a mastery of both Eastern and Western knowledge, had the quaint habit of speaking English as if he had learned it from reading aphorisms found in fortune cookies. Yet he was supposed to be a positive portrayal! That is, he represented a European American's ideal image of an Asian American projected on to the silver screen: intelligent, passive, polite, self-effacing, and effeminate. [28] With the possible exception of intelligence, none of his vaunted attributes ranked high on the American scale of manhood. Small wonder that Asian American cultural nationalists, particularly men, were offended. Equally galling was the fact that in forty-seven feature-length movies, Charlie Chan had been played by European American actors; though his sons were played by Asian Americans. The incongruity was not lost on Arthur Hu, the neoconservative critic, who remarked: "Everyone complains about Charlie Chan, but who noticed the supreme irony in that while the elder was a white man playing a Chinese, number-one son was a Chinese playing a straight white American kid?" [29] After the coalition organized a massive telephone campaign to the San Francisco mayor's office, the filmmaker abandoned plans for filming in San Francisco's Chinatown.

A more recent effort to challenge stereotyping was the *Miss Saigon* controversy, which began as a protest over the so-called adhesive-tape phenomenon: the casting in Asian roles of European American actors who use tape (or some prosthetic device) applied to the temples and cheekbones and "yellowface" makeup to approximate the appearance of Asians. [30] By casting only European Americans, even as Asian characters, Asian American actors are denied meaningful roles. Asian Americans have since shifted the emphasis of the protest from equal employment opportunities for Asian American actors to the play's racist and sexist images. (In *Miss Saigon*, all the Asian roles were negative, with men portrayed as sleazy pimps and subhuman soldiers and women as bar girls and low-class prostitutes.)

Miss Saigon is a loose adaptation of Puccini's tragic opera *Madama Butterfly* to the Vietnam War. In July 1990, Actor's Equity Association condemned the proposed casting of Jonathan Pryce, an English actor, to re-create on Broadway his leading role from the London production as an Eurasian pimp: "The casting of a Caucasian actor made up to appear Asian is an affront to the Asian community. . . . [It is] especially disturbing when the casting of an Asian actor, in this role, would be an important and significant opportunity to break the usual pattern of casting Asians in minor roles."[31] Equity pointed to a clause in its production contract, in which all parties agreed "to continue their joint efforts toward, and reaffirm their commitment to the policy of nondiscrimination, and to an ongoing policy of furthering the principles of equal employment opportunities."[32]

Led by the Pan Asian Repertory Theater, a coalition of fifteen Asian American community organizations, including the New York chapter of the Asian American Journalists Association, the Asian American Legal Defense and Education Fund, and the Chinese Progressive Association, came out in support of Equity's position. The coalition argued that though an European American actor could play "the Engineer" (the name for the Eurasian brothel owner), it was essential that there be "a good faith effort to audition Asian actors for the role."[33] For Tisa Chang, the artistic and production director of the Pan Asian Repertory Theater, the "real issue is not who gets cast, but that any organization continue to perpetuate and encourage stereotypes at the expense of artists of color, which borders on 19th-century imperialism."[34] For Vincent Tai, a board member of the Asian American Theatre Company, the exclusion of Asian Americans from principal roles was simply a variant of the "glass ceiling" effect, whereby Asian Americans find it difficult to advance beyond a certain level in corporations and institutions.[35]

Not all Asian Americans supported Equity's position. Frank Chin, the iconoclastic playwright, thought the struggle silly, since Asian American actors were fighting to play stereotypical roles. Furthermore, he believed that "once a production—any production, even a racist one—is mounted, then a producer should be allowed to proceed as he likes. In other words, he supported the creative freedom of the producer."[36]

Cameron Mackintosh and his associates maintained that casting Pryce in the lead was purely an artistic decision, shifting the dispute away from economics and equity. In addition, they argued that Pryce was being rejected solely on the basis of his race and condemned Equity's action as "reverse discrimination" and a violation of its own principle of nontraditional casting "encouraging producers to cast nonracially defined roles with performers of talent, regardless of skin color."[37] Their arguments displayed a lack of understanding of and sympathy for the concept of affirmative action, which gives preferential treatment to people of color who have historically been excluded from employment and educational opportunities and continue to suffer from discrimination in American society. Affirmative action differs markedly from past laws that consciously discriminated against *entire* groups of people solely because of their race. Affirmative action policies were conceived as correctives to centuries of injustice. Unfortunately, in the process a few European Americans would be hurt, an unavoidable price that had to be paid in order to achieve greater equality and justice. In the theater community, affirmative action took the form of nontraditional casting, which was conceived as a means of increasing employment of minority actors—not as a means of enabling European American actors to play minority roles.

Even though Equity was forced to reverse itself when Mackintosh threatened to cancel *Miss Saigon*, in the long run, the controversy will probably benefit the Asian American community. For one thing, it has instilled in Asian American theater artists a sense of solidarity. They have organized themselves into such groups as Asian Pacific Alliance for Creative Equality to work for the casting of Asian Americans in Asian roles. For another, it may lead to fewer European American actors masquerading as Asians on stage, more Asian American actors being offered leading as well as meaningful roles, and the eventual elimination of dehumanizing and degrading stereotypes.

Reclaiming the Past

While refuting racial stereotypes has been a necessary part of forming an Asian American identity, so also has been learning what is accurate. An informed understanding has been even more important for Asian Americans themselves than for other people, since it has influenced their self-concepts and their children's. After all, what one was heavily influences what one is and will be. Historically voiceless, Asian Americans have needed to reclaim their history, find significance in it, and make it known to others. Through a more accurate understanding of their history, they hoped to find a voice, one that embodied a more meaningful and complex identity.

Community scholars and artists have been preserving Asian American heritage through local studies, documentaries, songs, posters, murals, plays, dances, historical societies, archival resources, ethnic museums, and other community-based projects. They brought to their task invaluable assets: scholars, their network of local informants and access to local records, resources that have taken a lifetime to develop; artists, an expressive media to illuminate and validate alternative representations of the Asian American experience. Both have been motivated by the belief that when people interact with information about their past, they can better interpret and understand the present and gain a feel for the future. The process affirms their individual and group identity, countering the sense of "otherness" that has marked the Asian American community; and, most significantly, it empowers them, freeing them from the dominant society's definition of who they are or should be. These scholars and artists see themselves as a vital link between the past and the future, their work a permanent memorial to earlier generations and a stable foundation for later ones.

Community scholars and artists have consciously involved local residents in documenting and interpreting their own history, an activity that engenders empathy and respect for others. They write social history from the bottom up, giving voice to the silent and educating the Asian American community about itself and answering explicitly the question of whose history scholars are reconstructing. Such efforts reflects the Movement's democratic thrust. A central activity has been to record, before they die, the recollections of the *lo wah kue* (a Cantonese expression for old overseas Chinese) of America's Chinatowns; the *issei* (first-generation Japanese Americans) who leased farmland in California and elsewhere in the American West; the *manong* (a Filipino term meaning "elder brother" that refers to all first-generation immigrants) who worked up and down the West Coast; and other early immigrants. It is a difficult task, since most of the elders are dead and those who are still alive are reticent about telling their story, which they consider private as well as insignificant. Community scholars and artists perceive such recordings to be an important task because these life stories constitute the building blocks of Asian American history and culture. Future listeners will learn about their roots and derive strength from that knowledge.

Community scholars are publishing their own studies, usually highly descriptive, in an effort to reconstruct the past, often for no reason other than its intrinsic value to the community. They focus their attention on specific Asian ethnic groups and research subjects that are integral to these communities: for Chinese Americans, the legacy of exclusion; for Japanese Americans, the trauma of the concentration camps; for Filipino Americans, the penurious and painful lives of Filipino migrant workers; for Korean Americans, their contribution to Korea's independence movement against Japan. These works often explore the human costs of racism in America. They demythologize the United States as *the* land of opportunity that welcomed the wretched of the earth to its shores and recapture the emotional aspects of the Asian American experience, which are often overlooked or treated abstractly in academic tomes.

Island: Poetry and History of Chinese Immigrants on Angel Island, 1910–40 is an example par excellence of community scholarship.[38] In the late 1970s, Him Mark Lai, a Bechtel Corporation engineer; Genny Lim, a housewife and nascent poet; and Judy Yung, a librarian in the Asian branch of the Oakland Public Library, felt that the story of the Chinese who passed through Angel Island, the harsh Ellis Island of the West, needed to be told. From 1882 to 1943, most Chinese were excluded from entering the country. The few who could enter had first to submit to intense questioning and scrutiny on Angel Island, where all aspiring immigrants were detained upon arrival. The core of *Island* is the poems that Chinese immigrants wrote and carved on the walls of their barrack prisons. These poems, 135 of which have survived, tell of the "pain, loneliness, suffering and anger from being incarcerated in that hell-hole interrogation station."[39] They are of significant literary value and constitute the beginnings of Asian American culture. Augmenting the translations are interviews with Chinese who had undergone the harsh treatment, and with immigration officials and social workers who once worked there. *Island* inspired a number of other artistic works: Felicia Lowe's docudrama, *Carved in Silence*; Genny Lim's play, *Paper Angels*; Loni Ding's film, *Island of Secret Memories*; and Betty Wong's musical narrative, "Bright Moon Rising," which was produced for Festival 2,000 in San Francisco.

Like the scholars, community artists have also been reconstructing a past that many Asian Americans have been silent about, preferring to repress the painful memories that they have lived with all their lives. For Japanese Americans, one of those memories is the internment camps of World War II. Loni Ding's film, *The Color of Honor: The Japanese American Soldier in WWII*, offers one of the most comprehensive looks at the internment. Inspired to make this feature-length documentary by the San Francisco hearings on redress for former internees, she felt that it was "extremely important to deal with the contradictions of battle and liberating towns when your family is locked up at home."[40]

In the film, Ding "recovers the voices of those who wrestled with the wrenching contradiction of being incarcerated by their own government, yet called to serve in its military." [41] What makes the work so significant for the Japanese American community, as well as others, is how she deals with the issue of honor. In addition to the men who served in the 442nd Regimental Combat Team, which became the most decorated unit in U.S. military history, and those who served in the Pacific Theater as members of the little-known Military Intelligence Service, which contributed decisively to the defeat of Japan, she discusses the thousands of draft resisters and army protesters who were willing to go to federal prisons in order to challenge the constitutionality of the concentration camps. As members of the Fair Play Committee at the Heart Mountain Relocation Center, they refused to serve in the military as long as their families remained imprisoned, becoming the largest group of Americans ever to resist the draft until the Vietnam War. As her film makes clear, this choice was as courageous and honorable as serving in the armed forces. For those who took this different path and have had to endure stigma and self-doubt ever since, the film is a vindication of their courageous choice.

Recovering the history of forgotten victims and unsung heroes is important work to be sure, but it can also be depressing. An exception to the focus on how Asian Americans have been victimized is Arthur Dong's *Forbidden City, USA*, a documentary about an internationally acclaimed Chinese nightclub in San Francisco. The film successfully preserves a piece of Asian American cultural history, but it does so in an entertaining way.[42] Dong was interested in portraying Asian Americans having fun. In this Asian American counterpart to the Cotton Club, Chinese American talent performed in all-American production numbers. These entertainers were rebels, for they had to face the Chinese community's opprobrium for dancing and singing in public, and at the same time challenge segregated show business, with its stereotype of Chinese as speaking only pidgin English, having bowed legs and no rhythm. Forbidden City was a unique club that "exploited and exploded stereotypes": It exploited them by promoting itself as an "exotic" form of entertainment and exploded them by providing a venue for Asian Americans who sang like Frank Sinatra and Sophie Tucker and danced like Fred Astaire and Ginger Rogers.

In his column in *Asian Week*, William Wong raised a query about these Chinese American performers that is germane to the development of Asian American culture in general: Were the Forbidden City performers "true to their ethnicities—somehow reflecting their root cultures, or were they " 'selling out' their cultural backgrounds simply for employment"?[43] It is a controversial question, one with which Asian American cultural activists have been grappling. The plight of Asian American actors, who must choose between playing roles they find objectionable or be unemployed, has even been the subject of a play: In *Yankee Dawg You Die*, Philip Kan Gotanda explores what it means to be an Asian American actor through the interaction between an older actor who has been forced to accept demeaning roles—"Ching Chong Chinamen houseboy, the stereotypical evil Japanese World War II general, the Fu Manchu villain from outer space"—in order to make a living, and a younger actor who will accept only "roles he thinks are correct, are dignified."[44] In the course of the play, both men peer into each other's personal and professional souls, becoming more understanding and tolerant in the process. Gotanda hopes that the play's audience will no longer look at an Asian American and see a stereotype; instead, he would like them to see the Asian American as "a complex human being who is also unique because he or she is an Asian-American in this country."[45]

In addition to local studies and creative works, community scholars and artists have helped found various community-based organizations dedicated to the preservation of the Asian American past. Three examples are the New York Chinatown History Project in New York City, the Japanese American National Museum in Los Angeles, and the Filipino American National Historical Society in Seattle, each on a "cultural rescue mission" to challenge the dominant society's implicit contention that Asian Americans led insignificant lives.[46]

The New York Chinatown History Project (NYCHP) is the only major Chinese American historical research group on the East Coast.[47] Officially incorporated in 1980, it actually traces its beginnings to the Basement Workshop, where its co-founders, Charlie Lai and John Kuo Wei Tchen, former student activists, had met four years earlier.[48] Like other people at the Basement, for a time *the* Asian American cultural organization on the East Coast, they wanted to contribute to the community in some significant way. But how? They had become skeptical about the efficacy of existing community activism and "constantly asked each other . . . Who are we organizing? . . . What makes us think that something *we* want is right for the community?"[49] Since much of the radical politics in the community at the time had degenerated into sophomoric sectarianism, they had to turn elsewhere. The Chinatown History Project proved to be the alternative that they were looking for.

In 1978, Tchen, who was serving as coordinator of Basement's Asian

American Resource Center, applied for and received a grant from the New York Council for the Humanities to mount a major multimedia exhibition on Chinese in America called "Images from a Neglected Past: The Work and Culture of Chinese in America," which opened at the Chatham Square branch of the New York Public Library. According to Lai and Tchen, "the response was tremendous. Seniors would hike up those three steep flights to look at the exhibit. And many would begin to tell us their life stories. . . . It became very obvious that: one, there wasn't much publicly available material on the history of Chinatown; two, residents were deeply interested in the community's past; and three, those who have lived in the community are the real experts on the experience." [50] Inspired by this response, they decided "to establish an organization devoted to synthesizing the role of history with community-building"— the New York Chinatown History Project, which became, in effect, a vehicle for presenting a dissenting view of American society, that of the oppressed Chinese in America.[51]

Tchen and Lai decided that one of the things that the Chinatown community needed was a place—a physical and intellectual space—where people could come to raise and answer questions about themselves and the Chinatown community. They had a populist perspective, emphasizing the daily life of ordinary Chinese (as opposed to the elite), for they were convinced that working people had something significant to say. They assumed that the masses who lived and worked in Chinatown led "dynamic" rather than "passive" lives. They further believed that

> not only do all of us naturally look back to our personal past when we get older—something beautifully expressed in the traditional Chinese saying "falling leaves return to their roots"—but from a practical standpoint, we cannot improve the present unless we understand the past. Understanding the community's history, then, is not a luxury that should be left to the few who have the time and inclination, it is a necessity for all who wish to move positively into building a decent future.[52]

NYCHP is probably best known for its excellent exhibits on various aspects of community life, especially those less studied and understood, such as the lives of laundry and garment workers. In their own elliptical way, these exhibits have constituted an indictment of racial *and* class oppression. In December 1984, NYCHP opened its first exhibit, "Eight Pound Livelihood: History of Chinese Laundry Workers in the U.S.," which, as the title indicates, was about people who labored long hours in Chinese hand laundries. Mounting such an exhibit was difficult because many members of the community, including laundry workers themselves, would just as soon forget that racial barriers had forced them to enter such a low-esteem occupation and spend their lives doing such arduous work. "One embittered, elderly laundry man waved [NYCHP researchers] out of his store screaming, 'Laundries have no history!' "[53] He was wrong. The ubiquitous laundries provided the major occupation of immigrants and thus played an important part in the social history of Chinese Americans. (The same could be said for the contemporary garment industry, which employs thousands of immigrant Chinese women and is the subject of NYCHP's "Both Sides of the Cloth: Chinese American Women in the New York City Garment Industry.") Over a dozen such exhibits, including ones on other Asian Americans, have "actively made public the validation of these experiences to the lifeblood of the community's history."[54]

Since its establishment in 1980, the NYCHP has developed an enviable reputation in the local community as a place where "personal possessions and stories can be transformed into a part of the collective memory."[55] In attempting to explore the complexity of the New York Chinese experience, the project has very deliberately placed it in the cultural pluralist context of the city. As Tchen pointed out:

> We've taken a strong cultural geographic approach of looking at how a space has had a succession of groups, often at the same time, making the streetscape a variety of homes for different cultures. We've deliberately resisted a straight cultural nationalist history and favored looking at history from a perspective of hierarchical segments and constructed experiences. Hence, the Chinese in New York are acknowledged to have multiple cultural influences and identities both within the Chinese experience (e.g. a Chinese cigar maker from Cuba, or a Chinese from Toishan who stayed in S.F. for years and then migrated to New York) and also cross-culturally (e.g. lots of early Chinese New York men, many of whom were sailors, married Irish women).[56]

In 1991, Fay Chew, the executive director, and the board of directors decided to broaden the scope of NYCHP and changed its name to the Chinatown History Museum (CHM).[57] It will be devoted to the Chinese diaspora in the Americas, extending its interest beyond the New York metropolitan area to include Chinese settlements throughout the Western hemisphere. In addition to its greater geographic scope, CHM will also be a "dialogue-driven" rather than a "collections-driven" facility, emphasizing collaboration with the intended audience and reflecting its needs, instead of basing its activities on what material is available in the collection, as is the case with many traditional museums. This concept came out of the project's effort to reflect on and improve its first ten years of work. With the change from NYCHP to CHM, it is becoming a permanent part of the community that it cares so much about.

At the same time that the Chinatown History Project was being established, on the other side of the country there was a concerted movement to found a relatively traditional museum dedicated to documenting and preserving the Japanese American experience.[58] That the impetus for this effort came from the *nisei* rather than the *sansei* probably explains, in part, its conservative character. In 1980, Bruce T. Kanji, president of the Merit Savings Bank, and other leaders in the *nikkei* (Japanese American) community "raised funds to commission a feasibility study for a 'National Museum of Japanese American History.' " Meanwhile, *nisei* veterans who had been responsible for bringing an exhibit on the Japanese American soldier in World War II to the Los Angeles Natural History Museum set up the 100th/442nd/MIS Museum Foundation to build a "Japanese American Heritage Museum." Since both groups shared similar goals, they decided to merge in 1985 as the "Japanese American National Museum" (JANM).

JANM had an auspicious beginning, receiving important assistance from various public agencies: Senator Art Torres introduced a California Senate bill that resulted in a state contribution of $750,000, the Community Redevelopment Agency provided a matching grant of $1 million, and the City of Los Angeles leased the historic Nishi Hongwanji Buddhist Temple in Little Tokyo to the museum for the sum of $1 a year. The temple was an ideal choice for the museum's permanent site. Besides providing 33,000 square feet of space, it has immeasurable symbolic value. Built in 1925, it is the oldest existing Buddhist temple in the city and an integral part of the Japanese American community. During World War II, it was used as a household storage facility for interned Japanese Americans; after the war, it served as a temporary hostel for many who returned from the concentration camps.

During the 1980s, when most community-based organizations were scrambling to survive, JANM's ability to acquire such significant support was remarkable, suggesting that the Los Angeles *nikkei* community has come a long way politically. The prospect of JANM enhancing Little Tokyo's attraction as a tourist spot probably played a role as well. But to become a reality, the museum needed much more money. For that, it had to depend on the resources of the *nikkei* community itself. Under the leadership of Irene Y. Hirano, the former director of T.H.E. Clinic for Women, JANM launched a sophisticated capital campaign to raise $24.1 million. Assisting in this endeavor were a succession of national campaign steering committees whose membership reads like a Who's Who of the Japanese American community and included Japanese executives such as Akio Morita, chairman of the Sony Corporation. During the first phase of the campaign, JAMN raised $10.2 million to renovate the temple, establish an initial exhibit area, and provide operating funds; during the second, it will try to raise $13.9 million to construct a pavilion that will add 65,000 square feet to the museum, placing it in the "world class" among historical and cultural museums; to expand exhibitions and public programs; and to establish a $5 million endowment to pay for general expenses.

Another national effort to preserve Asian American heritage is the Filipino American National Historical Society, a spin-off of the Seattle Demonstration Project for Asian Americans (DPAA), a community-based research/advocacy organization.[59] During the 1980s, DPAA focused on the history of Filipino and Korean Americans, two groups that had been overshadowed by the more numerous Chinese and Japanese Americans. It began the "Forgotten Asian Americans" project, a national oral history project supported by a $125,000 grant from the Division of Special Programs of the National Endowment for the Humanities. The DPAA is known nationally for its photographic exhibits of Filipino and Korean Americans and its publication *Filipinos: Forgotten Asian Americans*, by Fred Cordova. The latter is a pictorial essay that traces the history of Filipino Americans from 1763 to 1963 through rare photographs and oral histories.

When its application for a third year of funding for the DPAA was rejected, ostensibly because the project was too ambitious, the participants in DPAA decided to carry on without public assistance and finish transcribing the one hundred interviews they had conducted with Filipinos and Koreans. Meanwhile, the Filipino American participants wanted to continue building the new network of intellectuals they had developed, to return the results of their research to the community, and to record the history of Filipino Americans. In

1982, Dorothy L. Cordova,[60] a long-time community activist, conceived the idea of a national historical society to carry on the work of the project; hence the founding of the Filipino American National Historical Society (FANHS) three years later.

FANHS's mission is "to promote understanding, education, enlightenment, appreciation, and enrichment through the identification, gathering, preservation and dissemination of the history and culture of Filipino Americans."[61] It accomplishes this through a national office that serves as an information clearinghouse and depository of materials on Filipino Americans and provides various public services. Through its annual conferences, FAHNS has also nurtured future scholars for the field of Filipino American Studies by providing workshops and panels on how to do research. In 1987, FANHS focused its first meeting in Seattle on the theme "Who/What is a Filipino American." As Fred Cordova has observed, for Filipino Americans there is always an identity crisis.[62] Within the Movement, they feel like stepchildren and are ambivalent about identifying with other Asian Americans, who until recently were predominantly Chinese and Japanese Americans. As a "brown" people, they would have felt out of place at the Berkeley "Yellow Identity" conference; indeed, some Filipino Americans feel that they have more in common with Chicanos, with whom they share a Hispanic heritage and Catholic religion. Rather than continue to be "a minority within a minority,"[63] some of them feel that they should be an independent group, especially since their portion of the population is growing rapidly.

In 1988, to celebrate the 225th anniversary of Filipino settlement on the American continent, FANHS held its meeting in New Orleans, the locale of that settlement. Most people assume that Filipinos began arriving in the United States in the early twentieth century as agricultural laborers or later as professionals; in fact, as Marina Estrella Espina has shown, as early as 1763 there were Filipinos (the so-called Manilamen) living in southeastern Louisiana.[64] They were the earliest Asians to cross the Pacific in the Spanish galleons that plied between Manila and Acapulco and the first to settle in what is now the continental United States.

In retrospect, it seems odd that NYCHP, JANM, and FANHS should have emerged during the 1980s, a difficult decade that saw decreasing federal support for nonprofit, community-based organizations. Within the context of the Asian American Movement and community, however, the 1980s was the right time. Since its inception, the Movement had instilled ethnic pride in individual Asian Americans and raised the ethnic consciousness of the entire community. A natural outcome was the conviction that the Asian American past was worth preserving for posterity. After twenty years of searching for their individual and collective identities, Asian Americans finally took steps to preserve and exhibit their recently recorded history.

Constructing a Collective Culture

Whereas Asian American activists have had little difficulty in accepting the need to refute stereotypes and reclaim history because challenging distorted images cleared away some of the psychological impediments to the development of an authentic Asian American identity, and recovering their history laid the foundation for a more authentic sense of themselves, they also realized the need to create an Asian American culture to give form and substance to that identity. But doing so has proven to be controversial, for within the Movement there have been two competing though interrelated approaches to Asian American culture: political and aesthetic.

During the early years of the Movement, the political approach to cultural development predominated, and it continues to have a strong following among activists. It was heavily influenced by Mao Tse-tung's "Talks at the Yenan Forum on Literature and Art" (May 1942), which defined the theoretical basis for artistic production in the People's Republic of China. Mao said in essence that art must meet first a political requirement and only secondarily aesthetic criteria. In the milieu of the late 1960s and early 1970s, the political approach had considerable appeal to newly politicized Asian American activists, many of whom thought that the long-awaited social revolution was imminent and wanted to be at the front of the anticipated changes rather than lag behind them. Any qualms they had about combining politics and culture were pushed aside by the urgent issues of the period—the vicious war in Vietnam and the malignant social conditions in Asian American communities.

The political approach emphasized the Asian American artist's moral responsibility to the community and the social purpose of an artist's work. For some cultural activists, this meant that Asian American writers (as well as other artists) should serve as "cultural ambassadors" and bear the burden of speaking for their people. Consequently, "their fictional characters must be shining role models. . . . And because the history of Asian Americans has gone largely untold for decades, some feel that Asian American writers have the artistic duty to shatter stereotypes and honor the historical record with religious fervor." [65] For others, it meant supporting the unity of the Asian American Movement and its struggle for social change and addressing community concerns. The political approach has resulted in vital and unvarnished works protesting the victimization of Asian Americans and celebrating their resistance to oppression.

Fred Wei-han Ho (formerly Houn), a musician and one of the ardent proponents of this approach, argues that Asian American art should consciously reflect the "experiences, history, and life conditions" of Asian American communities,[66] which historically were mainly working class. Asian American art should be about them; certainly, it should be meaningful and pertinent to them. Its relevance comes from inspiring "a spirit of defiance, of class and national pride to resist domination and backward ideology" and from transforming the working class from "a class-in-itself to a class-for-itself." [67] Ho has contributed mightily to that end through Asian American jazz, expanding its limits by including other cultural art forms within Asian musical traditions, especially folk forms, and from without, notably African and African/American forms.

Aion, the first Asian American magazine, was one of the earliest expression of the political approach to art. It was born in 1968 during the San Francisco State strike, but its two issues were published in 1970. According to Janice Mirikitani, who was radicalized by the antiwar movement, *Aion* was an effort "to combine the political consciousness of the day and Asian American culture, the things that the young people were into at that time." [68] Its purpose was to move readers from complacency, the seedbed for "cultural destruction," to participation in the "international movement to end the exploitation of all Third World peoples and work to create our own revolutionary culture in this country." [69] It offered readers a potpourri of essays, photographs, poems, and other socially informed works. Perhaps the most polemical was a statement by Alex Hing, minister of information of the Red Guard party, titled "The Need for an United Asian American Front."

Less rhetorical but more effective was A Grain of Sand, one of the first cultural groups to reflect the social and political issues of the Asian American Movement. It consisted of Chris Kando Iijima, Nobuko Joanne Miyamoto, and "Charlie" Chin, Asian American troubadours influenced by the social-protest music of the period.[70] According to Chin, Miyamoto was the most militant of the three: "Inspired by the Panthers, she felt that the Asian Movement, too, had to stand up around issues such as racism and U.S. aggression in Viet Nam, that Asian Americans had to make their voices heard, to get off their knees and no longer be a quiet minority." [71]

The trio sang at Movement events across the country, at protest demonstrations, on college campuses, and at activities in support of community-based organizations. They inspired other Asian American cultural groups, such as Yokohama, California, on the West Coast, whose members agreed with them that "music has the power to touch; at the same time it can move people collectively while striking some emotion deep within an individual." [72] In 1973, the trio recorded *A Grain of Sand: Music for the Struggle by Asians in America*, the first Asian American album. The dominant themes of the twelve songs on the album were the antiwar movement and Asian American identity.[73] Like others who have taken the political approach to Asian American culture, they made the social message of their songs explicit. A statement accompanying the record explained their perspective on the relationship of politics to culture: "Recently there has been a tendency to separate culture from politics, that one can have a "cultural" presentation without being "political." We believe that distinction is false. . . . Asian American culture in America must . . . move toward revolutionary culture; otherwise it moves toward reactionary culture." [74]

Soon after *A Grain of Sand* was released, the group disbanded; but its members have continued to make music, individually and sometimes together. "Charlie" Chin continued Asian American folk culture through one-man shows such as "ABC" (American Born Chinese), with songs and monologues about being Chinese American. In 1982, he and Iijima recorded *Back to Back*, an album in the tradition of "talk story" and folk music "that was shared in farm labor camps, around campfires along the Transcontinental Railroad, and under the stars that were looked at and dreamed upon by Asian Pacific people whether in Mother Asia and the Pacific, or here in the good old U.S. of A." [75] Miyamoto is the only one of the three who has made the performing arts central to her life. In 1978, she founded Great Leap, Inc., a nonprofit, community-based organization committed to presenting the experiences of Asian Americans "with shows that blend dance, music and drama." [76] Great Leap's most ambitious project has been *Talk Story: A Musical Odyssey of Asians in America*, a multimedia musical featuring short scenes that depict the life of Asians in America, from the early immigrants to the fourth generation.

During the middle 1970s, Asian American artists began to move away from the political and toward the aesthetic approach, a trend reinforced by the 1980s' obsessive preoccupation with ego and materialism. When the antiwar movement ended in the United States with the victory of the North Vietnamese and the South Vietnamese's National Liberation Front in 1975, the major political focus for cooperative activity among Asian American activists disappeared as well. The sense of crisis that had gripped them began to dissipate, and political activism began to decline. Without the implicit political constraints imposed by the exigencies of the late 1960s and early 1970s, Asian American artists no longer felt compelled to produce art that supported the struggle against various governments. They were tired of producing so-called politically correct art, or "socialist realist" art, which sought to propagate certain ideas in order to mobilize the masses behind a specific cause. Besides, even artists attracted to the idea of combining politics and art found it difficult to achieve such a goal in practice. And without the stirring social issues of the late 1960s and early 1970s, political art was difficult to justify.

The aesthetic approach is consciously individualistic, emphasizing the development of personal style and technique. To use the Maoist expression, it is "art for art's sake," rather than for politic's sake. Although aesthetic Asian American artists share the same themes (identity, cultural conflict, alienation, etc.) as political ones, they are less concerned with the political content of their work than with whether it fulfills their artistic vision and standards. They are also often more interested in exploring the universal rather than the particularistic aspects of these concerns and seek to make them recognizable to as wide an audience as possible, including non-Asian Americans. In recent years, being able to "cross over" to a general audience is considered a mark of artistic maturity as well as a means toward commercial success. Even if their works are based on their experiences as Asian Americans, as is usually the case, these artists try to speak to broad human concerns.

Among Asian American artists, writers have received the most attention.[77] Frank Chin, father of modern Asian American literature, pioneered in the development of Asian American culture, paving the way for the aesthetic approach. As an "angry young man," he decried and defined the dominant society's oppression of Asian American artists (though he was speaking specifically about writers). From the beginning, he assumed a "defiant stance . . . toward white assimilation, imitation, and paternalistic white racist evaluations of Asian American writing."[78] As far as he was concerned, "an artist should be judged on his own terms, and to apply the traditional Western criteria [or, one might add, political criteria] to his work is irrelevant and unfair."[79]

Chin has called for and written works that reflect Asian American history—a history that is a "valiant, vital part of the history of the American West," but one that Asian Americans "under the stress of white racism, have forgotten or wish to forget in their eagerness to be assimilated into the majority culture."[80] He also advocates a culture that reflects an Asian American sensibility, one that is neither Asian nor white, and a language that "coheres the people into a community by organizing and codifying the symbols of the people's common experience."[81] In his writings, Chin believes he has, through the use of a distinctive Chinatown argot, "captured the rhythms and accents of Chinese America without which its culture cannot be truly represented."[82] Whether or not he has done that, it is at least certain that he has circumvented conventional literary and stylistic modes of expression and created one that he can call his own.

Chin's contribution to Asian American culture is incalculable. His provocative plays have achieved a number of "firsts." *Chickencoop Chinaman* was the first Asian American drama to be produced by the "legitimate" theater, and *The Year of the Dragon* was the first to be shown on national television.[83] His exploration of Asian American identity in his writings and his outspoken opposition to the exclusion of Asian Americans from American culture have inspired others to try their hand at creating unfettered literary works. But while Chin has achieved acclaim in the Asian American community, he has never been able to attain mainstream popularity. Much to his chagrin, this accomplishment was reserved for an Asian American woman—Maxine Hong Kingston.

In the history of Asian American culture, the 1976 publication of Maxine Hong Kingston's *The Woman Warrior: A Memoir of a Girlhood among Ghosts* was a watershed event. A critically acclaimed work, it became "the most widely taught book by a living author in U.S. colleges and universities."[84] In this work, Kingston intertwines myths and legends from traditional China with autobiographical reminiscences to dramatize a girl's struggle (presumably her own) to resolve her identity crisis as a Chinese American, that is, to mediate the demands of both traditional Chinese culture, as interpreted by her parents, and contemporary American culture. But as her verbal tapestry unfolds, it is evident that her identity cannot be divided simply into Chinese and American halves, even for analytical purposes. As one critic put it, "her identity in the book is not separable from culture and family, but knotted with the stories she has inherited from them and which she transforms in the retelling to suit her own needs as a Chinese American." [85] Kingston has written an engrossing and elegant narrative, one that has earned her an enviable reputation as one of the country's most original and provocative writers. She has attained national recognition, and her works are considered great novels about an Asian ethnic experience in America's pluralist society.

Unfortunately, Frank Chin has been engaged in a diatribe against Maxine Hong Kingston. It reflects the larger rift between cultural activists who advocate an Asian American artistic sensibility and look to Asian America as a source of inspiration and those they brand as assimilationists, "mostly academic artists, certified, trained and socialized in the prevailing European-dominated aesthetic and sensibility." [86] The roots of the conflict lie in Chin's apparent obsession with countering the image of Asian American men as emasculated, a result of their willingness to assimilate into the majority culture: "The white stereotype of the acceptable Asian is utterly without manhood. Good or bad, the stereotypical Asian is nothing as a man. At worst, the Asian-American is contemptible because he is womanly, effeminate, devoid of all the traditionally masculine qualities of originality, daring, physical courage, and creativity." [87] Dedicated to restoring the lost manhood of Asian American men, Chin is adamantly opposed to anyone who aids and abets their cultural castration. For him, the chief culprit in this process has been Kingston, whose very success condemns her, since in his eyes, only a person guilty of collaborating with the "enemy" can be accepted by them. He accuses her of being an "assimilationist who caters to all the stereotypes," calling her writing "border town whore talk" and those who enjoy her work (a phrase that more or less covers most of the reading public) "ignorant or racist or both." [88]

Kingston has conceded that her work may have been misunderstood and has been concerned about the "patronizing tone coming from white book reviewers . . . [who] left the impression that *Woman Warrior* was a tour guide's inside look at a strange, exotic people." [89] Nonetheless, she believes that what Chin and others like him are *really* saying is that Asian American women should not be writing at all.[90] It is the same problem that African American women writers, such as Alice Walker, author of *The Color Purple*, have had to face from their male counterparts.

Chin and Kingston have paid one another the literary compliment of satirizing each other: in the "Afterword" of his anthology of eight short stories, *The Chinaman Pacific & Frisco R.R. Co.*, Chin parodies Kingston with "Unmanly Warrior," who turns out to be Joan of Arc as a six-foot-four, 225-pound male homosexual; in Kingston's novel *Tripmaster Monkey: His Fake Book* the protagonist, Wittman Ah Sing, a would-be writer living in Berkeley during the 1960s, is modeled on Chin.[91]

The tense relationship between them notwithstanding, both Chin and Kingston have inspired other Asian American writers, who have been creating works of increasingly high quality and receiving literary accolades for them.[92] These later works have for the most part taken the aesthetic approach, showing "artistic vision and sophistication—a break from the angry writers of the '60s who often toed the 'correct' political line."[93] At the same time, they have been, in their own inimitable fashion, challenging stereotypes and creating "imaginative worlds in which they—not white culture—shape the language and motifs."[94] As the poet Li-Young Lee noted: "We still have to create literature without pandering or making it seem exotic. We still have to create art."[95] What has allowed them to escape literary ghettoization has been their ability to employ their ethnic sensibility to describe aspects of the Asian American experience that appeal to a common humanity.

The underlying impetus for the Asian American Movement was the search for identity and the creation of a new culture. Unlike European Americans, who could incorporate their ethnic identity into their sense of being American, Asian Americans had to create an entirely new identity: the Asian American. They resolved their "identity crisis" by directly challenging the distorted images that have diminished them as individuals and degraded them as a group, replacing them with more accurate ones based on historical knowledge about themselves, and creating a pan-Asian counterculture that reflects their values and experiences. In so doing, they instilled pride and self-esteem in their generation. This process in turn awakened ethnic sensibilities and led to a sense of cultural freedom that gave birth to their own forms of expression, enriching the multicultural mosaic that is America. Among these have been notable literary works equal to any produced by members of the dominant society. Given their history of marginalization, some people wonder whether this acknowledgment of Asian American literature is an example of cultural affirmative action or simply an aberration. Only time will tell. Meanwhile, Asian Americans have contributed significantly to the broadening of American culture.

An accompanying consequence of these changes was that Asian American women became aware of a second layer of their identity. As they fought side by side with men against racial injustice in America, they became aware of the equally pernicious problem of sexism. They realized that they suffered from an additional form of oppression, one that was particularly difficult to deal with because it was rooted in Asian patriarchal culture and nurtured in American sexist society. Moreover, raising the issue of gender inequality would and did give rise to accusations of disloyalty to the newly emergent Asian American community, distracting its members from the main conflict against racial inequality. As the next chapter shows, in spite of these impediments, women activists decided to start their own social movement for equality and empowerment within the larger Asian American Movement. In secure and supportive women's groups, they educated themselves about the relationship of racism, sexism, and class oppression in the Asian American community as well as the wider society.

3 Race versus Gender:
The Asian American Women's Movement

Hey, Brother, I've been thinking.
I've been hoping that some day,·
   some day you'd see.
I've counselled, been quiet, I cook,
   I clean, I buy it.
And now I'm ready for some time for
   me.
      —"Say What You Will"
      Back to Back music album

The Asian American women's movement has been and still is one of the most dynamic elements within the Movement. Its participants have been mainly middle-class Asian American women responding to oppression in both their ethnic and mainstream societies—as individuals, in small informal groups, or as members of large structured organizations. Though the Asian American women's movement has never been a single entity with a unified theory and agenda, it has promoted personal and group empowerment and continues to struggle for the right of Asian American women to participate equally in a pluralistic society that has yet to be fully realized in the United States. Begun as a desire for sisterhood and in reaction to sexism in the Movement, it has gone through two overlapping phases, evolving from a relatively homogeneous local phenomenon into one that is internally diverse but national in scope, in which women from many Asian ethnic groups integrate local, national, and international concerns.

During its first phase, Asian American women started informal women's groups for mutual support and political study. Out of these groups came projects that attempted to ameliorate the conditions of women, giving the women's movement visibility and legitimacy in the Asian American community. But these informal women's groups met too sporadically, were too uncoordinated, too unstructured, and too localized to be politically effective. During the second phase, the women's movement moved beyond the Asian American Movement to become a recognizable force in its own right. Instead of a few informal women's groups, there are now many formal Asian American women's organizations with interregional links and national visibility and an unprecedented opportunity to improve the status of Asian/Pacific women throughout the country. And these formal organizations have attracted many more women, albeit mainly those with professional occupations and interests. Still, many of the issues as well as the participants remain the same. The best-attended workshops at conferences continue to be the ones on man–woman relations. Quite a few of the current leaders trace the roots of their activism back to their involvement with their ethnic communities and the Movement, including left groups. That is why new organizations continue to support "progressive causes."

The Asian American women's movement has been mistakenly viewed as one of the token ethnic groups within the mainstream women's liberation movement; in actuality, it was independent and parallel.[1] Most women activists joined exclusively Asian American groups or organizations, though some "struggled against racism/sexism, in the absence of a 'critical mass,' usually through coalitions with other women of color."[2] While the Asian American women's movement certainly has roots in the women's liberation movement, they are shallow ones. As a predominantly European American phenomenon grappling with the "feminine mystique," that is, the belief that a woman's role should be that of a housewife–mother, and advocating employment outside the house as a solution to it,[3] the women's liberation movement initially seemed irrelevant to Asian American women whose self-image and self-esteem came from attachment to family. And, whether they wanted to or not, many of them were already working outside the home, usually in low-wage occupations in a racially stratified labor market, to supplement the family income. The tendency of European American feminists "to polarize the sexes, encourage narcissism, and deprecate individual obligation to others"[4] alienated Asian American women who identified closely with their ethnic community. Though European American feminists bracketed sexism with racism (and attributed both to the existing social structure), through a mixture of ignorance and indifference, they all but forgot the latter. They spoke of universal sisterhood, yet their actions reflected their racial biases, a problem that persists to the present. As Patricia Collins has noted, "Even today African-American, Hispanic, Native American, and Asian-American women criticize the feminist movement and its scholarship for being racist and overly concerned with white, middle-class women's issues."[5] Since the 1960s, however, white feminists have increasingly interacted with women of color and have become more sensitive to minority issues and concerns. Meanwhile, their call for removing social barriers and for a reconsideration of gender roles in society struck a responsive chord in many Asian American women activists.

The Asian American women's movement has been consistently concerned with improving the role and status of Asian American women and is thus a social movement in its own right rather than an appendage to any other movement. The first half of its history had two stages: Asian American women gathered together in informal groups that were either "rap sessions" or "study groups"; later, these groups evolved into women's projects that made tangible contributions to their ethnic communities. After experiencing a brief decline during the mid-1970s, the movement experienced a resurgence and has become one of the most dynamic dimensions of the Asian American Movement. Except for the periodic emergence of small groups on college campuses and elsewhere, the latter half of its history has been characterized by large organizations with bylaws, elected officers, and steering committees. Because many of the current leaders came out of the early days of the women's movement, however, they have generally tried to emphasize the consensus politics of the 1960s, preferring group leadership and decision making over individual leaders. But in addition, as feminists, they stressed the process as much as the results, believing that "with mutual, sisterly support . . . participation in decision-making [would] help each other develop various skills (chairing, expressing opinions, defending points of view)."[6] Except for explicitly political groups, such as the Organization of Asian Women, which has adopted "principles of unity," they have consciously refrained from adopting ideological principles in order to appeal to a wide range of people.

It was primarily the contradictions in the Movement that gave rise to the Asian American women's movement. The Movement proved to be a double-edged sword, for it not only challenged the dominant society's race-based institutions and values but also prompted a critical examination of its own gender-based attitudes and actions. Women activists became aware of their limited role in the Movement and their multiple forms of exploitation and oppression in society. If they challenged traditional gender relationships and set up separate women's groups, they were perceived as disloyal to their ethnic group. Though "making waves" was initially greeted with dismay, they discovered that in the long run it had a beneficial effect. By developing their potential as people and demanding equal participation, they became better able to contribute to the Asian American Movement and community. In the beginning, then, the Asian American women's movement was mainly interested in fostering "sisterhood" and challenging the Asian American patriarchy manifested in the Movement.

Sisterhood Is Powerful

From the start of the Asian American Movement, it was evident that most men activists considered women to be inferior and relegated them to secondary roles, reflecting the strong patriarchal values of both the Asian American community and mainstream society. Men were usually the spokespersons, while women performed the so-called traditional tasks of brewing coffee and taking notes.[7] A case in point was *Gidra*, the first and, in many respects, the most progressive of the Asian American alternative newspapers. In 1969, the first year of the newspaper's existence, the sex ratio of the staff was more or less equal, but gradually fewer women volunteered. By the paper's last year, 1974, there were almost twice as many men staffers as women. Furthermore, except for the years when it published two issues on the Asian American women's movement, there were twice as many men contributors as women. According to Colin Watanabe, this gender distribution was probably caused by sexism, a subject never adequately addressed by the staff.[8] He thought that though some men staffers had enlightened attitudes toward women, it was difficult for them to change old habits. They told sexist jokes and engaged in other juvenile behavior that made the newspaper office unpleasant for women. Others noted that the men had little consciousness of women's issues and were socially immature.

Because of their own low level of feminist and political consciousness, most women staffers tolerated this situation. They also accepted a work environment geared toward men, who often scheduled important tasks late in the evening or worked through the night. Most women simply did not have the flexible schedules of their male counterparts. They found it difficult to maintain non-traditional roles over an extended period of time and were under pressure from parents and peers to return to school or establish families. Only women who were assertive and had strong identities were able to attain leadership roles.

Women activists resented their exclusion from leadership positions and became increasingly frustrated in their efforts to assert themselves within Movement organizations and activities. It was an oppressive situation. Evelyn Yoshimura aptly summed it up: "Eventually it became clear that even within the Movement, where we were talking about creating a different kind of society . . . there were problems with women not being taken seriously, or their work not being looked at in the same light, or women being accepted as leaders by men, especially in the early stages." [9]

During the first years of the Movement, some male activists tried to rationalize this situation by pointing to their own oppression, arguing that they had a "right" to the sexual services of "their" women, after years when Asian women were excluded from the country. Moreover, they saw services from women as "just compensation" for the sacrifices they were making on behalf of the "people." It was a specious argument, one advanced by male chauvinists in the social movements of the 1960s. Naturally, women activists found it galling that a social movement devoted to equality should regard the female half of it as unequal. They justifiably resented being referred to "in sexual contexts only and as sexual conquests." [10]

In this sexist climate, Asian American women's groups emerged spontaneously. Often women working on various campus and community projects simply identified with each other and sought the support denied them by their so-called brothers. Sometimes a blatant act of sexism in which a "sister" had been ill used led to a confrontation and moved the women to organize their own support groups. Among many such incidents, one that occurred at the Japanese American Community Services–Asian Involvement Office in Los Angeles became a local cause célèbre. During introductions at a meeting there, "one guy got up and said I'm so and so, and then said this is my wife and she doesn't have anything to say." [11] There was an audible gasp in the room, especially from the women present, and people began to take him to task for his condescending comment. It appears that the man had not intended to denigrate his wife but was trying clumsily to spare her the ordeal of speaking in public. In any event, afterward women got together to discuss the incident and its implications. They felt that the undercurrent of sexism was "holding back the Movement" by ignoring a huge reservoir of energy and creativity—Asian American women.

The earliest Asian American women's groups were the ubiquitous "rap sessions"—usually small, informal, and ethnically homogeneous, attracting mainly American-born, college-educated Chinese and Japanese American women. Female variants of those held among Asian American activists in general, these sessions provided a supportive and secure environment where participants could express their frustration, pain, and anger as an oppressed people and share their experiences, feelings, and hopes as women. Rap sessions also provided an opportunity to discuss candidly the inferior and secondary roles to which women had been relegated in their community and in the Movement itself. Miya Iwataki pointed out that in these groups, "women began talking about years of scotch-taping eyelids to create a double eyelid fold then carefully painting it over with heavy strokes of Maybelline black liquid eyeliner . . . and checking out each other as potential sources of competition for Asian men." [12] She also noted that a major topic of discussion was man–woman relations. Women activists began noticing that male activists tended to have "quiet and unassuming, usually non-active 'girl friends' " and wondered why.

Another type of Asian American women's group, which often evolved from the "rap session," was the study group. Women's study groups were small and intense gatherings that delved into a diverse body of literature. The participants were driven by several interrelated impulses: (1) They felt that they had been betrayed by an educational system that had ignored or distorted Asian American history and culture; (2) they quickly tired of airing their complaints and wanted to understand the root causes of their oppression; (3) they wanted to hold discussions "without having the 'male oppressor' present, so that women could be free to examine problems and issues in a mutually supportive environment";[13] (4) since contemporary culture appeared morally and politically bankrupt, they wanted to develop alternative perspectives on American society. This last aim gave many Asian American women's study groups an explicitly political character.

Among some of the more ambitious and active women, there was a desire to develop a Marxist–Leninist–Maoist, rather than feminist, perspective. Inspired by women revolutionaries in Vietnam and China who, by definition, had a sophisticated ideological understanding of national and international affairs, they sought a political understanding equal to that of the men, who themselves were groping for a radical perspective. A mastery of ideology was a prerequisite for leadership within certain Asian American organizations, which were becoming increasingly political. One Asian American woman, who belonged to a "Thursday night group," recalled: "In reality, the content of those study groups centered around overall political issues, and not as much, really, on the women's question. It was a safe place for women to look at the political questions that were being studied in the larger Asian American organizations." [14]

The women would first get together to read well-known radical works, such as Friedrich Engels's *The Origin of the Family, Private Property, and the State* and Mao Tse-tung's "On Contradiction," then try to apply what they had learned to their ethnic communities. For many, such literature was indispensable for analyzing local, national, and international events. Some concluded that class, rather than race and gender, was responsible for their oppression. Once again, women's issues became secondary, only this time to ideology.

While some Asian American women were satisfied with these separate groups and their emphasis on "consciousness raising" or "left politics," others began looking for ways to maintain group solidarity while doing something tangible, something that went beyond "talk" and addressed the problems they had been discussing. They wanted to prove to themselves (and to men, who sometimes saw these groups as divisive "bitch sessions") that they were capable of making a contribution to the community on their own. So they set up women's projects.

There were basically two kinds of Asian American women's projects: educational programs that focused on women and outreach programs that tried to ameliorate their condition. Often one evolved out of the other. Among the former were Asian American Women's Studies courses and publications. In such courses, women sought "knowledge and relief to the uneasiness of being Asian women." [15] As one group of women put it: "We faced a dilemma. We were not satisfied with the traditional Asian roles, the white middle-class standards, nor the typical Asian women stereotypes in America. We wanted our own identity." [16] For that reason, these courses "focused on questions of Asian American women's roles in society and on the personal and political development of class members." [17] In addition, they emphasized social analysis, collective action, and community resources.

In Asian American publications, feminists tried to communicate with other women so that they would know that they had kindred spirits, and with men so that they might better understand and appreciate the struggles that women were going through. Among these various publications, the best known is the *Asian Women* journal. In 1970, a group of women who met in a proseminar on Asian women at the University of California, Berkeley, began to meet informally "to critically examine and discuss [their] roles as Asian women."[18] One of the first things they learned was that other Asian American women were meeting around the country. They decided to share their thoughts, ideas, and experiences with others through a journal. In the course of working on it, they deepened their identity as Asian American women and learned "that personal experiences are not private but common to all women" and that "out of common experiences political struggle is created."[19] In other words, they believed that the problems they faced were universal and rooted in society, and as such could be solved politically. In spite of delays and distractions, *Asian Women* was published a year later and quickly became required reading for activists. It has since attained the status of a classic in the field of Asian American Studies.

Among the outreach programs established by Asian American women, one of the most significant was the Los Angeles Asian Women's Center. During the early 1970s, when the Asian American Movement was in its "serve the people" phase, women activists realized that there was a real need to reach out and help their sisters. Such alarming statistics as "one out of every three [drug] overdoses [in Los Angeles] were women" convinced them that "Asian women faced a special form of oppression" and desperately needed social services designed explicitly for them.[20] So, in 1972, the Center was established to provide a drug-abuse program for women. Its workers were committed to creating an institution that was on guard against cooptation. Like other Asian American alternative grassroots organizations that had emerged during this period, the Center emphasized consensus decision making, provided multiple services, and was wary of federal funding. Instead of having the usual administrators, it had an egalitarian coordinating committee. Although it was originally funded by the Department of Health, Education, and Welfare to provide a drug-abuse program for Asian Sisters (another of the women's projects of the period), the staff decided to expand its services to include child care, health, education, and counseling. In order to have the personnel necessary to staff these programs, it collectivized salaries, allowing it to expand from only four to five women to seventeen full-time workers—a remarkable achievement even for this idealistic period. As Miya Iwataki, a former director of the Center, noted, "it was women who were the only ones to try to test federal funds in this way."[21]

In 1976 the Asian Women's Center closed, mainly because it attempted to accomplish too much. Besides delivering diverse services to women, it served as the hub of the Asian American women's movement in Los Angeles, providing women activists with a hospitable environment for their work. Unfortunately, there was tension between those who wanted to provide services and those who wanted to organize Asian American women around various issues. Even employees felt somewhat compromised by working in a federally funded project, as well as dismayed by the web of rules and regulations that seemed to be designed to hinder rather than enhance their services to the community. Evidently, there was a shallow commitment to the original purpose of the Center, for when federal funding ended there was little interest in finding alternative sources to maintain the Center.

Since then, other agencies have been established to assist Asian American women. One that retains a grassroots character is the New York Asian Women's Center, which, in spite of its name, has no connection to the Los Angeles Asian Women's Center.[22] It began as a hotline in 1984 and is the first project on the East Coast designed to address the problem of battering in Asian American communities, a issue that has been part of the European American women's movement for quite a while. Its direct services consist of multilingual hotline counseling for battered women, advocacy, and a network of safe homes. Its community education program includes presentations and workshops that address the economic and cultural realities faced by Asian American women, especially working-class women, who constitute the vast majority of its clients. Because of the tremendous demand for its services, in 1987 it moved to institutionalize itself—a difficult feat in New York City's precarious fiscal situation.

Arguably the most neglected and least active Asian American women have been working-class women, most of whom are recent immigrants and refugees concerned with subsisting in the United States. The challenge for the women's movement in particular as well as the Asian American Movement in general is to encourage the participation of these women and ensure that their interests are adequately represented. Two organizations that work with them are Asian Immigrant Women Advocates (AIWA) in Oakland, California, and the Chinese chapter of the Coalition of Labor Union Women (CLUW) in New York City. Since 1983, AIWA has served low-income Asian immigrant women concentrated in entry-level positions within the San Francisco Bay Area's garment, hotel, restaurant, electronics, and nursing home industries.[23] It provides employment-related education and leadership training that will ultimately facilitate organizing immigrant women. In 1984, the Chinese chapter of CLUW began as an effort by Chinese garment workers to get their union, the International Ladies Garment Workers Union, to provide more services.[24] The motivating issue was the demand for day care for preschool children, most of whom were forced to spend the day in the sewing factories with their mothers. Eventually, the ILGWU provided a day-care center. Meanwhile, Chinese garment workers founded a local chapter of CLUW so that they would have a stronger voice in trade union matters and women's issues. The irony of having "to form a women's chapter to promote women's causes inside this essentially women's union"[25] has not escaped the attention of community activists. It illustrates, among other things, how mainstream organizations ignore the interests of Asian Americans.

The impact of the early groups and projects was limited to the personal and political development of a few Asian American women. The rap sessions and study groups raised participants' self-esteem and self-confidence and helped them understand the social roots of racism, sexism, and class conflict. The community projects gave them opportunities to overcome feelings of powerlessness, fight things that have traditionally oppressed them, acquire leadership skills through practice, and affirm their identities as whole, equal persons. They forged friendships and bonds of sisterhood that were often able to survive the tumultous politics of the mid-1970s and laid the basis for future Asian American women's organizations.

"The Times They Are a-Changin' "

During the mid-1970s, the United States entered a conservative period, one that saw social movements disappear or decline and many idealistic activists transform themselves into materialistic "Yuppies" (young upwardly mobile professionals). A generation's "shining moment" had passed. As discussed in Chapter 7, while the nation headed politically toward the right, the Asian American Movement was pulled paradoxically to the left, only to become mired in sectarian strife. The women's movement was caught in these internecine conflicts as well. Many women activists forsook the Asian American women's movement and joined Marxist–Leninist organizations. Convinced that the oppression of Asian American women was class rather than gender based and that the liberation of women lay in the overthrow of capitalism, they lost interest in women's groups, devoting their time instead to educating and recruiting women into their parties or mass organizations.

The fate of two Asian American women's groups illustrates the damage these sectarian struggles caused. In 1975, a women's group based in Chinatown that was linked to one of the left groups and an informal women's study group that emerged out of the midtown United Asian Communities Center formed a coalition to participate in the citywide International Women's Day march and rally. Afterward, they met to discuss forming a single women's organization in New York City, one that would be more ideological and cohesive. But the session quickly disintegrated when some women insisted that the political line of their group be the ideological foundation of the proposed organization or there be no organization at all. One distraught woman, "shocked at the dictatorial method and the suddenness of its demise," came away exclaiming, "My god . . . they've eliminated the whole women's movement, Asian women's movement overnight!" [26]

Nevertheless, the Asian American women's movement was able to outlast these sectarian struggles and adapt to the changing times. Many women activists began working within the framework of the wider society. They were regularly asked to represent minority or women's concerns, and some were appointed to various local and state women's commissions. Besides, they "no longer had the luxury of campus life in which to nurture a movement and were tied to responsibilities of labor force participation, many in professional occupations." [27]

In spite of the changing climate in the nation and community, some Asian American women determined to continue organized groups such as Asian Women United-San Francisco (AWU–SF), the Organization of Asian American Women (OAW), and the Organization of Pan Asian American Women, Inc. (Pan Asia). The first two represent different strands in the women's movement: AWU–SF, interest in education; and OAW, interest in political study. Both are small local organizations consisting mostly of women with strong ties to their ethnic communities who have participated in the Asian American Movement yet have managed to remain apart from its internal conflicts. In contrast, Pan Asia was a harbinger of a different trend—the move toward embracing mainstream women's issues. Its comparatively diverse membership is dispersed throughout the United States, and the majority of its members became involved in feminism after the mid-1970s.

AWU–SF was founded in 1975.[28] It differed from past groups in significant ways: It consisted of a handful of middle-aged, middle-class professional Asian American women; and it incorporated as a nonprofit organization in 1980, thus becoming eligible to apply for federal grants. It began as a mutual-support group for a handful of women who had been involved in community issues. One of its early undertakings was to teach a women's course for Berkeley's Asian American Studies program, and its primary purpose is now to produce high-quality educational materials about Asian American women, such as the four-part video program *With Silk Wings*. Its most recent work is *Making Waves: An Anthology of Writings by and about Asian American Women*, which was modeled on the *Asian Women* journal mentioned earlier.

AWU–SF encountered difficulties during the 1980s when its older members were experiencing burnout; fortunately, because of their firm commitment to the organization and its purpose, they were able to hang on until replacements could be recruited. Another problem was that under the Reagan administration, federal funding evaporated, and the group had to rely on royalties from past projects to fund its latest one, a video on Asian American women artists.

OAW has its roots in the feminist theory weekly study group from the United Asian Communities Center in New York City. In 1976, the members began to call themselves the Organization of Asian Women when they participated in coalitions or endorsed events.[29] Originally, practically all of them were in their mid-to-late twenties, and most had a history of involvement with their ethnic communities and the Asian American Movement. Now, OAW includes new members, many of whom were active in the Asian American student movement on the East Coast. Ultimately, they hope to develop a theory of Asian women's experiences. One of their ongoing projects has been an audiovisual history of Asian American women called *Tapestry*. Thus far, they have produced *Tapestry, Part I*, a slide show focusing on the history of working-class Chinese and Japanese women during feudal times, and *Tapestry, Part II*, a slide show and video on Asian women in America up to 1950. They are currently working on Part III, which will bring the history up to date.

OAW devotes much effort to organizing coalitions and forums around significant community, national, and international issues. Because of the unpleasant experiences some members had with "ultra-left politics, pre-party organizations and their front groups, and pseudo-coalitions controlled by these groups,"[30] they are understandably cautious about those they work with. A few of the older and more experienced members consciously seek to insulate themselves from Asian American Movement politics; all of them try to carve out an independent identity as a political women's organization. In recent years, OAW has found it increasingly difficult to function because its members have been preoccupied with family matters. As with AWU–SF, it has managed to continue by recruiting new members.

Pan Asia's origins can be traced back to the National Conference on the Educational and Occupational Needs of Asian and Pacific American Women sponsored by the National Institute of Education and held in San Francisco during August 1976.[31] After the conference, participants from the Washington, D.C., area met informally, and in December of that year they decided to become a formal organization. While its founders came mainly from the West Coast and Hawaii and were active in grassroots issues, Pan Asia consists mainly of professional women. Its distinguishing feature is its emphasis on national public policy issues, especially those that affect Asian American women. It monitors and supports legislation concerning child care, women's equity, and parental leave, among other goals. It aims to ensure the participation of Asian American women in all aspects of society, especially in areas where they have been traditionally excluded or underrepresented. It stresses networking with Asian American women across the country and with diverse organizations and coalitions in Washington, D.C.; since 1987, it has expanded its contact with women of color and national public policy organizations. Its strength is its members' expertise in finding their way through the federal bureaucracy to gain access to programs and policymakers. Pan Asia members provided initial support and leadership for the 1980 National Conference of the Asian/Pacific American Educational Equity Project and the National Network of Asian and Pacific Women, both of which are discussed later in the chapter. In recent years, it has focused on immigrant and refugee women because their needs are so pressing. As of 1991, it is the only national pan-Asian women's organization and Asian American public policy group based in Washington, D.C.

Women activists who joined AWU–SF, OAW, Pan Asia, and the other organizations that emerged during the mid-1970s kept the embers of the Asian American women's movement alive. They were soon followed by cultural activists, who added another dimension to the women's movement—aesthetics. Cultural activists created artistic works that affirmed their own identity as Asian American women and enriched the life of the Asian American community as well. To support their struggle to break free of social constraints on cultural expression and to nurture their creative talents as artists and writers, they founded small groups and collectives. Two well-known ones were Pacific Asian American Women Writers–West, a Los Angeles group consisting mostly of Japanese Americans; and Unbound Feet, a San Francisco group consisting of Chinese Americans. While recognizing that art is a highly individualistic endeavor, both groups believe that mutual support has helped them develop their writing abilities and resulted in a greater awareness of themselves as Asian American women.

Pacific Asian American Women Writers–West (PAAWWW, pronounced "pow"), established in the summer of 1978, seeks to foster and sustain the artistic development of women writers of color; to promote, perpetuate, and preserve Pacific Asian American literature, history, and arts; and to develop larger audiences for the artistic endeavors of Pacific Asian American women writers.[32] It began as an informal gathering of writers and other artists, all with some experience in the creative arts, including some actresses who were seeking scripts as well as wanting to learn to write. Besides the basic desire to write well, the women shared a common dismay at the "inequitable and unreal portrayal of Pacific Asian American people by the mainstream media" and the "need to correct this slanted representation by developing, expressing, and promoting a truer picture of our cultural reality."[33]

At the urging of Emma Gee, a well-known activist with roots in Asian American Studies, PAAWWW members began to share their prose and poetry with the community. Starting with a presentation of their works at the Amerasia Bookstore, which was followed by other requests for dramatic readings, they began to develop serious artistic performances on subjects ranging from immigration to American concentration camps during World War II.[34] This approach had its drawbacks, however. Producing programs had become an end in itself, consuming time and energy that could otherwise be spent in creating literary works, and meetings often focused on the administrative aspects of the organization or on preparing for a performance. Still, these cooperative ventures had "crystallized . . . their power as a group," endowed them with a collective identity, and given "newer members a chance to expose their writings and others to expose their talents."[35]

PAAWWW has evolved into "a multi-dimensional and dynamic group of professional and novice writers from a variety of backgrounds and life experiences. Ranging in age from the 20's to the early 50's, they include actresses, community activists, academicians, a secretary, and a French pastry chef." [36] Its atmosphere of mutual respect attracts some of the most talented Asian American writers in the area. At any one time, about a dozen active members are willing to attend meetings, sponsor social activities, and participate in cultural and community events, creating an "atmosphere of mutual support, criticism, encouragement, and just plain fun." [37] But, there are limits to what the group can do. Evidently, once they venture outside the purely artistic realm, the members encounter difficulties. Though they have talked about producing a book of their writings, which would be a natural project for a writers' group, they have failed to do so because of lack of money and commitment. At the moment, no one is prepared to take responsibility for raising the money and carrying out the other tasks necessary to bring the project to fruition.

PAAWWW has been able to survive and thrive because it understands and accepts its organizational limits. It recognizes that it consists of temperamental and individualistic artists whose primary interest is in their imaginative endeavors, rather than in the organization per se. While it realizes that its strength lies in its constant striving for consensus, it is willing to support the individual artistic proclivities of its members. This has resulted in a constant stream of creative energy, taking the group into unexplored areas. Perhaps PAAWWW's most attractive feature is its autonomy, its ability to determine its own fate. As Momoko Iko noted:

> All of us have been associated with larger, more prestigious situations, but we have not been in control. Here, we understand and control the decision-making process. It's extremely important to an artist to know that an organization exists to accommodate you rather than you the organization. . . . We maintain the right . . . to tire of an activity, to seek nourishment in another way, to retreat, change our minds. It's a necessary structure for artists; otherwise, we'd all take our marbles and go home.[38]

In comparison, Unbound Feet has fared less well than its southern California sisters. In 1978, Genny Lim and Nancy Hom decided to organize a poetry reading at the Chinese Culture Center and asked four other Chinese American women—Kitty Tsui, Nellie Wong, Canyon Sam, and Nanying Stella Wong—to join them. The reading was an unexpected and unqualified success, so much so that in 1979 they decided to form a group of their own, with five of the original women, plus Merle Woo. At the suggestion of Hom, they called themselves Unbound Feet, a metaphor that would serve to reflect their Chinese heritage, one that traditionally bound the souls as well as the feet of its women, and their liberation as women and as writers.[39]

Unbound Feet wrote and performed principally in the San Francisco Bay Area. Initially, members recited their individual poems; they wrote poems on a common theme for specific readings. For example, a program titled "Yellow Daughter" addressed the implications of being both an Asian American and a daughter. Within a short time, the collective's presentations became quite sophisticated. The writers no longer just walked on stage and read their work; instead, they rehearsed their performances, opening and closing with a ritual chant, choreographing their movements, and memorizing their dialogues. They were rapidly evolving into a professional performance group with a following, especially among Asian American feminists, and invitations from outside the Bay Area. For instance, they were invited to perform at the opening of the Los Angeles Women's Building.

Members of Unbound Feet perceived themselves as pioneers in the field of Asian American women's literature, with a responsibility to express women's experience on stage as completely as possible. By articulating their stories, they hoped to make them part and parcel of Asian American folklore. As Genny Lim recalled, "Unbound Feet tried consciously to create a new mythology for Asian American women."[40] They considered collecting their material into a book that would be published by Isthmus Press, the publishing arm of Kearney Street Workshop, a grassroots arts organization that believes that art can contribute to progressive social change. But either fears of possible censorship by a male editor or internal conflicts within the group compelled them to withdraw their manuscript, putting an end to a potentially powerful work by and for Asian American women.

As they grew personally and professionally, the need for mutual support that had originally brought them together diminished. They began to develop different priorities as people and as artists. Some of the members developed a commitment to radical feminist politics; others developed an equally strong commitment to their families, trying to juggle the demands of being both young mothers *and* political artists. It was only a matter of time before these internal differences resulted in the dissolution of the collective. Apparently, what precipitated the demise of the group was the desire of one member to use a poetry reading at the Asian American Studies program, University of California, Berkeley, as an opportunity to lambast the program and the then Ethnic Studies Department chairman, L. Ling-chi Wang, for not renewing her contract.[41] Ostensibly, the department had let her go because she had reached a four-year limit to her employment agreement; she claimed her dismissal was due to her sexual preferences, her socialist feminist politics, and her criticism of the program.[42] Though sympathetic, three members of the group were unwilling to use the performance for such a personal purpose; the other three felt betrayed when their "sisters" opposed this request. Afterward, there were public denunciations of the three who had refused and accusations of homophobia. For Unbound Feet, it was an inglorious end to what had been a glorious group in the Asian American community.

Asian American women writers have been among the first to break out of the Asian American literary ghetto and achieve popularity in the wider society. Maxine Hong Kingston and Amy Tan, unquestionably the most famous, have been published by major presses and their books have appeared on bestseller lists.[43] In addition to commercial success, both women have received rave reviews from critics, who have conferred on them the status of major American authors. The literary establishment has given Kingston prestigious awards: *The Woman Warrior* received the National Book Critics Circle Award for nonfiction (even though it is principally a work of fiction) in 1976, and *China Men* received the National Book Award in 1980. They have even set the standard in some publishing houses: Kingston has reported that aspiring authors have been receiving "Maxine Hong Kingston rejection letters" suggesting that they read her works for clues on how to succeed commercially, and Tan has told of "an editor at a big publishing house who recently sold his colleagues on a promising unknown by calling the writer 'another Amy Tan.' "[44] In spring 1991, booksellers anxiously awaited Tan's second novel, *The Kitchen God's Wife*, hoping that it would singlehandedly revive an interest in literature and stimulate the sale of books.

Kingston was undoubtedly the pioneer. Though she has written several books, she is still best known for her first work, *The Woman Warrior*, "a brilliant collage of myth, memory, fantasy, and fact on growing up female and Chinese American in a family dominated by a strong-willed mother."[45] It creatively intertwines folktales and history to express her personal concerns as a

Chinese American woman. It is a timely book with timeless themes, touching on "a sensitive contemporary nerve, as we all search for our roots and try to understand how family structure has affected a woman's understanding of herself."[46] What accounts for its universal appeal is its theme of an estranged mother–daughter. As one critic noted: "The intricate pattern of love and hate, of anger and pride that bound mother and daughter together across a growing cultural and emotional gulf weaves its way through every chapter of this book and accounts . . . for its peculiar attraction."[47]

While *The Woman Warrior* deals with both racism in American society and sexism in Chinese society, the latter predominates and is what enthralls the reading public. The problem of sexism in the Chinese American community is central to Kingston's consciousness,[48] and criticism of Chinese patriarchy is primary in her book. Kingston portrays Chinese women as victims and victors.[49] On the one hand, she recounts stories (real and imagined) about Confucian China's oppression of women, which reduced them to virtual slaves whose sole purposes in life were to obey silently the men in their family and to procreate male heirs. On the other hand, Kingston talks about women as warriors: Fa Mu-lan (Cantonese for Hua Mulan), a legendary fifth-century Chinese woman who disguised herself as a man and assumed her father's place in battle against foreign invaders; and her own mother, Brave Orchid, an independent and indomitable woman who raises her family in anti-Asian America, no mean feat. Naturally, Kingston perceives herself also as a woman warrior, but one who wields a pen rather than a sword, speaking truth to patriarchical power— appropriately for one who is a self-declared pacifist as well as a feminist.

Amy Tan's *Joy Luck Club* likewise deals with interconnected cultural and generational conflicts. There is the inevitable East versus West theme, crystallized in an observation made by one of the main characters: "I wanted my children to have the best combination: American circumstances and Chinese character. How could I know these two things do not mix?"[50]—or, as one critic notes, "the contrast between Chinese suffering and strength, American ease and unhappiness."[51] But it is the alienation between immigrant mothers and their American-born daughters that is paramount. Instead of Kingston's single mother–daughter dyad, Tan has four. The novel consists of stories about their lives and loves, the most important of which is that between mother and daughter. It is evident that Chinese mothers are strong and active, a characterization that challenges the stereotype of traditional Chinese women as weak and passive. In order for them to endure their nightmarish and oppressive existences in pre-1949 China, they had to possess inner strength. In sharp contrast, their daughters are depicted as diffident and disoriented. Meanwhile, in the story but "on the periphery are some of the most worthless men this side of *The Color Purple*."[52]

To put it mildly, some Asian American men take exception to the way they have been depicted in books by Asian American women. They have castigated Kingston, Tan, and others for portraying Asian men as misogynists in order to appeal to European Americans. With the publication of *China Men*, Kingston counters such charges by portraying the male members of her family (and by extension other Asian American men) as complex individuals and in a sympathetic light. Like other determined immigrant men who left their native lands to establish themselves and their families in America, they were courageous pioneers who braved hardships and dangers. For Chinese men, these problems were exacerbated by the anti-Asian atmosphere of the American West, which Kingston makes clear with a chronology of anti-Chinese laws. Even the title speaks to their manhood, for it refers to them as men from China, redefining the perjorative slur "Chinamen."

Tan, however, has inadvertently played into the hands of those who accuse her of promoting stereotypes of Asian men. In *Kitchen God's Wife* she chronicles the brutal and miserable life of Winnie Louie, a victim of an arranged marriage. The inhuman behavior of her husband, Wen Fu, is aided and abetted by a society that ignores the plight of women and therefore perpetuates it. But as one reviewer observed, Wen Fu is "a man of such one-dimensional malevolence that one can regard him as a caricature."[53]

While Kingston, Tan, and other women writers were attaining recognition in the wider society, international and national social forces eventually led to the revival of the Asian American women's movement and greater recognition of it by the women's liberation movement.

On the Move Again

In the late 1960s and early 1970s, most Asian American women found the European American women's liberation movement irrelevant in their ethnic communities.[54] They perceived European American feminism as something for middle-class white women engaged in male bashing. At that time, they were more concerned about their racial than their gender identity. Evelyn Yoshimura noted that a lot of Asian American women she worked with "felt a distinction between what [they] were going through, the issues that [they] were raising, the questions [they] were raising and the . . . feminist movement." [55] Preoccupied with the passage of the Equal Rights Amendment, the women's liberation movement ignored the concerns of women of color, such as "sterilization abuse, racial stereotypes, prostitution on U.S. military bases abroad, welfare mothers, wages for housework, etc." [56] The differences were evident at the Vancouver Indochinese Women's Conference (April 1971). When "a lesbian group criticized the Indochinese women for not taking up the question of homosexual oppression in Viet Nam . . . in the midst of napalm, tiger cages, and other American atrocities," [57] the parochialism and pettiness of the women's liberation movement were made manifest. Asian American women who have tried to work with European American women activists were rebuffed every time they introduced the issue of race and how it was affecting them. As late as 1974, when Ying Lee Kelley, as a member of a minority women's panel at a San Francisco women's event, said that her fight was first against racial oppression, then sexism, "she was roundly booed by some women in the audience who considered the conference a strictly 'women's affair' and wanted no discussions on racism." [58]

But the attitudes of both European American and Asian American women did change slightly. Both groups began to realize that while their concerns were culturally diverse, they shared the basic problems of women in a male-dominated world. In the course of coming into contact with Asian American and other women of color, European American women became increasingly sensitive to their concerns and were willing, after a struggle, to take their priorities into consideration. Still, "conscious and rigorous efforts have not been made by many of those active in white feminist organizations to recruit Asian American women and other women of color openly, to treat them as core groups in the movement, and to incorporate them in the organizational policy and decision-making levels." [59]

Meanwhile, many Asian American women activists had also become disillusioned with and alienated from the Movement, mainly because of the polemics and struggles over who had the most correct theory and practice. Some of them found solace among their Asian American sisters and became interested in feminist theories. Equally significant was the arrival of a new generation of women activists with middle-class aspirations and interests. Unlike their predecessors, they could relate to the issues that the European American women's liberation movement was raising, such as pay equity, domestic violence, and wider career choices.

Then came the International Women's Year (IWY) events in 1975. President Gerald Ford established a commission to gather data, make recommendations, and represent the country at the IWY Conference in Mexico City (19 June to 2 July 1975). Believing that women should work out their own agenda, Congresswomen Patsy Mink of Hawaii and Bella Abzug of New York drafted a bill proposing that a conference be held in every state and territory to identify issues and elect delegates to a U.S. national women's conference, the historic Houston Conference in November 1977. Because of the enthusiasm and interest generated by the Mexico City conference, the bill was passed. These mandates created a climate favorable to activities focusing on education, economic, and policy issues related to women. For example, the Women's Educational Equity Act (WEEA), passed in August 1974 and renewed in November 1978, would provide grants and contracts for national, statewide, and other significant projects. WEEA has been the prime funding agency for the educational projects of AWU–SF, and the events that eventually led to the founding of the National Network of Asian and Pacific Women.

International Women's Year activities involved thousands of women, many of whom had no previous experience with the women's movement, and gave birth to new women's organizations. A case in point is the Organization of Chinese American Women (OCAW). Pauline Tsui, one of its charter members and its current executive director, traced her involvement to 1975, when she served on the advisory committee of the U.S. Center for International Women's Year and was co-chair of the group to observe IWY at the Defense Mapping Agency, where she worked.[60] Her experience raised her consciousness about the problems confronting Asian American women. She recognized the need for a Washington, D.C., based organization that could tap federal resources to address the problems of Chinese women, the group with which she was most familiar. So she got together with other Chinese American women working in the capital. Their collective efforts resulted in the formal establishment of OCAW in spring 1977.

OCAW, which now has two thousand women members in cities throughout the nation, was at first affiliated with the Organization of Chinese Americans

(OCA). Unfortunately, OCA and OCAW had an uneasy relationship, since OCAW perceived itself as an equal partner rather than an auxiliary unit, and the two had different priorities.[61] OCA acts as an advocacy group addressing national issues such as civil rights and immigration laws. OCAW, in contrast, functions primarily as a service organization, providing direct assistance to its professional and immigrant members. So, in 1987, the two groups had an amicable divorce. According to Tsui, "OCA initiated the separation by taking away OCAW's autonomy which OCAW had for ten years. Consequently, members of OCAW responded by ending our affiliation."[62] The split illustrates the difficulty some Asian American women have had in balancing commitments to their ethnic group and their gender.

Preparations for the 1977 Houston conference stimulated the emergence of other Asian American women's organizations, mainly on the East Coast, but also in Chicago and the Seattle, King County, area. Esther Kee of the Democratic party convened a meeting of Asian American women at the Transfiguration Church in New York's Chinatown to prepare for the state's IWY conference (July 1977), which would choose delegates for the national conference. Out of this meeting came the Asian American Women's Caucus, which later represented New York Asian American women at Houston.[63] Although the caucus continued afterward, many of its members became disillusioned when they perceived it as a vehicle for Kee's political ambitions in the Democratic party.[64] In 1978, these dissidents broke away to form Asian Women United–New York (AWU–NY).[65]

In the beginning, AWU–NY was a grassroots feminist organization committed to educating Asian American women and the community about issues important to their lives through forums, discussions, and workshops. In recent years, it has been interested in establishing a personal support network. As Becky Hom noted, "the women in AWU are more involved in their personal lives. Their life cycle is more in tune with the life cycle of women, where women are at, at their chronological age."[66] Because it is one of the few viable Asian American organizations in New York City and consists mainly of politically inexperienced women, various left political groups have tried periodically to influence the thinking of these women on different issues. But members experienced in dealing with Marxist–Leninist groups are careful to present a political balance.

The main impetus for the revival of the Asian American women's movement was the Houston conference. Its key contribution was to raise people's consciousness about Asian American women's issues and to create a climate hospitable for the emergence of new Asian American women's organizations, rather than to produce activists. The presence of so many Pacific Islanders— Hawaiians, Samoans, and Guamanians—at Houston made Asian American women aware of the need to broaden future organizations. Altogether there were seventy-four Asian–Pacific American delegates and nine delegates-at-large at Houston, a 2.7 percent representation.[67] Since most were selected from the general Asian–Pacific American female population, especially those involved in electoral politics, rather than the women's movement, only a few spoke out on Asian–Pacific American women's issues. Still, as part of the Third World women's coalition, they made their presence felt. This coalition struggled with European American women delegates to have their concerns of "visibility, identity, and equality" included in the overall plan of action.[68] After many compromises and concessions, the coalition got its "Substitute Minority Women Resolution" adopted. The Asian–Pacific American women portion of it reads: "Asian/Pacific American Women are wrongly thought to be part of a 'model minority' with few problems. This obscures our vulnerability due to language and cultural barriers, sweatshop work conditions with high health hazards, the particular problems of wives of U.S. servicemen, lack of access to accreditation and licensing because of immigrant status and to many federally-funded services."[69]

Some of the Asian–Pacific American women delegates "went on to become active in or founded women's groups, political groups or local action groups revolving around some of the concerns identified in Houston."[70] Perhaps more important, they felt the need for a network of Asian American women to ensure that their issues would be addressed at the national level.

In 1979, Tin Myaing Thein, a member of Pan Asia and of President Carter's National Advisory Committee on Women, obtained a $168,149 WEEA grant to focus on the educational and employment needs of Asian–Pacific women.[71] It was a pivotal project, one that would set in motion a revival of the Asian American women's movement. Thein contacted Asian–Pacific women leaders to discuss organizing regional conferences in California, Hawaii, and New York. In spite of some ambivalence about a project that came "down" from the national capital rather than "up" from the Asian American communities, veteran women activists were initially interested in participating. Long-time activist Emma Gee wrote:

I was first attracted to the idea of participating in the proposed state conference, because I thought our existing network of Asian/Pacific American women in California and other places, built over the past decade, could draw in new people. And by working together collectively, we could develop good working relationships in the long struggle for meaningful change in our society, assuming, of course, we shared at least some similar goals.[72]

Later, many of the "Old Guard," a sobriquet conferred on older Asian American activists by newer ones, dropped out because they disagreed with Thein's "work style." Believing that "proposals involving women and minorities are not created out of a vacuum or by single individuals" but were "the result of long and continuing *community* struggles," they took issue with her alleged unwillingness to share basic information and her attitude toward "federally-funded grants as a form of private property" and questioned the disbursement of the budget.[73] Furthermore, they raised questions about the beneficiaries of the project: "It is still unclear, after much discussion, whose needs this conference will serve. It is important that the very people whose needs are to be addressed should be active participants in planning the conference, such as low-income immigrant women workers."[74] The regional conferences seemed to them to be geared to the needs of middle-class Asian–Pacific women, especially professionals, rather than working-class women.[75] They were apparently echoing the sentiments of an earlier period, instead of reflecting the working-class issues embodied in the Asian–Pacific American section of the minority resolution adopted at the Houston conference. In short, the Old Guard made the classic criticism of federally funded projects and challenged Thein's control of this one.

Other Asian–Pacific women Thein had contacted maintained their interest in establishing a regional or national Asian–Pacific women's group. Irene Hirano, one of the organizers of the regional conference in California and a former co-chair of the National Network, observed that the women she met throughout the state "were enthused" and "thought that the timing was right."[76] Indeed, the eight hundred women who attended the state conference held in Los Angeles and the subsequent establishment of several new Asian–Pacific women's organizations in California proved Hirano correct—the time was right.

This conference, as well as the other regional meetings in New York and Hawaii, culminated in the National Conference of the Asian/Pacific Americans

Educational Equity Project in Washington, D.C. (15–17 August 1980). Sally Li Young, chair of the New York delegation, noted that "for us, this is Houston," a view shared by many.[77] Among other things, the participants adopted a resolution to promote a national network of Asian and Pacific women's organizations. It drew heated debate in the caucus meetings and on the assembly floor.[78] While people agreed on the need for such an organization, there was considerable argument over its structure and membership. Because of the existence of earlier organizations and the absence of a national leadership, they decided that the proposed network should serve as an umbrella organization consisting of independent groups that could maintain their autonomy and identity, yet come together to address mutually pertinent matters.

Another issue was Pacific Island women. From the beginning, their representatives were involved in planning and founding the National Network. After all, they were "sisters" from the same part of the world and had similar experiences in the United States. Having them aboard would broaden the scope of the organization, a politically sound move. Although they were relatively few in number, they made their cultural and physical presence felt. Feelie Lee, former president of the Asian Pacific Women's Network–Los Angeles, vividly recalled:

> The Asian Americans outnumbered the Pacific Islanders, it was like four out of every five were Asian Americans. But in terms of actual physical size and stature, the Pacific Islanders totally overshadowed us. These brown skinned, majestic women with their leis, long gowns constituted a tight-knit group, sitting as a caucus. Whereas the Asian Americans— at least three generations old—sat in their silks and suits, grappling with political issues that were so new to them. The visual contrast as well as class differences underscored the differences in goals and strategies that would emerge even more in later years.[79]

Pacific Islanders appreciated the potential benefits that their ethnic communities could derive from a national organization and worked to ensure that they as a group distinct from Asian Americans would be included "in every stage and level of the network." [80] Strong women at the founding conference forcefully articulated their concerns and engendered considerable empathy from the Asian American women. Feelie Lee noted, "it looked [like] they were there to establish their identity and define their needs against a generation of porcelain dolls."[81] After a three-hour debate, the founding members decided that the network's leadership should be equitable rather than proportional. So leadership positions in the National Network were divided evenly between Asian Americans and Pacific Islanders. Pat Luce, director of the National Office of Samoan Affairs and a former co-chair of the National Network, noted that the Pacific Islanders "felt that there was parity" and "the structure allowed [them] to have a voice in it."[82]

Nevertheless, Pacific Islanders had a difficult time exercising the leadership they worked so hard to acquire. Pacific Islander leaders found it difficult to attend the six follow-up meetings that were held around the nation. Since the National Network was underfunded, which was especially so in the beginning when individual dues were only $5, leaders had to donate time, resources, and money. Asian Americans were better able to do this than Pacific Islanders, who were usually strapped for resources and preoccupied with problems in their own communities. Moreover, Pacific Islanders lacked consistent leadership at the top, making communication difficult. Their inability to participate fully made it difficult to safeguard and promote their interests.

In 1982, the National Network of Asian and Pacific Women was officially inaugurated in La Jolla, California. By design, it serves as an umbrella organization that meets only twice a year. It consists of over two dozen member organizations and several thousand members. It tries to provide its members with a means of maintaining regular communication with each other through national conferences and newsletters, assisting women in establishing their own organizations, educating them about social and political issues through the activities of its member organizations, and giving national visibility to certain issues. It has also received two grants from the Department of Education: $40,000 to develop an Asian American women's curriculum primarily for private colleges, and $147,000 to study the problem of Asian mail-order brides and military wives. But the latter, discussed later in this chapter, became an albatross around its neck and involved it in litigation that threatened to destroy the organization.

The National Network has benefited from the mainstream establishment's practice of using national organizations to reach specific constituencies. For example, it, along with other Asian and Pacific women's groups in Washington, D.C., was called to plan a White House briefing focused on Asian and Pacific women's issues. The network viewed the 20 May 1985 briefing as a singular opportunity "to establish its credibility, show strength in numbers, knowledge through skills and issues, and organization through a united approach." [83] The three-hour briefing was less than ideal, though participants used the opportunity to inform and educate the White House staff; the most valuable aspect of the visit was the prearranged visits to government agencies and with key legislators after the briefing, which allowed participants to have in-depth discussions with "relevant personnel in the nation's capital." [84]

The National Network has had its share of problems. It has been castigated for catering to middle-class women who are mainly interested in enhancing their employment opportunities. The Old Guard believes that class issues are more important than gender ones and thinks it should emphasize working-class women. In contrast, the National Network believes that the type of community activism characteristic of the first phase of the women's movement was ineffectual and that it will be the professionals, rather than the workers, who will be in the vanguard of social change in the United States. Besides, its leaders claim, when it organizes activities that focus mainly on middle-class women, it is merely responding to the wishes of the majority of its members. The leaders can also claim, with considerable justification, that many of their general activities, such as combating stereotypes, benefit *all* Asian–Pacific women.

But insiders have also taken exception to the National Network's emphasis on middle-class issues and concerns. The Pacific Islanders, who are primarily concerned with their working-class communities, have found the National Network's activities largely irrelevant to their needs. Their political development and priorities are markedly different from those of Asian American women. The Samoan community, for example, did not begin to organize regionally until the mid-1970s, when it held a Samoan Leaders Community Conference in California.[85] Its women, who are often the main catalyst for change, are more concerned with community issues, which they are just beginning to address. Along with other Asian–Pacific Americans, they have lobbied to get the U.S. Census Bureau to recognize separate Asian–Pacific groups. The census data told a disturbing tale of pervasive poverty and low educational achievement among Pacific Islanders in America. The statistics documented what these people already knew, that they were "falling through the cracks" in American society. Unlike their Asian American sisters, who are mainly interested in the problems of underemployment and admission to colleges, Pacific Islanders are concerned about unemployment and high school dropouts. In short, Pacific Islanders are involved in basic "survival" issues.

The National Network is a fundamentally flawed organization: It is structured so that Pacific Islanders have political parity with Asian Americans, yet Asian Americans make up the majority of the members; and the two groups have different, though overlapping, agendas. Much to the organization's credit, it agrees that the Pacific Islanders certainly have a right to complain about the failure to respond to their needs. Ultimately, it went the direction of OCAW and formed two separate organizations.

In the late 1980s, the National Network was embroiled in litigation that threatened to destroy it. A few days after the White House briefing, a Chinese–Filipino woman, in collaboration with the National Network's chairperson, submitted a hastily written proposal to study the problem of mail-order brides and military wives—without consulting the national leader, who learned of the proposal only after the National Network received a $147,000 award. On examining the proposal, some leaders wanted to return the award because the project was poorly conceived, with an inadequate methodology and unrealistic deadline. Moreover, they had heard disquieting allegations that the project director had previously misused monies entrusted to her and had falsified her credentials on the application. Finally, they decided to retain the grant and try to fulfill its purpose, but replaced the project director. She, in turn, promptly sued the National Network and its leaders. While the suit had no merit and was dismissed in court, it was a nuisance that drained the organization of financial resources and demoralized its members.

The case illustrates the National Network's inherent contradictions and fragility. Like other national organizations faced with bureaucratic and funding deadlines, it was caught between individual control and grassroots accountability, a situation exacerbated by a lack of effective communication within its own governing board and between the board and member organizations.

While the National Network is in transition, its member organizations are still active. They have always been the strength of the network, attracting large numbers of previously apathetic women. During the mid-1980s, those in California have been especially active and have established a statewide body called the California Asian/Pacific Women's Network.[86] Its priorities have been child care, women refugees, and media stereotypes of Asian American women. Among its members the Asian/Pacific Women's Network–Los Angeles is the largest group with a membership close to six hundred women (and men), most of whom are in the professions. In spite of its numbers, it has tried to foster close personal bonds through an active mentor program. It has engaged in mainly educational activities, sponsoring workshops on personal development, social issues, and professional growth. One of its most visible areas of concern has been the problem of mail-order brides from Asia. It and its sister organization, the Pacific and Asian American Women Bay Area Coalition, are well known for their annual scholarships, given to Asian–Pacific women who are seeking to pursue a life change, and for their Women Warrior Awards, which honor distinguished individuals in business, government, education, the arts, and the sciences who have contributed to the advancement of Asian–Pacific women.

The Asian American women's movement has been able to endure and expand because of its willingness to include the growing numbers of Asian ethnic women from various groups and adapt to changing issues of importance to them. It has politicized these women, instilling in them a desire for equity and equality and motivating them to become active in the Movement. As participants in the Movement, they have influenced Asian American organizations, making them more sensitive to women's issues. Many of them have become leaders in the Movement, bringing to it their political experience and feminist perspective. They have been less successful in influencing European American feminist organizations, though that too will change as issues and policies affecting women of color receive greater public attention.

One of the vehicles for nurturing both Asian American women's identity and ethnic identity has been the alternative press. As the next chapter shows, such publications played an early and indispensable role in the development of the women's movement and a distinct pan-Asian identity, legitimating them even before they had gained popular acceptance. In the course of reporting on the day-to-day activities of Asian American women and men and commenting on their actions and concerns, alternative press publications promote the pan-Asian concept; in researching the past and discussing the present circumstances of Asian Americans, they provide a historical and contemporary basis for a collective identity. By serving as cultural media, they contribute to the definition of who is an Asian American, giving that term shape and unity, in the process creating a constituency for themselves.

Speaking Out:

The Asian American Alternative Press

Usually only sensational news—
such as gang violence, Chinatown
sweatshops, or the massive influx of
immigrants and refugees—arouses
curiosity or attracts the attention of
the predominately white media
establishment.

—Editorial, *East/West*

From the beginning, Asian American activists were attracted to the printed word and appreciated its power to move people emotionally and politically. Those with a heightened ethnic consciousness saw newspapers, magazines, newsletters, and journals as means of reaching out to others and voicing long-suppressed personal feelings. Those working in campus and community groups saw periodicals as a means of gaining visibility, disseminating information about their own activities, and publicizing their perspective on national and international issues. Those belonging to Marxist–Leninist organizations saw the press as a political instrument that could preach revolution—that is, a radical restructuring of values and institutions.

Underlying these various attitudes was the well-founded belief that, historically, the mainstream press had spoken for the European American majority, while Asian Americans, as well as other people of color, had been largely ignored. When the latter did make the news, the information about them was often disparaging, or they were depicted in a demeaning manner. Equally disquieting was the tack taken by the traditional Asian ethnic press, which touted the achievements and promoted the preservation of a particular ethnic group's heritage, while overlooking common interests and experiences and ignoring pressing social issues and concerns.[1] Even worse, some Asian ethnic newspapers in America were used by certain Asian governments to spread political propaganda and report on the loyalty of individuals and organizations in the immigrant communities.[2]

Both the mainstream and Asian ethnic presses often stifled unpopular ideas and refused access to people working for social and political change. Consequently, there was a cry for an alternative press that would present the Asian American community with a diversity of perspectives, stimulate people to ponder contemporary social issues, and mobilize them for specific social actions. A plethora of publications emerged to meet these needs, but most were ephemeral and practically all have been ignored in works dealing with the "dissident" or "alternative" press of America.[3]

Three of the most influential Asian American periodicals were *Gidra*, *Bridge* magazine, and *Amerasia Journal*. All of them trace their origins to the Asian American Movement, were influenced by it, and made contributions to it. Founded by students, they were read by the first generation to perceive themselves as Asian Americans. They relied on volunteers (though *Amerasia* soon professionalized its staff) and reflected an ethnic–regional character. Even though their distribution was limited, copies managed to find their way to readers living in isolated communities. Often they were the main communication link between Asian American activists working on common causes in different parts of the United States, unifying the Movement and Asian Americans, thereby enhancing existing community organizing efforts.

Gidra, the first radical Asian American newspaper, was a raffish-looking tabloid published monthly in Los Angeles from 1969 to 1974. Because of its limited resources, it was mainly a local paper that provided some coverage of California and the rest of the West Coast. Originally conceived simply as a "forum for discussions of issues confronting individuals of Asian ancestry in contemporary America,"[4] it provided reports on events in the Asian American community and essays on a variety of timely subjects. It was soon followed by others, like *Rodan*, a San Francisco clone. Across the continent was *Bridge*, a New York Chinatown-based bimonthly magazine that started in 1971, changed to a quarterly in 1976, and lasted till 1985—a long time for a Movement publication. Initially aimed at overseas Chinese, it broadened its focus to Asian Americans. In his obituary for *Bridge*, Bill J. Gee noted that its "forty-two issues . . . represent a running account of Asian American history up to this very day, an invaluable source of information to future historians of these times." [5] Since *Gidra* and *Bridge* were explicitly aimed at a popular audience, they had more in common with each other than they did with *Amerasia*, which is still being published by the Asian American Studies Center at the University of California, Los Angeles. It is the only field publication of Asian American Studies and is one of those rare professional journals that consciously eschews academia and tries to publish well-researched, quality scholarship in a form that is accessible not only to scholars but also to students, professionals, community activists, and other interested laypeople.

Gidra

Founded during the 1960s, *Gidra* was considered by some people to be the journalistic arm of the Movement. In a survey of Asian American periodicals, Rocky Chin noted that "if there is an 'Asian-American Movement' publication, it is *Gidra*, the most widely circulated Asian American newspaper-magazine in the country." [6] It was prominent and creditable enough to be included in the Federal Bureau of Investigation's counterintelligence program. The FBI's Los Angeles field office described the paper as "mildly militant (and sometimes obscene) in nature and espouses all yellow power issues. It reports regularly on Asian American activities on the California campuses as well as other areas of the country and has proved to be a wealth of information concerning the identities of organizations and individuals devoted to these causes." [7]

In February 1969, after their proposal for a community newspaper had been turned down by the UCLA administration, five Asian American students— Dinora Gil, Laura Ho, Mike Murase, Tracy Okida, and Colin Watanabe— decided to pool their meager resources to publish their own newspaper. [8] All third-generation Asian American students at UCLA, they had been members of such early Asian American organizations as Oriental Concern, had worked with the UCLA Asian American Studies Center, or both. Originally they were torn between "Yellowstone" and "Epicanthus" for a title, names that would reflect their newspaper's pan-Asian emphasis. To break the deadlock, Tracy Okida suggested "Gidra"—which, he explained, was a huge bug, the hero of a

Japanese monster movie. The students accepted the name without reservation and made its namesake—a slant-eyed caterpillar wearing a conical bamboo peasant hat and wielding a pen—the paper's mascot. It was an odd name for a newspaper, for it had no known meaning; Jeffrey Matsui of the *Pacific Citizen* thought that it was merely "Ardig" spelled backward, a word without meaning.[9] The absence of meaning gave it an existential appeal, since the students wanted to define the paper in the course of its development; perhaps unconsciously, they hoped that the paper, like a chrysalis, would experience a metamorphosis and become like a butterfly—one of nature's most beautiful beings.

In April 1969, the first issue of *Gidra* rolled off the press. It had no clearly articulated editorial policy. Initially, there was some discussion about the need for one—or, at least, for a detailed statement of objectives. A few staff members wanted the paper to have some sort of ideological perspective but could not agree on one; others felt that any such perspective might alienate people. Gradually, however, the staff developed certain tacit ideas that determined the direction of the paper: the value of collectivism, the importance of Asian pride and identity, and the need to change the country's economic and political system. Different political perspectives notwithstanding, the editors at least agreed that something must be done to disseminate accurate information about Asian Americans and to enhance existing community organizing efforts. They felt there was an obvious need to start a dialogue about local concerns as a first step in bringing about social change.

In keeping with the spirit of the 1960s, *Gidra* staff members usually made major decisions collectively, after extensive open discussions that reflected an informal, consensus-building approach to decision making. But a core group consisting of the most important staff members dominated the process and, in effect, created a hierarchy. Some members openly discussed their discontent in the paper, while others found it difficult to challenge the core group, preferring to avoid conflict and criticism. In this atmosphere, *Gidra* staff as a whole rarely confronted problems openly and directly, and seldom evaluated personnel or procedures.

During the latter part of 1971, a system of rotating monthly coordinators was established to resolve this organizational issue. Dean Toji recalled: "One or two people were responsible for cracking the whip and hassling people to get their articles in. They stayed up all night, ate lots of polly seeds and Lucy's burritos, and smoked a lot of cigarettes (mostly Kool Milds, for some reason— I preferred Camel straights). This was called Coordination. But each month, the coordinators would be different people from ones before, selected on the basis of who could go without sleep in the next month." [10]

The few editorials were usually penned by an individual who wanted to discuss an issue, though several people would comment on the draft for style and substance. By the end of 1971, "fine print messages," an idea conceived by Tracy Okida, began appearing in lieu of editorials.[11] These vignettes were placed discreetly at the bottom of the page below the staff lists. "Da Blurb," as these messages were sometimes called, revealed the "journo-political" headaches experienced by the staff during that month. More often than not, they were pessimistic maunderings about life in general and *Gidra* in particular and presumably served as a catharsis for the writer. Apparently, the rigors of publishing a monthly periodical, anxieties over funding, and uncertainties of relying on volunteers were taking their toll.

Gidra had a press run of about 4,000 copies, with about 900 to 1,300 local subscribers, with the West Coast, state of California, and city of Los Angeles having the greatest concentration. The number of actual readers probably exceeded these figures, since issues circulated among several people. Most were college students, especially those involved with the Movement. Many of the papers were given away to passersby on the street or placed on the doorsteps of homes in certain neighborhoods such as the Crenshaw district. Copies were also sent to contact people across California and the United States for sale or for free distribution.

A total of 247 different individuals at one time or another volunteered to serve on *Gidra*'s staff. Though their ages ranged from eleven to fifty-one, most were young adults from California. Some participated because they perceived the paper as a conduit for ideas and information within the Asian American community, others for the satisfaction of seeing the paper well received. For yet others it was an organizing tool that could be used to bring about social change. Many volunteers were already involved in the Movement, and the articles they wrote were usually about its activities. Joining the staff gave them an opportunity to work and socialize with others who shared similar values and commitments. Colin Watanabe noted that *Gidra* "had a certain amount of social attraction for Asian Americans who were looking for an alternative to fraternities and sororities." [12] Dean Toji recalled that "*Gidra* was extremely open on a personal level (just come in, and do some work, hang out). It was easy to be accepted as part of the group. The 'collective spirit' which was spoken about so much then, was . . . very real. That sort of collectivity was liberating rather than confining. And, [it] was fun." [13] Getting an issue out often depended on people's personal loyalty to others on the staff.

While *Gidra*'s large number of volunteers speaks well of its reputation as a community newspaper and the openness with which it welcomed newcomers, it was also a source of weakness. On the one hand, fresh volunteers enabled the paper to survive, since it had money only for supplies, printing, and postage, not for salaries; on the other hand, an organization that relies solely on volunteers cannot expect to have a reliable staff or to make plans for the future. Frequent turnovers in personnel were organizationally disruptive. New people had to be trained, and there were disparities in the levels of staff expertise, political development, and understanding of Asian American issues. Furthermore, this turnover caused format changes that appeared to some readers as personal whimsy and made the production of each issue a constant challenge.

The large number of volunteers also masked the narrow ethnic makeup of the paper's personnel. In spite of its intentions to be a publication for and by Asian Americans, its staff and contributors consisted mainly of young Japanese Americans—friends, and later friends of friends, of its UCLA founders. During its first year, 78 percent of its staff and 68 percent of its contributors were Japanese Americans; in its last year, the figures were 91 and 67 percent, respectively. This staffing pattern influenced the kinds of articles that were published. Many articles reported Japanese American events; more important, many reflected specifically Japanese American concerns or sensibilities, even though they were often placed in a larger Asian American context.

During its brief existence *Gidra* went through two perceptible phases, each of which was associated with a core group that served as the center of the paper. The first was devoted to learning the technical skills required to publish a newspaper, to defining what kind of paper it wanted to be, and, consequently, to defining what it meant to be Asian American and involved in the Asian American Movement; the second was devoted to covering the antiwar movement, counterculture lifestyles, and radical politics. As one phase gradually displaced the other, the direction of the paper changed in significant ways.

The first phase focused on the Movement, the issue of identity, and Asian American Studies programs. Activists accused colleges and universities of institutional racism, of contributing to the widespread ignorance and misconceptions about Asian Americans, and of facilitating the assimilation of a few individuals while abandoning the rest to poverty and isolation, a pernicious process that exacerbated problems afflicting Asian American communities. *Gidra* had a symbiotic relationship with one of the most prominent of these programs, the Asian American Studies Center at UCLA. During its first year, it published many articles about the Center and other Asian American Studies programs, as well as the need to make the educational system more responsive to the needs of Asian Americans. It advocated making the college curriculum more relevant to Asian Americans and encouraged students to enroll in Asian American Studies courses, which would instill in them a sense of pride and dignity. It even published essays that had originally been written for Asian American Studies courses.[14]

The Center reciprocated by donating office space and equipment, providing monetary subsidies in the form of service contracts, and using articles from the paper as instructional material. Some of these articles were reprinted in *Roots* and *Counterpoint*, two popular Center anthologies that were widely used in introductory Asian American Studies courses.[15] Over one-fifth of the selections in *Roots*, for example, were from early issues of *Gidra*.

Besides publishing articles about Movement activities, *Gidra* provided a vehicle for explaining exactly what this phenomenon was. In its inaugural issue, Larry Kubota initiated a public discussion of Yellow Power, which he defined as "Asian Americans seeking greater control over the direction of [their] lives. It also expresses a determination to effect constructive changes in the larger society." [16] In other words, the Movement emphasized self-determination and the creation of a more humanistic society. Later, Amy Uyematsu defined Yellow Power as a collective ethnic political effort to achieve local self-determination through a unified Asian American community.[17] Such political power would enable Asian Americans to resist oppression and improve their socioeconomic situation.

The issue of identity led to several controversial articles the first year. In a lengthy letter and follow-up article, David Ota vehemently opposed an ethnic identity and argued that "Japanese-Americans" should dispense with their hyphenated appellation and assert their American heritage through the use of the cumbersome but unambiguous term "Americans of Japanese descent." [18] Instead of following the example of African Americans, he proposed they should

emulate European American ethnic groups whose members had gained acceptance by embracing Americanism. He described his proposal as a synthesis of
militant patriotism with liberal motives.

The late Steve Tatsukawa was the first to respond to Ota's proposal.[19] He
criticized Ota's assumptions that the United States was a democracy and noted
that the real issue was power. For him, the goal was "self-determination."
Asian Americans needed to go beyond the question of identity, which he saw
as an indulgence, and to participate in a "revolution," which he equated with
rapid and radical social change. Only in this way would they solve their socioeconomic problems. The most cogent critique, however, was offered by Frank
Kofsky, a historian at Sacramento State College, who pointed out that Ota had
overlooked the problem of endemic racism in American society.[20]

While some people overlooked or discounted the issue of race in America,
those working for *Gidra* did not. Their most celebrated as well as earliest case
was the Los Angeles Board of Supervisors' dismissal of Thomas T. Noguchi,
the "coroner to the stars," for mismanagement. *Gidra* depicted him not just as
a person suffering from injustice but as an Asian American who was willing
to speak out, to oppose racial discrimination openly. In the eyes of the staff,
his unwillingness to accept his fate apathetically made him a rebel, one who
contradicted the popular belief that Japanese Americans were inherently quiet.[21]

For the *Gidra* people, as they were known, the first phase of the paper's
history was an exhausting but exhilarating one. They had established the paper
as a medium of expression for the Asian American community by expressing
that community's concerns and announcing its activities. They had made it the
premier newspaper of the Asian American Movement by describing what the
Movement was and discussing where it was headed. But their most notable
achievement was simply making it through the first year.

Before entering its second phase, *Gidra* went through a transitional period
that lasted from about the middle to the end of 1970, a period influenced by
the paper's support of a May 1970 student strike. The Asian American Student Alliance at UCLA had organized a general strike on campus to protest the
American military's invasion of Cambodia, the subsequent killing of students
at Kent State and Jackson State, and the "police riot" at UCLA. The Asian
Strike Committee had used the *Gidra* office as a center for its protest activities,
and some of its members stayed on to help publish the paper. Bruce Iwasaki,
for instance, became aware through his work with the committee that *Gidra*

might be a means of addressing Asian American concerns off campus and a medium for disseminating his own political ideas, especially about the Vietnam War. With so many antiwar activists on its staff and the country concerned over the expansion of the war, it was natural for *Gidra* to shift its emphasis from who Asian Americans were to why Asian Americans opposed the war. Ethnic concerns were overtaken by national events.

As it entered its second year, *Gidra* began to experience major turnovers in personnel. In 1970, 127 different people, including, for the first time, some without a college background, gave their time and talent to the paper. Some of the original members left to pursue different activities, often related to the Movement, and were replaced with others. With their departure, a second core group evolved that was larger than the first. With these changes in personnel, there was also a decided shift in emphasis, from campus to community concerns, from personal identity to group organizing, and, in a general sense, from history and psychology to sociology and politics. The paper's issues were now the antiwar movement, counterculture lifestyles, and international perspectives.

Gidra had earlier come out publicly against the war. In its December 1969 editorial it condemned the My Lai massacre and urged Asian Americans to participate in the third nationwide Vietnam Moratorium by joining an unprecedented Asian American demonstration against the war organized in Los Angeles by the newly founded Asian Americans for Peace. It disagreed with the government's foreign policy in Southeast Asia, which it found politically and morally bankrupt. And it propagated the belief that the Vietnam War was part of a historical pattern of genocide against Asians at home and abroad. Pat Sumi argued that the atrocity committed at My Lai was not simply an unfortunate accident of the war but had precedents as early as the Philippine–American War (1898–1902), which was referred to as America's first Vietnam.[22] But the most often cited example of this pattern of killing Asians was the atomic bombings of Hiroshima and Nagasaki. While the atomic bombs and the mass internment of 120,000 Japanese Americans in concentration camps during World War II were rationalized as "military necessities," according to *Gidra* they were really the result of racial prejudice.

Toward the end of 1971, as a result of readers' criticisms and suggestions, the staff decided to tone down its negativism and rhetoric and present constructive counterculture alternatives. *Gidra* began publishing practical pieces on such topics as how to raise a garden and how to repair a toilet, articles meant to encourage self-reliance and provide alternatives to the patent "price gouging" and "profiteering" of American society. These pieces reflected the staff's disillusionment with the competitiveness and hypocrisy that characterized both European American and Asian American societies. For their efforts, they were accused of imitating the "white hippie counterculture" and forsaking the "revolution." Some critics felt that the paper was on the periphery of the Movement, since it appeared merely to describe rather than to participate in it.

This accusation was unwarranted. From the beginning, the paper had encouraged the development of a distinctive Asian American culture and an understanding of the complex relations among people in the Movement. Many of its pieces shared a conviction that contemporary society was intellectually and emotionally sterile and that there had to be a meaningful alternative. Moreover, it is clear that the staff did not see culture and politics as incompatible. Bruce Iwasaki argued that the "Woodstock Nation and the Third World Nation are not separate, mutually exclusive camps within the Asian movement" and that "a genuine alternative culture eschewing middle class materialism, restrictions, and authoritarianism in favor of greater permissiveness in sex, drugs, appearance and art forms is of profound importance to the movement." [23]

In order to provide more in-depth coverage of certain topics, *Gidra* began publishing a series of theme issues on specific segments of the population, important community concerns or activities, or trends in the Movement. The first topical issue, in January 1971, focused on Asian American women and grew out of International Women's Week. It contained pieces that explored the economic and psychological exploitation of women, indicting men for their complicity but placing the blame squarely on the shoulders of American capitalism. This edition went a long way toward legitimating women's concerns within the Movement. It became a standard practice for Movement periodicals to set aside at least one number for women. [24]

Another topical issue was youth oriented and had a "street" perspective. [25] It reflected the involvement of high school students who had been hired by *Gidra* through a Neighborhood Youth Corps program and high school dropouts who had joined the paper. The most moving issue was that on the "middle generation," which contained some of the most highly personal articles *Gidra* ever published. [26] A public avowal that young people had finally come to appreciate their parents' struggles, the articles symbolized reconciliation and pleaded for greater communication between generations. Special issues, however, were eventually "abandoned in order to have a wider coverage of events and personalities within each issue." [27]

During its second phase, *Gidra* developed more of an "international perspective" on the Asian American experience, attempting to place it within a larger political context. Here again, Asian American antiwar activists asserted that racial injustices at home were connected to imperialism abroad: To understand the former, one had to understand the latter. A reflection of this international perspective was stories about Japan and China. Given the predominance of Japanese American staffers and contributors, it was natural for them to be personally interested in Japan; but their stories, less than flattering to the land of their ancestors, focused on its dependence on the United States. They paid particular attention to Okinawa, the largest of the Ryukyu Islands, which was being returned to Japan in 1972 after being used as a base for the training and recreation of American troops headed for Southeast Asia.[28] They criticized the United States–Japan Security Pact, which they felt facilitated America's aggressive imperialist policies in Asia, and covered American demonstrations against Prime Minister Sato's government, which ratified it.[29] There were also stories about Japan itself, especially about what was thought to be a resurgence of Japanese militarism and its relationship to American imperialism.[30]

Since Asian American activists were alienated from America *and* Japan, they gave their affections to China. The People's Republic of China was viewed as *the* revolutionary country. It was admired for liberating itself from Western domination in 1949 and for its ongoing efforts to establish an egalitarian society. At the time, China was in the throes of the Cultural Revolution (1966–1976), which seemed to be a struggle to maintain revolutionary values and oppose the bureaucratism that had stifled other revolutions. (Now that the Cultural Revolution has been discredited, that tragic episode in China's recent history is referred to as the "Decade of Destruction.")

In 1972, the interest in an international perspective eventually led some of the *Gidra* people to organize a political study group called the Westside Collective, which focused on the objective conditions of Asian Americans, the goals toward which they should work, and the means to achieve them. They divided their efforts into six-week sessions with rotating chairs and a recess and evaluation after each session. They also moved into a house and entered into a group-living arrangement. The combination of political study and collective living made them a cohesive entity. Ironically, studying political matters did not lead to a more politically focused newspaper; instead, it made the *Gidra* people ask whether their publication had outlived its usefulness. By April 1974, they and the other members of the staff concluded that it had.

In hindsight, Mike Murase thought that *Gidra* ceased publishing because the staff felt that it was time for the paper to evolve into something else.[31] After its closing, the staff continued to meet regularly, first twice a week and later less frequently, to evaluate their experiences and consider some alternatives, including a weekly paper that would focus on local community events, a series of occasional papers or pamphlets dealing with specific issues, a literary anthology, and an Asian American news service. *Gidra*'s fate reflected what was happening in the Movement, for in the mid-1970s Asian American groups felt the need for reflection and self-appraisal. Since the paper's demise, many *Gidra* staffers have continued their involvement in the Asian American Movement and progressive issues.[32] They have also stayed in contact with one another. In spring 1989, some of them met to discuss a twentieth anniversary edition, which they published a year later.[33]

Gidra lasted five years, no mean feat considering that most dissident newspapers fold after only a few months. Its demise was due, in part, to its success. It had inspired other Asian American newspapers and magazines, which then competed with it for subscribers and volunteers; it had also encouraged various campus and community activities, which then competed with it for labor and resources. Potential workers often preferred to participate directly in activities rather than write about them. Over the years *Gidra* attracted fewer and fewer people willing to spend part of their lives on a Movement newspaper, making the work more difficult for those who did. Meanwhile, the core staff members were getting older and were understandably concerned with such mundane matters as making a living and raising families. Since working for *Gidra* was never meant to be a career, they had to look elsewhere.

Bridge

As *Gidra* was closing its doors, *Bridge* had just mailed out its most popular issue to date. It featured "Media: Racism in the Comics" and was the only issue ever to sell out completely.[34] The editor reaffirmed the staff's commitment "to do its work of being a bridge—between the various Asian American groups, with their different backgrounds and experiences, and between Asian Americans and American society in general" and observed that in the absence of a paid staff and organizational support, its survival was "near miraculous."[35]

It is uncertain who conceived of *Bridge*.[36] Most people credit Danny N. T. Yung, the charismatic founder of Basement Workshop, which published the magazine until 1979. Yung was an urban planner who wrote the Ford Foundation funded *Chinatown Report, 1969*, and was looking for additional means of disseminating his research. Hence the inception of the magazine, whose first issue (July–August 1971) did have an article on Chinatown based on the *Report* and the *Chinatown Health Survey*.[37] While it is unclear how instrumental Yung was in the birth of *Bridge*, there is little doubt that he played a significant role in its development, especially in the areas of fund raising and artwork.

Others credit the idea to Frank Ching, a copy editor at the foreign desk of the *New York Times* and later the Beijing correspondent of the *Wall Street Journal*, and until 1974 the managing editor of *Bridge*.[38] Ching himself, however, attributed the idea to Peter Chow, who had the "grandiose goal" of publishing a magazine for Chinese in the United States and eventually those in the rest of the world.[39] He recalled that Chow talked to Yung and later Margarett Loke, who later became an editor at the *New York Times Magazine* and the person mainly responsible for editing the first issue, about the venture. Loke brought Ching aboard as a fellow writer and editor. But Chow claimed to be only one of several people who started *Bridge*.[40] He did serve as the coordinator of the first issue, was on the editorial board for the next two issues, and managed the printing shop that printed it. Because he felt that the magazine needed a more formal organization to ensure its long-term viability while others were more "worried about issues . . . action . . . ideology," he dropped out after a year.[41] Ironically, Chow, in his capacity as director of Asian Cinevision, which assumed stewardship of the magazine in 1981, would be the one to preside over *Bridge*'s demise.

Danny Yung, Frank Ching, Margarett Loke, and Peter Chow, like most of the others who helped establish *Bridge*, were well-educated, Cantonese-speaking sons and daughters of middle- and upper-middle-class families in Hong Kong. They had attended university in the United States and had developed a political awareness and social consciousness in college. Unlike their *Gidra* counterparts, they tended to hold professional positions while volunteering to work on the magazine. Having regular occupations made it possible for them to work on the magazine longer than the *Gidra* people, who at some point had to get on with their lives. Most of them served on the editorial rather than the production side of the magazine. Because of their common background and experience, they socialized with each other and were later perceived as a clique by some of the staff. Though *Bridge* did somewhat better than *Gidra* in putting together a diverse staff, the predominance of a single ethnic group was still palpable. *Bridge*'s staff members in its initial years were mainly foreign-born Chinese Americans who were joined by young American-born Chinese and other Asian Americans—a reflection of its location in New York's Chinatown and its aim to reach overseas Chinese. But the individuals who worked for *Bridge* did so for basically the same reasons as those working for *Gidra*. Since *Bridge* relied on volunteers, it also encountered some of the same organizational problems as *Gidra*.

Like many other overseas Chinese students who became politicized while they were studying in the United States, the *Bridge* editors were initially concerned exclusively with issues concerning China and Chinese. They were interested in such activities as the Tiao Yu Tai movement, the effort to get the People's Republic of China admitted into the United Nations and to normalize its relations with the United States, and the opposition to the Kuomintang control of Chinatown. Fluent in English and ambivalent about returning to a British colony where they would be hard pressed to find a position commensurate with their education, they viewed the United States as an alternative home. As a matter of course, they developed an interest in the social problems of the Chinese in America.

They became involved in *Bridge* because they wanted to apply their skills (in writing, graphic arts, and other areas) to serve the community. The community in this case was New York City's Chinatown, which the *Report* and subsequent studies had shown to be a ghetto with innumerable maladies. Unlike the older immigrants, who felt the powerlessness of being a minority people in a hostile environment, or the newer immigrants, who were bewildered and preoccupied with making a living, the *Bridge* staffers had the confidence and capability to change things. Moreover, they felt that it was their responsibility to do so. In some respects, then, *Bridge* was an outgrowth of Chinese cultural nationalism, but one that was colored by an Asian American experience.

Originally, *Bridge* was to serve the overseas Chinese community. This intention was manifest in its logo, the Chinese character *qiao* (literally, "bridge")—

an ideal ideogram, for it could serve as a pun on the one hand for "sojourn," which when used in conjunction with the character *hua* (China) meant overseas Chinese. In its first editorial, Margarett Loke wrote: "Isn't it about time the terrible aloneness of the Chinese is destroyed? And a bridge built—between Chinese and Chinese, between Chinese and the larger society? We believe it's time to build such a bridge. To provide a platform open to all viewpoints. To be a medium through which readers themselves would approach solutions to problems. To stimulate and emphasize interaction and involvement." [42]

But *Bridge*'s effort to close the cleavages between Chinese drew fire from Frank Chin, who argued that "Americanized Chinese who've come over in their teens and later to settle here and American born Chinaman have nothing in common, culturally, intellectually, emotionally." [43] His criticisms were expressed in an exchange of letters with Frank Ching in 1972 and 1973, a lively correspondence that raised timely questions about the existence of an Asian American sensibility and cultural identity. The controversy began when Chin took umbrage at a *New York Times* article written by Ching's colleague Ralph Blumenthal. The article, originally focused on Chinatown and performers from Hong Kong and Taiwan, had been revised at Ching's suggestion to include mention of Frank Chin as an indigenous example, but it otherwise ignored the contributions and concerns of Asian American writers and artists.

Chin and Ching exchanged increasingly vitriolic letters that revealed some fundamental, and perhaps irreconcilable, differences in attitude toward Asian American culture. Chin's central concern was to maintain his "Chinaman cultural integrity." [44] As far as he was concerned, those who thought that Chinese Americans were interchangeable with Chinese were simply ignorant; furthermore, "the writing of Americanized Chinese is just as racist as white writing, when it deals with Chinese America." [45] Ching acknowledged the indisputable differences between Chinese and Chinese Americans, but took exception to Chin's criticisms of the magazine (though he chose to overlook the implicit personal attacks on himself and the other editors). He replied:

> Let me explain that the purpose of *Bridge* is not, as you put it, to bind
> you to the immigrants. The purpose of *Bridge* is to foster a sense of soli-
> darity and to promote understanding among Asians, whether Chinese,
> Japanese, Koreans, etc. And within the Chinese-American commu-
> nity there are many who were born and raised in this country and many

others who were born and raised abroad. We recognize the differences
in experiences and attitudes between them. But you cannot exclude the
foreign-born Chinese-Americans and say you have nothing in common
with them. Your father is a foreign-born Chinese-American. You have
at least that much in common.[46]

Some readers commented on the correspondence: Edward Liu characterized
Chin's letters as "tantrums" designed to draw attention to himself, and Clifford
Boram thought Chin's criticism of *Bridge* as "dull" was unwarranted.[47]

Bridge's audience gradually changed from overseas Chinese to Asian
Americans. The person primarily responsible for this shift was Danny Yung.[48]
Having attended the University of California at Berkeley before coming to New
York City, he brought back with him a lot of Movement material and, more
important, a heightened awareness of the common experience of Asians in
America. Wanting a magazine that would raise the social consciousness of
Asian Americans, he made a conscious effort to persuade others at *Bridge* to
recruit writers and staff who were of Filipino, Japanese, Korean, and other
Asian ancestry, who became involved mainly in the artistic and cultural aspects
of the magazine. For example, David Oyama, a journalist and later an actor
and theatrical producer, was brought in to succeed Frank Ching as the head of
the magazine in 1974 and stayed until the end of 1977.

It took the *Bridge* staff several years to make the transition to a full-fledged
Asian American publication. Not until about 1973 did a significant number of
feature articles deal with the experience and concerns of non-Chinese Asian
ethnic groups or Asian Americans in general. From 1971 to 1975, 61 percent of the feature articles were on a "Chinese" topic and only 22 percent
on Asian Americans.[49] Volume I focused mainly on ethnic Chinese, though
there was a perceptible shift from overseas Chinese to Chinese Americans—
graphically announced on the cover of the second issue, which showed a white
shirt washed in a Chinese hand laundry, captioned "Yellow Identity White
Washed?" It was made explicit in Frank Ching's editorial, "An American in
Disguise," a reference to the book of the same title written by Daniel Okimoto.
Ching wrote: "It is important that Chinese-Americans, especially the younger,
more aware, generation, feel that they are a part of this country and work to
change it in whatever way it needs changing. This is one purpose of *Bridge*
Magazine—to bridge that gap between Chinese-Americans and Americans in

general. Another purpose is to bridge the gap between various groups within the Chinese community itself." [50] The magazine was to be a "powerful tool of self-expression for a previously often silent and often passive minority." [51]

By issue 4 of volume I, it had broadened its focus to include all Asian Americans and replaced its logo with the subtitle "Magazine of Asians in America." But it continued to emphasize ethnic Chinese subjects, particularly Chinatowns. The change was, as one editorial noted, a "slow and inconsistent" process.[52] A breakthrough of sorts occurred with the last issue of the first volume, which depicted on its cover the anguished face of a Japanese American behind barbed wire and contained several articles on the internment.[53]

As the editors solicited articles on other Asian ethnic groups, they began to provide an Asian American perspective on national issues. For many readers, this was *Bridge*'s raison d'être. Beginning with volume II (late 1972) its editorials dealt with Asian American Studies, anti-immigration legislation, busing, and other issues that adversely affected the Asian American community. Volume III included a significant number of feature articles on specific non-Chinese Asian ethnic groups as well as on Asian Americans in general, and devoted special issues to themes such as the Asian American women's movement (winter 1978 and spring 1979 issues).[54] Under the editorship of Genny Lim and Judy Yung, the issues published several thoughtful historical and contemporary essays that addressed those concerns that were "universal to women yet unique to Asian women" [55] as well as several poems by or about women.

During the early 1970s, the central national issue was the Vietnam War. Like the *Gidra* people, the *Bridge* editors focused on the racial dimension of the war and its implications for Asian Americans. They repeated Indira Gandhi's question, "Would this sort of war or the savage bombing which has taken place in Vietnam have been tolerated for so long had the people been European?" [56] As far as they could tell, the only positive side to the war was that it had raised the consciousness of Asian Americans and stirred them to protest. The antiwar articles and editorials culminated in 1975 with a special issue, "Vietnam in Retrospect," which was jointly published by *Bridge* and the Vietnam Resource Center. It featured "U.S. Involvement in Vietnam" by Noam Chomsky, "The Last Days of America in Vietnam" by Ngo Vinh Long, and "The American Peace Movement" by George Vickers.

More than anything else, *Bridge*'s early and regular coverage of electoral politics, mainly presidential politics, expressed its commitment to an Asian

American perspective on national issues. This interest set it apart from other Asian American publications. Except for 1980, when *Bridge* was experiencing internal difficulties, the magazine made it a point to publish an issue on each presidential race. The 1972 elections were the first. *Bridge* wanted to publish the views of major political figures on Asian Americans, but the only presidential candidate to respond was George McGovern. Perhaps to avoid the embarrassment of being ignored again, *Bridge* reversed this procedure for the 1976 campaign and offered the presidential candidates the views of Asian Americans. It provided much more coverage and published informative reports on Asian American community involvement in the elections.

Initially, *Bridge*'s main interest was simply to encourage Asian Americans to vote. During the 1972 election, the editors outlined the "grave" problems confronting the nation and noted that "it is incumbent upon all of us to make whatever contribution we can toward the solution of these problems. For some, this may take the form of direct action. For many, however, their power to influence events lies in the ballot." [57] By 1976, the editors advocated greater community involvement in the electoral process:

> The majority of our people have become so alienated, isolated, and intimidated by the social and political processes of our society that they are skeptical of becoming involved in political activities. Yet, the political arena provides the greatest leverage for alleviating the ills and injustices of our society.
>
> We must begin to assert ourselves politically. And we can begin with voter registration drives, invitations to political leaders to address our community organizations, and submission of position papers to public officials.[58]

To a large extent this exhortation reflected an already increased Asian American involvement in the electoral process, which in turn was due to the Democratic party's initiative to get African Americans and other people of color to support Jimmy Carter, its presidential candidate.

Besides providing an Asian American perspective on national issues, *Bridge* was noted for its coverage of Asian American culture. From the first issue, which had a section specifically on the arts, *Bridge* allocated considerable space to culture, and many well-known artists and writers had their work published in it. Poets Wing Tek Lum and Lawson F. Inada, for example, were occasional contributors. Early pieces on culture, intended to give readers something light and diverting, dealt with popular Chinese culture. For example, the serialization of Robin Wu's translation of Chin Yung's "Flying Fox of Snow Mountain," a Chinese version of an American Western, responded to the growing fascination of Chinatown youth (and others) with the martial arts, as did articles on the cult of Bruce Lee, the star of kung-fu movies. But gradually, the magazine moved away from Chinese culture and toward Asian American culture.

Many of the early articles on Asian American culture focused on the discrimination against Asian American writers, artists, and performers and the stereotyping of Asians and Asian Americans. The problem of prejudice toward Asian Americans in the arts was addressed directly by Albert Pacetta, a member of New York State's Human Rights Appeal Board. In his guest editorial, "Asians for Asian Roles," he noted that the "exclusion of Asian Americans from the entertainment industry [was] flagrantly apparent"[59] and that they should be given the opportunity to perform. Most of the articles on stereotyping focused on the image of Asians and Asian Americans in the media and how it affected children. Knowing that media images and portrayals of Asians directly affected the self-esteem of Asian Americans and how they are perceived and treated by others, Movement members began to organize themselves into groups to monitor these images.

After the Vietnam War ended in 1975, *Bridge* allocated more space to the works of Asian Americans. The breakthrough occurred in October 1976 with an issue on Asian American poetry, which was noteworthy for several reasons: It set a precedent for special issues on culture; it demonstrated the wealth of writing that was available; it prepared the public for forthcoming anthologies and collections; and, perhaps most important, it gave Asian Americans a forum in which they could voice their experiences in that "heightened form of expression which is poetry."[60] In many respects the special issue complemented the earlier articles that decried the barren, unidimensional images of Asian Americans, for it showed their creativity and complexity. To paraphrase David Oyama, who edited the issue, it was a significant "part of a culture in the act of discovering itself."[61]

This trend toward an emphasis on Asian American culture was hastened under the stewardship of Asian Cinevision (ACV), a community-based media arts center that took over the publishing of *Bridge* in 1981. ACV, which needed a publication that would give it greater visibility, described its new journal in a

Publisher's Note as "a vehicle for creative expression and one forum through which Asian American perspectives can react and interact"—reversing the order of its original priorities. It was natural for ACV to organize the magazine around its national network of media artists and writers, giving it an editorial board composed of literary figures such as Diane Mark, a poet and historian who served as editor-in-chief pro tem for the last five issues. The new editorial board decided to devote one of the magazine's four annual issues to Asian American literature, since there were so few forums for emerging writers. In 1985, Mark received an Editor's Award from the Coordinating Council of Literary Magazines. She felt that it had been "given as much to *Bridge* the magazine" for its celebration of Asian American literature.[62] Ironically, that same year the effort to promote culture ended when *Bridge* abruptly expired from fiscal ills.

The absence of a firm financial base of support was a perennial problem for *Bridge*. Advertising, the foundation of profit-oriented commercial magazines, was nil. Although the editors had created a position for a business manager, no one "fulfilled that function in a way that it should be performed."[63] Advertising was never systematically sold. The staff had little enthusiasm or optimism about supporting the magazine through advertisements, and businesses were reluctant to advertise in a "literary and somewhat political magazine" with such a small subscriber list.[64] *Bridge* was simply not that kind of publication. In a message to its readers in the October 1976 issue, the editors and staff explained:

> We have expended much effort at various times to attract advertising and promote the magazine during the past five years. Because of the relatively small circulation dispersed over a nation-wide area, it has been difficult to attract advertising. Those advertisers who generally buy space in the local ethnic press—restaurants and small businesses—find the market too dispersed. National advertisers find the readership too small. Our greatest hope, therefore, is to increase our readership and circulation nationally and in certain selected local markets—New York, Los Angeles, and San Francisco are our most promising areas of concentration.[65]

Instead, *Bridge* relied mainly on individual and institutional subscriptions and private and public funding organizations to pay its expenses—sources of support that were never adequate. At its peak, it had an estimated seven hundred subscribers, but that eventually dwindled to four hundred, with approximately 40 percent representing institutions and libraries. "From the first issue on," according to Frank Ching, "the magazine has had a hand to mouth existence. On at least one occasion, we passed the hat around and asked our own staff to donate money so that the next issue could be published." [66] In order to publish the first issue in 1971, Danny Yung approached An Wang (of Wang Computers) for a special donation.[67] Two years later, the magazine was forced to make an appeal to its readers for assistance, a plea that resulted in "an outpouring of letters and checks" that helped it overcome its immediate crisis.[68]

In 1977, in order to cover *Bridge*'s expenses, Danny Yung and Priscilla Chung, both of whom worked for the magazine and served on the Advisory Board of the Asian American Mental Health Research Center (AAMHRC), arranged for *Bridge* to publish a special section featuring the work of the Center. The AAMHRC (later called the Pacific/Asian American Mental Health Research Center) was a "community-based research center, sensitive to the research needs of Asian and Pacific Islands communities it serves." [69] The editors were ambivalent, thinking the Center's research too academic for *Bridge* and raising questions about whom that work served. But the need for funds overrode their reservations. They reluctantly agreed to sell AAMHRC a certain number of pages so that its researchers could have a vehicle to publish some of their findings. The editors rationalized this arrangement in the following manner:

> The purpose of this joint effort is to bring together the best resources of both organizations for the benefit of the entire Asian American community. We hope that this special section will serve as a compelling case for other Asian American organizations to acknowledge their differences; realize that for the most part these differences are more procedural than substantive; and then begin to work together for the common cause of the Asian American community. Events turn too quickly for us to continually debate esoteric methodologies rather than address the exigencies in our community.[70]

Even though the articles that the AAMHRC prepared were more technical than the usual work appearing in *Bridge*, they were for the most part timely and significant, particularly William T. Liu and Alice K. Murata's "The Viet-

namese in America." This five-part series provided Asian Americans with up-
to-date information on the arrival and settlement of the Vietnamese refugees
in the United States. Highly critical of the resettlement process, it informed
people that "much of the $450 million voted by the Congress for the resettle-
ment of refugees went to the administration and to voluntary agencies" rather
than the refugees themselves.[71]

In 1978, *Bridge* made a purely monetary arrangement with Winberg Chai,
chair of the Asian Studies Department at the City College of New York
(CCNY), who agreed to buy a certain number of issues in exchange for the right
to publish the work of the Asian American Assembly, a research project for the
development of a City College-run community service program for Chinatown.
These brief and uninspiring articles, mostly reports made at the assembly's
second annual conference (held in May 1978 in New York City), did little more
than promote the organization. The issues were to be distributed to students
enrolled in Asian American Studies courses as a way of introducing them to
the magazine.[72] While the arrangements with AAMHRC and the CCNY Asian
Studies Department helped defray the production costs of a half-dozen issues,
they also left the magazine with a reputation for being too academic.

In 1979 *Bridge*'s fiscal situation worsened when its long-standing relationship with the Basement Workshop abruptly ended. At that time the Basement
was experiencing numerous internal difficulties, not the least of which was
financial. After it severed ties, the magazine was forced to suspend operations for a while. In 1981, it resumed publishing under the auspices of Asian
Cinevision.

During the intervening period, *Bridge* lost many subscribers. When it resumed publishing, even long-time readers failed to renew, presumably because
they considered *Bridge* unreliable and irrelevant. During a period of escalating
expenses, this loss of readers proved fatal. After many years of just getting by,
Bridge finally succumbed to its economic woes, squeezed to death by increasing production costs and a decreasing revenue base. In the first half of 1985
alone, the magazine suffered from a deficit of nearly $20,000, equivalent to
the deficit for the entire previous year. As a nonprofit community organization,
ACV found this financial hemorrhage unacceptable, so it made the difficult
decision to suspend publication.

Bridge's experience suggests that the long-term existence of a Movement
publication depends on whether it can find a home in a financially stable insti-

tution. *Amerasia* was able to do just that when it became part of UCLA's Asian American Studies Center. This strong institutional base made it possible for it to secure a place for itself among professional journals.

Amerasia

Amerasia Journal grew out of interaction between activists on the West and East Coasts—specifically, out of the Yale Asian American Students Association (YAASA), which was founded in 1969 by Yale students who had been active on the West Coast and wanted a support group on campus.[73] YAASA engaged in typical Movement activities: organizing Asian American conferences, developing courses, and campaigning for the repeal of Title II of the Internal Security Act. Four of its activists—Rocky Chin, Lowell Chun-hoon, Don Nakanishi, and Glenn Omatsu—were interested in starting a journal. They were aware of *Gidra* and the emergence of other Movement publications on the West Coast, especially in the San Francisco Bay Area, and had learned that the Basement Workshop was planning to publish *Bridge* magazine. They concluded that what was needed was a national publication that would disseminate social science research relevant to Asian Americans and give Asian American scholars an outlet for their work. They also wanted a publication that had a literary dimension. Such a journal would serve as a resource for the new Asian American Studies courses and programs being established around the nation, as well as for the Asian American community. The result was *Amerasia*. Its general goals were stated in the March 1971 inaugural issue: "to accurately assess our past, to attain a clear knowledge of our present situation, and to pose plausible, well-defined visions of our future."[74] In that issue it featured "New York Chinatown Today: Community in Crisis" and "The Political and Economic Effects of Urban Renewal on Ethnic Communities: A Case Study of San Francisco's Japantown," articles that sought to dispel the myths surrounding specific communities and to document their current problems. These two articles conveyed a sense of urgency that caught the attention of Asian Americans. Since then, however, *Amerasia* has published relatively few articles assessing the social welfare needs of Asian Americans.

During its early years, *Amerasia* published some articles that generated heated controversy, most notably Stanley and Derald Sue's "Chinese American Mental Health and Personality."[75] On the basis of "personal observations, clinical impressions, and available research findings" the authors concluded that traditional Chinese values conflicted with American middle-class values and led to serious psychological problems among Chinese Americans (and, by extension, other Asian Americans who shared similar cultural backgrounds). They constructed a typology of three personality types—the traditionalist, the marginal man, and the Asian American—which they proposed as a theoretical framework for assessing community mental health problems and as the basis for further research.

Ben Tong, a fellow psychologist, reacted with a scathing critique, "The Ghetto of the Mind: Notes on the Historical Psychology of Chinese America." [76] Castigating the Sues for their ahistorical approach to the problem of mental health, he offered an alternative thesis: In order to live in the anti-Asian milieu of the United States, Chinese had to act meek and mild and stay within the secure confines of the Chinatown ghetto. This thesis appealed to Asian Americans because it placed the blame on the oppressors rather than their victims. Tong, whose reputation was enhanced by the controversy, aggressively defended his position; the Sues, admitting the value of his criticism, tried to place their analysis in historical perspective.

Like most Movement projects, the journal began with more enthusiasm than resources. There was a dearth of funds, publishable articles, and staff time. The first problem was temporarily solved through the financial contributions from Chun-hoon and Nakanishi, who pooled their summer incomes to finance the publication, and donations made by members of the Chun-hoon family. The second, the founders dealt with by publishing two pieces of their own and encouraging fellow Yale students to contribute work. The third was never worked out satisfactorily; there were simply too many things that needed to be done, and no one had the time and energy to focus on just one project. As with *Gidra* and *Bridge*, launching *Amerasia* required personal sacrifices by those involved.

Fortunately for the future of *Amerasia*, it was eventually transferred to UCLA's Asian American Studies Center. Like other Ethnic Studies programs, the Center traced its origins to the mass movements for social change and justice of the 1960s. A tacit aspect of its mission was to support Movement activities. The Center and YAASA agreed to co-publish *Amerasia* for a year, with Chun-hoon, who had been accepted as a history graduate student at UCLA, serving as its editor. After that, the Center began publishing *Amerasia* alone. It was a mutually beneficial arrangement: The Center gave the journal institutional support and legitimacy, and in return the journal served as one outlet for the Center's scholarly research.

While *Amerasia* had found a permanent home, there were still some difficult years ahead. Money was no longer a problem, but it continued to suffer from a scarcity of articles and limited staff time. Like all new publications, it initially received few good manuscripts. The established scholars dealing with Asian American themes were submitting their work to traditional academic publications, and there were not yet many Asian American Studies scholars producing significant work, a problem that only time would solve. Because the early editors were students, with little previous experience as writers or editors, they found working on the journal difficult. Furthermore, the Center's publications staff often placed a higher priority on other projects, particularly *Counterpoint*, an introductory Asian American Studies text that was finally published in 1976. Consequently, *Amerasia*, which was originally a quarterly, published only one issue a year between 1973 and 1976. Its pivotal year was 1975. UCLA had just completed its five-year review of the Asian American Studies Center, and the staff had concluded that the next five years would be a critical period in the Center's long-term survival; so they tried to strengthen its various components. For *Amerasia* that meant hiring a permanent editor who would place it on a sound footing and ensure that it became a scholarly (though not necessarily conventional) journal that was published regularly. Although some at the Center thought it advisable to employ a faculty person, they eventually agreed on a nonacademic—Russell Leong.

Leong is a third-generation Chinese American with both activist and professional publishing credentials. He had participated in the Third World Strike at San Francisco State and worked on Asian American publications. In retrospect, Leong believes that he was probably hired on the strength of his editing and writing abilities and for his contacts with other writers. Given the spirit of the times, his politics must have also played a major role in his hiring. In any case, he has satisfied the Center staff's expectations and has been the person mainly responsible for the journal's development. In consultation with former staff members, he implemented several basic changes. To improve the journal's quality, he established an editorial board to offer advice and solicit manuscripts, instituted a formal review process for the manuscripts it receives, worked to get articles indexed/abstracted in various publications, made the book review section a regular feature, and added an annual bibliography. In addition, *Amerasia* has tried to publish special issues at least once a year, expand its readership, and make a concerted effort to change its regional character by soliciting articles from places besides the West Coast. *Amerasia* has about nine hundred subscribers, half of whom are institutions and libraries.

Amerasia has always sought to be both a professional field journal that disseminated research in Asian American Studies *and* a community publication relevant to Asian Americans.[77] It recognized the responsibility of academic researchers to respond to community needs; thus, it is "an interdisciplinary journal, [that is] challenged—and beset—by the same conditions which face all university publications" and "a forum for critical research and commentary, a conduit for creative expression, and a source for archival materials such as translations, biographical, and historical accounts, [that] serves the broader Asian American community."[78] Excellence in research and writing is not enough to get an article published in the journal. The overriding criterion is whether it begins to "uncover the wrong questions divorced from social reality and to raise new questions rooted in it"—in other words, to develop and disseminate new perspectives on the Asian American experience.[79]

Amerasia's articles generally fall into three broad categories—historical, social science, and literary expression and critical commentary—with historical pieces predominating. The early prevalence of historical articles reflects the research at the Center and the predominance of historical research in Asian American Studies. Some outstanding examples of historical works employing new perspectives are "Asian Immigrant Coal Miners and the United Mine Workers of America: Race and Class at Rock Springs, Wyoming, 1907," by Yuji Ichioka, "Black Reactions to Chinese Immigration and the Anti-Chinese Movement: 1850–1910," by David J. Hellwig, and "The Search for Spies: American Counterintelligence and the Japanese American Community, 1931– 1942," by Bob Kumamoto.[80] A research associate at the Center, Yuji Ichioka has had the time and freedom to pursue his own projects without the usual institutional constraints. His work is especially valuable for its exceptional command of immigrant-language materials such as newspapers, letters, organizational records, and other primary sources that represent the immigrants' own perspective on events and experience.

Other examples of ground-breaking scholarship are Gary Y. Okihiro, "Japanese Resistance in America's Concentration Camps: A Reevaluation" and Arthur A. Hansen and David A. Hacker, "The Manzanar Riot: An Ethnic Perspective," both of which offer radical interpretations of resistance in the concentration camps.[81] Okihiro dismisses earlier explanations of internee's behavior that stressed the Japanese sense of "loyalty" or feelings of "helplessness," instead seeing the resistance activities at Poston and Manzanar as "continuous and . . . effective" acts that expressed the internee's tendency "to resist externally imposed changes of their institutions."[82] Hansen and Hacker, using the "perspectivist model," focus on the cultural meaning of the Manzanar Riot within the Japanese American community.

Special issues of *Amerasia* have served as an opportunity to publish works reflecting "alternative" and "revisionist" perspectives. For example, the 1980 issue on Hawaii highlighted some of the neglected areas of the islands' history and society. Franklin Odo, the consulting guest editor, noted that the articles "reflect directions of inquiry, which, if further developed, may lead to alternative interpretations and more authentic images of ethnicity, race, class, and labor in Hawaii . . . authors . . . attempt to provide perspectives based on the experiences and attitudes of Asian and Native Hawaiian groups themselves."[83] These articles went a long way in fulfilling *Amerasia*'s early commitment "to collect and publish the best and most provocative material we can find on Asians in America."[84]

While the criteria for the selection of poetry and short stories necessarily differ from those for scholarship, *Amerasia* still prefers works that reflect a critical perspective, that have some message and meaning. Besides meeting the conventional standards for coherence, structure, and language, to be accepted for publication literary pieces must manifest Asian American sensibilities and worldviews. Because of their perceived popularity, especially among students, the journal has begun putting out at least one entire issue a year on literature (and intends to do the same for other creative arts such as graphics and photography). In 1991, it published "Burning Cane," an Asian Pacific student literary collection containing a variety of literary forms: "fictionalized vignettes, missives, essay, satire, and, in many instances, taken on a new personae: of a mother, father, brother, sister, lover, pen pal, etc., to direct their narratives."[85]

Amerasia's preference for articles that look at Asian Americans in new ways is to a certain extent a reaction to earlier scholarship that viewed their experience from an "assimilationist perspective," focusing on the ability of Asians to adapt and blend into American society.[86] Scholars attributed any failures in assimilation to various Asian cultural traits, rather than to flaws in the American social system. That is, they upheld the status quo. The articles that *Amerasia* publishes have consciously taken a different tack, placing the Asian American experience within a broader national and international context and reinterpreting it in terms of such theories as institutional racism, internal colonialism, and Marxism–Leninism. They tend implicitly to advocate basic structural changes of American society.

While *Amerasia* has been in the vanguard of innovative scholarship, it has fared less well in capturing the diversity of the Asian American communities. From 1971 to 1986, 44 percent of its articles were on Chinese American themes and 21 percent on Japanese American ones; most of these articles were written by members of those ethnic groups. This imbalance reflects the fact that during the early 1970s scholars were studying mainly Chinese and Japanese Americans, the most prominent Asian American groups at the time. It also reflects the demographics of the field. As two of the older Asian American groups, the Chinese and Japanese Americans have had more time to develop humanities and social science scholars. It was natural for these scholars to focus on topics that were of personal as well as professional interest. Besides, their ethnicity undoubtedly facilitated their access to data on their own communities and enabled them to bring their personal experience to bear on their research. Since scholarship on an Asian ethnic group appears to depend on the number of scholars in that group, it will be a while before there is a significant body of literature on some of the smaller and newer Asian American groups. An exception has been the recent studies on Southeast Asian refugees that were mainly done by non-Southeast Asians.

Still, since the mid-1970s, the journal has evinced a gradual but perceptible shift toward articles dealing with other Asian ethnic groups, especially Korean and Filipino Americans. First-generation Korean Americans have been particularly prolific researchers, much to the benefit of Asian American Studies. Since much of the interest and research of Filipino Americans is on the Philippines, such work may become part of the emerging literature on the Pacific Rim rather than Asian American Studies. *Amerasia* has done less well in publishing articles on Southeast Asians. Even though there have been a number of studies on this subject, it was only in 1983, with Jacqueline Desbarats and Linda Holland's "Indochinese Settlement Patterns in Orange County," that *Amerasia* printed its first such article, five years after the "Vietnamese in America" series appeared in *Bridge*. By way of explanation, Russell Leong notes that there have been two recurrent problems with much of the scholarship on the newer immigrant and refugee communities:

1. Much of it tends to be "needs assessment" type of reports state/ federal commissioned. Thus, the work is usually limited in terms of wider theoretical and demographic, as well as political implications. These reports tend to reach similar conclusions—need for bilingual and culturally sensitive staffing, and so forth.

2. A great deal of the research on refugees and immigrants is a result of white scholars obtaining funding, and hiring native-language speakers to do the field research, surveys, etc. Not that scholarship by Anglo scholars is inherently biased, but the point is that they have many more avenues for publication. Also, we would like to see research (more of it) done by members of the groups themselves. This all has to do with the crucial and sometimes delicate distinction between being the *subject* and the *object* of research.[87]

Usually, articles on groups other than the Chinese and Japanese have been published in special issues devoted to them rather than in theme issues focusing on such topics as racial or class conflict. The special issue on "Emerging Ethnicity: The Korean and Hmong Communities" is a case in point.[88] Predictably, articles and issues that focus on the lesser-known groups and subjects are the most popular precisely because there is little available on them.

As it enters the 1990s, *Amerasia* has expanded to publish three times a year. The third issue will incorporate a forum format that will allow it to "bring new voices to the pages of the journal" and "take positions on the current social, cultural, and political issues of these times," enabling it to go beyond the corridors of academe.[89] For example, its forum on "War and Asian Americans" brought together materials written and compiled during the Persian Gulf War in 1991.[90] It began with an editorial by Alexander Saxton, who skillfully deconstructed President George Bush's "embrace of the Rambo Syndrome," an ideology of white supremacy that has replaced the Anglo-American hero with a European American ethnic.[91]

Amerasia Journal stands alone as the professional journal of Asian American Studies. Its major contributions have been to increase our knowledge about Asian Americans, to legitimate Asian American Studies scholarship, and to provide resources for Asian American Studies courses. It has to a certain extent shaped the field by disseminating research, especially historical pieces, that have a "revisionist perspective." It has given visibility to the research of the Asian American Studies Center's faculty and research associates, and in so doing has enhanced its campus and national reputation. It is considered the best of UCLA's ethnic journals, with many of its historical essays being cited by scholars and its creative writing reprinted in literary works.

Gidra, *Bridge*, *Amerasia*, and other alternative press publications helped to close the communication and cultural gaps between Asian Americans. By starting a dialogue about the Asian American community and contributing to the development of a pan-Asian culture, they gave Asian Americans a sense of their own integrity and identity as a people. These publications made Asian Americans aware of the social forces that influenced their communities and called for militancy toward those with political power. The authors published in these presses have argued that in order for Asian Americans to advance themselves in an ethnically pluralist society, it was essential that they become a unified group conscious of its own special interest and prepared to engage in collective action to bring about social change.

Since these publications were founded, some things have changed and some have not. The mainstream and Asian ethnic presses now regularly use the term *Asian Americans* and occasionally place their stories in a pan-Asian context. The conventional press now does a better job of covering news and events in the Asian American community. An editorial in *East/West* even complimented the *San Francisco Chronicle* for its series of articles on Chinese and Vietnamese American communities, though it noted in passing: "The SF Bay Area mainstream press, as a rule, doesn't give adequate coverage to news and events in the Asian American community. Usually only sensational news—such as gang violence, Chinatown sweatshops, or the massive influx of immigrants and refugees—arouses curiosity or attracts the attention of the predominantly white media establishment. The coverage of even these events is usually superficial, if not distorted." [92]

The Asian ethnic press, in contrast, has been more sensitive to the problems and concerns within the Asian American communities. As Russell Leong has observed, "the ethnic press . . . has come of age in terms of community coverage" and even particular Asian-language newspapers are expanding their coverage to other Asian American groups because "there is the realization . . . that what happens to members of 'another' Asian group concerns them as well." [93] Some of them choose to paint a unidimensional image of Asian Americans, however, *AsiAm* and *Rice*, glossy West Coast monthlies aimed at Asian American professionals and entrepreneurs, for example, have been criticized for promoting the "model minority" stereotype. One pundit noted that "some people feel that the highly successful image" of Asian Americans that *Rice* projects "reflects only a small, very successful minority of the Asian-American community and masks the fact that many Asian-Americans are still struggling." [94]

For many Asian American activists, instilling ethnic pride and developing a pan-Asian identity were insufficient; some of the more extreme elements in the community thought that these goals were actually counterproductive, for they deflected people from the more significant goal of social revolution. As far as the radicals were concerned, the community needed effective counterinstitutions, rather than "culture." The first counterinstitution that the activists established was Asian American Studies. As the next chapter documents, Asian American Studies faculty, staff, and students have been making up for decades of academic neglect during which Asians in America were at best a marginal topic of study. The intensity of the struggle to establish Asian American Studies convinced many that it was a "revolutionary," rather than a "cultural," institution. But to the extent that professors rostered in Asian American Studies programs in colleges and universities published research critical of the existing political and social order, they were part of the "cultural revolution" of the late 1960s and early 1970s.

5 Activists and the Development of Asian American Studies

struggling
to educate
and inform
about
how Amerika
screwed
us
—Gay Eng
  "Asian American Studies"

As a result of their participation in the Third World strikes at San Francisco State College (now San Francisco State University) and the University of California at Berkeley in 1968–1969, Asian American student activists gained the right and responsibility to define an entirely new field of inquiry—Asian American Studies (AAS)—whose very existence challenged the "traditional, unidimensional, minority-negating perspective of Western-based history and experience."[1] Besides taking the prevailing Eurocentric interpretation of the country's origins and development to task, they became part of the ongoing struggle to re-vision America as a multicultural society. At State, AAS became part of a School of Ethnic Studies; at Berkeley, of an Ethnic Studies department.[2] Overnight, erstwhile student leaders were thrust into the role of faculty, with the prerogative of setting curriculum requirements, hiring personnel, and approving tenure. They carried out their responsibilities with a volatile mixture of idealism and inexperience. Besides broadening the existing body of knowledge to include Asian Americans, they wanted AAS to reconsider the origins, methods, and limits of learning about Asian Americans and other people of color and in the process to redefine the way knowledge in general has been produced, constructed, and used to understand the human experience. Moreover, they wanted AAS to become involved directly in the effort to solve the problems of the Asian American community and the larger society.

In keeping with the ideals of the 1960s and as a matter of sheer necessity, they minimized the distinctions between faculty and students, and faculty/ students and community members, making it possible for virtually anyone to become a college professor. In the early years, there were few Asian American Studies scholars available (and practically none with firsthand experience in an Asian American community). Often they hired faculty whose main credential was political involvement and participation in local community organizations rather than excellence in teaching and research. So it is hardly surprising that their ranks were initially filled with political activists rather than professors and that the early years were full of political strife rather than professional development.

Since 1968, AAS programs have found Ethnic Studies departments to be nurturing environments, providing them with considerable autonomy and protection from external attacks as well as an intellectual community that supports their scholarship. A concomitant development of AAS programs has been the inclusion of Asian Americans in Equal Opportunity Programs (EOPs) and other affirmative action programs that have provided much needed services to students. Through the EOPs, many disadvantaged Asian American students have been able to obtain tutoring, counseling, and financing.

San Francisco State and Berkeley were only the beginning. During the early 1970s, Asian American students and community members in California and the rest of the nation demanded that similar AAS programs—or, at least, AAS courses—be introduced on their campuses. Many of these efforts began with a single student who had the vision, commitment, and skill to organize Asian Americans into a group that could press the college administration to respond to their interests. Effective campaigns led first to experimental courses taught by undergraduate and graduate students, community leaders, and existing faculty and then to more extensive programs housed in traditional departments (usually history or sociology) in arts and sciences colleges.

City College of New York (CCNY, later City University of New York), long regarded as the "proletarian Harvard," was the scene of the most dramatic of the poststrike struggles for an AAS program.[3] In March 1971, a group called Concerned Asian Students staged a three-day takeover of Goethals Hall, which housed the Asian Studies Department, to force the administration to accede to its demands for greater Asian American access to the college. The demonstrators were later joined by African American and Puerto Rican students, and by Asian Americans from other campuses and the community. They succeeded in setting up an AAS program within the interdisciplinary Asian Studies Department—the only such arrangement in the country. The program was given four new faculty, a counselor, and a community liaison administrator. Although the demonstrators wanted the department to be a predominantly AAS program rather than an Asian area studies program, the emphasis remained on Asia, since the department chair and most of the faculty were Asian area specialists. During the devastating 1975 New York City fiscal crisis, the program was severely cut back, a victim of the "last hired, first fired" phenomenon. By 1978, Betty Lee Sung was the sole surviving faculty member in Asian American Studies at CCNY.

The widespread push for AAS was brief, lasting from 1968 to 1973. Because programs were founded primarily for political rather than academic reasons, college administrators made only shallow and tentative commitments to them. Foes and friends alike perceived AAS, which implicitly provided an "ideological justification for changing existing arrangements of privilege and power,"[4] merely as a temporary political concession to radicals. It was hardly surprising, then, that when the national economic decline began in 1973, signaling the end of a period of expansion in higher education and the start of years of retrenchment, administrators began to renege on the agreements they had made earlier. They were reluctant to "expand or even continue what they [saw] as basically innovative and experimental 'fringe' programs."[5] As budgets were reduced, traditional departments "began to accuse Asian American Studies and other small programs of usurping resources that were, according to them, rightfully theirs."[6] In the competition for scarce resources, these departments questioned the curriculum and credibility of AAS programs and challenged the legitimacy of AAS as a field of inquiry.

Movement critics also questioned the relevance of AAS programs that were moving away from the original vision of student- and community-controlled programs and toward an academic one. AAS programs had to justify their existence to the community as well as the academy; at the same time they had to decide whether they were accountable to one or the other, since shrinking resources precluded serving both. Most decided to phase out their innovative student–community components and assume a more conventional academic role. It was a process that gave rise to an institutional identity crisis of the first magnitude. At its crux was the perennial question: What is the role of AAS in institutions of higher education?

The Meaning of Asian American Studies

Nearly all AAS programs have had four purposes: (1) raising the ethnic consciousness and self-awareness of Asian American students; (2) disseminating new educational materials on Asian Americans; (3) developing radical social and political perspectives and research on Asian Americans; and (4) providing culturally sensitive services to Asian American students and communities. Originally, the attainment of these goals was to involve faculty, staff, students, and community members. But as AAS programs evolved, roles became differentiated and regularized. Student influence began to wane as radical Asian American student leaders became faculty members or left school. Increasing numbers of rank-and-file students experienced a surfeit of activism and returned to traditional academic and social pursuits. Community influence also declined as local leaders devoted more of their scarce time to other pertinent matters, including earning a living and raising a family. By the late 1970s, student and community involvement had all but disappeared, and power was wholly in the hands of the faculty. As AAS programs became institutionalized, traditional educational standards began to prevail; hence the increasing importance of research and scholarship, even at schools that stressed teaching. AAS faculty members, like their colleagues, became concerned with securing tenure, a process that has promoted the development of regular courses and the publication of scholarly work.

Of the four purposes, AAS programs have been most effective in raising the ethnic consciousness and self-awareness of students, mainly through their courses. Under the popular rubric of "The Asian American Experience," programs have offered introductory courses on identity and history as a means of socializing and politicizing their students, most of whom were U.S.-born Asian Americans. These courses were a natural extension of the so-called consciousness raising, criticism and self-criticism, and political study sessions that activists had engaged in during the 1960s. They instilled pride in students by informing them of their history without the demeaning distortions of Eurocentric scholarship. They emphasized the similarities in the historical experiences of all Asian groups (though the examples have usually been confined to Chinese, Filipinos, Japanese, and Koreans), especially their oppression by European American society and their resistance to it. They clarified the meaning of racial inequality in American society. Heightening consciousness has remained an essential feature of AAS programs. But as increasing numbers of Asian American students come from the post-1965 immigrant and post-1975 refugee population, this goal has become more difficult to achieve, since most students now have strong Asian national identities and are more concerned with events in their homeland. The shared experiences of Asian Americans hold little interest for them because, as one AAS faculty member noted, they think of themselves as "immigrants" rather than "ethnics."[7] But to the extent that AAS has provided a social and historical framework for understanding American society, many students still find it useful and personally meaningful.

Naturally, as a brand-new field of study, AAS initially suffered from a dearth of educational materials. There was a crying need for articles, monographs, and documents to use in courses. Individually and in groups, faculty began to gather together what there was. Predictably, there was much more on Asians than on Asian Americans. Except for some significant works on Asian immigration and communities published by non-Asian scholars, what little there was on Asian Americans was either dated or derogatory. AAS programs had little choice but to produce their own materials.

The primary producer has been the Asian American Studies Center at UCLA. Its classic *Roots: An Asian American Reader* was the mainstay of practically all AAS courses in the early 1970s. Its publication, *Amerasia Journal*, has become a national interdisciplinary journal of scholarship, criticism, and literature on Asian Americans. Its leadership in this area can be traced to the program's inception. Unlike most other AAS programs, the one at UCLA was not created out of direct action against the school administration by radical Asian American students. In fact, it was to preempt that possibility that in January 1970 Chancellor Charles Young's staff designed the "American Cultures Project," which established Asian American, Black, Chicano, and Native American Studies Centers. A publications program was a natural complement to the research mission of the Asian American Studies Center.

AAS programs have been slow in developing alternative theoretical per-spectives. While addressing the identity crisis of Asian American students and reviewing their historical roots remain staples in the AAS curricula, other top-ics, such as community issues and institutions, literature and art, and studies of race and gender have been gradually added. The emotion-laden diatribes against racism in America have given way to thoughtful critiques of American social, economic, and political systems. Wishing both to legitimate AAS as a field of inquiry and to counter the ascendant assimilation ideology, which had eroded self-respect and inculcated self-hatred, scholars searched for new paradigms to explain the Asian American experience. But the search was de-layed because AAS programs were preoccupied with staying alive within the academy and were involved in popular political struggles such as the antiwar movement and were entangled in New Left politics within the Asian Ameri-can Movement. Only in the late 1970s and 1980s did the field begin to publish significant historical and social science scholarship.

Ironically, this scholarship rarely included community research. There are of course various explanations for this conspicuous lacuna. In some cases, it was simply a matter of choice. Malcolm Collier, an AAS faculty member, ex-plained that at San Francisco State, program staff worked, rather than wrote, on applied community problems; the absence of any real writing on the subject stemmed from a "higher priority [given] to producing for community than for academy; general reluctance to make easy generalizations about what we knew to be complex issues; and distrust of the process of research for research'[s] sake." [8] But according to Betty Lee Sung, an AAS faculty member at the City University of New York (CUNY), "the reason why most social scientists have not done community research is that they do not speak the language, hence cannot penetrate the community to get at the real picture." [9] Sadly, another rea-son is that community research has little credibility and even less prestige in the academy. [10]

The least successful aspect of AAS programs has been the failure to main-tain an ongoing involvement with Asian American communities, even though it was largely in the community's name that activists organized campus strikes and marched in demonstrations. Commitment to the community (and the asso-ciated aim of social change) has become attentuated. It remains strongest on campuses near an actual community (i.e., Chinatown, Little Tokyo, Manila-town, and today, Koreatown and Little Saigon). For those programs physically removed from an Asian American community, it has become mainly an ideal discussed in the past tense.

Originally, AAS programs perceived themselves as a positive force for social change in what they considered to be nothing more than ghettos. Indeed, many had anticipated that they would be in the vanguard of the struggle to agitate on behalf of the interests of the Asian American community. Among other things, they intended to reverse the "brain drain" that had left the community leaderless and powerless. Students were usually required or encouraged to become involved in community issues and activities, mainly through social service projects. The idea was to imbue students with a sense of who they were and where they came from so that they would be motivated to return to the community and join the struggle to solve its myriad problems. The minimum expectation was that students would engage in activities that supported Asian American interests.

In the beginning, the symbiotic relationship between campus and community seemed to work. AAS programs channeled university resources into the community, set up projects to address perceived problems, and provided the community with needed technical services.[11] They made certain that community issues and perspectives were represented in the curriculum, usually by inviting community members to serve as instructors or to sit on various AAS committees or by sending students to serve as interns in community-based organizations and to do field work in a community. In the latter case, the pedagogical rationale was that one learned through practice and that " 'learned' knowledge was better than 'taught' knowledge." [12] The community component of the Asian Studies Department at CCNY was one of the most active. The department received two Field Foundation grants totaling $50,000, which were given to students to start community-based projects such as the Basement Workshop. The department also sponsored summer courses: "Community Analysis and Action," "Asians and American Law," and community practicum classes that were supposed to provide students with direct experience in the Chinatown community. For example, students participated in the 1973 street fair in New York's Chinatown and compiled information pamphlets on housing, immigration, and workers' rights. It soon became clear, however, that some of these classes were a way of enlisting students to staff various day-care, youth, housing, and health programs in the community rather than teach them about the community—in short, surrogate social service agencies rather than real college classes. Students went into Chinatown intent on changing it, often without the slightest understanding of its deep-rooted traditions and institutions. Later, some student activists realized that CCNY's AAS program could not solve the problems of the community and that the "community people themselves will be the main component in broad social change." [13] In any case, the community component, along with most of the AAS program at CCNY, fell victim to the retrenchment that followed the 1975 New York City fiscal crisis.

Within a few years, the participation of AAS programs in community groups and activities had begun to wane, though the ideal persisted. Happily, one reason for the decline was that many community groups no longer needed the resources or assistance of AAS programs. They had learned the necessary community development techniques and strategies and were quite capable of implementing them. Often, too, what AAS programs could provide in the way of assistance was inappropriate to community needs, and vice versa, so that maintaining a relationship was pointless. In such instances, the result was an amicable divorce, with little rancor or regret.

Less fortunately, some of the projects set up in the community went awry. Occasionally, students went into the local community with a misguided missionary zeal, adding to problems instead of alleviating them. Some community workers in San Francisco's Chinatown, for example, complained of "elitist students who think gloriously of how they can organize and work on the gang kids in Chinatown, and how heavy they are." A variant was students who enhanced their self-image by equating themselves with the "community" and speaking on its behalf, even though their roots were shallow and their commitment recent. Unlike actual community residents, they had the choice of leaving, and most eventually did.

More serious problems were the development of a dependency on AAS programs for funding and labor and a tendency to equate campus-organized programs with the "community" and make them ends in themselves, while other needs were neglected. This was one of the main reasons that San Francisco State eventually curtailed its involvement with the community. Faculty members decided to limit the program's formal involvement to contributing money occasionally to community causes, continuing some tutorial programs, and sponsoring a few select student internships and field-work projects. They believed that the "services AAS provided to AA students through courses, advising, and other support services *were/are* themselves an important form of community action, just as legitimately a community activity as running a child care center . . . there was also an ideological strand that took the position that students should engage themselves in community as *community members* not as 'students.' " [14] Later, they tried to generate community input through a Community Advisory Board, but without success. As a body without decision-making responsibilities, the board lacked power and purpose; its members merely offered individual advice. As with most other AAS programs, State's work in the Asian American community continues through the efforts of individual faculty members.

An exception to this general trend has been the Student/Community Projects (S/CP) unit of the Asian American Studies Center at UCLA, which has "historically provided a vital link between research, student activities, and the various Asian and Pacific Islander communities in the Los Angeles area." [15] Among its projects was the Asian Pacific Community Research Roundtable, where community representatives met with academicians to match research interests with community needs. S/CP also implemented a pilot project to develop an undergraduate field studies course that would fulfill an AAS requirement and maintain a community internship program. Its ability to survive, indeed flourish, can be attributed to several factors. First, it has been an integral part of the Center from the beginning, with the task of working with students to improve the community. Unlike other AAS programs, where students have been intimately involved in governance, the Center has channeled student energy and enthusiasm into S/CP. Second, it has maintained an openness "rooted in the belief that the S/CP office was there for everyone's use no matter what political orientation or whether they were community oriented or a fraternity or sorority." [16] Third, S/CP has had a series of exceptionally dedicated coordinators. Each brought a particular style of leadership to the unit, from maverick activism to the "empowerment and development of a new generation of scholars, community service workers and organizers . . . to utilize their academic skills to address social and community problems." [17] Warren Furutani, the well-known community activist, spent over four years as S/CP coordinator, serving as a role model and mentor for students interested in community activism. Fourth, it has adapted to changing circumstances, for example, by working with the new immigrant students at UCLA despite their Asian, rather than Asian American, orientation. The student groups that S/CP has sponsored have served as "big sisters and brothers" to new students on campus.

The general decline in community involvement raised serious questions about the fundamental goal of AAS—so much so that by July 1973 that purpose became the focus of the Second National Asian American Studies Conference held at San Jose, California, whose theme was "Asian Studies: A Tool of Control or Tool of Change." Penny Nakatsu, the keynote speaker, argued that "survival in the academic world alone as a goal with no foundation in principle is self-serving and self-defeating," and asked: "Is mere survival of a program and academic legitimation the only questions which we must need ask?" [18]

To be sure, there were other questions to be asked, but for most of her colleagues in AAS, the first issue was the survival of AAS. Until that was dealt with, all others were moot. Indeed, in the beginning AAS programs were fighting for their lives. They had to deal not only with those in the academy who opposed them but also with internal factions that wanted to control the program for their own political purposes. A central point of contention became governance: Who was in charge, who made the decisions, who had a voice, and how loud was that voice?

Nowhere were these conflicts more manifest than at San Francisco State and Berkeley. At both schools, Asian American activists committed to the growth and development of AAS spent the early 1970s defending their programs against hostile elements and developing a firm foundation. It was a sobering experience. Among other things, they learned that acquiring power was easier than exercising it.

The Politics of Survival

The activists who administered the AAS program at San Francisco State were typical of their generation—they had an avid interest in campus politics, held counterculture values, and had strong ties to the community.[19] Out of the decision-making styles of the Asian American communities from which the people came and the principle of "self-determination," they evolved an informal two-tiered system of governance: a central planning council that was responsible for overseeing the program, and area planning groups that were responsible for developing courses in Chinese, Filipino, and Japanese American Studies. Underlying this system was a curriculum that emphasized the unique experiences of each group, from which would evolve broader issues and concerns that affected them all as Asian Americans. Later, the program shifted to a faculty-governed program, making the area planning groups obsolete.

As part of this commitment to maintaining the integrity of individual Asian ethnic groups, each area planning group developed a distinct orientation. Chinese American Studies, the largest component of the curriculum because of the predominance of Chinese American faculty and students, has consistently emphasized the teaching of critical perspectives, analytic skills, and political–organizing strategies to prepare students for working in Chinatown. It has also paid the most attention to student participation in community activities. Filipino American Studies began with a "homeland" focus, that is, on Philippine politics, but later shifted to teaching about contemporary Filipino American problems and issues. Japanese American Studies began with an interest in ideological issues, placing the Asian American experience in a larger international context and discussing the implications of such significant economic systems as capitalism. By the mid-1970s, it had changed its focus to teaching Japanese American history.

The area groups shared a camaraderie that dated back to the Third World strike, a commitment to the AAS program that that struggle had created, and a belief in open communication and collective action. But the harmony eroded as conflicts arose over how best to ensure the long-term existence of AAS. One early fight, in 1970, was over the development of an Asian American Studies major and the use of Asian American Studies courses that satisfied the college's general education requirements for graduation.

One way to survive, some argued, was to develop a major in AAS because it would enhance the credibility and status of the program. Opponents, who included a majority of the people in area planning groups, argued that a major in a traditional department and a minor in AAS would make it easier for students to find jobs. Furthermore, they argued that the Asian American community would be better served if the students, trained in a wide array of disciplines, used their skills to obtain influential occupations in such fields as government and law. Finally, in their view a major would compel the program to offer certain courses regularly, taking away some of its curricular flexibility. Since the proponents of an AAS major were unable to attain sufficient support, no major was proposed.

Another possible way to ensure survival was to use AAS courses to fulfill the school's general education requirement. During this period, many colleges and universities were liberalizing their degree requirements, giving students greater choices in what they could study. In reexamining its general education requirements, State offered the AAS program an opportunity to include AAS courses among the requirements. Proponents argued that this move would guarantee high enrollments and that, anyway, AAS courses should be part of a student's liberal education. Opponents countered that enrollments would remain satisfactory without this boost and that faculty should develop courses for their own sake rather than just to meet criteria for required courses. Besides, the change would engender considerable debate over which courses should be selected for this purpose.

The proponents managed to persuade the others to their point of view; ever since, the inclusion of its courses in the general education requirements has become the mainstay of the AAS program's survival strategy. In 1981, this strategy was imperiled by the San Francisco State administration's decision to revise the general education requirements.[20] The proposed revision was clearly intended to restrict the use of AAS and other Ethnic Studies courses to meet the general education requirement. Under this threat, the AAS program completely redesigned itself, creating new courses and dropping old ones. The result was a coherent curriculum that was superior to the potpourri of courses previously offered and was much more attractive to students. It met not only the AAS program's educational goals but the new general education requirements as well. Programmatically, the AAS program did pay a price for these changes. Because the administration limited the number of courses from AAS that could meet the general education requirements, it was forced to reduce the number of courses on Asian ethnic groups and offer more general Asian American ones.

Another potentially divisive issue was whether the program should promote a particular political ideology. In the effort to start the program, this question had gone unanswered. But in 1973 the new leaders of the Japanese American Studies group resurrected the issue. Protorevolutionaries with an anti-imperialist and antiracist political agenda, they were influenced by romantic images of Asian revolutionaries defending their homelands from imperialist aggressors, rather than a commitment to a specific set of beliefs. They wanted AAS to explore the possibility of adopting a political ideology. Presumably, such discussions would further politicize the program and increase its involvement in the community, where revolutionary struggles were seen as most intense. But the Chinese American Studies group, which argued for a diversity of political principles, was able to veto the adoption of a single perspective. As a result of this defeat, some Japanese American Studies group members dropped out of the program and joined the J-Town Collective, where they became involved in the struggle over the redevelopment of Nihonmachi (Japantown). In refusing to adopt a single political philosophy, San Francisco State's AAS program probably avoided getting embroiled in the sectarianism that was causing political havoc on other campuses, such as the University of California at Berkeley.[21]

The Politics of the "Revolution"

At Berkeley, Asian American activists divided themselves into two opposing camps: Marxist revolutionaries and militant reformers.[22] For nearly a decade, they struggled for control of the AAS program, leaving disorder in their wake. The chaotic conditions caused many of the early activists who had come to the program "with energy, idealism and love" to leave, feeling "scorned, defeated, and burned out." [23]

Among the Marxist revolutionaries, there were those who perceived AAS as a potentially "revolutionary" program, a subversive element within the university that was committed to raising the students' consciousness about the capitalist exploitation and oppression of Asian Americans. Equipped with this newfound ethnic and class consciousness, they thought, students would return to the Asian American community to change it.

Other Marxists thought that AAS was essentially irrelevant; the revolution was imminent, and the main revolutionary thrust should be working in Asian American ghettos, where social conflicts were sharpest and political results quickest. They viewed AAS as a convenient vehicle for convincing idealistic students to leave school to work in the community and a way of recruiting them into community organizations. It was an anti-intellectual stance, one that falsely counterpoised "academic work" and "progressive work."

In general, the Marxist revolutionaries had a visceral contempt for institutions of higher learning, which they perceived as bourgeois places that produced "technological coolies" who did exotic war research in the so-called military–industrial complex or were "running dogs" who served America's capitalist class. They were convinced that the AAS program would eventually be suppressed for its politics or coopted by the administration, a prophecy their actions seemed determined to fulfill. Consequently, they sought to exploit the AAS program for the resources it could provide in the present and were unwilling to plan for its long-term survival and development within the university. They made a mockery of the educational program by ignoring the professed purpose of the courses, dispensing with any rigor, and giving out good grades to anyone who enrolled. They hired personnel who were transient and unqualified to teach. Some of the English-language instructors, for example, barely knew English, a farcical situation that could hardly benefit the students, who desperately desired to learn the language so that they could better their socioeconomic situation in America. Community-oriented programs—the "Asian-American Communities" course, the field-work assistants program, and community projects in San Francisco Chinatown, Japantown, and Manilatown—were irresponsibly managed. As many as eighteen community projects operated at one time, a number that gave rise to difficulties in supervision and coordination. Furthermore, these projects had little relationship to course work. Many of the Marxist revolutionaries worked as field-work assistants simply to receive salaries. To add insult to injury, they demanded part of the salaries of the regular faculty as well, arguing that working for the "revolution" was more important than providing students with an education.

Militant reformers were also committed to the growth and development of the Asian American community, but they thought that they could best aid this process by graduating students: It was through the students that social change would occur. Academic work was political work, according to them, for it raised the political consciousness of people and provided them with critical perspectives. Citing Antonio Gramsci's argument that Italy had had the preconditions for a revolution but failed to produce one because the people lacked a class consciousness, militant reformers maintained that scholarship could help create that consciousness. Simply milking the program for resources, as the Marxist revolutionaries were wont to do, would lead not only to intellectual bankruptcy but also to political suicide.

Originally, the militant reformers wanted Berkeley to become an authentic "community college," that is, a school that served the local community. This meant that its "course content, admission standards, and scholastic requirements should be geared to the needs of community youth . . . research activities should be directed at solving, not contributing to community problems." [24] Later, they grudgingly accepted Berkeley for what it was, an elite research university, but one that could be changed from within to meet the long-term needs of the Asian American community. They believed that "fundamental social change requires life-times of commitment, sacrifices, careful planning and analysis, and step-by-step attainment of goals." [25] The role of AAS in this change was to educate students; provide research data and analysis with a Third World perspective; and participate in and support community, national, and international movements for social change. To be prepared for power, students needed not only a commitment to improving the community but also skills in critical analysis, skills through which they could come to understand the true conditions of Asians—as well as other Third World people—in America. Such analysis included learning about the patterns of development in American society that have affected Asian American communities and individuals. Militant reformers carried out community research that served "to illuminate the *linkages* which exist between the root causes of our minority status within the United States and the international position of the United States, especially in relation to Third World countries." [26] In addition, militant reformers advocated direct participation in planned and responsible community work, channeling students into community projects. In short, they saw AAS as the Asian American Movement's intellectual arm, responsible for challenging the values and perspectives of the dominant society through research, teaching, and service.

In order to save the program from being destroyed from within or marginalized from without, the militant reformers carried out a 1972 coup against one group of revolutionaries belonging to Wei Min She (WMS) and a 1977 purge of another group of revolutionaries belonging to I Wor Kuen (IWK). In April 1972 a group known as "the 8" carried out a coup against the Campus Community Council (CCC) and took control of the program. "The 8" saw the CCC as an inadequate form of governance. Theoretically, the CCC consisted of representatives chosen for their ethnic consciousness, progressive politics, and, most important, commitment to the community—three qualities that ought to have made them effective leaders. But, except for the first CCC, which consisted of the original Asian American leaders of the Third World Liberation Front, the council was woefully ineffective.

The CCC, on the surface, appeared to be an idealistic, innovative, dynamic, democratic structure designed to prevent vested interests from emerging in the AAS program and from becoming a creature of the university administration. In reality, it was an anarchic system in which decisions, including those dealing with personnel, were made at meetings attended by fifty to a hundred people (faculty, staff, students, and community people—and, for that matter, anyone else who happened to attend), with no provision for their implementation. The absence of clear lines of authority made administrative paralysis inevitable.

Furthermore, this ultrademocracy gave students and transients great influence in the program, even though their knowledge of the university was superficial and their understanding of the long-term consequences of decisions and actions unclear. A case in point was their misunderstanding of academic tenure. When the subject of granting "tenureship" to a professor arose at a political education meeting, they assumed that tenure was merely "lifetime employment," and "everyone agreed that the issue of tenureship should be decided on a political basis." [27] To most professors, of course, tenure is the principal guarantor of academic freedom, a prized privilege that ensures their right to teach what they believe, to espouse unpopular causes, to act on knowledge and ideas without fear of retribution from anyone. Indeed, it exists to protect professors from just those people who would decide matters on a "political basis."

Perhaps more important, students did not have to live with the consequences of their decisions, since they eventually left the university, but the faculty remained and were held accountable. This state of affairs resulted in declining morale as the program became bogged down in an endless series of exhausting meetings, characterized by dwindling attendance. The coup attempted to address this problem by abolishing the CCC and replacing it with coordinators empowered to make decisions.

Although many people involved in the AAS program considered the takeover by "the 8" illegal, they accepted it when they realized that the program was at a virtual standstill, with important personnel decisions in limbo. But while the coup temporarily stabilized the administration of the program, there were still problems connected with the curriculum and teaching staff that were left unresolved. From 1973 to 1975, there was an effort to regularize the decision-making process and develop a systematic means of recruiting faculty and staff.[28] In 1975, one of the crucial developments was the appointment of Sucheng Chan, assistant professor, to the Academic Senate's Committee on Courses of Instruction, a position that allowed her to serve as a "power broker" between this important university committee and the AAS program.[29] In this capacity, she was able to educate the Committee on Courses on the academic legitimacy of AAS and to assist AAS faculty in redesigning their course proposals to improve their chances of approval. Through her efforts, over thirty courses were approved, without which no Bachelor of Arts degree in AAS could have been possible.

Meanwhile, members of WMS became increasingly influenced by the Revolutionary Union's focus on the role of the multinational working class in the revolution, a position that would distinguish WMS from it arch rival within the Asian American Movement, IWK, which was mainly interested in the role of racial minorities in the working-class struggle in the United States. In 1975, WMS dissolved itself and merged with the Revolutionary Union to form the Revolutionary Communist party, wrote the students off as "bourgeois," and abandoned the college campuses to pursue other forms of political work.[30] At Berkeley, the departure of WMS created an opportunity for IWK and other Marxist groups, such as the mostly Filipino Katipunan ng mga Demokrati-kong Pilipino (KDP, Union of Democratic Filipinos),[31] to insinuate themselves into AAS.

During the next two years, IWK tried to gain control of the program through "the proliferation of bureaucratic committees which were accountable to no one and accomplished little."[32] This tactic made the management of the program difficult, if not impossible; furthermore, it made AAS increasingly vulnerable to external interference. Since AAS appeared unable to govern itself, the university administration intervened repeatedly and subjected its curriculum and faculty to constant scrutiny. Such actions threatened the program's autonomy and the principle of self-determination on which it was based. Faculty members found the situation intolerable, so in 1977, led by a group dubbed the "faculty 7," they exercised their administrative authority and purged the program of those who would impede it.

IWK tried unsuccessfully to reverse the purge by waging a propaganda campaign against the program on campus and in the community, disrupting classes and committee meetings and intimidating and harassing students, staff, and faculty. Though IWK justified its every action in terms of the "community's interest," the community gave its overwhelming support to the militant reformers. The 1977 confrontation virtually ended the Marxist revolutionaries' involvement in Berkeley's AAS program and had the unforeseen consequence of discrediting their claims to community support. Ever since, AAS at Berkeley has been under the control of tenure-track faculty. In retrospect, the purge of the Marxist revolutionaries may have saved the program from going into academic receivership.[33] The continuous chaos might have resulted in the Berkeley administration either assuming control of the program or closing it down.

In spite of external enemies and internal rivals, AAS at Berkeley has survived and even flourished. It has developed into a nationally known academic program. Its faculty members have been able to produce significant scholarship, which is why most of them have received tenure. They have also played a major role in the creation of Berkeley's Ethnic Studies doctoral program, the first of its kind in the country. Berkeley graduates are likely to be the future faculty of Ethnic Studies programs around the country and will shape the field.

AAS not only made it through the 1970s, but reached a milestone in its professional development with the establishment of the Association for Asian American Studies in 1979.[34] Douglas W. Lee and others started the association with the intention of making AAS a nationally recognized field of study. Like other professional organizations, the association has had its share of problems. In the early 1980s, few people were interested. Some identified more with their disciplines than with AAS. (This may have been a career choice, since they received little credit for attending an annual meeting of a field whose origins were suspect and whose legitimacy was questioned.) Others felt the field lacked intellectual vigor. While AAS was far from moribund, neither was it pulsating with life. Few scholarly works were being produced, so there was little to discuss. A core of leaders, however, kept the association going (and for their pains they have been perceived as a clique).

During the late 1980s, a surge of activity reflected increased interest in multicultural education in California and elsewhere, the growing numbers of graduate students looking for a venue to present their work, and swelling student activism.[35] And a new generation of radical Asian American students had emerged earlier in the decade to perpetuate the legacy of their predecessors and renew the demand for social justice.

Asian American Studies Redux

During the latter half of the 1970s, the demand for social justice that had given birth to the civil rights movement diminished dramatically. Ethnic Studies programs contracted and consolidated, and fewer than half of them survived into the next decade. Forced to function in an academic "ghetto" on the margins of the curriculum, they were surrounded by unsympathetic and often hostile departments. With the coming of the Reagan presidency (1980–1988) and the conservative interlude, the plight of AAS programs worsened. In the politically inhospitable climate of the 1980s, there was a backlash against racial-minority communities and a degradation of their concerns. On the national level, it was evident in the administration's conscious effort to weaken the social gains of the 1960s in the name of privatization; on the local level, in the frequent reports of violence against people of color; on college campuses, in the precipitous increase in racial incidents.

"Reagan's Children: Racial Hatred on Campus," the title of an essay by Jon Wiener in *The Nation*, captured the malevolent spirit of the times. Wiener discussed the resurgence of racism on college and university campuses during the 1980s, the Reagan administration's abetting of it, and the strategies that activists were using to combat it.[36] Ernest L. Boyers's study for the Carnegie Foundation for the Advancement of Teaching, "Campus Life: In Search of Community," revealed that 24 percent of college presidents surveyed felt that racial tension was an important problem: "Groups [were] dividing themselves along racial lines that [were] more brutal than in the past." [37] No one was spared. Asian American students were attacked for "curve busting" on grade scales and for raising the level of competition for jobs in such fields as math, science, and engineering.[38]

Meanwhile, the Asian American population had changed dramatically, becoming larger and different in character. With heavy immigration resulting from the Immigration Act of 1965 and the influx of over 700,000 Southeast Asian refugees since the end of the Vietnam War in 1975, Asian Americans increased from 1.4 million in 1970 to 3.8 million in 1980 and 7.3 million in 1990, representing 2.9 percent of the total U.S. population.[39] Barring major changes in U.S. immigration policy, Asian Americans could number almost 10 million in the year 2000. This phenomenal growth has also given the Asian American community a new diversity reflected in the emergence of such Asian American communities as Koreatown and Little Saigon, as well as new Chinatowns. Except for Japanese Americans, Asian Americans have become a predominantly immigrant population.

Since the mid-1970s, Asian American college enrollments have risen by an astounding 126 percent; moreover, the students include increasing numbers of immigrants and refugees.[40] Many can be found in elite institutions: From 1976 to 1986, the percentage of Asian American freshmen at MIT climbed from 5.3 to 20.6; at Harvard, from 3.6 to 12.8; at Stanford, from 5.7 to 14.7.[41] Because they constitute a large (and in some cases the largest) ethnic-minority student group on some college campuses, they have suffered from overt anti-Asian sentiment and covert ceilings on Asian American student admissions. Even though their needs have grown along with their numbers, services for them have declined or disappeared. They have also been selectively denied the protection of affirmative action programs and excluded from equal opportunity programs. Requests for assistance have sometimes been met with referrals to the foreign student office, reminding Asian Americans that they remain "perpetual foreigners" in their own country. Such actions have been justified by the widely held belief that Asian Americans are a "model minority," one that can succeed (indeed, flourish) in college without the assistance afforded other people of color. They are also regarded as a unique group because when the various subgroups are lumped together, Asian Americans have become overrepresented, rather than underrepresented, on many college campuses.

From this new wave of Asian American students has come another generation of activists, one determined to defend the gains made since the late 1960s. The new activists have responded to the repeated attacks on racial-minority programs throughout the country in general and those on college campuses in particular. They have pursued the general goals of their 1960s predecessors: strengthening identity and pride, promoting history and culture, and ending individual and institutional racism. But they have focused their energies on educational reform and embraced such causes as establishing AAS courses and programs, making Ethnic Studies a general education requirement, opposing quotas on the admission of Asian American students, and increasing faculty diversity.

This generation of radical Asian American students has been markedly different from its predecessor. As beneficiaries of the earlier effort to establish AAS courses and programs, these students have been deeply concerned about racial discrimination and are committed to social change. They have been a more diverse group, reflecting the demographic changes in the Asian American population. U.S.-born descendants of pre-1965 Asian immigrants (mostly Chinese and Japanese) have been outnumbered by the sons and daughters of post-1965 immigrants and recently arrived refugees. Except for *sansei* holdovers from the previous era, fewer Japanese Americans are now involved in radical politics. The new generation has also tended to be a more affluent group, with many members coming from upper-middle-class backgrounds, which is why much of the renewed student activism has occurred in Ivy League schools on the East Coast or at prestigious universities such as Berkeley and Stanford on the West Coast. Most students from working-class backgrounds have been too busy working and studying to be politically involved; at most, they have joined

Asian ethnic organizations to participate in cultural and social activities. The conservative political climate of the 1980s and, more important, the experiences of their parents with communism in Asia made Asian American student activists with immigrant and refugee backgrounds much less sympathetic to Marxist–Leninist and Maoist solutions to such social problems as racism.

Asian American activists resurrected the student movement first on the East Coast. On 2 April 1977, they held a "pan-campus conference" at Yale University "to improve student organizing by exchanging information and by systematizing contact between [Asian Student Organizations]." [42] The meeting was a major event, attracting students from as far away as Oberlin College. As originally conceived by the organizers, it was supposed to be a multifaceted conference; instead, it became dominated by the "Bakke issue." Allen Bakke had accused the University of California Medical School at Davis of engaging in "reverse discrimination" for having a special admissions program that gave "preferential treatment" to minority students who were "less qualified" than himself. *The University of California* v. *Bakke* eventually reached the U.S. Supreme Court. Asian Americans and other Third World students were deeply concerned about the pending decision. Opposition to *Bakke* proved futile. On 28 June 1978, the Court ruled that Davis's special admissions program was in violation of Title VI of the 1964 Civil Rights Act and the Fourteenth Amendment of the Constitution and ordered the university to admit Allen Bakke.

To promote intercampus communication and mutual support, the Yale conference established the Intercollegiate-Liaison Committee (ICLC), which organized a Unity Conference at Princeton University for the following year. As the name suggests, the conference's main aim was to rally Asian Americans around such issues as the *Bakke* case. Participants discussed the implications of the case for the admission of minority students into colleges and universities around the country, as well as affirmative action programs in general. An immediate issue was the threat by colleges to eliminate presession orientations for students of color. At the Princeton conference, the ICLC established the East Coast Asian Student Union (ECASU), a network of Asian American student organizations at mainly Ivy League schools and private colleges along the East Coast. ECASU was followed by the establishment of the Asian Pacific Student Union (APSU), which evolved from the Asian Student Union on the West Coast, and the Midwest Asian Pacific American Student Association Network (MAPASAN). With the establishment of these three regional networks, the Asian American student movement not only experienced a resurgence but also reached a higher level of organizational development.

ECASU, APSU, and MAPASAN have sought mainly to foster communication among Asian student organizations on college campuses in their respective regions and to pursue the interests of Asian American students by integrating social, cultural, educational, and political activities. One of their major goals has been to strengthen AAS. In spring 1984, ECASU organized a task force on AAS to investigate the possibility of establishing courses and programs on the East Coast and to identify the resources available to students. Three years later, the establishment of AAS courses and programs became a top priority of its spring 1987 conference, whose theme was "Education for Action." In this endeavor, ECASU joined with the Asian American Resource Workshop, a community-based educational organization in Boston. Together they held workshops on campuses to educate Asian American students about the need for AAS and to assist them in building programs on their campuses.

An example of students organizing to advocate an AAS program is the Massachusetts Institute of Technology Asian American Caucus, a pan-Asian group of undergraduate and graduate students. The caucus was founded in fall 1988 specifically to promote AAS as a means of developing Asian American consciousness on campus. Its members felt that the "foundation for Asian American consciousness primarily begins with having the opportunity to study and debate the historical and contemporary experiences of Asians in the U.S." [43] Its immediate goal was to convince the administration to offer one regular AAS course—a first step toward meeting the needs of MIT's Asian American students. Even though they made up 18 percent of all undergraduates in 1989, support services or classes for Asian American students had been "nonexistent." Nor were there any plans to provide these programs, even though the school was interested in developing a multicultural environment.

As a result of these various efforts, considerable interest in AAS has developed on the East Coast. New courses have been introduced at Boston University, Brown, Cornell, Harvard, Hunter, Princeton, Smith, Tufts, the University of Connecticut, the University of Massachusetts at Boston and Amherst, and Wellesley. Some of these have served as the foundation for full-fledged programs. One of the newest and most successful has been at Cornell, where the first Ivy League AAS program was established in 1987.[44] It began with an article in the campus newspaper about Asian Americans that led to an informal meeting between the provost and several Asian American faculty. Faculty member Lee C. Lee used the opportunity to request monies for an AAS program. On 1 July 1987, with a $100,000 budget and a staff of three, Lee inaugurated Cornell's AAS program, "a University-wide program within the College of Arts and Sciences to promote teaching, research and cultural activities related to Americans of Asian heritage." [45] Like other AAS programs, it offers basic courses on aspects of the Asian American experience; it also advocates incorporating specific Asian American issues and topics into the regular curriculum. In addition to its teaching mission, the program provided monies to encourage research on Asian American topics and a place where those interested in Asian American culture and arts can interact socially. Asian American students on the East Coast have pointed to Cornell's AAS program as a model for what they want at their schools.

On the West Coast, the struggle to strengthen AAS has taken a different tack. The emphasis has been to broaden the scope of AAS from a set of courses for interested Asian American students to making an AAS or Ethnic Studies course a graduation requirement for all undergraduates. Proponents have argued that studying about people of color should be an indispensable part of college students' education, since doing so prepares them to live in a culturally pluralist and interdependent society. In spite of the reasonableness of this argument, the campaign to make Ethnic Studies a part of the general education requirement at various colleges across the nation has met stiff resistance. As Sucheng Chan, who has participated in the building of AAS at three University of California campuses, explains it, the campaign challenged the "very structure of power within the university" and raised issues about who gets to "define reality," calling into question the "ideological foundations of society in general and the university in particular." [46]

The campaign has experienced some success. Such requirements already exist in some schools, such as San Francisco State University, the University of California at Santa Cruz, Santa Barbara, Irvine, and Riverside (within the College of Humanities and Social Sciences), the University of Colorado at Boulder, Washington State University, Bryn Mawr, and Barnard. On 25 April 1989, after two years of heated debate, Berkeley's Academic Senate voted 227–194 to impose an "American Cultures" requirement.[47] This requirement— effective with the 1991 freshman class—can be met by taking courses on at least three of five ethnic groups in American society: African Americans, Chicanos, Asian Americans, Native Americans, and European Americans. The proponents allayed suspicions that the requirement was a political ploy to expand the influence of the Ethnic Studies Department by designing it so that any department could offer courses to meet it. From the perspective of the Ethnic Studies Department, this strategy had three advantages: (1) It forced the other departments to diversify their curricula to include courses on ethnic minorities, a form of "intellectual affirmative action"; (2) it placed Ethnic Studies faculty members in the position of consultants to their colleagues, thus enhancing their status and enlarging their network of contacts at the university; and (3) it allowed the Ethnic Studies Department to avoid becoming merely a service department. As one of the most prestigious schools in the country, Berkeley may set in motion the widespread adoption of similar requirements throughout California and the rest of the United States.

Besides defending and expanding AAS, the new generation of Asian American activists has been involved in opposing tacit quotas against Asian American students and increasing the diversity of the faculty. In a survey of twenty-five universities, mainly in the Northeast, the ECASU Joint Admissions Task Force found some disturbing patterns: (1) The number of Asian Americans applying to colleges in the late 1970s and early 1980s had doubled, but the number of applicants admitted had increased only slightly, if at all; (2) the percentages of Asian Americans being admitted continued to lag behind admission rates for all other groups, including European Americans; and (3) the most recent Asian American students tended to come from the middle and upper classes.[48] The task force concluded that biased admissions processes made it extremely difficult for the average Asian American high school student to be admitted to the colleges surveyed and nearly impossible for those who were poor, from inner cities, or both. The problem was laid at the feet of admissions officers who had accepted the model minority myth, which portrays Asian Americans as having succeeded in America despite a long history of being subjected to rampant discrimination and ignores the "difficulties faced by Asian-American students on the grounds that youngsters who are doing so well academically cannot possibly need any special help."[49] The problem persisted throughout the 1980s. For example, in January 1988, information from Harvard indicated that over the past decade, 13.3 percent of Asian American applicants had been admitted—a rate 3.7 percent below the admission rate for European American students; moreover, for any given year, the combined math and verbal College

Board scores for Asian Americans were typically forty points higher than for European Americans admitted.[50]

In 1984 at the University of California at Berkeley the problem of "quotas" against Asian American students was made manifest.[51] That year, a group of concerned Asian American community leaders noticed that there was an alarming drop of 231 Asian American freshmen, even though the number of Asian applicants had been rapidly rising and their qualifications improving. They formed an Asian American Task Force on University Admissions (AATFUA) co-chaired by Judges Ken Kawaichi and Lillian Sing. The task force's report claimed that Asian American enrollment in the freshman class at Berkeley had dropped by 20.9 percent and attributed the decline to a major change in admissions policy in 1984—the end of guaranteed Berkeley admission to Equal Opportunity Program (EOP) applicants, most of whom were Asian Americans.

In November 1987, Berkeley appointed a Special Committee on Asian Admissions to "examine the issue of whether there has been or is now significant bias, either conscious or unconscious, against Asian American freshman applicants in the undergraduate admissions policy at Berkeley."[52] In February 1989, the committee, chaired by William Shack, released its report. It found that in order to deal with a huge influx of freshmen applicants the university had initiated policies that adversely affected Asian American applicants. It concurred with the AATFUA's 1985 report that the removal of EOP protection had significantly affected Asian American admissions. Furthermore, it noted that the university had also raised the minimum grade point average (GPA) required for automatic admission, but not the minimum college entrance test scores. Since Asian Americans were more likely to be admitted on the basis of their GPA, while European American applicants often possessed better test scores, this policy change prevented an additional seventy-four Asian American students from being admitted in 1984. But the committee also claimed that its investigation "found nothing remotely resembling a 'quota' on the admission of Asian Americans at Berkeley. Nor have we found statistical evidence to support an inference of significant long-term bias against Asian Americans."[53]

Asian Americans were highly critical of the Shack report. AATFUA and the Student Coalition for Fair Admissions (SCFA) claimed that the Shack committee had "decided to minimize the wrongdoings of 1984 by statistically distributing them over a period of seven years and also by using legal jargon to exonerate the University."[54] Members of the SCFA, incensed at the Shack report's failure to hold anyone accountable for the discriminatory admissions policies, called the report a "whitewash." [55] Chancellor Ira Michael Heyman apologized for the insensitive way his staff had responded to concerns expressed by Asian Americans but refused to admit any wrongdoing.

The Asian American community's outcry over possible quotas against Asian American students led the U.S. Department of Education's Office of Civil Rights to look into alleged anti-Asian admissions quotas at the University of Pennsylvania, Carnegie-Mellon University, Evergreen Valley College in San Jose, the Math Department in the University of California at Los Angeles, and Harvard. The on-site investigations had the salutary effect of forcing the schools to perform self-evaluations to ensure that their admissions process was nondiscriminatory.

Unfortunately, some people have used the controversy over quotas against Asian Americans to attack affirmative action programs. Arthur Hu, a neo-conservative pundit who writes the provocative column "Hu's on First" in *Asian Week* argued that affirmative action programs resulted in colleges and universities admitting less-qualified minority applicants at the expense of more-qualified European Americans and Asian Americans. [56] The latter's cultural values, he argued—specifically, their emphasis on education, individual effort, and discipline—explain their success in contemporary American society. Conservative Congressman Dana Rohrabacher (Rep.–California) charged that several colleges and universities, including Berkeley, UCLA, Harvard, Stanford, and Brown, had set upper-limit quotas for Asian Americans *and* had used affirmative action programs to admit other "underrepresented" minorities in order to achieve "ethnic diversity." But Rohrabacher's motives were suspect: During a Heritage Foundation forum, he admitted having used the Asian American cause as "a vehicle to show that America has made a mistake on affirmative action." [57] Both Hu and Rohrabacher appear less interested in seeing that Asian American applicants receive fair treatment than in dismantling affirmative action programs.

Asian American students have also been deeply concerned about the lack of faculty diversity and its implications for the kind of education they have been receiving. As members of Third World coalitions, such as Students United for Diversity at Berkeley, they have claimed that the "systematic censorship of minorities at the University and the female perspective within the academic experience at Berkeley results in churning out students who are academically functional but socially and culturally illiterate"[58] and have demanded that the faculty reflect the multicultural population of California. While full-time minority teachers have increased by 34.3 percent at Berkeley, the increase has been greatest among nonfaculty members and low-ranking faculty.

The issue of tenure brought the question of faculty diversity to a head. Among racial-minority faculty members in the United States, Asian Americans have fared worst in obtaining tenure. The American Council on Education found that though the number of Asian American faculty members had doubled between 1975 and 1985, their overall tenure rate was below the national level.[59] Asian Americans had the lowest tenure rate among all minorities at 61.2 percent, followed by African Americans at 61.7 percent, and significantly lower than European Americans at 72 percent. Furthermore, those with full-time tenured positions tended to be foreign-born Asians (who outnumbered American-born Asians 10 to 1). Yet administrators perceive that Asian American faculty members, like their student counterparts, may be "overrepresented."

A case in point is the University of Colorado at Boulder. In a 1986 memorandum to the president, an associate vice-president for human resources said, "It is important to note that there is strong representation of Asian faculty members relative to the number of other minority groups. If Asians are excluded from the minority faculty statistics, the percentage of minorities in faculty ranks may be reduced by almost one-half."[60] The chancellor of the Boulder campus noted in his 1985–1986 affirmative action report that while problems existed in the representation of Asians on the faculty, still the emphasis should be on increasing the representation of other ethnic groups. Consequently, there was a tacit policy to exclude Asian American faculty from the campus "special opportunity program" for the recruitment of minority faculty, a situation that has since been corrected. This erroneous perception was based on the relatively large number of Asian Americans holding faculty titles.[61] In the University of Colorado system, there were sixty-eight Asian Americans with faculty titles, compared to forty-nine Hispanics, the second-largest minority group; moreover, fifty of the Asian Americans were on the university's flagship campus in Boulder and thus relatively visible. But only thirty-eight of the Asians and thirty of the Hispanics held tenure-track appointments.

Students have singled out the denial of tenure to Asian American faculty as a significant struggle because it symbolizes a "glass ceiling," that is, "a barrier through which top management positions can only be seen, but not reached."[62]

This ceiling has held back qualified Asian Americans from attaining positions of authority in all occupations. When Helen Choi, co-chair of Berkeley's Asian American Political Alliance, said during a sit-in at the Berkeley Department of Architecture office, "If you're Asian, you can work hard and study hard, but you're just going to crack your head against the ceiling like Marcy [Li Wang] did," she was voicing the widespread concern that Asian Americans have had about the absence of fairness in American society.[63] Choi and her schoolmates realized that unless they shattered this artificial barrier, they too could be held back from reaching the positions they merited.

The two most important tenure battles have been those of Don Nakanishi and Marcy Li Wang. In fall 1987, Don Nakanishi, a well-known Asian American activist since his undergraduate days at Yale, was denied tenure by the UCLA Graduate School of Education. His critics charged that his pioneering research on Asian Americans and electoral politics, and his work on such controversial topics as Asian American undergraduate admissions, affirmative action programs, and anti-Asian quotas, was "esoteric" and "irrelevant," hence unworthy of tenure. Nakanishi challenged UCLA's decision, and his case immediately became a cause célèbre in the Asian American community. In spring 1989, after almost three years of struggle, which included two personnel reviews and five separate faculty votes, he finally received tenure and promotion to associate professor. Nakanishi's attorney, Dale Minami, said that the turning point came when Chancellor Charles Young saw "the breadth and significance of Nakanishi's support in his own community," which saw his struggle as a "fight for intellectual diversification, for the development of AAS programs, and for the presence of Asian Americans at all levels in higher education, not only at UCLA but also on campuses elsewhere."[64]

The Marcy Li Wang case was markedly different.[65] Wang was a typical professor who devoted herself entirely to her work, publishing articles in major journals in her field and garnering an impressive record of professional accomplishments. Yet, in 1985, Berkeley's College of Environmental Design turned her down for tenure. Wang felt that the decision was based not on her alleged lack of merit but on her colleagues' perception that "she was an outspoken 'troublemaker' who refused to adhere to the department's unwritten cultural rules."[66] In other words, she had been judged on subjective criteria that discriminated against women and minorities. In 1986, going through the established procedure, she appealed the decision to the Academic Senate's

Committee on Privilege and Tenure, which found evidence of procedural violations. Yet in 1988 she was denied tenure a second time. She has appealed this decision as well and the case is still pending. Meanwhile, her case has received relatively little publicity, unlike that of Nakanishi, who had been continuously involved in the Asian American Movement and whose fellow activists immediately came to his assistance. When people did learn of Wang's plight—that she was a victim of both racism and sexism—a coalition of students from many organizations came to her assistance, as did community groups such as Chinese for Affirmative Action and the Berkeley Asian Task Force.

After the Third World strikes, Asian American student activists turned their attention to managing the AAS programs they had wrested from resistant school administrators. They had to navigate a tortuous path between external forces that questioned the legitimacy of AAS as a scholarly field and internal forces that threatened to undermine AAS programs. Much of the turmoil concerned how to make AAS pertinent to the community. On the one hand, there were self-styled revolutionaries who considered AAS merely a temporary guerrilla base in enemy territory where they would return resources, notably students, to the community. They agreed that the panacea for the community's problems was the imminent "revolution"—but disagreed among themselves about what change the revolution would bring and how to carry it out. These differences led to bitter sectarian conflicts both in the community and on the campuses, where Marxist groups alienated AAS faculty from students, and both from university administrators. On the other hand, there were reformers who accepted AAS as an educational institution. They believed that the long-term needs of the community would be best served by carrying out the traditional mission of higher education—instruction and scholarship—though from an Asian American perspective. Teaching Asian American students about their culture and history would raise their ethnic and political consciousness and instill in them a commitment for social change in their community. Researching Asian American topics would challenge the dominant society's assumptions about the Asian American community.

The faculty eventually gained control of AAS programs and governed them with an eye toward their long-term survival. With a mixture of reluctance and relief, they abandoned the original vision of student- and community-controlled AAS programs as unrealistic. Except for student representatives on various committees, there is seldom any meaningful student voice left in AAS program governance. And except for individual faculty, staff, and student participation in the community, the links with the community have become tenuous. At present, it usually requires a major crisis for AAS programs to work closely with either students or community members. But they continue to heighten the ethnic and political consciousness of their students and to sensitize their schools to Asian American issues and concerns. In the process, they have earned the reputation of being among the most radical and socially relevant units in the university.

One of the major lessons AAS participants have learned from these early struggles was that though AAS could help bring about change in the community, channeling resources and students there, it was beyond the capacity and outside the mission of academic programs to provide social services. What they could provide was hardly sufficient to solve the multitude of problems in the community and doing so often jeopardized the programs by contravening the rules and regulations of the university. While a few Asian American students have managed to make a place for themselves in the community, most were transients with little understanding of its social realities and little long-term commitment to its development. As the next chapter shows, the community would be better served by having its own organizations and programs.

Chanting such slogans as "Dare to Struggle, Dare to Win," Asian Americans across the country protested against the Vietnam War, which they perceived as imperialist and racist. Antiwar protests such as this one in New York City in 1972 served as an early vehicle for developing inter-Asian coalitions that were national in scope. *Bob Hsiang photo © 1992*

Asian American political activists considered S. I. Hayakawa's support of the Vietnam War and his authoritarian policies as president of San Francisco State College during the Third World strike anathema. Here Asian Americans protest the Japanese American Citizens League's decision to invite him as a keynote speaker. *Connie Hwang photo*

Decades of silence over the unjust incarceration of 120,000 Japanese Americans in concentration camps during World War II were pierced by the persistent questions of third-generation Japanese Americans, shown here holding a candlelight service at the Japanese Buddhist Church in New York City, February 1992, to commemorate the fiftieth anniversary of Executive Order 9066. The signs indicate the names of the concentration camps and the states in which they were located.   *Photo © Corky Lee*

"We are the children of the migrant worker/ We are the offspring of the concentration camp. Sons and daughters of the railroad builder/ Who leave their stamp on Amerika." So sang "Charlie" Chin, Joanne Miyamoto, and Chris Iijima, shown here in concert at Folk City, Greenwich Village, New York City, April 1971. The lyrics are from *A Grain of Sand*, one of the earliest Asian American Movement albums.   *Bob Hsiang photo © 1992*

A significant part of the effort to resist cultural oppression and assert ethnic pride has been the repudiation of stereotypes. Here Asian Americans protest the racist and sexist images in the Broadway musical *Miss Saigon* in New York City, April 1991. The photograph of "My Sister" is of a Vietnamese National Liberation Front fighter from the Vietnam War era. *Photo © Corky Lee*

The Asian American women's movement was a response to racism in the women's liberation movement and sexism in the Asian American Movement. Here Asian American women form their own contingent in the International Women's Day parade, New York City, March 1983. *Photo © Corky Lee*

Inspired by community activists, more than 500 Asian Americans, young and old, foreign born and American born, joined forces in San Francisco in 1973 to protest the federal government's proposal to cut child-care funding. *Connie Hwang photo*

Responding to the call "Serve the People," a host of mainly young Asian Americans volunteered for community-based organizations that provided needed social services. Here an Asian American activist administers a blood pressure examination during the Chinatown Health Fair in Columbus Park, New York City, August 1973. *Photo © Corky Lee*

Asian American women workers, long exploited by the garment industry in the United States, were encouraged to fight back by the Asian American Movement. In 1974, Chinese garment workers of the Greater Chinese American Sewing Company went on strike to protest poor working conditions and fight for their right to unionize. Through sheer persistence, they finally attained a favorable settlement ten years later. *Connie Hwang photo*

The 1982 killing of Vincent Chin by two unemployed auto workers, who received the lenient sentence of three years' probation and a $3,000 fine, outraged the Asian American community. Groups protested the judgment and the increasing incidence of violence against Asians across the country. On the tenth anniversary of Chin's death, some 500 people attended a commemorative service in Confucius Plaza, Chinatown, New York City, June 1992. Names on the mock tombstones represent other victims of anti-Asian violence. *Photo © Corky Lee*

6

"To Serve the People":
Reformers and Community-Based
Organizations

You're never going to make a lot of
money—and you aren't going to
change the whole world. You aren't
going to make Republicans into
Democrats and change capitalists into
socialists . . . but you can help some
often alienated people to improve their
lives. There's nothing wrong with that.
— Harold Lui, director,
Chinatown Health Clinic

Responding to arguments that legal desegregation was not enough to guarantee full participation in American society for minorities, in January 1964, President Lyndon B. Johnson declared a War on Poverty. He established the Office of Economic Opportunity and spent billions of dollars on antipoverty programs, creating nearly two million new jobs. The War on Poverty was prematurely terminated by Richard Nixon in 1974; but while it lasted, it was a catalyst for change in the Asian American community, as it was in the African American community. It gave birth to many community-based organizations that provided social, health, and legal services; offered job training and educational opportunities; and initiated self-help programs. Unfortunately, when it ended, many of these organizations were forced to twist in the wind until they were able to find substitute sources of funding. Those that endured went on to become major community institutions and their directors important community leaders. They became political power bases for Asian American reformers.

As is well known, the War on Poverty was intended mainly to help African

Americans living in urban ghettos. Its primary goal was to change so-called human wastelands into viable communities, but it overlooked a fundamental fact: African Americans were looking for ways to leave the slums, not ways to improve them. The War on Poverty did provide many of them with a passport out of the ghettos. Asian Americans were equally anxious to flee the ghetto, and the War on Poverty also provided some of them with a means of escape, but there was a crucial difference—as old residents left, new groups of Asian immigrants and refugees flooded in. For each Asian American who departed, several Asian immigrants arrived, looking for a place to call home even if it was only the tenements. The War on Poverty coincided with the liberalization of immigration laws. The Immigration Act of 3 October 1965 abolished the national origins quota system, removing discriminatory restrictions on Asian immigration to the United States. Consequently, the number of Asian Americans jumped from 891,000 in 1960 to 1.4 million in 1970, 3.8 million in 1980, and 7.3 million in 1990.¹ This demographic difference made the War on Poverty particularly pertinent to the Asian American community.

Unlike most U.S.-born people of color, who have suffered years, indeed generations, of oppression and have been caught up in the pernicious "culture of poverty," that is, a self-perpetuating cycle of poverty, Asian immigrants and refugees came to America with imagination and energy, looking for a brand new start. For them, the antipoverty programs offered material resources and moral support, enhancing their ability to survive in American society and easing their adjustment to it. For educated Asian Americans, the antipoverty programs also offered opportunities for professional development and, more important, employment. The heads of many community-based organizations providing direct services to Chinatown residents, for example, have been Asian nationals with higher education, often the holders of graduate degrees from American professional schools. Besides their academic credentials, they also have the bilingual–bicultural background necessary to work effectively among first-generation Asian Americans. Those able to secure a position with an antipoverty program acquired an entree into the Asian American middle class.

The War on Poverty changed the political landscape of the Asian American community. Reformers, most of whom in the beginning were Chinese and Japanese Americans, realized that the causes of poverty were political as well as economic. Any solution necessarily involved changing the distribution of political power within the community as well as between it and the dominant society. The War on Poverty's reliance on "community action" to eliminate poverty offered reformers a chance to acquire political power in the Asian American community because it called for not only local control of programs but also for the "maximum feasible participation" by the poor themselves, rather than the traditional elite.[2] It charged local planning councils to consult with poor people to ascertain the sort of services needed in their area, rather than simply ask traditional organizations what poor people required. Membership in these local planning councils empowered Asian American reformers by giving them a chance to sponsor community-based organizations that were outside the control of the existing community power structure.

With federal funds, reformers founded many pan-Asian and Asian ethnic organizations to provide social services needed in their communities. For example, between 1969 and 1972, they started an estimated sixty community-based organizations in Los Angeles County alone.[3] Most of these were social service organizations that were similar to the agencies serving the dominant society. Such organizations were necessary because Asian American communities had been largely ignored. When existing human service institutions did respond to an Asian American community's needs, it was often too little, too late. Employing a few bilingual–bicultural personnel in welfare departments, public schools, and law-enforcement agencies was clearly inadequate to meet the needs of Asian American communities.

Social Service Organizations

Chinese American reformers were among the earliest Asian Americans to avail themselves of the War on Poverty in order to establish social service organizations. They were usually older, second-generation Chinese Americans who had acquired a college education (usually the first in their families to do so) or middle-class Chinese nationals who were working for an advanced degree in the United States. Since many of them held professional positions, they were guided by the corporate values of their professions as well as the middle-class values of American society. At the same time, they were influenced by the moderate civil rights movement of the early 1960s and wanted to integrate Chinese Americans into the existing social order. They shared a pragmatic perspective that saw the War on Poverty as a chance to improve conditions in the country's Chinatowns and obtain some economic justice for residents there. They also shared a political perspective that considered the pursuit of political empowerment as an inherent feature of a democratic pluralist society. As long-time Chinatown residents or Chinese nationals, they understood traditional Chinese-style politics, with its emphasis on personal connections, well enough to bring about change in the community. As educated individuals, they understood how to work with the dominant society and its institutions to help the Chinese American community.

Chinese American reformers joined local planning councils to ensure that their communities were included in the War on Poverty. In 1965, for example, Larry Jack Wong, Alan Wong, and other community activists helped establish the Chinatown–North Beach Economic Opportunity Council.[4] The council managed a million-dollar antipoverty fund that supported such programs and agencies as Self-Help for the Elderly (discussed later in the chapter), English-language classes, and a Planned Parenthood drop-in clinic. The council stood as a challenge to the authority of the traditional elite represented by the Chinese Consolidated Benevolent Association (CCBA, also known as the Chinese Six Companies in San Francisco), an all-male hierarchy of fraternal, district, family, business, and charity organizations. Since some of the most visible community activists were local church leaders, the CCBA could not label them "communists," an accusation that had effectively silenced past opponents. They were called other names, however. Alan Wong, who was then executive director of the YMCA, recalled that they were branded "radicals and trouble-makers," though he considered himself a reformer whose actions were guided by Christian values.[5]

In order to participate in the antipoverty programs, reformers had to challenge the popular perception of Chinese Americans as a "model minority" able to succeed in American society without public assistance and of Chinatowns as thriving communities. As the largest and best-known Asian ethnic enclaves, Chinatowns have come to symbolize the Asian American community. This image of Chinese Americans was touted in articles such as "Success Story of One Minority Group in U.S." in *U.S. News & World Report*: "One such minority, the nation's 300,000 Chinese-Americans, is winning wealth and respect by dint of its own hard work. . . . Still being taught in Chinatown is the old idea that people should depend on their own efforts—not a welfare check—in order to reach America's 'promised land.' "[6] San Francisco's Chinatown, for instance, was promoted as a " 'self-helping' community of successful businessmen, studious and obedient children, hierarchies made legitimate by quaintness and tradition, and a generally docile, contented, respectable populace." [7]

This misperception was abetted by the CCBA, which, for reasons of pride and profit, concealed the community's problems behind a mask of probity. It and its member organizations have traditionally provided welfare services to Chinatown residents. But it lacked the knowledge and money to meet the community's needs, so it chose simply to ignore them. According to the students of the Intercollegiate Chinese for Social Action, the leadership's denial of problems resulted in Chinatown's being left out of San Francisco's Model Cities program, which would have provided money to rehabilitate the community.[8]

In contrast, Chinese American reformers were willing to admit that the country's Chinatowns—especially those in San Francisco and New York, the largest, oldest, and best known—were nothing more than "glittering ghettos" with pervasive problems, places that people fled from at the earliest opportunity.[9] Behind the facade for tourists were deteriorating slums. In San Francisco's Chinatown, 77 percent of dwellings were substandard by city codes. Decaying tenements built over a half century earlier, after the great San Francisco earthquake of 1906, they were owned by absentee landlords, mostly Chinese. The adjacent financial district steadily encroached on the old tenements, decreasing the number of low-rent housing units. In New York's Chinatown, 62 percent of those surveyed in the *Chinatown Study Report* (1969) reported that their apartment houses had not been painted in the past three years (a breach of the city's rent-control law); 35 percent reported rats and mice in their homes, and 76 percent cockroach infestation.

As one might expect from such deplorable conditions, Chinatown residents suffered from maladies prevalent in slums: malnutrition, trachoma, tuberculosis, alcoholism, and depression. According to a report by the San Francisco Department of Public Health, the tuberculosis rate in Chinatown was twice the national and state average.[10] It had the sad distinction of having the highest tuberculosis (and suicide) rates in the nation. According to the *Chinatown Health Survey* (1970), only about two-thirds of those interviewed in New York's Chinatown were covered by health insurance. The rest were simply too poor to afford medical attention.

Residents led precarious lives. In San Francisco's Chinatown, 15 percent were looking for work. In New York's Chinatown, only an estimated 3 percent were unemployed; but in both cases, residents were dependent on a stratified labor market and confined to limited job opportunities in Chinatown. The *Study Report* noted that in New York's Chinatown 35.5 percent of the men worked in Chinese restaurants and 75 percent of the women worked in garment factories. As part of their tacit agreement with employers, they usually worked more than forty hours a week and at least a twelve-hour day.

In an interview with the San Francisco State College Study Team investigating the causes of the Third World strike at San Francisco State, Mason Wong, president of the Intercollegiate Chinese for Social Action, succinctly summarized Chinatown's condition:

> The fiction is that the Chinese have never suffered as much as, say, the black or brown communities in this country. . . . Rather, the Chinese community has the same basic problems as all other nonwhite communities. The only thing different is that it has neon lights and a few tourist restaurants, which is all that white people want to know about our community. Yet these restaurants are staffed by illiterate Chinese who work fourteen hours per day, six days per week, for starvation wages. The only way to survive in our community is exploit each other, hence the myth of the successful Chinese businessman. This exploitation is perpetuated at the expense of the Chinese immigrants who can only find work in the sweatshops, laundries and restaurants in Chinatown.[11]

To deal with these problems, Chinese American reformers established community-based organizations. Three that were founded in the 1960s and have become quite influential are New York City's Chinatown Planning Council (CPC), San Francisco's Self-Help for the Elderly (SHE), and Chinese for Affirmative Action (CAA).[12] Originally, CPC and SHE were started by private institutions for the benefit of Chinatown residents: CPC traced its origins to the Community Services Society of New York City and SHE to Beatrice Schiffman of the San Francisco Council of Churches. CAA was started by a group of Chinese American student and community activists. All three posed an implicit challenge to the entrenched Chinese American establishment.

The traditional elite was wary of outside forces intervening in community affairs and preferred the facade of a self-reliant, self-sufficient Chinese American community. It wanted to promote the image of a safe ethnic enclave attractive to visitors and was prepared to prolong the community's problems in order to avoid losing face and political power. Charles Wang, who served as the president of CPC for many years and who in 1991 became the vice-chair of the U.S. Civil Rights Commission, recalled that the CCBA engaged in a disinformation campaign, questioning the validity of the Cattell report (discussed in the next section) and alleging, on the basis of the report's red cover, that CPC members who supported its recommendations were communists. Beatrice Schiffman, who served as SHE's first executive director, recalled that the "Six Companies felt outsiders were invading their turf and maverick savings and loan manager J. K. Choy felt that he could serve the elderly better from his storefront service operation at SF Federal Savings and Loan." [13] Henry Der, the current executive director of CAA, observed that during its early years, his organization was likewise misunderstood. People attributed to it "unfounded political agendas" and perceived it as "a radical organization seeking to overthrow either community or public institutions." [14] Eventually, CPC, SHE, and CAA earned the respect, if not the affection, of the traditional Chinese establishment, which has grudgingly recognized the contributions they have made to the Chinese community.

Chinatown Planning Council

In 1962, Stuart H. Cattell published *Health, Welfare and Social Organization in Chinatown, New York City*, a social anthropological study of "the underlying network of obligations and responsibilities of traditional Chinese culture" that affected health and welfare in Chinatown.[15] He reported that the Chinatown community was suffering from tremendous social problems, "problems that were deliberately hidden from view by Chinatown's established leadership," problems that might be exacerbated by any impending changes in the immigration laws.[16] And he concluded that the "most pressing need in Chinatown is an effective community organization which would bridge the gaps between the numerous voluntary associations and thereby break the log jam of conflicting interests and inaction which is holding up the solution of many problems." [17] Such a community organization would consist of "public spirited people" outside the traditional Chinatown leadership, which had failed to solve past problems. Acting on Cattell's conclusions, a group of mainly second-generation Chinese American social workers, educators, and others got together in 1965 to establish the Chinatown Planning Council.

In its first year, CPC held numerous meetings to decide how to bring in the skills and resources that the Chinatown community needed. Meanwhile, the circumstances were so urgent that its members volunteered to serve as interim counselors until they could be replaced by a full-time paid staff. During its first phase (1964–1968), CPC encountered the classic problems of a new organization: Its purpose was only dimly understood, so there was some confusion as to what services to offer; its staff was for the most part untrained, so service delivery was hampered; and its initial board of directors was politically weak, so support was limited.

Gradually, CPC solved these internal problems. CPC, which later changed its name to the Chinese-American Planning Council, has since focused on providing integrated personal services that will move its constituents to self-sufficiency or, in the case of the aged and ill, to programs that allow them to live with a measure of decency. Thus, CPC offered adult education courses, day care, support services for the elderly, youth counseling, housing mediation, and even a modest cultural arts program that provided workshops and free concerts for various age groups—a diversity of services that has proven to be both a strength and a weakness. To manage these programs, CPC hired Allen B. Cohen to serve as general director. He, in turn, recruited a professional staff with social service training and experience, including Charles Wang, who later succeeded him. Finally, CPC put together an effective board of directors.

War on Poverty funds gave CPC its start. In summer 1965, it obtained funding for a Head Start project. Since then, it has opened twelve centers providing day care for more than fourteen hundred children and funded mainly by the New York City Agency for Child Development. In fall 1965, it received a $76,000 grant to provide translation, employment referral, supportive counseling, ombudsman services, housing assistance, and help with a variety of government programs for Chinatown residents. It was able to renew this contract annually. When fiscal crises came, as they inevitably did, CPC managed to weather them by applying successfully to a variety of public and private funding sources for grants that could be used to defray some of its general expenses as well as to fund specific services. Paradoxically, it has actually done comparatively well during lean years. In a tight fiscal environment, funding agencies emphasize accountability and tend to award grants to organizations with a known track record. For that reason, CPC has been able to compete successfully with rival organizations for increasingly scarce dollars. Its staff has had the technical ability and in-depth knowledge of funding agencies to allow it to tap many financial sources, making it the largest social service agency in New York's Chinatown, with an annual budget of $12 million.

Unfortunately, CPC has evolved into a large and impersonal entity committed to its own well-being, sometimes at the expense of its clients. It has been accused of abusing immigrant workers enrolled in its Intercity Remodeling and Apartment Repair program, which began in September 1986.[18] Ostensibly, the program was to train new Chinese immigrants for the construction industry by having them repair and renovate buildings owned by the city. Each worker was supposed to receive one year of training; one day a week was devoted to learning English in the morning and construction skills in the afternoon, and the rest of the week was spent rehabilitating buildings. But according to the National Labor Relations Board (NLRB), the so-called training program provided little training and very few jobs. Instead, CPC was found guilty of unfair labor practices.

Workers saw themselves as exploited employees, rather than students, so they demanded improved working conditions, benefits, and actual job training. Later, they formed the CPC Independent Workers Union, which the NLRB certified as the exclusive collective bargaining representative for these employees. Meanwhile, CPC still maintained that they were trainees and not workers, challenged their right to organize, and "graduated" them. The former workers claimed that their summary termination was retaliation for demanding the basic right to establish a union. They fought back with street demonstrations and called for a boycott of CPC fund-raising functions. In the end, the federal courts upheld the right of the workers to form a union.

CPC has become New York Chinatown's largest social service agency, but at the expense of its original mission. It has committed the classic mistake of equating the organization's self-interest with the interest of those it serves. Misusing immigrant Chinese workers has tarnished its distinguished record of service to Chinese Americans; it needs to reexamine its purposes and change its practices if it is to restore its credibility in the community. It is fortunate that CPC has survived the scandal, for New York's growing Chinatown community has come to depend on its many social services.

Self-Help for the Elderly

Other social service agencies, such as Self-Help for the Elderly, have managed to avoid CPC's fate; as Beatrice Schiffman noted, "the humanity has not left [SHE] . . . and it has left a lot of agencies."[19] SHE has a tightly focused mission—to provide a better quality of life to the seniors in San Francisco's Chinatown. Since opening its doors in August 1966, SHE has developed into a "one-stop multi-purpose senior services agency" that serves as a safety net for many of San Francisco's aging Chinese residents.[20] With seven centers, it serves as a vital link between the elderly and the community. And none too soon. Between 1965 and 1975, there was a fourfold increase in the number of elderly Asian–Pacific Islanders Americans, with over 55 percent of them concentrated in California and Washington, and 14 percent of them living in or near poverty.[21]

Initially, SHE was an agency in search of a constituency. During its formative period (1966–1971), it had to overcome several obstacles before it could deliver services to its putative clients. First, it had to assess the elderly's needs and, more important, allay their apprehensions about possible deportation, a legacy of anti-Asian laws. It spent considerable effort in reaching out to senior citizens, developing a rapport with them and educating them about SHE's services. In the beginning, its meals program served only fifty clients; by the middle 1980s, it served two hundred thousand meals, including twenty thousand to handicapped and homebound seniors, each year. It provided various services to twenty-five thousand seniors annually.

Among SHE's early accomplishments was its challenge of the eligibility guidelines of the San Francisco Welfare Department. SHE established the right of permanent residents to obtain public assistance, a change that benefited other minority communities as well. In 1971, SHE participated in the First White House Conference on the Aging, where its director, Sam Yuen, explained the need for bilingual–bicultural services for elderly ethnic-minority people. SHE became a model aging program serving a particular ethnic community. Throughout the 1970s, its work was recognized by local and national magazines.

As part of the Older Adult Unit of the San Francisco Council of Churches, SHE received $128,000 of funding from the Economic Opportunity Council. When the War on Poverty ended, SHE nearly closed its doors. Even as SHE was being touted as a model for emulation during the 1970s, the Nixon administration undermined it when it cut Economic Opportunity Council funding. The staff received no salaries for several months as they applied for grants from the United Way, San Francisco Commission on the Aging, Comprehensive Employment and Training Act, and San Francisco Foundation. While the organization was able to weather this fiscal storm, others lay ahead: The Reagan administration cutbacks proved to be even more traumatic because SHE had expanded during the intervening decade and was forced during the new crisis to reduce its staff severely. To ensure financial stability and continuity in services, Anni Chung, who assumed the directorship in 1981, established a fund-raising committee that has been quite creative in raising revenues.

SHE has had its share of political battles, none more trying than the Pineview controversy. Anni Chung and her staff saw affordable housing for seniors as SHE's highest priority. In 1983, they began planning the Pineview Housing Project, a federally funded project that would provide seventy housing units as well as a senior center and other facilities for low-income seniors and physically handicapped residents. If Pineview was approved by the San Francisco Planning Commission, the U.S. Department of Housing and Urban Development would provide $5.4 million in construction loans and $24 million in rent subsidies throughout the forty-year mortgage period. Since the project involved land use in space-starved Chinatown, it would affect the entire community. In retrospect, it is apparent that SHE failed to do the necessary groundwork to gain the cooperation of the community for this politically charged undertaking.

Tenants at the site protested the project and the San Francisco Board of Supervisors, unwilling to rezone the area from a public-owned property to a commercial and residential mixed-use district, rejected it. Proponents saw the venture as a precedent-setting step forward in cooperation between nonprofit groups and commercial property developers, one that would serve as a model for future housing development and reconstruction in Chinatown. Ironically, opponents criticized Pineview on precisely the same grounds, arguing that it would set a precedent for many more commercial high-rises that would lead inexorably to the destruction of Chinatown. Fay Wong of the Chinese Progressive Association linked Pineview to the "rapid commercialization and gentrification in every U.S. major city over the past two decades, including the Boston and New York Chinatowns." [22]

SHE then decided to move Pineview above the Broadway Tunnel. No opposition was expected from community groups, since the new site would "not be taking light or air away from anyone." [23] But resistance arose anyway: The Broadway Tunnel Park Committee wanted a park at the site, and parishioners of Our Lady of Guadalupe Church protested that the housing development would obscure their church and aggravate traffic and parking problems. This time, Pineview was able to rally the support of most of the Chinatown community and nearly all the San Francisco newspapers, including *Asian Week*, the *San*

Francisco Chronicle, *East/West*, the *San Francisco Examiner*, and *Progress*. Consequently, both the San Francisco Planning Commission and the Board of Supervisors gave a rare unanimous approval to Pineview. In a last ditch effort to end it, opponents forced a public referendum (Proposition X) on the lease of air rights over the tunnel, but to no avail. Voters approved Pineview by a two-to-one margin. The Lady Shaw Senior Center, as the senior housing facility was finally called, was finished in fall 1990. On the occasion of its opening, Anni Chung was moved to say, "If a community supports a project, no matter how hard it is, it can be accomplished." [24] SHE had obviously learned an important political lesson from the Pineview controversy.

Chinese for Affirmative Action

Like CPC and SHE, Chinese for Affirmative Action (CAA) was born in the social ferment of the 1960s and received War on Poverty funds. But CAA also resembled Asian American alternative grassroots organizations in that it was established mainly by politically conscious preprofessionals who were willing to employ some of the social movement strategies of the 1960s to achieve their goals, including a reliance on the community for strength and sustenance. Perhaps most important, it eventually went beyond the physical limits of San Francisco's Chinatown and developed an Asian American perspective and identity, though it retained its ethnic name and local base.

In early 1969, a small band of community activists and young people, predominantly college graduates, were aware that the most pressing problem encountered by newly arrived immigrants was finding jobs that paid at least the minimum wage. They "sensed the need for an advocacy group on behalf of Chinese Americans who, like other minority groups, were subtly and systematically denied equal opportunity in many sectors of society." [25] Since the Six Companies had abdicated responsibility as advocates for Chinese Americans and were oblivious to the demographic and social changes occurring in Chinatown, these activists founded CAA, principally to fight for fair employment of Chinese.

During its first five years, CAA was a service and informal advocacy organization. Naturally, based in San Francisco's Chinatown and having a membership of mainly Chinese Americans, it provided direct services to Chinese in the Bay Area. Its Skills Bank, for instance, offered counseling, English tutorials, and job-placement services to over fifteen hundred clients annually. "After a preliminary analysis of the workforce and a study of evidence of employment discrimination, the early leaders identified five specific occupational targets for immediate action: building trades, service industry, mass media, finance and insurance industry, and civil service at local, state, and federal levels." [26] These sectors were selected because they were big employers and excluded Chinese Americans.

CAA's baptism in the area of employment discrimination was the Holiday Inn case. Even though a $13 million, twenty-seven-story Holiday Inn was being built in the heart of Chinatown, Chinese Americans were denied jobs on the construction site. A survey of the workforce indicated that "only three Chinese apprentices out of a total of more than 220 journeymen and foremen—that is, 1.3% Chinese—are on the payroll even though the surrounding population is almost 100% Chinese"—and this after eighteen months of continuous negotiations between Chinese community representatives and Cahill Construction Company, the general contractors.[27] Evidently Cahill, its subcontractors, and the San Francisco Redevelopment Agency had all failed to comply with the guidelines of the City's Affirmative Action Program—"a program designed to recruit, hire, train and retain minority workers in building trades, especially in projects involving public property and funds." [28] Ironically, the building was called the Chinese Culture and Trade Center because the third floor was to be used "to provide the proper atmosphere and facilities for the development of cultural perspective, self-awareness and community understanding and participation among Americans of Chinese ancestry." [29]

While CAA was ultimately unable to convince Cahill to hire Chinese to construct the building, in cooperation with the Chinatown–North Beach Human Resources Development Center and the San Francisco Human Rights Commission, it did convince the Holiday Inn management to employ local residents in the hotel.[30] It also acquired the standing to influence the building trades in San Francisco: CAA later acquired positions for Chinese journeymen and apprentices, assisted the Office of Federal Contract Compliance of the U.S. Department of Labor to conduct public hearings on employment discrimination, and worked with other minority groups to negotiate an affirmative action plan for the city's building trades. Its long-term success can be attributed to its firm commitment to equal employment and its tenacious negotiating style. This early victory "provided the impetus for other, expanded civil rights battles which involved strategies such as taking on the established economic and political power structure through aggressive negotiation, demanding the enforcement of civil rights by local, state and federal compliance agencies, and exerting public pressure on the media." [31]

By 1973, CAA had some successes. It became recognized as a legitimate community-based organization, the Chinese American counterpart to the National Association for the Advancement of Colored People (NAACP), with increasing membership and support. In 1974, under the leadership of Henry Der, the newly appointed executive director, CAA increasingly emphasized its role as an advocate of Chinese American rights. Later, though it continued to bear the name Chinese for Affirmative Action, it broadened its vision to encompass the larger issues of empowerment and equity for Asian Americans in general.[32] It played a major role as a resource center and information clearinghouse for victims of discrimination as well as those interested in civil rights issues.

By the 1980s it was evident that much of CAA's work was relevant to the larger Asian American community and that what happened to other Asian ethnic groups around the country affected Chinese Americans, as the 1982 Detroit murder of Vincent Chin tragically proved. CAA was the Asian American community's prime advocate in the passage of the Voting Rights Act of 1975 and the extension of the act in 1981–1982; in May 1986, it organized the "Break the Silence" conference and coalition that focused on anti-Asian violence; in fall 1986, it worked with other civil rights groups to educate citizens on the dangers of the "English-only" movement in California and nationwide; and it helped organize the National Coalition for the Accurate Count of Asian Pacific Americans to deal with a proposal by the U.S. Census Bureau to eliminate the specific listing of Asian and Pacific Islander on the race question on the 1990 census. With its executive director serving as a member of the Asian American Task Force on University of California Admissions, CAA has increased community awareness of discriminatory admissions policies and has helped pressure the university into admitting that its changes in policy had very likely harmed Asian American applicants. It has also joined other Asian American civil rights groups to urge the "federal civil rights enforcement officials in Washington, D.C., not to exploit Asian American complaints about university admissions quotas as a vehicle to undermine and attack (student) affirmative action programs for underrepresented Afro-American, Hispanic and American Indian students." [33] CAA's efforts to ensure that Asian American students will be treated fairly in the college admissions process have won it the support of the community, particularly Asian immigrant parents. In sum, CAA is much like the alternative grassroots organizations founded at the same time as social service organizations, watching out for the Asian American community's civil rights and representing its interests locally and nationally.

Alternative Grassroots Organizations

Besides community-based organizations that delivered direct services to a physical community such as Chinatown, alternative grassroots organizations identified with the larger Asian American community. They worked to empower the community so that Asian Americans could break through the constraints imposed by the dominant society and control their own destiny. Most were founded by second-generation Asian American college students (or graduates) influenced by the increasingly militant student movement of the late 1960s. These young reformers viewed the War on Poverty and other federal programs with deep suspicion; some even perceived them as a domestic counterpart to the counterinsurgency programs being employed in Vietnam and other Third World countries to pacify "restless natives." [34]

In their view, federal programs supposedly had several subversive functions: First, they divided, weakened, and, finally controlled racial-minority communities in the United States, pitting one group against another and making it impossible for them to cooperate against their common oppressor. Second, they changed self-reliant communities into dependent ones, eroding the self-confidence of the people living there. Third, they turned community activists into government employees with a "9-to-5" mentality. Or, as one critic put it, "revolution is transformed into rhetoric and takes on a curious capitalistic mentality cushioned with wall to wall carpets, laid out on IBM typewriters and financed on credit." [35] Perhaps most insidious, they believed the programs intended to coopt community leaders and monitor community dissidents. In short, in the paranoid political climate of the late 1960s, some activists thought that federal programs were part of "a full-blown neo-colonist strategy to keep Asian American communities tamed, divided, controlled and useful to the dominant society and its beneficiaries." [36]

Instead, young reformers placed their hopes in alternative grassroots organizations that challenged the existing power structure through the support of the "people," that is, the discontented masses. Presumably, such community support would protect them from the threats and blandishments of mainstream society. But the practical requirements of founding essentially antiestablishment organizations in the Asian American community and sustaining them through voluntarism and self-reliance proved daunting. While this process was in keeping with the democratic sentiments of the era, it also made these institutions inherently unstable, since they invariably encountered difficulties in recruiting and retaining volunteers and in soliciting support from a resource-poor community. Much to their credit, they tried.

Among the most active alternative grassroots organizations have been Basement Workshop and the Asian Law Caucus, both established in the 1970s, and the Committee Against Anti-Asian Violence, which was organized in the 1980s. The cultural nationalists who helped to found Basement Workshop believed that reclaiming and creating an Asian American culture was an essential precondition for social change in the community. They appreciated the need for an environment that would encourage Asian Americans to learn about their history and heritage. They provided an ideological framework in which people could resolve their ambivalence about being Asians in America and affirm their identity as Asian Americans. But some of them discovered that, paradoxically, Asian American culture as it was expressed in the 1960s and early 1970s was inimical to making an Asian American cultural organization a permanent part of the community.

In contrast, the lawyers and law students who established the Asian Law Caucus were better prepared to institutionalize their organization in the Asian American community. They realized that, historically, Asian Americans have been excluded from equal protection under the law. Though most laws that discriminated against Asians have been erased from the statute books or lapsed from nonuse, the legacy of inequality and injustice continued. So they shared a collective vision of opening a nonprofit public-interest law office to defend the community. Furthermore, they had the practical competence needed to realize it and, unlike cultural nationalists, fewer fears about being coopted by the dominant society. On the contrary, it was they who planned to coopt the established judicial system in order to protect the interest of the Asian American community, which they did and do, with panache as well as professionalism. Their record of service, which can be measured in tangible ways, attracted volunteers, especially those interested in legal careers.

The founders of the Committee Against Anti-Asian Violence (CAAAV) never envisioned an ongoing organization when they sponsored the first New York City area forum on violence against Asians in spring 1986. They had a modest goal—to educate the community about the increasing incidence of anti-Asian violence. But it became evident that a network was needed to oppose anti-Asian violence and that such a network would have the support of the Asian American community. CAAAV became the main Asian American group in the emerging multiracial movement for justice in New York City. Because of its firm commitment to the principle of justice and consistent leadership in anti-Asian violence issues, the organization has continued to develop. And after four years of doing so as an all-volunteer group, CAAAV finally moved to make itself a permanent part of the community by hiring a full-time organizer in 1990.[37]

Basement Workshop

The archetypal alternative grassroots organization was the Basement Workshop (1971–1986).[38] Initially, Basement served as a focal point for socially conscious and politically active Asian Americans, mainly second-generation Chinese Americans and third-generation Japanese Americans interested in projects to improve the quality of life in New York's Chinatown. It served as an umbrella organization for individuals interested in working on art projects and in organizing the community around issues of education, employment, housing, and health care. Later, it became exclusively a community arts and culture organization. Basement's fifteen-year history was shaped mainly by the energy and imagination of its volunteers and the support of the Chinatown community. This proved to be an advantage especially in the beginning, when it attracted volunteers with unfettered ideas and boundless energy, and a disadvantage later, when such individuals became scarce and support from the community waned. Still, Basement has a singular place in Asian American history, for it served as the conduit for activism on the East Coast and a catalyst for the development of Asian American culture.

Basement's origins can be traced to the Asian American Resource Center, established by Danny N. T. Yung to house the information that he and a group of fellow urban planners at Columbia University had gathered for the *Chinatown Report, 1969*, a Ford Foundation project. Yung and his colleagues intended to continue compiling information about Asian American communities, as well as finding a way to disseminate it. *Bridge* magazine, discussed in an earlier chapter, was conceived of as one way to do this. Apart from the information located at the Resource Center, which in the beginning consisted of "an orange crate and a four drawer filing cabinet" in the damp basement of a Chinatown tenement,[39] its importance lay in serving as a hospitable place for Asian Americans searching for meaning during troubled times: local youths looking for worthwhile activity in the ghetto that was Chinatown, activists looking for people with a progressive political agenda to work with, and writers and artists looking for an audience that would appreciate their work. They constituted a critical mass of young Asian Americans who became the heart and soul of Basement Workshop.

Learning that Chinese living in turn-of-the-century tenements in lower Manhattan had a higher rate of tuberculosis, hepatitis B, parasitic infections, and hypertension than the general New York population, in summer 1971 the Asian Americans gathered in that basement organized the first Chinatown Health Fair: several testing and information booths, which eventually evolved into the Chinatown Health Clinic. The fair attracted a group of artists, writers, and musicians who wanted to help out. Afterward, they started the Basement Workshop project, after which the community-based organization was later named, to work on "Yellow Pearl."

Yellow Pearl began as a modest project to mimeograph music, with illustrations and additional poetry and prose, but developed into an appealing collection of the earliest examples of Asian American culture. Many of those associated with the project were young people from Chinese American families outside Chinatown, and they were perceived as intruders who came into the community with preconceived notions about its problems and ways to solve them. Fortunately, the tensions between those from the outside and those from within Chinatown were never serious enough to jeopardize the project. Yellow Pearl found its way to different parts of the country, introducing Asian American culture to the uninitiated and Basement Workshop to the population at large, though it was mainly the Asian American community that took notice of it.

In the beginning, Basement Workshop relied heavily on individual initiative and group support. People were encouraged to follow the counterculture spirit of the 1960s and "do their own thing," and they did. But that free-spirited approach, with its sense of immediacy and preoccupation with the present, militated against planning for the future and boded ill for the group's institutionalization within the Asian American community. Governance, such as there was, was in the hands of "an unwieldy collective . . . which moved along month by month with a great deal of yelling." [40] By the middle 1970s, Basement was in a quandary over whether it should become a formal community organization or remain an informal collective of activists. Those who wanted to place Basement on a more secure financial footing and to set up stable management procedures were vulnerable to accusations of being bureaucratic and self-aggrandizing. Fay Chiang, a poet, was accused of being an "organizational misleader and a sell out to the people in the face of federal and state funding." [41]

As a result of increased funding from foundation, corporate, and government sources, Basement expanded pell-mell. In the early 1970s, it supported the overhead of four locations: three loft spaces and a storefront. It published *Bridge* magazine and sponsored the Amerasia Creative Arts program, which designed a series of workshops in silk-screening, photography, dance, music, and creative writing. It managed the Asian American Resource Center, which later became the basis of the Chinatown History Project founded by Jack Tchen and Charlie Lai. Through its Community Planning Workshop program, Basement started weekly survival English and citizenship classes for two hundred adults, an after-school arts and crafts program for forty children, and a Neighborhood Youth Corps intern program each summer. Without fully realizing it, Basement was becoming an unwieldy, multidisciplinary organization. In retrospect, it appears that Basement's growth outstripped its means. It would have been wiser to plan its development systematically, rather than allow it to grow unchecked.

Exacerbating Basement's internal problems was the sectarianism of the mid-1970s, a subject explored in detail in the next chapter. Observing that Basement was mired in a controversy over its purpose and direction, members of Asian Americans for Equal Employment, which served as a front organization for the Asian Study Group, a Marxist–Leninist organization, saw it as ripe for takeover. Basement was clearly a major political prize: It had attracted Asian American activists from all over the city and had been involved in progressive community issues. Its artists regularly supported controversial causes by providing publicity materials, graphics, and posters. Staying up all night printing two thousand posters to support a demonstration at City Hall against police brutality was the sort of work that brought out the best in its volunteers.

Two camps emerged within Basement: those who wanted it to serve as a vehicle for community arts and resources and those who wanted to use it for partisan political organizing.[42] The political dissension resulted in divisions among those within the organization as well as those in the community who supported it, which included practically all the Asian American activists in the area. Fay Chiang, who served as Basement's director for many years and was caught in this upheaval, bitterly recalled:

> In June 1975, I attended a meeting where a position paper drafted by the members of the partisan group was read to me accusing me of selling out the community to the federal and state government by accepting arts funding. In the old lingo, I was the victim of an organizational purge. At the end of the meeting I was literally pinned to the floor as I tried to protest. The body of 75 people left in hysteria. For several months I was harassed and followed about the streets of Chinatown, as this group tried to "break" me.[43]

In summer 1975, Basement physically departed Chinatown in order to escape the hostile political climate, in which neither the left nor the right was "speaking to issues dealing with the very real needs of [the Chinatown] community and its people, but rather the needs and the righteousness of each political party's beliefs."[44] Perhaps in reaction to the political struggles in the community, as well as to make the organization more manageable, Basement reduced the scope of its activities. It focused mainly on Asian American culture, allowing artists an opportunity to create works that reflected Asian American experiences and sensibilities without political constraints.

In 1977, Basement attempted to move from the chaos that characterized its early years to a stable corporate organization, one that emphasized planning and accountability. Among other things, it made plans to purchase a building to serve as a permanent home. It tried consciously to institutionalize itself, calling for an active board of directors, a professional staff, and revision of its bylaws. At the same time, it tried to retain the goals that had evolved over the years. But the effort came to nought because people were unable to agree on its future direction. Worse yet, Basement began to fall apart organizationally. By 1979, the situation seemed slapstick: "Board members resigned, staff departed, the organization was over $25,000 in debt, the bookkeeper went to Florida (with the books), the IRS was banging on the doors, former employees were screaming for back pay and the creditors were threatening court suits."[45] During the

1980s, Fay Chiang tried to overcome the spirit of failure that permeated the organization, rehabilitate it, and restore it to its former glory. Programs were limited to a reading series, gallery, dance classes, and concerts, with a focus on the work of emerging and professional artists. Among other things, she paid artists fees and gave them a place to display their work to the public.[46] Initially many of them refused to participate, lest association with Basement tarnish their careers and reputations; eventually, they came around. But it was too late. Chiang was unable to halt Basement's downward spiral. Her efforts only raised serious questions about whether Basement was still a community organization.

According to one prominent Asian American artist and activist, Chiang and her colleagues had changed the basic character of Basement.[47] They decided that Basement should support Asian American artists interested in creating high-quality work regardless of political content; or, to use the political vernacular of the period, to create "art for art's sake" rather than art for the Asian American community's sake. They were, this artist presumed, responding to the significant shift in funding away from so-called ghetto arts programs to mainstream-oriented programs that sponsored well-known artists, individuals who belonged to the "downtown performance arts scene." [48] A more charitable interpretation is that Chiang and her associates were reacting to the sectarianism of the 1970s. In the poisoned political atmosphere that had developed within the Asian American Movement, people with a pronounced political posture became suspect became they could very well be harboring hostile intentions toward Basement.

In any case, critics complained that Basement supported apolitical artists who saw it as a way to enhance their careers and repelled political artists who wanted to create a culture that enhanced the Asian American Movement. There was a backlash from community activists who thought that Basement had betrayed them and abandoned its commitment to "serve the people." [49] Sadly, they expressed their displeasure in unseemly ways. An opponent who belonged to the New York State Council for the Arts, for instance, conducted a lengthy diatribe against Basement's application for funding, opposing an increase of $10,000 that would have raised its funding to $35,000, the difference being a big loss for a nonprofit organization.[50] Obviously, the sense of solidarity that had characterized the Asian American Movement in its infancy had disintegrated.

The death blow was delivered by the Reagan administration. During Reagan's conservative presidency, when community-based organizations in general and minority ones in particular were chronically underfunded, artists discovered that it was impossible for them to make a living (as well as do their own creative work) and manage Basement at the same time. Consequently, Chiang found it too difficult to develop a board of directors and staff, operate artistic programs, and raise funds for the organization, a problem she shared with other alternative grassroots organizations.[51] With regret and, perhaps, relief, she and her associates closed Basement Workshop on 15 May 1986.

Basement Workshop played a significant role in the Asian American Movement, nationally as well as on the East Coast. It served as an important center for activists seeking support for their political and cultural activities. It was one of the first community-based organizations to embrace the concept of an Asian American identity, history, and culture. It was influential in introducing the concept to hundreds of young people who "hung out" at its various facilities, motivating many of them to become involved in the Movement. Its continuous involvement in the creation of Asian American culture may be Basement's most important legacy. It provided a place for artists to practice their craft, to teach their skills to others, and to display their work. In so doing it gave them unprecedented public exposure, increased their access to public funding, and paved the way for greater public acceptance. Finally, it served as the model for other Asian American community-based organizations, such as the Asian American Resource Workshop, which was founded in 1979.

Besides culturally oriented organizations such as the Basement Workshop, Movement activists appreciated the need for alternative grassroots organizations that could fight forthrightly for equality and justice in American society. The Asian Law Caucus and other Asian American nonprofit public-interest law offices have been among the most effective in doing this.

Asian Law Caucus

The Asian Law Caucus, the oldest and best-known Asian American community law organization, has been the inspiration for those that followed it.[52] The caucus has provided legal representation to the Asian American poor, educated Asian Americans about their legal and civil rights, trained law students in community-focused legal work, and engaged in litigation against institutional racism. Though the caucus has had its share of internal difficulties and has gone through trying times, it has been more successful than most alternative grassroots organizations in establishing itself as a permanent part of the Asian American community.

The caucus was founded in August 1972 by a small group of idealistic lawyers and law students who initially came together in opposition to the Vietnam War, representing Asian American conscientious objectors. They stayed together because they believed in public-interest law and the need for legal services in the Asian American community. Among the founders was Ken Kawaichi, a visionary who conceived the idea of a community-based legal organization and proposed a five-year plan for its realization. As it turned out, a community law office was indeed established in Oakland, but as a result more of youthful impulse than of mature planning. Garrick Lew recalled that after a strenuous game of basketball, the founders saw a vacant storefront across the street and decided then and there to rent it with the money that Dale Minami had made from representing draft resisters.[53] It would be fair to say that the Asian Law Caucus had its birth on a basketball court and was paid for by the antiwar movement.

During the caucus's first three years, Dale Minami acted as managing attorney, securing the first foundation grants that kept the organization solvent as well as serving as lead counsel in many of its early lawsuits. The staff consisted of either volunteers or people paid through the federal Comprehensive Employment and Training Act. In keeping with the spirit of the times, they made decisions collectively and led a precarious financial existence. Their first major case was *Chann v. Scott*. In fall 1972, the caucus filed a class-action civil rights suit against the San Francisco Police Department for arbitrary dragnet arrests of Chinatown youths. Lew recalled, "They couldn't tell the kids apart, felt they all 'looked alike.' So, they wanted to sweep all the Chinatown youths and begin dossiers on them—whom they hung out with, whom they talked to. Well . . . this was illegal, unconstitutional." [54] They were able to force the police to cease conducting sweeps against Chinese American youths, even though the suit was dismissed two years later.

In 1975, the caucus opened an office in San Francisco's Chinatown, eventually increasing its caseload by more than 200 percent. From that point on, the caucus averaged five hundred cases and more than a thousand consultations annually. In 1981, the San Francisco Neighborhood Legal Assistance Foundation closed its doors, tripling the demand for the caucus's services in its Oakland headquarters. Because of the immigrant character of the Asian American community, the majority of its clients have been recent immigrants, refugees, or people who spoke limited English. Many were "tenants facing exorbitant rent increases in one-room residential units or working below minimum wage standards in garment sweatshops in Chinatown." [55] One of the caucus's major victories was a settlement against a major garment manufacturer for unlawful labor practices on the part of its subcontractor (*Ha et al.* v. *T & W Fashions*). By the 1980s, protecting the rights of immigrants became a central concern as the country experienced a resurgence of nativism. Life became increasingly precarious for immigrants denied employment because they spoke with an accent or held only permanent resident status.

In the 1980s, the caucus reassessed its priorities, deciding "to specialize in high-profile legal issues with the greatest potential impact on Asian Americans." [56] Occasionally that meant being involved in cases that affected other people of color. Its involvement in the effort to stop government plans to evict undocumented aliens from public housing, to obtain a preliminary injunction to end Immigration and Naturalization Service raids, and to form a statewide committee against the "English-only" amendment to the California State Constitution provided more immediate aid to Latinos, but established important legal precedents that would protect the rights of Asian immigrants as well. The caucus also became increasingly political as it became involved in areas such as labor, housing, immigration law, senior rights, and criminal defense. [57] It went beyond the simple eviction cases of the past to broader issues such as land use, preservation of housing, and fighting the demolition of buildings. Among its successes in these areas was the passage of an ordinance to prevent Chinatown residential hotels from being demolished (Oakland Conversion Ordinance).

Perhaps the caucus's most satisfying achievement was the *coram nobis* cases (also known as "internment cases"), based on an obscure provision of federal law that permitted a "petition for a writ of error coram nobis," legal jargon meaning that the "original trial was tainted by 'fundamental error' or that the conviction resulted in 'manifest injustice' to the defendant." [58] Together with other attorneys, including those working for the Asian American Legal Defense and Education Fund, the caucus successfully filed writs to overturn the wartime convictions of Fred T. Korematsu, Gordon Hirabayashi, and Min Yasui. For the Japanese American attorneys involved in the *coram nobis* cases, "it became both a personal obsession . . . as well as a legal and political issue because [it was their] parents who were interned." [59] In affirming the convictions of these Japanese Americans, the U.S. Supreme Court had upheld the military's authority to deny a specific racial group its civil and constitutional rights. Justices Owen Roberts, Robert Jackson, and Frank Murphy filed dissents. [60] In his dissenting opinion, Justice Murphy wrote that the exclusion order "goes over the very brink of constitutional power and falls into the ugly abyss of racism" and that such a thing "is unattractive in any setting, but is utterly revolting among a free people who have embraced the principles set forth in the Constitution of the United States." [61] Along with the *Dred Scott* case, these convictions represented "what is by consensus the low-water mark in the history of the Supreme Court's treatment of civil liberties." [62]

But, as the *coram nobis* attorneys later found out, the Supreme Court's decision stood on "a factual base of fraud and deceit." [63] They had discovered documents that revealed that high officials and government attorneys had lied to the Supreme Court and knowingly suppressed, altered, and destroyed key evidence in order to ensure the convictions of the three men. Furthermore, the evidence showed that "officials knew that the claims of espionage and sabotage were false, and that the racial argument that Japanese Americans were prone to disloyalty was baseless." [64] The bitter irony, of course, was that the government officials' willingness to employ racism to make the Japanese Americans scapegoats for the nation's early defeats, notably the destruction of the Pacific fleet at Pearl Harbor, made them kindred spirits to the Axis enemies they fought against in World War II. The legacy of the *coram nobis* cases was to strengthen civil rights in the United States. Judge Marilyn Hall Patel, the federal judge who heard the reopened *Korematsu* case, noted:

> As historical precedent it stands as a constant caution that in times of war or declared military necessity our institutions must be viligant in protecting constitutional guarantees. It stands as a caution that in times of distress the shield of military necessity and national security must not be used to protect governmental actions from close scrutiny and accountability. It stands as a caution that in times of international hostility and antagonisms our institutions, legislative, executive and judicial, must be prepared to exercise their authority to protect all citizens from the petty fears and prejudices that are so easily aroused." [65]

While the Asian Law Caucus and similar organizations could be counted on to use the legal system to defend the Asian American community, the Vincent Chin tragedy proved that more was needed to protect the Asian American community. On 19 June 1982, Vincent Chin, a young Chinese American draftsman, was killed by Ronald Ebens and Michael Nitz, both of whom were unemployed autoworkers. Before bludgeoning him to death with a baseball bat, they "reviled Chin with racial obscenities and, believing him to be Japanese, allegedly blamed him for layoffs in the automobile industry"—a classic case of using Asians as scapegoats for the country's economic problems.[66] Ebens and Nitz were sentenced to three years' probation and a fine of $3,780. Asian Americans, especially Chinese Americans, were outraged by the lenient sentences. It seemed like a return to the nineteenth century, when Chinese received no protection under the law, a situation succinctly reflected in the derogatory expression "Not a Chinaman's chance." "Justice for Vincent Chin" became a rallying cry in the Asian American community, which demanded that Ebens and Nitz pay for their crime. Americans for Justice, an alternative grassroots organization, managed to get the U.S. Justice Department to indict them for violation of Chin's civil rights. In June 1984, a U.S. district court jury acquitted Nitz but found Ebens guilty and sentenced him to twenty-five years in jail. Unfortunately, during the appeal and retrial, Ebens was acquitted of all charges. Perhaps the only good thing to come out of the case was to make Asian Americans realize that they could not depend solely on the judicial system to protect them and that organized community groups would be needed to oppose anti-Asian violence.

Committee Against Anti-Asian Violence

In the wake of the Vincent Chin tragedy, there was growing concern in the Asian American community over pervasive and pernicious anti-Asian violence, as well as increasing public attention to it. In spring 1986, activists belonging to the Organization of Asian Women, Organization of Chinese Americans, and the Japanese American Citizens League came together to consider ways of dealing with this important issue. They consciously invited diverse Asian American groups in order to have the broadest possible participation. Together they formed the Committee Against Anti-Asian Violence (CAAAV) to voice the Asian American community's concerns about anti-Asian violence and police brutality in the New York City area.[67] At the time, CAAAV was one of many community organizations formed to combat racially motivated violence, which received national attention when Michael Griffith, an African American, was killed by a mob of white youths in Howard Beach in December 1986.

On 18 October 1986, in New York City, the group sponsored a half-day educational forum on "Violence against Asians in America." [68] It emphasized the root causes of anti-Asian violence and the importance of "building coalitions and bridges across diverse racial, economic, and political communities, and initiating *proactive* in addition to reactive strategies." [69] The forum drew 250 people of different political persuasions and from different sectors of the community, many of them former community activists who had dropped out of the Movement because of exhaustion or had been driven out because of sectarianism, but were now ready to return.

In follow-up meetings, forum organizers found considerable community support for a local network of organizations and individuals to oppose anti-Asian violence in New York City. Under the leadership of Mini Liu [70] and Monona Yin, who served as co-chairs, CAAAV focused on advocacy work for victims, community mobilization, documentation of incidents, public education, lobbying, and coalition building. The first case they worked on occurred in January 1987 when two European American police officers forcibly entered Wong's and Woo's apartment, assaulted four family members, and arrested them on false charges. CAAAV launched "a campaign combining community mobilization, public relations, pressure on various government agencies, and development of a legal strategy" that led "to the . . . dismissal of all charges against the victims." [71] Two years later, in a separate civil action charging the police with violating their federal and state constitutional and statutory civil rights, members of the Wong and Woo families settled out of court for $90,000. This success immediately defined CAAAV as a credible community-based organization. Since then, it has repeatedly demonstrated its ability to mobilize Asian Americans as well as other people of color to oppose racial violence and police brutality.

CAAAV's success can be attributed mainly to its leaders, all of whom have been Asian American women. As a result of the mutual trust and respect developed by their earlier association in such groups as the Organization of Asian Women, they have been able to provide coherent leadership. Culturally sensitive and politically mature, they have accepted their own limitations, such as lack of language skills and social contacts necessary to work in certain Asian ethnic enclaves. They are fully prepared to work in tandem with groups such as Korean Americans and Asian Indian Americans on cases that affect their communities directly, sharing with them their experience in dealing with the criminal justice system, community organizing, and media relations, without insisting on controlling the entire effort, as some organizations are wont to do. Meanwhile, they have tried to increase their effectiveness by translating their brochure into several Asian languages and to organize bilingual community outreach teams.

They have also been quite astute in avoiding some of the political problems that have adversely affected community-based organizations. During their first year, for instance, they braced themselves for possible incursions from Marxist–Leninist organizations. By exercising firm control over the group's activities, they prevented any possible takeover attempts and squelched sectarian outbreaks of the sort that had marred the "Justice for Vincent Chin" campaign. Except for claiming credit for work that CAAAV did, opportunistic revolutionaries have not posed much of a threat to the organization. And since no outside group manipulated CAAAV, it could mediate between rival political organizations in the community. As a nonpartisan group, CAAAV provides a safe place for independent community activists to do progressive work.

The Economics of Reform

Both social service organizations and alternative grassroots organizations, but especially the former, have encountered financial obstacles. Social service organizations have bigger budgets than grassroots organizations and depend heavily on outside sources because their clients are too poor to pay. Social service organizations have large and costly staffs, many of whom are college trained professionals. They have more clients, most of whom are from the working class and depend on them for services—even in some cases for basic subsistence. It is small wonder that social service organizations are perennially preoccupied with raising money. Most of their financial support has come from public sources, particularly the national government. While federal funds were a boon in the beginning, giving rise to many worthwhile programs, they later proved to be a bane. The Chinatown Planning Council has discovered to its dismay that relying principally on publicly funded programs has several decided disadvantages: First, these monies are frequently earmarked for something other than "trained social workers, youth workers or community organization staff who could bring that additional professional expertise to bear on the problem." [72] So CPC staff members often find themselves working in human services areas for which they are unprepared. Second, in order to acquire funds, CPC has had to modify its programs to fit the funds available (a fact that partly explains its multifaceted character). Third, unless a grant was renewed or replaced, the particular program it paid for eventually expired, even though the problem it dealt with persisted. Fourth, the drive for monies can become an end in itself.

Self-Help for the Elderly also initially benefited from federal funds but suffered severely when they were no longer available. SHE has had little choice but to diversify its funding base, relying increasingly on the community. Comparatively speaking, Asian Americans continue to esteem their elders, so SHE has found it easier to raise money from the community, most often at organized banquets in Chinatown, than have other organizations. Today SHE has an operating budget of $5 million and a staff of 180 people. Only about 60 percent of the budget comes from the federal government, a figures that appears to be about average for a social service organization.

Chinese for Affirmative Action is smaller than CPC and SHE. Its direct services have been restricted mainly to helping low-income minority clients find employment in the public and private sectors. Since its main mission has been civil rights advocacy on behalf of all Asian Americans, which is less costly than direct services, it can get by on its annual membership fees, fund-raising events in the community, and grants from private foundations and corporations.

Depending on annual membership fees has its limitations. While some Chinese Americans, especially those belonging to the professional class, have supported CAA, many have not—for instance, recently arrived immigrants and refugees. The poorer ones, preoccupied with staying alive in American society, have been unable to contribute time or money; the affluent immigrants have denied the need for civil rights advocacy. Their very success, which they attribute solely to their individual efforts, makes it difficult for them to comprehend the value of affirmative action programs. But this pattern is changing as a result of the recent controversy surrounding alleged quotas restricting their children and other Asian American students from attending the University of California at Berkeley and other prestigious campuses.

Perhaps more problematic has been obtaining the support of foundations and corporations. In this difficulty, CAA has quite a bit of company. The Asian Pacific Planning Council of Los Angeles found that Asian American organizations got a disproportionately small share of private grant monies allocated for minority programs.[73] In 1990, private foundations gave only $4.2 million, or

.17 percent of their total of $2.42 billion in grants, to Asian American agencies, even though these agencies served an ethnic community that constituted 2.9 percent of the population. Asian Americans did better with corporations, community, and family foundations, which gave them 2.4 percent of the $188.5 million awarded to minorities nationwide.

There are various reasons for this phenomenon. One of the popular explanations is that foundations and corporations have accepted the "model minority" myth and believe that Asian Americans have fewer problems than non-Asian groups. According to Kathy Owyang Turner, assistant director of CAA, foundations share a common belief that Chinese Americans are parsimonious. Since Chinese Americans are unwilling to support their own causes, why, they ask, should the foundations?[74] Robert Lee notes that this misperception was based on the first generation of Chinese in America, who were too poor to give because they were paid less than non-Asians.[75] In his study "Philanthropy and Pluralism, Misconceptions and New Findings about Chinese American Philanthropy," he points out that Chinese Americans, including the less affluent, have exhibited great generosity. Citing the huge sums of money contributed to earthquake victims in the Bay Area in 1989, Mexico in 1985, and China in 1980, he stresses that "Chinese will give when the proper appeal is made" and that "their trends for donations reflect neo-Confucian ethics that support the spirit of giving."[76] He also points out that this perception of parsimony is changing and that the number of foundations aiding the Chinese is growing.

Other social service organizations, having learned the harsh lesson taught by a succession of conservative administrations, have sought alternative means of support. Some have established income-generating enterprises such as the Koryo Village Center project of the Korean Community Center of the East Bay (KCCEB), established in 1977 by a group of social workers, students, teachers, and clergy to serve the rapidly growing Korean-speaking community in Oakland.[77] In November 1986, KCCEB purchased a 24,000-square-foot lot with a 5,000-square-foot vacant building in North Oakland, which it planned to convert into a commercial and cultural site, with space for expanded social service programs. The commercial component was designed as a "small business incubator" to stimulate small business growth and development. The cultural component was to consist of a center that could host conferences, meetings, recitals, and art exhibits. It would provide a physical gathering place for the Korean American community and a way to introduce Korean culture to others.

The Koryo Village Center, a "for-profit" venture, allowed KCCEB, a "nonprofit" community-based organization, to avail itself of sources that support community economic development such as the James Irvine Foundation, which provided a $100,000 capital grant in April 1987. It will also enhance KCCEB's long-term ability to offer sustained social services to the community by providing a regular source of income. Bong Hwan Kim, then executive director, also hoped that Koryo Village would lead other minority communities to improve their "social and economic positions . . . by taking charge of projects like this and taking the responsibility to see that they become successful instead of just leaving opportunities for private speculators." [78]

Alternative grassroots organizations also received support from public sources, including War on Poverty funds, but they depended less on public money. Some wanted it that way. Activists were ambivalent about financial assistance from government agencies (and corporate foundations), which they thought was mainly a means of exercising control over minority communities. They preferred to rely on "the community (an expression that served as a mantra for many activists)"; they believed the community could accomplish anything, given proper leadership—that is, given *their* leadership.

What support these groups actually received was mainly from a small sector of the community—the Asian American middle class. Middle-class residents who appreciated the need for a pan-Asian identity could afford to contribute money, and, more important, college students could afford to donate time. In the late 1960s and early 1970s, many college students felt more than a little guilty that their parents had been able to leave the ethnic community for the safe, prosperous, but sterile suburbs where they were the only people of color in the neighborhood. When they reached their majority, many began to gravitate toward Asian American communities in search of their ethnic roots. The quest often led them to alternative grassroots organizations, where they worked as volunteers. As long as there was a steady stream of such volunteers, these grassroots groups could continue to operate, even on shoestring budgets. The rub was that community support was far from constant and often changed with economic and political circumstances within and outside the organization.

Basement Workshop was a classic case: Circumstances changed it from an exemplary community-based organization committed to creating a distinctive Asian American culture into one serving mainstream-oriented Asian American artists. It changed because it could not put into effect an administrative structure that made survival and growth possible; insulate itself from the sectarianism in the Asian American Movement, which among other things discredited the political dimension that distinguished Asian American culture; or retain community support, which, after all, is what made it an alternative grassroots organization.

As a community-based organization that provided preprofessional training or professional experience, the Asian Law Caucus has found it easier to recruit and retain volunteers and to institutionalize itself in the Asian American community. In 1975, after successfully pressuring United Way to make it a member agency, the caucus achieved financial stability. In 1980, Don Tamaki, who was hired as executive director, developed a diversified funding base. In 1983, he was succeeded by Peggy Saika, a former social worker who was given the difficult assignment of placing the caucus on a sound administrative basis. Among other things, that meant creating internal structures to facilitate decision making; implementing a sound financial management system; developing a good relationship with the board of directors; and making plans for the future instead of simply reacting to crises, as most alternative grassroots organizations do.

Since CAAAV is younger than the other groups discussed here, it is difficult to know whether it will succumb to the problems that have afflicted other alternative grassroots organizations. It remains a comparatively small, mainly volunteer organization that emphasizes building bridges in the Asian American community and forming coalitions with other people of color. It has been able to develop an extensive support network of eighteen groups, and in 1988 it reorganized, creating a more flexible structure that allowed volunteers to join different work committees. In 1990, Milyoung Cho was hired as its first full-time organizer and coordinator. Trained at the Center for Third World Organizing in Oakland and a co-founder of Action for Community Empowerment, she also had contacts in the Korean American community and experience with multiracial organizing. In January 1991, after raising $14,000 to support its internal changes, CAAAV moved into its first office. "The move to reorganize and institutionalize comes none too soon,"[79] since bias crimes against Asian Americans had more than doubled from 1989 to 1990. According to partial data from the New York City Police Department Bias Unit, there had been a 680 percent increase in anti-Asian bias crimes since the inception of CAAAV.

Reformers, in both social service organizations and alternative grassroots organizations, constituted a new local elite, deriving political power from their control of these new community-based organizations. Gradually they assumed the traditional elite's role as representatives of the Asian American community and spokespeople to the wider society. Those working with social service organizations had the most political clout. Part of their political influence and social status resulted simply from their being college-educated professionals who headed major community institutions. But their ability to attract significant resources, in the beginning mainly War on Poverty funds, made them a power to be reckoned with. They demonstrated an understanding of government bureaucracies (and presumably the dominant society, though that is less certain) and an aptitude for gaining access to decision makers. Since they served mainly the working class, providing direct services that strengthened immigrants' chances of survival in American society, they commanded the moral high ground as well. They were shrewd enough to establish at least a working relationship with other elements in the community, including the traditional elite. Thus their erstwhile enemies became allies, if not necessarily friends, in matters that affected the community. All this is to say that they were able to institutionalize their organizations and make them an integral part of the Asian American community.

In contrast, alternative grassroots organizations have had a difficult time in finding a permanent place for themselves in the Asian American community. Their advocacy role—trying to make the welfare bureaucracy, police department, and other human service institutions more responsive to the needs of the community—has been less salient to and less appreciated by the community than direct services. The programs they did offer appealed mainly to the middle class, especially college students interested in such intellectual issues as identity, culture, and civil rights. Also, they tended to perceive themselves as an oppositional force to the established order within the community, an important role, to be sure, but one that eventually alienated some of them from the very community they hoped to help. For both social service and alternative grassroots organizations, financial problems have been a constant worry. Periodic fiscal crises resulting from federal cutbacks, especially during the conservative Reagan and Bush administrations, have given rise to disillusionment and a belief that the government's commitment to ending poverty in America is shallow and the resources it is willing to commit are inadequate to accomplish any mission meaningfully. Community-based organizations have learned that relying on federal largess placed them and the people they served at risk, and have therefore emphasized self-reliance. Still, an interventionist federal government with progressive social policies can contribute to the well-being of racial-minority communities. Through the national government's involvement in the Asian American community, many people have found some means to improve their lives. With the steady influx of Asian immigrants and refugees, the government needs to increase its support of community-based organizations if these new arrivals are to receive the help necessary to make them meaningful members of an ethnically pluralist America.

In the Asian American Movement, reformers and their community-based organizations have often been openly ridiculed for being, well, "reformist." According to their revolutionary rivals, their programs were by definition nothing more than a palliative on festering sores in the Asian American community. True, reformers had no panacea for the community's problems, nor did they ever claim to have one. They devoted themselves to delivering human services and providing scarce resources that improved lives in the community. And, as Harold Lui, director of the New York Chinatown Health Clinic, once observed, there was nothing wrong with that. Revolutionaries, in contrast, argued that only a comprehensive sociopolitical transformation of the nation would solve the problems of the Asian American community. But, as the next chapter discusses, they were hard put to carry out this solution.

7   The Emergence and Eclipse of Maoist Organizations

> "What is the correct strategy for
> organizing Asian Americans?" It's
> ridiculous to think in terms of a one-
> dimensional strategy. The sectarian
> says: "Your heads are in a wrong
> place. You should be into this, rather
> than that." There might be some truth
> in what he says, but to try to make the
> diverse reality of the Asian American
> experience fit into a single, narrow
> mold of analysis is foolish, and
> becomes destructive to achieving
> any kind of real unity.
>   —"Asian Nation," *Gidra*

Some members of the early phase of the Asian American Movement had received their political baptism in the New Left student movement.[1] They constituted some of the Movement's most politically progressive elements, bringing with them pertinent parts of the New Left's ideology, goals, and tactics; but they also brought with them its problems, notably sectarianism. In the late 1960s, Students for a Democratic Society (SDS) and similar groups were rent over whether the New Left should continue to be a coalition of locally based groups that adhered to the ideal of participatory democracy or should move toward a centrally controlled organization.[2] Under the influence of European existentialists such as Albert Camus, author of *The Rebel*, and American intellectuals such as C. Wright Mills, author of *The Power Elite*, members of the New Left had originally embraced the humanistic socialism of the young Karl Marx as far better suited to the circumstances of postindustrial America than the later, Old Left emphasis on a vanguard party stressing working-class militancy. During the early 1960s, they deemed Marxism–Leninism "dated and irrelevant," rejected the so-called scientific socialism of the Second and Third Communist Internationale as "dogmatism," and focused on personal liberation. Indeed, they had a profound distrust of anything that was beyond their personal control, believing it would become corrupt. But by the late 1960s, because of their inability to stop the Vietnam War, many members of the New Left became disillusioned with idealism. Frustrated with the slow pace of change in American society, they sought speedier solutions to the social problems with which they were struggling. As a result of their experiences in the civil rights and antiwar movements, many of them focused increasingly on the nature of American state and society and began a reappraisal of Marxism–Leninism, which seemed to offer a comprehensive explanation for and a way to solve these problems. Concluding that the capitalist system of the United States was responsible for creating injustice at home and aggression abroad and that conventional means of change, such as the electoral system, was ineffectual, they advocated the elimination of capitalism, through violence if necessary.

As SDS and the New Left in general disintegrated over how best to change America and degenerated into what Todd Gitlin aptly called "screaming factions,"[3] Marxism–Leninism–Mao Tse-tung Thought (henceforth referred to as MLMTT, a cumbersome acronym popular during the 1970s) became the ideology of choice. Rejecting the moralism and idealism of the early New Left as a "petty bourgeois" phenomenon, radicals followed what they believed to be the "science of revolution." In doing so, they unwittingly resurrected, more or less, the style of the Old Left. In the wake of the New Left's decline, a plethora of radical political organizations emerged. There were the infamous Weathermen, whose nihilism captured the popular imagination and whose terrorism captured the attention of the police. There were also groups that wanted a new New Left that was better organized and more disciplined than its predecessor, one that was able to acquire political power and effect serious social change. Generally discounting ethnic nationalism (and, by extension, America's ethnically pluralist ideals), they focused on capital–labor relations. Each group usually began as an informal collective that evolved into a national organization through the consolidation of smaller left groups. Each was committed to building a single, unified left movement in the United States, preferably under its own organization's leadership. Consequently, the various groups were in competition with one another to establish a new revolutionary party that would displace the moribund Communist party, U.S.A. The new party would, it was hoped, fulfill the original mission of overturning the nation's monopoly capitalist system, which had given rise to imperialism, and replace it with a socialist one that would be rational, humane, and able to redistribute society's wealth equitably.

These new radical organizations, such as the Progressive Labor party, Revolutionary Communist party, and the Communist party (Marxist–Leninist), reverted to classic communist methods, establishing clandestine, conspiratorial, Leninist-style organizations. They believed that socialist consciousness was not a natural attribute of the working class but a characteristic of professional revolutionaries, who would inject that consciousness into the masses. In other words, their cadres would be a class-conscious proletarian vanguard that would lead and educate an American working class that had been seduced by and integrated into the capitalist system.

Marxist–Leninist organizations everywhere practiced democratic centralism, a system in which decisions were made by a central committee at the top and relayed down to the rank and file. "Democratic" meant that decisions were made by majority vote in the central committee of the party and that individual cadres could pass their opinions up the chain of command. "Centralism" meant that decisions were made by the leaders and were binding on all party members. In practice, the tendency was to emphasize "centralism" over "democratic," presumably because of real or imagined exigencies. Discipline was imperative and dissent impermissible. The process fostered fanaticism, which manifested itself in self-righteous behavior and the active intolerance of liberals—traits evident in the endless arguments among friends and foes alike.

The new Marxist–Leninist parties in the United States implicitly agreed with Lenin that the principle of "broad democracy" in party organization was nothing more than a "useless and harmful toy."[4] They saw no historical precedent for participatory democracy in revolutionary organizations. Besides, mass democracy only made a party organization vulnerable to infiltration by the "Red Squad" of local police forces, the Federal Bureau of Investigation, and other internal security agencies. Agencies like the FBI did indeed operate counterintelligence programs to infiltrate radical organizations,[5] but the most threatening enemies proved to be other Marxist–Leninist organizations. The revolutionary parties had few qualms about using the broad democratic principles of other groups to influence them and even to seize control over them. These activities were as disruptive in the New Left as the "hostile takeovers" of corporations were on Wall Street during the 1980s.

The decline of the New Left and the emergence of Marxist–Leninist organizations were manifested in the Asian American Movement as well. Never fully comfortable in white-dominated organizations such as SDS and inspired by ethnic nationalist groups such as the Black Panthers, Asian Americans began founding their own radical left groups. In the beginning, Asian American activists were chiefly concerned with building pride and resisting oppression. After developing a heightened consciousness of themselves as members of an oppressed racial minority, many returned to "the community"—the Chinatowns, Little Tokyos, and Manilatowns that had continued into the 1970s—to help their people achieve self-determination and self-reliance. But many became dissatisfied with reform and wanted to get at the root causes of community problems. At this point, they moved away from a concern with ethnic consciousness and toward a commitment to revolutionary change.

In their search for self-determination, many Asian American revolutionaries were inspired by the national liberation movements in Asia. Dubbing the Asian American community an internal colony that needed to be liberated, they wanted to emulate the Viet Cong, who were waging an effective guerrilla war against American imperialism in Vietnam. Better yet, they wanted to model themselves on the Chinese Communists, who had freed the Chinese people from Western and Japanese imperialism and made the country into a regional power. They found inspiration in the fact that under the Chinese Communists, the People's Republic of China (PRC) had the potential to become a superpower on a par with the United States and the Soviet Union. Moreover, the PRC supported armed revolutionary movements in Third World countries and constituted an alternative within the communist world to the Soviet Union, which was condemned for revisionism, that is, embracing capitalist values and practices. Indeed, the enthusiasm for the PRC was so widespread that it became fashionable among American leftists to don so-called Mao suits and spout Maoist aphorisms found in the *Quotations from Chairman Mao Tse-tung*.[6]

Like most people in the New Left, Asian American revolutionaries had a romantic view of the PRC. Among their most compelling images was one of a China that had eliminated hunger for the first time in its long history; in reality, the Chinese people still suffered from starvation, the worst period being the famine of 1959–1961, but few Asian American revolutionaries seemed aware of that. Asian American revolutionaries admired the Great Proletarian Cultural Revolution (1966–1976) as an effort to maintain China's revolutionary integrity, identify with the "masses," and avoid the bureaucratic sclerosis that had doomed other socialist states; they could not see that, in actuality, it was a political power struggle that brought the country to the brink of civil war.

Asian American revolutionaries believed that what made the Chinese powerful was Mao Tse-tung's Communist party, which had creatively mixed MLMTT with aspects of Chinese culture and emphasized identification with the "masses" to create a strong and united China that would be able to take its proper place in the world. Many concluded that America needed a similar party and ideology. They spent much of the 1970s studying MLMTT and laying the groundwork for such an organization. Often Maoist sects had their beginnings as study groups in which members read the canonical works and examined other ideas and documents that were circulating in the radical community.

Most of these radical study groups eventually disappeared or were absorbed by national organizations. Though most collectives were small and short lived, some became dissatisfied with their local role and aspired to become the new revolutionary party that would replace the allegedly defunct CPUSA. As one radical who belonged to Fan Di observed, "We didn't have the power to be 'The Party.' Everyone was claiming to be 'The Party' at that time."[7] Only a handful of these groups attained prominence outside their local area. Among the most significant Maoist sects in the Asian American Movement were the Red Guard party, Wei Min She, I Wor Kuen, and the Asian Study Group.

The Red Guard Party

The earliest and best known of the revolutionary groups was the Red Guard party.[8] It consisted of the more politicized elements of Leway, a youth organization discussed in Chapter 1. Its beginnings were similar to Leway's in that it resulted less from a conscious design than from circumstances—in this case the "police riot" in San Francisco's Chinatown during the Chinese New Year's festivities in February 1969. Members of the then defunct Leway were trying to maintain public order at the celebration, but some of the more belligerent police on duty took exception to their effort and arrested one of them, an action that provoked the wrath of other youth, who promptly "unarrested" their friend. Tom Wolfe, in his sensationalized piece "The New Yellow Peril" provided a vivid description of what happened: "The Red Guard has mounted the barricades. . . . It's the crowd versus the Tac squad. Boys in black surround the paddy wagon. Bottles, bricks and all sorts of shit rain down from the rooftops. Cats are throwing cherry bombs dipped in glue and studded with broken glass . . . suzy wong flower drum song no tickee no tong war no wonton." [9] Wolfe was wrong about one thing: There was no Red Guard, at least not at that time. The Red Guard party came into existence only after the melee.

Some of the youths went to the *Berkeley Barb*, a famous alternative newspaper of the period, to explain how the riot had occurred. In their side of the story, the riot was a struggle between the police and a revolutionary group— until then unheard of—called the "Red Dragons." In some respects the lie was less a prevarication than a self-fulfilling prophecy of the police—the expectation that a militant revolutionary group might develop out of an alliance between Leway and Wah Ching, the largest youth gang in Chinatown. Having announced the existence of the group, the storytellers decided to found one. One of the first things they did was to change its name. Red Dragon sounded too much like a Chinese secret society, so they adopted the name of the revolutionary youth then active in China—the Red Guards. While the Guards had certain parallels with their namesakes, they were really patterned after the Black Panthers, whose militancy and sexist attitudes toward women they embraced. (Red Guards too believed that since they would become casualties in the revolutionary struggle, "their" women should remain at home and raise revolutionary successors.) [10] The Black Panther Party for Self-Defense was founded in Oakland in 1966 by Bobby Seale, who served as its chairman, and Huey P. Newton, who served as its minister of defense.[11] The Panthers were organized along military lines and advocated armed resistance to racial oppression, especially the police, whom they perceived as an army of occupation in the black urban ghetto.

The Red Guards' goal was simple: community power. Alex Hing, minister of information, put it this way, "We're going to attain power, so we don't have to beg anymore." [12] Like the Black Panthers, the Red Guards perceived themselves as the defenders of their ethnic community and worked to achieve justice for its inhabitants. To free downtrodden Chinese from exploitation, they were prepared to confront the police. Their activities brought mixed results. The breakfast program attracted few Chinese children. Presumably, Chinese parents were too embarrassed to send their children or were able to feed them in spite of their poverty; so the Red Guards used the food to feed senior citizens at the park in Portsmouth Square. Still, the program probably won them the support of some members of the community, including criminals, who occa-

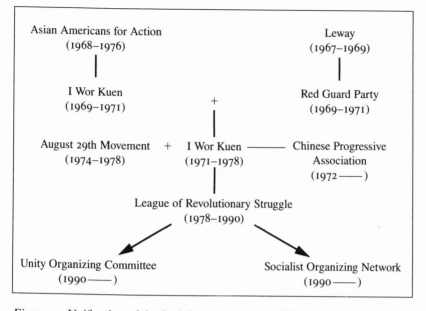

Figure 1: Unification of the Red Guard Party and I Wor Kuen

sionally donated food that they had stolen from local warehouses. But the effort to turn erstwhile street youths into revolutionary cadres was inherently flawed. As with most participants in the Asian American Movement, the former Leway members were more interested in finding a place for themselves in American society than in changing it in any fundamental way. After the Red Guard party merged with I Wor Kuen (see Figure 1), only a few of the Red Guards remained to do serious revolutionary work; the rest went on to find jobs and raise families.

The rallies at Portsmouth Square were probably the Red Guards' most significant community activity, certainly its most celebrated, for they tapped latent nationalist feelings (i.e., pro-PRC sentiment) of Chinatown residents and openly challenged the authority of the Chinese Six Companies, which was viewed as an extension of the Kuomintang (KMT, the Nationalist party) and its rump government in Taiwan.[13] In opposing the Six Companies, the Red Guards were one with the Chinese American reformers discussed in Chapter 5. Together, they eroded the authority of the traditional leadership, paved the way for other organizations, liberal and progressive, and ultimately helped to alter the power structure in Chinatown.

The Red Guards captured the imagination of Asian American student activists, most of whom were from the middle class and who romanticized street life, seeing street youth as one of the *éléments déclassés* that Mao Tse-tung was so fond of. As a young man, Mao had believed that members of the lumpenproletariat could be transformed by suitable political training into the vanguard of the proletariat. Revolutionaries belonging to Wei Min She, the Red Guard party's arch rival, disagreed. As far as they were concerned, youths who were, in their eyes, juvenile delinquents had no role in the revolution.

Wei Min She

In 1972, the Asian Community Center (ACC, see Chapter 1) had reached a critical juncture. Even though it had become a recognized force in Chinatown, its members were increasingly dissatisfied with reform and wanted to get at the fundamental causes of the community's ills. They came to believe that the "problems on the job, in the schools, or in the community [were] a direct result of the economic system of monopoly capitalism (imperialism)—a system controlled by a small class who owns the majority of wealth while everyone else works in one way or another for a living." [14] So that year they made an "organizational leap" and became Wei Min She (literally, Organization for the People). [15]

Wei Min She (WMS) described itself as an Asian American anti-imperialist organization committed to the "revolution." And ACC served as its "mass organization," an institution that allowed WMS to accommodate less political people and extend its influence into the Chinese community. [16] But in many respects, WMS remained ACC. According to Steve Yip, a WMS leader, ideologically WMS continued to focus on the local community, rather than anti-imperialist issues; organizationally, it continued to have a steering committee with decisions made by the membership, rather than a cadre organization that practiced "democratic centralism." [17] It took the group about a year to get beyond "reductionist thinking," that is, a community orientation, and become more "internationalist" in outlook.

Meanwhile, WMS involved itself in the Lee Mah electronics and Jung Sai garment workers' struggles for unionization. The radical press reported poor working conditions at Lee Mah and Jung Sai. [18] At both factories there were attempts to unionize workers. But at Lee Mah the effort was frustrated when the vote on unionization was declared null and void by mutual agreement between the Teamsters Union and the owner, and the latter began firing workers, most of whom had been sympathetic to the union. After receiving no further help from the Teamsters, the workers went to Chinese for Affirmative Action, which helped them hire a lawyer. At Jung Sai, on their third attempt, workers were able to get 90 out of 135 workers to sign pledge cards, allowing them to hold an election on whether or not to join Local 101, International Garment Workers Union (ILGWU), AFL-CIO. Apparently in an act of reprisal, the owners fired a union advocate, and on 15 July 1974 the workers went on strike to protest this action and other unfair labor practices and to demand better working conditions and the right to unionize. The strike lasted six months, after which the plant closed down and the work was contracted out to other shops. The workers brought a suit before the National Relations Labor Board, which finally ruled in their favor in 1983.

Wei Min She actively supported both the Lee Mah electronics workers and the Jung Sai garment workers. In the latter effort it was joined by other left groups, notably I Wor Kuen, and members of the Chinatown community. WMS saw these workers' struggles as the stirrings of a new class consciousness among workers in the community. It wanted to be the leader of the emerging workers' movement, a goal shared by other Asian American groups. But instead of working through the unions, as was usually the case, WMS worked independently, holding its own public demonstrations, trying unsuccessfully to link the Lee Mah and Jung Sai struggles, and during the Jung Sai strike establishing its own support committee in opposition to and in competition with the ILGWU.

This last move was in accord with WMS's long-term goal of establishing a multinational workers' movement that was separate from the American labor movement. But WMS's strategy was criticized by I Wor Kuen, which accused WMS of being opportunistic and placing its narrow organizational interests ahead of the workers. And the Jung Sai workers' strike committee found WMS's support committee sufficiently counterproductive to issue its own statement outlining three principles: "(1) Our demand is to join the International Ladies' Garment Workers Union; (2) final decision-making power lies with the workers strike committee; (3) *during the course of this labor dispute, we do not want to be dragged into any other political activities and/or propaganda*" [19] (emphasis added).

During its brief existence, WMS had numerous differences with the Red

Guard party and I Wor Kuen, which WMS considered ineffectual because of their lumpenproletariat base and preoccupation with narrow ethnic nationalist issues. But WMS discovered an affinity with the Revolutionary Union (RU; originally, Bay Area Revolutionary Union), founded in 1968 by Bob Avakian and other former SDS members as a militant, semiclandestine organization and heavily involved in the U.S.–China Friendship Association's efforts to normalize relations between the United States and the People's Republic of China. RU's objectives were the "development of a united front against imperialism, the fostering of revolutionary working class unity and leadership in struggle, and the formation of a Community Party based on Marxism–Leninism–Mao Tse-tung Thought, leading to the overthrow of the United States Government by force and violence."[20]

In 1975, deciding that it was ready to do more advanced revolutionary work, WMS merged with the Revolutionary Union to form the Revolutionary Communist party (RCP; see Figure 2). Under the leadership of Avakian, RCP anticipates the eventual overthrow of the U.S. government by violent means, a social upheaval that will be initiated by an economic depression or some other internal crisis. Meanwhile, RCP members spend their time honing their understanding of Marxist–Leninist theories. They also manage Revolution Books, a chain of bookstores probably modeled on Everybody's Bookstore, opened in January 1970 by WMS, in its earlier incarnation as ACC. Recently, they have engaged in such provocative actions as burning the American flag at rallies and demonstrations in order to ignite a "spark" that will start the revolution.[21] Ironically, burning the flag led the U.S. Supreme Court in 1989 to decree that the act was an expression of "free speech," hence protected by the First Amendment.[22] Among Asian Americans revolutionaries, RCP is known for supporting the discredited and disgraced "Gang of Four," which has been held responsible for the havoc wreaked by the Cultural Revolution in China.

I Wor Kuen

WMS's main political rival in the Asian American Movement was I Wor Kuen (literally, Righteous and Harmonious Fists). Founded in 1969 in New York's Chinatown, IWK was named after a peasant organization that tried to expel foreigners from China in the Boxer Rebellion (1900).[23] Its members identified with the "revolutionary spirit" of the Boxers and rejected the stereotype of

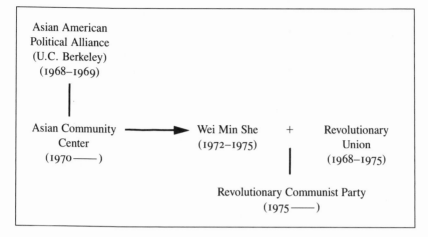

Figure 2: Radicalization of Wei Min She

Chinese as passive victims of exploitation. A militant group with revolution-ary aspirations, IWK traced its origins primarily to second-generation Chinese Americans who had participated in Triple A and Columbia University's Asian American Political Alliance.[24] Later, the group expanded to include foreign-born Chinese, some of whom were former youth-gang members that IWK members had worked with in Chinatown. IWK believed with Mao that mem-bers of the lumpenproletariat were potentially the vanguard of the revolution. That was the basis for its later unity with the Red Guard party.

IWK's militancy was a reflection of its members' earlier involvement in the student and antiwar movements and their distance from the Chinatown commu-nity. Some of them came from comparatively affluent families that lived outside Chinatown; hence they were less interested in addressing the social needs of the community and "less vulnerable to intimidation" from the conservative elite that controlled it. IWK's proposed long-term solution to Chinatown's problems was to replace the existing capitalist society with a socialist one. This was the last and most important goal of its "12 Point Platform and Program," an agenda similar to those espoused by the Black Panthers and the Young Lords, a Puerto Rican revolutionary group.

In February 1969, IWK opened a storefront in Chinatown to prepare the community for the "revolution," which during those heady days seemed im-minent. In January 1970, it began publishing a monthly bilingual newspaper called *Getting Together*, a highly rhetorical publication that stressed the need to organize Chinatown and transform it into a revolutionary base. The newspaper devoted much space to national liberation struggles around the world but paid particular attention to the People's Republic of China, with which it had a special affinity. It also carried reports on the oppressive conditions in Chinatown. As a political organ, *Getting Together* was quite conventional; still, it had considerable appeal to Asian American leftists who sympathized with its aspirations and understood its political jargon.

In the first issue of *Getting Together*, IWK members announced their revolutionary intent: "We are not out to demand this phony reform or that, but to fight for the total self-determination of the Asian people in Chinatown." [25] But it was humanly impossible to be in Chinatown without becoming acutely aware of the pressing need for reform. And IWK was astute enough to realize that ideology alone was insufficient to win the "hearts and minds" of the people there. Furthermore, providing social services in Chinatown would give IWK members an opportunity to work with and recruit Asian American professionals. Its health clinic was its most successful program because of the Chinatown residents' unattended physical and psychological problems, the worst of which was tuberculosis. IWK members learned to administer the simple TB tine test and began a block-by-block TB test canvass of Chinatown. People who showed signs of having TB were taken to area clinics for X-rays. Later, a clinic was opened in the IWK storefront to treat people and disseminate information on preventive health care.

Even though social service programs gave IWK a base in Chinatown, they were still secondary to mobilizing Chinatown for the revolution. To that end, IWK initiated or participated in a number of militant actions in Chinatown. One of its most notorious efforts was the Tourist Bus Demonstration, which was later perceived as an erroneous effort to protect the community from outsiders. On 19 April 1970, IWK began to protest the "presence of tourists who arrive[d] in Chinatown on tourist buses [and] ridicule[d] the Chinese and crowded the Chinese of Chinatown off the sidewalks." [26] IWK appeared to be emulating its namesake and was hell-bent on expelling "foreigners" from Chinese territory. Rockwell Chin has noted that the demonstration was misunderstood: It was aimed not at tourists per se but "against 'whistle-stop' tour groups which shoved people onto the streets and patronized only one restaurant (by prior agreement) on Pell Street." [27] In any event, it was considered a demonstration against all tourists and therefore an attack on the tourism industry—the economic foundation of the community. Local merchants and restaurateurs who depended on tourists for their livelihood felt threatened. The next day the Chinese Consolidated Benevolent Association draped a large sign in front of its building to welcome all tourists to Chinatown and added one more item to their growing list of grievances against IWK.

Meanwhile, IWK was struggling internally against "terrorist" and "ultramilitary" tendencies that would have relegated women to a subservient position in the organization.[28] A few of its members advocated the end of monogamy as a means to "liberate" relations between men and women, but others recognized this sophistry for what it was—a chauvinist ploy to exploit women sexually. By the time that the Red Guard party and I Wor Kuen merged and established a national organization in 1971, these tendencies had been corrected, strengthening the organization and paving the way for more of its women to assume leadership roles.

Its dearth of human and material resources notwithstanding, IWK decided to go national and opened a second storefront in San Francisco on 21 August 1971, thus becoming the first national organization dedicated to the fight for Asian American self-determination. For some Asian American radical groups, such as the J-Town Collective, this move signaled the beginning of a united Asian revolutionary movement in the United States.[29] IWK built on the foundation laid by the Red Guards, who had dissolved a month earlier and whose former members, including Alex Hing, brought to IWK a wealth of knowledge and experience. IWK's San Francisco branch sponsored activities similar to those in New York City. But these activities proved insufficient to mobilize the "masses."

IWK learned that there were limitations to being a Maoist group in Chinatown. As we discuss later, opponents like the Chinese Six Companies in San Francisco and the Chinese Consolidated Benevolent Association in New York City made life difficult as well as dangerous for IWK's members. More important, IWK could not attract adequate community support, despite its various social services. Rather than rally people, its revolutionary ideology and actions alienated them. Chinatown residents and organizations were wary about working with Maoists.

The solution was the founding, in spring 1972, of the Chinese Progressive Association (CPA).[30] Several years later, other branches were established in

New York City, Boston, and Los Angeles. Legally, CPA is a nonprofit "legal welfare organization to service the community."[31] Calling itself a "mass organization," it is supposedly a broad-based, grassroots group that progressive people of different political persuasions can join without committing themselves to carrying out the revolution. But the FBI considers it "a front organization" for IWK, to which several of its leaders belong.[32] Its primary purpose was to recruit IWK members and to carry out IWK's political agenda in Chinatown; its secondary purpose was to offer social services and serve as a community advocate. CPA members vehemently dispute this characterization: "The Chinese Progressive Association was never a 'front' group for any organization. Its politics, program and activities have been determined in a democratic way. There are many members of CPA with dual membership in other groups (including churches, clubs, the Democratic Party and left organizations)."[33]

During the 1970s, both purposes came together when CPA participated in the nationwide campaign to normalize diplomatic relations between the United States and the People's Republic of China. CPA (and by extension IWK) derived considerable benefits from the normalization drive, which appealed to the nationalist sentiments of Chinatown's residents. Among other things, it brought CPA into contact with community residents who identified culturally and emotionally with China and with a coalition of community organizations, including other Maoist groups, such as the Revolutionary Union.[34]

Besides the effort to normalize U.S.–China relations, which was finally successful in January 1979, CPA has sponsored some modest social service programs aimed at the working class in Chinatown, as well as political education programs to empower Chinese Americans to defend themselves against discrimination and fight for their civil rights. One of its more popular services has been its after-school program to teach Chinese to Chinese American elementary school children "as part of bridging the gap which develops when children go to public school."[35] In 1976, CPA experienced an internal political conflict over its direction, presumably over whether it should sponsor more reform programs or assume a more political posture in the community. CPA's political work is done by smaller groups, such as the Workers' Mutual Aid Committee, which offers counseling on workers' rights and general education for Chinese workers, and the Housing Committee, which assists residents in the area of tenants' rights.

Finally, CPA has also worked on a myriad of *ad hoc* issues that have cropped up over the last two decades. It has joined community coalitions to defend the I-Hotel, fight for redress and reparations for Japanese Americans, oppose the *Bakke* decision, obtain justice for Vincent Chin and Chol Soo Lee, work against the passage of the Simpson–Mazzoli immigration bill, support Jesse Jackson, and so on. Unfortunately, these occasions have also brought CPA into conflict with other groups, most notably its nemesis: Asian Americans for Equality, a mass organization whose origins can be traced in part to the Asian Study Group.

Asian Study Group

Among the major Maoist sects, the Asian Study Group (ASG) was probably the least known, even though it played a pivotal role in the Asian American left's eventual decline into sectarianism and violence. It replaced WMS as IWK's main political antagonist within the Movement. Unlike IWK and WMS, ASG was the brainchild of a single individual, Jerry Tung.

Tung's admirers consider him a brilliant thinker with an authoritative grasp of MLMTT. His early followers, most of whom were young and impressionable, were taken with his conviction and his ability to support arguments with precise references to V. I. Lenin and G. V. Plekhanov, a Russian social democrat who wrote on the economic development of Russia. Equally important, he had "correct" credentials. In 1969, he had been sent to jail for a year on twenty-nine counts of "conspiracy to riot." [36] His detractors were unimpressed and saw him as an unstable personality with suicidal tendencies.[37] Some speculate that his psychological problems are rooted in the lynching of his father by the Ku Klux Klan in 1951 in North Carolina—a theory that would at least explain the tragic confrontation between Tung's group and members of the Ku Klux Klan in Greensboro, North Carolina, in fall 1979.

During the New Left student movement of the 1960s, Jerry Tung was a member of the Progressive Labor party (PL) at the State University of New York at Stony Brook. For reasons that are unclear, Tung left PL in search of another radical organization to work with. But none proved to be receptive to his ideas, especially the need for a new party to replace the CPUSA, so in 1973 he formed his own organization in New York City—the Asian Study Group. ASG consisted of radical Asian American students from City College of New York and other campuses, including some who had participated in the

Third World strike at Berkeley. It was a self-styled antirevisionist collective that studied MLMTT literature. It was a relatively intellectual group consisting of mainly college students. All ASG members were required to study MLMTT to prepare them to wage an ideological struggle with their rivals, many of whom were at a disadvantage because their members were community activists without the benefit of higher education and extensive ideological training. Instead, the latter relied on their practical organizing experience and the "wisdom" encapsulated in the *Quotations from Chairman Mao Tse-tung*.

Among the materials that ASG members pored over, the most significant was Lenin's famous pamphlet "What Is to Be Done?" Like Lenin, Tung believed that the answer lay in establishing a vanguard party of revolutionaries. Tung advocated building a "true" communist party to supersede the defunct CPUSA, which he accused of having "punked out of going for the imperialist's jugular vein" after World War II.[38] His contempt for the CPUSA was shared by the New Left community, which considered it to be nothing more than a puppet of Moscow (therefore, a supporter of Soviet socialist imperialism), infiltrated by the FBI, and manipulated by both. But many in the New Left thought that establishing a party was premature; instead, they believed that the principal task was building a revolutionary, anti-imperialist mass base.

IWK, for instance, believed that "greater work needed to be done among the masses in order to firmly plant the roots for revolution" and publicly opposed what it called the ASG's "ultra-rightist line," criticizing it for "following in the footsteps of the Progressive Labor Party, and for belittling the mass work conducted in the Asian American Movement."[39] As far as the ASG was concerned, such criticism was simply jealousy. As one former member noted, "from the beginning when Jerry started his group, IWK could never forgive him. IWK was the top shot at the time; they thought they were the most advanced and the most committed among the Asians. And 'who the hell did he think he was to come in, fight with them, say they're wrong, start another group, and undermine their work?' "[40]

Tung thought that the Asian American Movement's "serve the people" programs were mere "Band-Aids" and that the many small Asian American collectives around the nation were engaged in sporadic and sophomoric exercises. What was needed was a centralized party, working with a carefully thought out plan—in fact, a vanguard party consisting of professional revolutionaries who recognized the necessity of class conflict for the eventual triumph of the working class.[41] Ideally, the party would articulate the general will of the proletariat; but its primary mission was to decide what would be the correct strategy for the liberation of the masses and then lead the struggle rather than rely on a spontaneous upheaval.

Building a revolutionary party meant abandoning the tactic of "uniting" (often a euphemism for taking over) the groups that came out of the New Left student movement and replacing it with the tactic of educating the "advanced worker." That involved going among the working class to "consolidate," that is, identify and recruit, these advanced workers, then educating them to become communist leaders. The competition for "advanced workers" was fierce. ASG had to compete with trade unions and community organizations as well as its New Left rivals for these workers. The scarcity of such people meant that it had to resort to such expedients as retooling its middle-class members by sending them out to work in industry, where they acquired working-class credentials and brought "correct politics to the historically predestined agency of change."[42] It was an earnest effort to legitimate themselves as a party of the working class and to distance themselves from their student movement origins. Some of these people did develop a working-class consciousness and identity. One member, for example, went to work as a steelworker for several years at U.S. Steel. While there, she was involved in union activity and was a founding member of a local committee organized to fight for women's rights in the steel mills. She was fully prepared to work in the mill for as long as it was required of her, but ASG ordered her as well as other Midwest members to go to New York City to work on other issues. For most ASG members, however, the stint in industry was a temporary political assignment and an indispensable part of a cadre's curriculum vitae. The fact that members could return to their middle-class lives if they wanted to (and after the sectarianism and violence of the 1970s, many of them did) made the experience essentially a piece of revolutionary theater in which they temporarily assumed the role of workers. Authentic workers have only one life to lead and one class to belong to.

Another method that ASG used to increase its numbers of "advanced workers" was to establish mass organizations in Chinatown that recruited people with progressive political interests. Unquestionably, its most effective front was Asian Americans for Equal Employment (AAFEE).[43] According to its own history, AAFEE was "founded in 1974 by a group of professionals, students, senior citizens and community residents who were concerned about the lack of Chinese construction workers employed building Confucius Plaza, the first housing complex funded with federal money." [44] But this is a self-serving (and perhaps self-deluding) interpretation that gives the illusion of broad community support from the beginning and masks the fact that AAFEE was used primarily as a vehicle for identifying, educating, and recruiting people into ASG.

Confucius Plaza was a 764-unit cooperative that included a school, day-care center, and some commercial outlets. It was being built by the DeMatteis construction firm. After being rebuffed by Al DeMatteis, who refused to accept a petition signed by eight thousand people calling for the hiring of more Asian Americans, AAFEE organized protests at the site. From 16 May 1974 onward, AAFEE demonstrated against job discrimination in the construction industry in general and at the Confucius Plaza site in particular. Its immediate demand was for the hiring of forty Asian American workers and an Asian American investigator to monitor hiring practices; its general demand was for "government, unions and contractors to remedy 'the century-old pattern of exclusion of Asian-Americans by establishing specific employment goals.' " [45]

The protests were meticulously planned and carried out and had the widespread support of the Chinatown community, as well as members of Fight Back, Black Economic Survival, and the Black and Puerto Rican Coalition. At the demonstrations, "several hundred pickets, from schoolgirls carrying their books to wizened members of the Chinese Golden Age Club, marched and chanted outside the Confucius Plaza construction site," displaying signs that said, "The Asians built the railroad: Why not Confucius Plaza" and "DeMatteis, you are a big racist." [46] Dozens of young protestors were arrested for trespassing and disorderly conduct when they climbed over the fence into the site or tried to block traffic. AAFEE believed that its "strategy of working with other minority groups and the tactics of protest, arrest, and rallies [were] essential in the struggle against De Matteis"—that this was what was needed to get him to the negotiating table. [47] It was a belief based in part on the recent history of other people of color. While such protests were new to Chinatown, they had been happening in African American and Puerto Rican communities in New York City throughout the previous decade.

The only group to withhold its support was the Chinese Consolidated Benevolent Association (CCBA). According to its chairman, Man Bun Lee, CCBA supported the aim of more jobs for Chinese but disagreed with AAFEE's methods, preferring negotiation to demonstration. Acting on that belief, he offered to negotiate with the DeMatteis organization and to set up a placement office for job seekers. He attributed the CCBA's position to generational differences: "This generation has education, they are more or less Americanized and they do things the American way . . . the older people try to do it the Chinese way." [48] (Presumably, Lee meant the conservative Asian preference for a low profile and indirect influence.) The CCBA's unwillingness to support such a popular cause reflected how out of touch it was with the community, and its inability to mediate the dispute with DeMatteis reflected its waning influence.

After months of protest, AAFEE triumphed, much to the astonishment of a community grown accustomed to suffering in silence. It was able to negotiate a settlement with DeMatteis, who promised twenty-four jobs to Chinese workers and got charges against the protestors dropped. As a result of these achievements, AAFEE became a credible community organization in Chinatown and a magnet that attracted activists. Rather than rest on its laurels, AAFEE planned on "more breakthroughs in other industries to include equal employment for Asian Americans." [49] But during fall 1974, it shifted its emphasis from equal employment for Asian Americans to civil rights issues. Apparently, ASG decided to broaden the scope of its political work in Chinatown and to challenge the traditional authority of CCBA through AAFEE.

Among the issues that AAFEE focused on, the most important was police brutality and harassment in Chinatown. The first case it protested occurred on 26 April 1975, when Peter Yew, an architectural engineer, was beaten by police during a minor traffic altercation.[50] Along with CCBA, AAFEE was part of a broad coalition to protest Yew's arrest and demand an end to "police brutality, oppression and racial discrimination." [51] But AAFEE also held its own protests—including one against CCBA, which it accused of having "sold out the people" in negotiations with City Hall. On 19 May 1975, about two thousand protesters demonstrated in front of CCBA headquarters, pelting it with eggs. In fall 1975, in order to garner more support, AAFEE members went around the country holding forums to discuss police brutality and the Confucius Plaza struggle. The strategy of shifting to civil rights issues was a success, for it increased awareness of racial oppression of Chinese Americans (and Asian Americans in general) and politicized Chinatown residents. Perhaps more important, it enhanced AAFEE's reputation as a community organization and nurtured a cadre of experienced political workers adept at managing mass movements in an Asian American community.

In 1976, Tung thought the time was ripe to establish a more advanced politi-

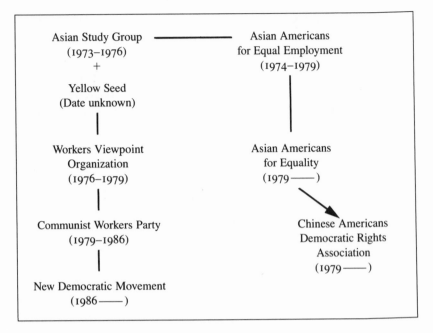

Figure 3: Evolution of the Asian Study Group

cal organization—the Workers Viewpoint Organization (WVO; see Figure 3). As one former member noted, it was an ironic choice of name since the "ASG didn't have whole-hearted faith in the views of the working class." [52] WVO was created mainly through the merging of ASG and Yellow Seed, another Marxist–Leninist collective, based in Philadelphia.

Toward the end of the decade, Tung was prepared to take the final step: establishing a new revolutionary party to replace the old CPUSA. But at this crucial juncture, AAFEE (now Asian Americans for Equality, or AAFE, a name change that reflected its broader concerns with civil rights issues yet retained a phonetic link to its past) experienced internal turmoil. In January 1979, twenty-six people resigned from it and established the Chinese American Democratic Rights Association (CADRA), a civil rights group based in New York's Chinatown. [53] They walked out because of disagreements over the work and direction of AAFE. Committed to providing social services to New York's Chinatown, they were resisting plans to establish AAFE chapters in Chicago, San Francisco, and Los Angeles, and to abandon Chinatown to work with members of the proletariat in general.[54] But AAFE, in a statement released to the press, said that it had "expelled" these dissidents because they opposed unionization, higher wages, and better working conditions (on the grounds that this program would drive away small shop owners and restaurant workers), because they wanted to build up AAFE by first offering social services and to bring in political analysis, and because they had distorted the history of the New York AAFE chapter and their own role in it. In the parlance of the New left, the central contradiction was between community-minded reformers who wanted to continue AAFE's social service programs and class-conscious revolutionaries who wanted to start a national movement. This contradiction led to violence.

In retaliation for an alleged beating of an AAFE member by CADRA people, WVO and AAFE members carrying lead pipes, iron bars, and hammers forced their way into CADRA offices, injured three persons, and damaged furniture during a 27 May 1979 demonstration. On 31 May 1979, WVO issued a leaflet "denouncing CADRA, I Wor Kuen, the National Association of Chinese Americans, the *China Daily News*, and the *Bei Mei Daily News* as 'the new Kuomintang.' "[55] A related incident occurred on 2 June 1979, at a demonstration in which thirty-five WVO and AAFE members picketed the *China Daily News* and broke down its door, apparently in retaliation for its refusal to publish AAFE's press releases. It was alleged that the Chinatown newspapers were forming a bloc with CADRA. On the following day, AAFE continued its attacks on CADRA by picketing its open-house reception.

Why WVO and AAFE felt the need to attack physically former members is uncertain. Peter Lau, president of CADRA, believed that the incident was staged by AAFE members to force the remaining members to reaffirm their allegiance to the group and end further desertions.[56] It was a desperate and foolish measure; as one editorial said, "even the conservatives know better than to drag their battles out into the open. This public display of internal disagreements only serves to exhibit weaknesses which are strategically 'un-cool' when confronting opponents."[57]

In spite of the fact that WVO had suffered a major setback, Tung decided to move to the last phase of his plan to establish a party. In October 1979, WVO was elevated to the Communist Workers party, U.S.A. (CWP).[58] Almost immediately, CWP engaged in provocative actions that would prove its undoing. The most dramatic and tragic was the Greensboro affair. Perhaps out of a mistaken belief that the route to a communist revolution was to challenge the Ku Klux Klan, Tung decided to hold a "Death to the Klan Rally" on 3 November 1979, in the African American section of Greensboro, North Carolina. Weeks before the rally, the CWP had called KKK members cowards and dared them to appear. Paul Bermanzohn, who had organized the protest march and served as its spokesman, publicly taunted the Klan, "We invite you and your two-bit punks to come out and face the wrath of the people," and handbills described the Klan as "the most treacherous scum element produced by the dying system of capitalism." [59] The KKK not only appeared but began to fire weapons, wounding and killing demonstrators.[60]

The Greensboro incident proved to be a political disaster and plunged CWP into a downward spiral. CWP initially derived considerable publicity from it: "Members were often in the news, threatening violence prior to marches and then attempting to disrupt the Democratic National Convention in 1980." [61] Trying to capitalize on the tragedy, it published a theoretical journal called *The 80's* and a collection of party documents and conference presentations forecasting an economic crisis that was supposed to dwarf the Great Depression and pave the way for the dictatorship of the proletariat. That crisis, of course, never materialized, a fact that raised further questions about CWP's judgment. Ultimately, the Greensboro incident failed either to enhance CWP's prestige or to instigate an insurrection; on the contrary, in the New Left community CWP became known for its aberrant actions. CWP members became increasingly demoralized and began to desert the party.

By the summer of 1984, CWP had reached its nadir. It suspended the publication of its political organ, *Workers Viewpoint*, and engaged in a reassessment of its ideology and practice. It was evident that CWP had made a fundamental shift in strategy when it endorsed Jesse Jackson's presidential bid and claimed that CWP martyrs were "forerunners of multinational unity in the South which Jesse Jackson's Rainbow Coalition is now striving." [62] Two years later, in 1986, CWP dissolved and reappeared in the guise of the New Democratic movement, an ill-defined entity with electoral aspirations. The latter has tried to gain influence in the Democratic party through local elections and through Jesse Jackson's Rainbow Coalition, and its president Bill Chong has played a prominent role in New York State Democratic party politics.

With the dissolution of CWP and the uncertain future of the New Democratic movement, Tung and his followers have transferred their operations to

AAFE. Naturally he occupies the senior position, serving as chairman of the board of directors. During the 1980s, AAFE not only recovered from the 1979 defections but tried to expand its influence in Chinatown by becoming a major opponent to gentrification, a form of redevelopment that has destroyed other Chinatowns. In 1981, AAFE filed a lawsuit in the New York Supreme Court challenging the constitutionality of a zoning variance called the Special Manhattan Bridge District, which allowed real estate developers to build luxury housing without building low- and moderate-income housing. In 1985, the New York Supreme Court declared "that the city had a constitutional obligation to use its zoning power to provide reasonable opportunity for low and moderate income housing." [63] But later, it was reversed by the State of New York Court of Appeals.[64] AAFE was more successful on 1 January 1986 when it became the first neighborhood preservation company funded by the New York State Division of Housing and Community Renewal to serve the Chinatown area. One of its major goals is to develop a master plan for residential and commercial land use in Chinatown that accommodated the community's history and culture, and its low-income residents.

Tung's involvement in electoral politics and community reform activities are part of what Asian American activists contemptuously call his "takeover from above" strategy, a grandiose version of the "takeover" tactics employed in the 1970s by the New Left. Its first phase is to have his followers join the Democratic party and the union movement, with the goal of capturing several state governments and union treasuries; its second phase is to use the monies in these treasuries to buy American Express; and its third phase is to have American Express take over its competitors.[65] Presumably, this Yuppie-style communism would eventually lead to a takeover of the United States and then the rest of the world.

Thermidorean Reaction

The emergence of Maoist organizations in Chinatown upset the community's political equilibrium. These organizations, along with liberal community activists, began to challenge the authority of the traditional merchant elite, namely, the CCBA, which had ruled Chinatown since the late nineteenth century. Even though the CCBA acts as the de facto representative of all overseas Chinese in the local area, it serves the interests of the traditional elite rather than those of the local population. It has, for instance, "completely and successfully [fought] every attempt that has been made to raise the wage levels of Chinatown workers." [66]

The CCBA maintained its power through a variety of means, especially as the intermediary to the world outside Chinatown. Whenever outside authorities dealt with the Chinatown community, they did so through the head of the organization, who was known as the unofficial "mayor of Chinatown." Its authority was further enhanced by an alliance with the Chinese Nationalist government, with which it shared a conservative ideology and politics. The symbiotic relationship of the two was manifest during the 1950s, when the CCBA took advantage of the anticommunist hysteria of the McCarthy period to "red-bait" its enemies, real and imaginary. During the 1960s, the CCBA tried this unsavory tactic again on the professionals in the newly established social service agencies in Chinatown. But the changing political climate in the United States made such simplistic and spurious allegations ineffective. Later, the CCBA tried to "coopt" the liberals, with some measure of success. It perceived, correctly, as it turns out, that the liberal-minded elements in social service agencies posed a potential threat to its own leadership of the community. But the CCBA reserved its greatest hostility for the Maoist groups committed to a radical transformation of the Chinatown community and its status in American society. These organizations returned the compliment and considered the CCBA their "main enemy."

Some CCBA members may have thought initially that the young cadres were simply working out Oedipal impulses. But the CCBA could not stand by as they began publicly supporting the PRC and disseminating its propaganda through literature and film. As Carmen Chow, one of IWK's best-known leaders, has noted, "when we showed *The East Is Red* and a thousand people came and stood up and sang the Chinese National Anthem . . . this really freaked out the KMT." [67] Such activities not only challenged the CCBA's authority but jeopardized its patron, since a renewal of political relations between the United States and the PRC could happen only at the KMT's and Taiwan's expense.

IWK took the worst of CCBA harassment. According to Virgo Lee, head of New York's Chinese Progressive Association, CCBA hired youth-gang members to intimidate IWK, breaking the windows of its storefront with such regularity that they were boarded up with red-painted planks. [68] The storefront was fire-bombed on three occasions. CCBA thugs threw bottles at IWK members from the rooftops in attempts to break up meetings and harassed people selling

Getting Together. They also took pictures of high school students who visited the storefront, and then went to their parents threatening to send copies to the FBI, raising the specter of unemployment and deportation. One plan, never implemented, was to "trash" the Federal Savings Bank and leave IWK buttons at the scene to incriminate the organization. CCBA's campaign of physical violence and disinformation would take its toll and deterred some people from participating in IWK activities, but it was ultimately unsuccessful in suppressing the group.

What did eventually force IWK to close its doors temporarily and reorganize was its failure to win the "hearts and minds" of the Chinatown community. IWK received support mainly from the marginal members of Chinatown: the young who were impressed with its militant assertion of racial pride, the leftists who had been active in the 1930s, and the old who simply wanted to be treated decently by someone. The rest of the community was ambivalent at best. While residents welcomed IWK's social services, they rejected its radical ideology. They were proud that China had "stood up," becoming a force to be reckoned with in the world, but they lacked enthusiasm for the society that the Chinese Communists had wrought. Unlike members of IWK, they actually knew something about the daily lives of the people on the mainland, either from having lived there or from the letters they received from relatives describing hardships there. Beyond the pro-PRC propaganda that IWK and other organizations disseminated, they saw a disquieting reality—a politically unstable and impoverished country.

Sectarianism

More damaging than the enmity of the conservatives were the sectarian struggles. At the start, the differences were, to use the Maoist expression, "non-antagonistic," capable of being worked out amicably. Radical groups held informal discussions and formal debates and forums to promote their ideological perspective and to persuade others that they understood the national and international issues better than their rivals. But by the mid-1970s exchanges became increasingly acrimonious, degenerating into sectarianism.

With the end of the antiwar movement in 1975 and the beginning of a conservative backlash, interest in the left and in revolutionary groups declined. As their ranks and resources dwindled, radical organizations became bitter rivals for power within the New Left as well as the Asian American Movement. Personal misunderstandings exacerbated the enmity between groups. Toward the end of the decade, intergroup communication had all but ceased and relationships had become "antagonistic." The legacy of these sectarian wars haunts the Movement to the present day.

The competition between groups was played out primarily in the ideological arena. During the early 1970s, when Asian American Marxist–Leninists were still on speaking terms, they discussed the possibility of an Asian nation (as some African Americans were arguing for a Black nation) within the United States. The national question, How can national minorities achieve liberation and end oppression? was one of the few Marxist–Leninist debates that dealt explicitly with Asian Americans. In 1972, East Wind (Los Angeles), a Marxist–Leninist collective made up of community workers from Japanese American Community Services–Asian Involvement, the Community Workers Collective, *Gidra*, and others active in the Asian American Movement in Los Angeles developed the so-called Asian nation line. Their basic idea was to build a "power base as Asians—culturally, geo-politically, economically, and as it becomes necessary, militarily," so that Asian Americans could forge their own "Asian nation–community" within the United States.[69] But theirs was not a narrow and nationalistic definition of "nation," since it was linked to other people of color and progressive European American groups. It was based on two premises: first, Asian Americans "of all kinds, regardless of where their heads are at must be reached out to, and touched"; second, "every form of activity, service, organizing, struggle and digging each other that makes us more aware of our oppression and also makes us feel more powerful and human is valid and legitimate as part of our movement."[70] In practical terms, the "Asian nation" line was mainly an ideological justification for organizing among Asian Americans and for establishing counterinstitutions to provide economic, cultural, and social services to Asian Americans during the "serve the people" phase of the Movement.

The controversy surrounding the "Asian nation" line became part of the larger discussion of the "national question," which Asian American radicals and others singled out as the "burning question of the day." They believed that U.S. imperialism was in retreat and that the main trend of the world was "revolution," an idea embodied in the popular antiwar slogan "Countries want independence, nations want liberation and the people want revolution." In 1968, the Tet offensive in Vietnam, a carefully coordinated series of communist attacks of extraordinary intensity and scope, and in 1969, Nixon's ill-fated

Vietnamization policy, lent credence to this belief. With the U.S. defeat in Vietnam imminent, some Asian American radicals believed that the oppressed nationalities, of which they were one, were at the forefront of "class struggle," the Maoist instrument for attacking the social underpinnings of U.S. imperialism. It was a significant view because it explained the relationship between the struggle of Asian Americans and the struggles of other Third World people, and the struggle of the masses of working people and progressive people.

But the Asian nation line was roundly criticized. Some New Left groups considered all work among oppressed nationalities of secondary importance unless it focused on "bread and butter" issues that could appeal to all workers. Asian American radicals were more sympathetic, but they too criticized it. Using Stalin's *Marxism and the National Question* and other materials and arguments, they concluded that there was no historical or material basis for an Asian nation in America. They concluded that even Chinese Americans, a group belonging to an identifiable geographic community, lacked the basis for a nation: (1) Chinatowns were perennial targets for urban renewal (these days "gentrification") and thus lacked a stable population; (2) Chinese Americans spoke different dialects and thus lacked a common language; (3) Chinatowns had no basic industries that could sustain an independent economy and thus lacked an "internal economic bond"; (4) Chinatowns were noncontiguous communities and thus lacked a common territory; and (5) different generations of Chinese Americans had their own cultural and psychological makeup and thus lacked a common culture.[71] Moreover, the emphasis on "cultural–national autonomy" would lead only to the political disintegration of the working class, destroying class unity. Asian American critics argued that "rather than face up to the question of the seizure of state power through proletarian revolution, the only way possible, cultural–national autonomy tends to avoid it, and diverts too much of the people's energy into 'cultural self-determination.' "[72] The opponents of the Asian nation line eventually won. By 1975, East Wind repudiated it, though the group continued to maintain that the elimination of national oppression was a major goal of the revolution.

The debate over the Asian nation and the national question was relatively benign and even constructive, for it allowed Asian American radicals to clarify their positions on national oppression and to affirm their commitment to a proletarian revolution. In spite of the criticism, it is evident that the line's implicit emphasis on ethnic nationalism explains, in part, the I Wor Kuen's support from some Asian American activists. Less benign was the struggle for

support within the Asian American Movement. Radicals often used community issues and organizations as opportunities for expanding their influence,
usually at the expense of their rivals as well as the Movement. They viewed
all Asian American groups as potential sources of recruits. Study groups were
particularly vulnerable because they provided a ready forum for promoting a
particular ideological perspective and an ideal means of identifying politically
"progressive" individuals for recruitment.

One of the few documented cases occurred in 1978 when I Wor Kuen and
Workers Viewpoint Organization were competing for dominance of the re-
surgent Asian American student movement. An early example of this rivalry
involved the Anti-*Bakke* Decision Coalition's principles of unity, which had
been adopted by the Intercollegiate Liaison Committee (ICLC) but opposed by
AAFE, a WVO mass organization. IWK members seized on the contradiction
as an opportunity to question AAFE's role in ICLC. IWK allegedly used its
position in the ICLC to exclude groups with different political perspectives,
notably WVO, from the Asian Students Unity Conference held at Princeton
University (31 March–2 April 1978), and attacked individuals who strongly
opposed or questioned its positions. One activist recalled:

> There were two major forces at work. First the IWK camp, who helped
> organize around the Bakke issue. By establishing the links with the stu-
> dents first by personal ties and by having effective and critical dialogues,
> they have heavily influenced many students' way of thinking. Second,
> we have the WVO camp. WVO was particularly small, but with IWK's
> coordinated efforts in curbing their influence, their attempt at grabbing
> "foothold" in the ICLC was effectively screened out.[73]

IWK was also blamed for undermining the East Coast Asian Student Union
(ECASU), an umbrella organization for Asian American student organiza-
tions along the East Coast that had emerged from the Princeton conference.[74]
According to the MidAtlantic region's "Draft Sum-Up of ECASU Split":

> IWK's opportunist and divisive role in the [Asian Student Movement]
> and [Asian student organizations], specifically ECASU. IWK's influ-
> ence in Asian student activities as manifested by their cadres'/sym-
> pathizers' role in the recent [Asian student movement] has finally de-
> veloped into the central issue which undermined the unity of ECASU
> and divided Asian students and organizations. IWK's attempt to seize

control of ECASU and undermine the genuine student elements and negate their efforts and talents must be analyzed, criticized, publicized & exposed.[75]

Lynn Yokoe's essay on the history of ECASU interpreted the split as the result of "A small group of individuals in the Mid-Atlantic who failed to work towards unity in the face of different opinions on how to build the network. Instead of trying to resolve the questions in an open and principled manner, they launched personal attacks on two representatives with whom they disagreed. Innuendo, suspicion and distrust predominated."[76] The evidence, however, seems to support the MidAtlantic region's charges that two ECASU members, ostensibly representing Asian student organizations at City College of New York and Hunter College, in actuality represented IWK, serving as conduits for its political policies and placing its interest ahead of ECASU's. As a former ECASU member recalled, "ECASU supposedly was a nonpartisan group, so people were . . . justifiably upset that . . . some people in ECASU were trying to manipulate ECASU to follow a certain party line."[77] What precipitated the internal crisis was the unauthorized use of the MidAtlantic/ECASU's mailing list to support a fund-raiser for the Progressive Chinatown Peoples' Association (PCPA), an IWK mass organization.

The two members were expelled; the MidAtlantic/ECASU separated from the New England/ECASU, which was considered to be under the control of Boston's Chinatown Progressive People's Association, another IWK mass organization; and the MidAtlantic collapsed, not to be revived until 1980, after a two year hiatus. In 1984, the MidAtlantic and New England regional groups once again joined together.

IWK's actions were hardly unique. Other radical organizations were guilty of similar practices, for they all subscribed to a Machiavellian political philosophy in which the end justified the means.

The League of Revolutionary Struggle (Marxist–Leninist)

In 1978, I Wor Kuen merged with the August 29th movement, a Chicano Marxist–Leninist organization, to found a new communist organization called the League of Revolutionary Struggle (Marxist–Leninist).[78] Later, they were joined by other groups: Seize the Time, East Wind, and the New York Collective in 1979; and the Revolutionary Communist League (Marxist–Leninist–Mao Zedong Thought) in 1980. The rationale for founding the league was the standard one: the need to develop a new revolutionary party to replace the CPUSA, which had failed to fulfill its responsibility to work toward the revolution. The league criticized the CPUSA for degenerating into a "revisionist" group that advocated electoral politics and promoted the interests of an imperialist Soviet Union. According to league members, since the mid-1950s the Soviet Union had betrayed its origins as the world's first socialist state to become an expansionist superpower on a par with the United States. It was ruled by a military bureaucratic elite that restored class exploitation and national oppression. Its rivalry with the United States was considered the greatest danger to world peace. The United States and Soviet Union were denounced with equal vehemence.

Like the other Maoist groups discussed earlier, the league considered itself the heir to the CPUSA and made becoming the "party" its central task. What made the league different from other groups was its emphasis on an alliance between the working class and oppressed nationalities, that is, people of color. Together they formed "the core of the united front against the U.S. monopoly capitalist class."[79] The oppression of minority-nationality people within the United States was, in their view, an integral part of a race-based capitalist system. The league sought to liberate these oppressed people by overthrowing the capitalist state and establishing a socialist state. Naturally, it recruited its members from racial-minority "mass organizations" within the ethnic communities and in the student and labor movements. While the league organized, agitated, and educated the members of mass organizations, making them increasingly radical, it worked assiduously to identify and recruit "advanced elements," meaning people with a progressive political outlook. It preferred to recruit "coalitionists" who believed that Third World people should work together for their common liberation, rather than "nationalists" concerned only about the problems in their own ethnic community.

The league had perceptible success in replenishing its ranks with credulous, idealistic students from such schools as Stanford, Berkeley, UCLA, University of California–Santa Cruz, San Jose State, and San Francisco State. It wielded considerable influence in statewide student organizations such as MEChA, the African/Black Student Alliance, and the Asian Pacific Islander Student Union.[80] Students who were recruited have described the process as secret and selective. After being singled out for recruitment, a student was invited to participate in a series of study groups, usually led by one or two league members and focused on socialism, Marxist theory, people-of-color movements, and student activism. Those deemed unworthy were no longer invited to meetings. At the start, a student was not informed that the study groups were sponsored by the league until he or she was invited to attend more advanced study groups, where the role of the league in progressive movements was discussed. To ensure maximum security, all invitations were issued through a single league member, who notified the student of study group meetings or other events—for example, speeches given by league leaders like Amiri Baraka, the well-known poet. If the student was "politically correct," he or she would be invited to apply for membership, a process that required writing an essay on why the new recruit wanted to join the league. Except for certain "public" members who spoke for the organization, usually those in leadership positions, its membership was kept secret because of the very real possibility of political repression.

The league's covert activities on college campuses were known to only a few people, mostly other Marxist–Leninists engaged in similar practices. Occasionally, students discovered that the league had tried to influence them for its own political purposes. For example, in 1989, Asian American students at the University of California at Berkeley became aware that as many as five "older students" were exercising excessive influence over the Asian Student Union (ASU) and leading it away from issues that the majority of students were interested in.[81] Their concern was "galvanized by the immediate issue of verbal and written assaults by the League against dissenting ASU members . . . intensified and made urgent by the League's rumour-propagation, innuendo, and disengenous criticisms."[82] In order to regain student autonomy, dissident students left ASU and together with others established the Asian American Political Alliance, (AAPA, named after the original group that had participated in the Third World strike two decades earlier). Ironically, AAPA has become *the* Asian Pacific American group on the Berkeley campus, much to the chagrin of those remaining in ASU.

Although losing its hold on the Asian American students at Berkeley was a significant setback for the League, the damage was contained. Understandably, Asian American students were reluctant to talk about the episode because they wanted to avoid being accused of "red-baiting" and McCarthyism. They were probably anxious to avoid reprisals as well, since the league had been known to engage in psychological intimidation and character assassination.[83] But a year later, the league's practice of infiltrating and influencing student organizations became a matter of public debate at Stanford University.

In February 1990, the *Stanford Review*, a right-wing student publication, published two articles: "Gordon Chang Connected to Maoist Cult" and "The League of Revolutionary Struggle: A Self-Proclaimed Revolutionary Vanguard."[84] The former drew attention to Gordon Chang, one of the league's leaders and a finalist for the Asian American Studies professorship in the History Department. A companion article depicted the league as a fanatical Maoist cult bent on the violent overthrow of the government. It cited league publications obtained from the Hoover Institution to prove that the organization was "dedicated to unifying all Marxist–Leninist groups, infiltrating and co-opting mass movements, and using this support to stage a revolution."[85] From the lurid headline to the unsubstantiated allegations, the articles appeared to be nothing more than *ad hominem* attacks on Chang by what was popularly regarded as a "notoriously inaccurate and inflammatory"[86] publication. Members of the Stanford University community properly saw the attacks as an attempt to infringe on Chang's First Amendment rights to free speech and an intrusion in the school's personnel decisions, both of which are considered sacrosanct in the university.

Two months later, however, articles on Chang and the league appeared again, this time in the *Stanford Daily*, the student newspaper. Michael Friedly, a senior staff writer, had completed an investigative report on the league and its presence on the Stanford campus.[87] Having heard that student leaders on campus constituted a clique belonging to a secret political group, he had decided to investigate this allegation to determine whether membership in this outside organization had affected the political process on campus. Over a period of three months, he had interviewed more than a hundred students, administrators, and people such as Harvey Klehr, a political scientist at Emory University and an expert on the American left. Most of the interviewees were committed to the empowerment of ethnic minorities, and many shared similar political perspectives with league members.

In the 18 May 1990 issue, Friedly wrote an article on the anonymous posters being distributed on campus maliciously attacking Chang as an "overseas Chinese muckety-muck in a Maoist party."[88] He added a sidebar, "Nationwide Organization Active Here, Students Say," which described the league and its activities on campus, especially its efforts to recruit students of color. Together, these two articles unleashed a public furor that was aired on the Op-Ed pages of the *Daily* during subsequent weeks. Charges of MaCarthyism and racism were leveled at Friedly for writing the articles and the editors for publishing them. Alleged league members defended themselves, and would-be recruits described the unsavory tactics. Even though most students had nothing to do with the league, they felt uneasy about a covert organization on campus that was using devious methods to influence them for its own political purposes. Students of color were especially aggrieved, feeling that they had been duped by friends and classmates belonging to the league.

A central concern was the extent of the league's involvement in campus politics. Friedly's sources reported that though the league had fewer than thirty members on campus, many of them were in positions that allowed them to shape student government policies and influence progressive politics on campus. Members had attained leadership positions in the Associated Students of Stanford University, the students-of-color organizations—MEChA, the Black Student Union, and the Asian American Student Association—and university staff positions.

Students were particularly concerned about whether the league had orchestrated the recent campaign to bring multiculturalism to Stanford and the occupation of university President Donald Kennedy's office. Beginning with the 1985 campaign to get Stanford to divest itself of stocks and bonds issued by firms doing business in South Africa, students of color had tried to bring multicultural values to the campus. In 1987, Stanford's centennial year, the Black Student Union, MEChA, the Asian American Student Association, and the Stanford American Indian Organization drafted a "Rainbow Agenda" and demonstrated in support of its demands. In 1988, they succeeded in changing the university's ethnocentric Western culture general education requirement. On 15 May 1989, they took over the president's office to emphasize the need for an Asian American Studies tenure-track professor; a full-time dean for El Centro Chicano, the Chicano student center; and a discrimination review board to act on complaints of racial slurs and incidents.[89] Fifty-five students, fourteen of whom were Asian American, were arrested for participating in this action.

Apparently, the league was heavily involved in the multicultural movement through its influence in the students-of-color organizations. The steering committee that planned the takeover of the president's office was "composed

entirely of League members or students who were in the process of becoming recruited by the League."[90] Stephen Ostrander, an activist committed
to progressive–liberal politics who participated in the "takeover," recalled:

> I first became suspicious of outside influence during and after the take-
> over. Many strangers suddenly appeared. A lot of information was never
> clarified.
>
> But it was the overwhelming rhetoric that led me to question indi-
> viduals I thought were my friends. In one of our many meetings after
> the takeover, Council of Presidents member David Brown, who was
> leading the meeting, constantly substituted "The Enemy" for "The Ad-
> ministration" in his remarks. When I objected to this, several people,
> who I now know to be League members, verbally assaulted me.[91]

Unfortunately, in its effort to enhance itself, the league had evidently eroded
the credibility of Stanford's multicultural movement, even among ardent supporters. Ostrander concluded: "The League, in its quest for revolution, has used
the struggle for multiculturalism as a front. As a result of their commitment to
politics rather than people, they have done more damage to multiculturalism at
Stanford than anyone else."[92]

The league mocked the struggle of Stanford's racial-minority community.
MEChA, the Black Student Union, and the Asian American Student Association have all experienced division along ideological lines, with moderates in
one camp and league members, advocating more radical policies and practices,
in the other. Its activities also alienated activists from progressive politics.
Richard Suh, a second-generation Korean American, resigned as chair of the
Asian American Students Association because of his disillusionment with the
league. In a commentary to the Stanford community, he said: "I decided at
some point that I felt like a lackey, because on a theoretical level [league mem-
bers] were fighting for . . . another agenda. I felt that the progressive politics at
Stanford were so dominated by this group, that I didn't feel independent unless
I disconnected myself from progressive politics for awhile."[93]

The Stanford scandal had significant repercussions within the league. According to a former member of the Chinese Progressive Association, the controversy over Chang's appointment to the faculty and the public debate over
the league's activities led to intense internal discussions about the organization
and its future.[94] Some members wanted the league to continue as a clandestine

Leninist-style organization; others wanted to replace it with another, more open political entity.[95] Evidently, the latter group prevailed: On 8 September 1990, at a national conference, the league disavowed Marxism–Leninism and decided to dissolve, disengage from radical politics, and devote its members' energies to electoral politics, specifically the left wing of the Democratic party.[96]

Since then, some have talked about the former league's decision to move into electoral politics as the beginning of a European-style social democratic movement. Others have sardonically referred to it as the "Cadrification of the Rainbow," that is, a move to gain control of Jesse Jackson's Rainbow Coalition. But any such effort is unlikely to succeed given the presence in the coalition of so many other revolutionaries, including former league rivals, who would recognize and thwart such an attempt. It is also pointless, given the improbability of Jesse Jackson's ever attaining the presidency. To the extent that it can influence Jackson's agenda and Jackson can influence the Democratic party, the former league can hope to make its presence felt.

It is doubtful that the Stanford scandal per se was responsible for the decision to dissolve the league. Instead, that decision must be understood in the context of the extraordinary events of 1989, the year that the West won the Cold War by default. It was the year that China destroyed its pro-democracy movement, Eastern Europe and the Soviet Union disavowed socialism, and East Berlin dismantled the Berlin Wall. It was the year that disillusioned Marxist–Leninists around the world, for it became patently obvious that socialism had led to bankrupt economies and communism to repressive regimes. With the overthrow of communist governments, the repudiation of Marxist–Leninist ideology, and the change from socialist economies to capitalist ones driven by market forces, the league was forced to rethink its commitment to the socialist model.

For Maoist groups like the league, the 3–4 June 1989 Tiananmen massacre of pro-democracy students was particularly disheartening. They, along with the rest of the world, watched with horror as their heroes, the Chinese Communists, murdered their young and lied about it afterward. In the wake of this atrocity, the league held a mass meeting in Oakland, and an editorial in its newspaper, *Unity*, asserted that the "vast majority of the students involved are patriotic and believe in socialism" and condemned the Chinese government's actions on the grounds that "it is not in the spirit of socialism, nor in the spirit of the Chinese Revolution and the Chinese Communist Party, to deal with contradictions among the people through the use of brute military force."[97] While the students in China were undoubtedly moved by nationalist sentiments, it is doubtful that they believed in socialism. On the contrary, like the demonstrators in Eastern Europe, they distrusted it. Indeed, for those who died on that fateful day, the government's repression was very much in keeping with the authoritarian "spirit of socialism" and the dark side of the Chinese revolution and the Chinese Communist party.

The Asian Americans who enlisted in the Red Guard party, Wei Min She, I Wor Kuen, and the Asian Study Group did so mainly to resist racism in America, not because they were committed to a communist ideology. Like those who joined reform organizations, they were embittered about the oppression and humiliation that Asian Americans had endured for over a century. They were inspired by the social movements in America and the wars of liberation in Asia, which heightened their consciousness of themselves as Asian Americans and provided them with alternative heroes with whom to identify. They found common cause with the Black Panthers, communist guerrillas, and other Third World people opposing American imperialism. They were some of the best and the brightest in the community, with the ability to enter American society at a level that their families could only dream about. But many refused to do so because they could not in good conscience be partners in what they believed to be the oppression of their people. Instead, they sacrificed potential careers, severed familial and friendship ties, and subjected themselves to austere lives in order to attain revolutionary ideals. But in giving themselves over to revolutionary organizations, they allowed themselves to be defined and diminished by those groups.

Without fully realizing it, Asian American radicals changed their focus from racism to capitalism. They believed that racial oppression was merely a tool of capitalists to divide working-class people and that the fundamental solution was socialism, the panacea, in their eyes, for America's ills. It was philosophically self-evident to them that socialism was morally superior, for it was based on the equal distribution of wealth, with Third World people receiving their fair share; capitalism was morally reprehensible, based as it was on the unequal distribution of wealth, with Third World people receiving the least. Before 1989, the verdict on socialism had yet to be reached. But the inequities that capitalism had wrought were manifest, especially in the ghettos. Revolutionaries were convinced that the exploitative capitalist economic system, along with the social and political structures that supported it, was beyond repair and needed to be thrown into the trash heap of history. They had exchanged their heightened consciousness of themselves as Asian Americans for what would prove finally to be the false consciousness of themselves as Maoist revolutionaries.

With the end of the Vietnam War, Marxist–Leninist organizations began to decline. With the dissipation of antigovernment sentiment and dwindling numbers of alienated youths, they found it increasingly difficult to sustain themselves, let alone grow. In this era of scarce revolutionary resources, rivalries became intense and antagonistic, degenerating into sectarian wars. The sectarianism of the 1970s accomplished little except to poison the atmosphere, tainting Asian American radicals of every political persuasion. For those who survived the period and continued to be active in the Movement, it was no longer possible to work with others without wondering about their hidden political agendas.

By the conservative Reagan era, the Maoist groups had withered. Except for the bookstores it operates, the Revolutionary Communist party has all but disappeared, with its members leading cloistered lives, immersed in the study of Marxism–Leninism–Mao Tse-tung Thought. Recently, it has been reported that RCP has formed an alliance with the Communist party of Peru, known worldwide as *Sendero Luminoso*, or "Shining Path," which is considered to be one of the most "secretive and savage revolutionary groups"[98] in existence today. The Communist Workers party has disappeared and reappeared as the New Democratic movement, of which little is heard, although as far as its rivals are concerned it is still the same old gang, trying to distance itself from its past and camouflaging its political intent. In an effort to legitimate themselves, CWP members have returned to college and resumed careers, joining the middle class and contributing to the economic system they so despise. The League of Revolutionary Struggle appears to be emulating the CWP and has reappeared as the Unity Organizing Committee, which includes most of its Asian American members.[99] Dissenters who disagreed with the original decision to dissolve the organization have founded the Socialist Organizing Network, which continues to uphold MLMTT.

Dissolution notwithstanding, both the CWP and the League of Revolutionary Struggle maintain a presence in Chinatown through their mass organizations. As Chapter 6 has shown, Asian Americans for Equality and the Chinese Progressive Association continue to compete for the "hearts and minds" of community residents through the very same kind of activities for which they used to ridicule Asian American reformers. Because of their history of sectarianism and commitment to communism, neither has succeeded in acquiring widespread support in Chinatown. Most community residents and organizations have been understandably wary of working with them. As a result, AAFE and CPA have become simply two more interest groups in the local community, with patently less power than traditional organizations like the Chinese Consolidated Benevolent Association and social service organizations like the Chinese-American Planning Council, which has been in the ascendancy in recent years.

Meanwhile, even before their dissolution, CWP and the League of Revolutionary Struggle tried to enlarge the scope of their activities by becoming involved in mainstream politics. They have followed in the footsteps of earlier communist groups in the United States that have tried to work through the Democratic party. As the final chapter shows, in the 1980s both organizations moved into electoral politics as a way of acquiring the political power that had eluded them earlier. Their decision to dissolve themselves was in part predicated on an earlier conclusion that working for a communist revolution in contemporary American society was a cul-de-sac and that Jesse Jackson's Rainbow Coalition, essentially an ethnically pluralist movement for social change, offered a better opportunity to promote their brand of progressive politics and socialist ideals.

8

From Radical to Electoral Politics:

The Asian American Odyssey

for Empowerment

> You, as Asian Americans, have a
> special role to play in any effort to
> change our country's policies. For
> you have seen so much of the worst
> side of our history.
>
> —Jesse Jackson (1984)

Asians in America have been a disenfranchised group throughout most of their history. As "aliens ineligible to citizenship," immigrants were denied the right to vote by the Naturalization Act of 1790, which stipulated that only "free white persons" could apply for naturalization, implicitly denying that privilege to people of color. After the Civil War, the laws were changed in 1870 to permit the naturalization of persons of African descent. The denial of the right of Asians to apply for U.S. citizenship was reaffirmed by the courts in such civil cases as *Ozawa* v. *U.S.* (1922), which stated that the privilege of naturalization extended only to white persons and persons of African origin. The only ones to escape the onus of "ineligibility" were persons of Asian ancestry born on American soil. In the course of opposing discriminatory laws, Chinese litigants established the important judicial principle that a person born in the United States of alien parents ineligible for citizenship was still an American citizen.[1]

Eventually, Asian immigrants attained the right to become naturalized citizens. In 1943, Chinese became eligible for citizenship when Congress repealed the Chinese exclusion acts as a goodwill gesture to China, a wartime ally. In 1946, Filipinos and Asian Indians were made eligible. Other Asians had to wait till 1952 and the passage of the McCarran–Walter Immigration and Naturalization Act, which eliminated race as a bar to immigration and naturalization.[2]

With citizenship came the right to vote. But elected officials and private citizens seem still determined to deny Asian Americans the franchise through the use of "English-only elections, literacy tests, racial gerrymandering, and physical intimidation and violence."[3] For their part, Asian Americans have been reluctant to join either the Democratic or the Republican party, since neither served them well in the past. Even though the Democrats proclaim that theirs is the party of the disadvantaged and seek to give access to those excluded from power, and the Republicans point to their party's pre–Civil War origins in 1854 and early premise of freedom, civil rights, and opportunity for all ethnic and racial minorities, both have been guilty of anti-Asian attitudes and actions.[4] As a result, most Asian Americans were politically apathetic during the immediate post–World War II era, limiting their activities to greying Democratic clubs that catered to established interests in Chinatowns and other Asian American communities and to national lobbying organizations like the Japanese American Citizens League. Few of them had political aspirations, and even fewer were elected to public office at any level.[5]

The notable exception was in Hawaii, where Asian Americans made up the majority of the population. Before World War II, Asians were active in local politics, and such men as Hiram Fong were elected to the territorial legislature; after the war, their ranks were augmented by returning veterans like Spark Matsunaga and Daniel Inouye, of the 100th Battalion and the 442nd Regimental Combat Team, respectively, who decided that they had earned the right to enter the political arena. Most of them joined a political coalition under the Democratic party that displaced the dominant European American oligarchy that had ruled the territory. When Hawaii became a state in 1959, Asian Americans were elected to both the U.S. House of Representatives and Senate, where they have ably served their state and nation.

Asian Americans on the mainland would also like to elect their own people to public office, but so far have had less success. With the passage of the Voting Rights Act (1965) and the politicization of the Asian American community during the 1960s, Asian Americans began to develop an interest in the problems and potential of the American political system. With their growing population and affluence during the 1970s, they became involved in electoral politics. A few mavericks were able to get elected: March Fong Eu became California's secretary of state in 1974; Norman Mineta and Robert Matsui won seats in the U.S. House of Representatives in 1974 and 1978, respectively; and S. I. Hayakawa won a seat in the U.S. Senate in 1976.

During the 1980s, increasing numbers of Asian Americans began to attain political office, usually at the local level—on the East Coast, Margaret Chin, Democratic state committeewoman of New York's 61st District, and S. B. Woo, lieutenant governor of Delaware; on the West Coast, Thomas Hsieh, supervisor of San Francisco, Judy Chu, councilwoman and mayor of Monterey Park, Michael Woo, councilman of Los Angeles, Warren Furutani, of the Los Angeles Board of Education, and others. Asian American activists, including erstwhile Maoists, began abandoning protest politics and entering electoral politics; much to the astonishment of the Asian American community, they too began to vie for public office. To understand these surprising and significant changes, one must examine the nature and potential of Asian American participation in the political process and their involvement in party politics, especially Jesse Jackson's Rainbow Coalition.

Asymmetrical Participation

The salient feature of Asian Americans' participation in the political process has been its asymmetry: They have been a major source of money but a minor source of votes. A study of minorities in California by Bruce Cain and Roderick Kiewiet found that Asian Americans there were more likely to give money than to vote.[6] Twenty-four percent of eligible Asian American voters in California contributed money to some political group in the 1984 election. Mervyn Field, director of the Field Institute for Public Policy, noted that while only 10 percent of the voters may be Asian Americans, as much as 20 to 30 percent of a candidate's campaign money may come from them.[7] During the early stages of Los Angeles Mayor Tom Bradley's 1986 campaign for governor, two $1,000-a-seat dinners sponsored by Asian Americans raised $50,000 each. An estimated 10 percent of his donations came from Asian Americans, though they constituted less than 6 percent of the population. That same year, in gratitude for his opposition to Ferdinand Marcos, Filipino Americans gave Democratic Congressman Stephen Solarz about $90,000, which amounted to 15 percent of all contributions, even though they represented only 1 percent of the voters in his district.[8] Asian Americans have been most generous to Asian American candidates: March Fong Eu got 75 percent of her campaign money from Asian Americans, S. B. Woo 70 percent, and Tom Hsieh 30 percent.[9]

Asian American contributions to national campaigns have been even more remarkable. In 1980, they contributed $2.5 million to Jimmy Carter's presidential campaign.[10] In 1984, they were second only to Jews in contributions to the Democratic party.[11] In 1988, presidential candidate Michael Dukakis, with the backing of Asian Americans, raised record amounts of money in California.[12] At a fund-raiser in Los Angeles Chinatown attended by 750 Chinese, Japanese, Korean, Cambodian, and other prominent Asian Americans, Dukakis collected more than $100,000 for his presidential campaign. It was the largest Asian American fund-raising event in California's history. It is little wonder that in political circles Asian American monetary contributions have achieved mythical proportions. But Asian Americans have been unable to translate this pocketbook power into political power. Financial contributions have not gotten them greater attention to their needs and concerns or increased access to political decision making. Even when legislation or policy decisions that had special implications for Asian Americans were being formulated, their interests have often been ignored or overlooked. Politicians realized that Asian Americans would contribute large sums and ask for nothing in return, except for having their picture taken with the candidate, a behavior that some political pundits perceived as "naive at best, stupid at worst." [13]

As Asian Americans have come to learn, money is no substitute for votes. According to the 1990 census, there are 7.3 million Asian Americans in the United States, a 108 percent increase since 1980; but while such growth makes them the fastest growing minority in the country, they still constitute only 2.9 percent of the total population and are considered a negligible factor in most elections. In theory, they could make a significant difference in a close national election, since most of this growth has occurred in such key electoral states as California, New York, Texas, and Illinois. This is particularly true of California, where Asian Americans are 9.6 percent of the population. It is also possible for them to be a "swing vote" in U.S. Senate races in those states where they are the largest or second-largest minority. They now outnumber African Americans in ten states and are even with them in three; they outnumber Latinos in three states and are even with them in ten.

But the advantage of being concentrated in certain states is counterweighed by the low registration and turnout rates of Asian American voters. The Cain/Kiewiet study found that only 55 percent of the Asian Americans it surveyed registered to vote, and only 48 percent actually voted.[14] In comparison, 84 percent of European Americans had registered, and 81 percent had voted. There are, of course, many noncitizens in the Asian American community, but even after the figures were adjusted for them, the number of eligible Asian Americans who voted in the 1984 election was only 69 percent—still lower than for their European American counterparts. The UCLA Asian Pacific American Registration Study found even lower Asian American voter registration rates for 1984, estimating that only 43 percent of Japanese Americans, 35.5 percent of Chinese Americans, 27 percent of Filipino Americans, 16.7 percent of Asian Indians, 13 percent of Korean Americans, 28.5 percent of Samoan Americans, and 4.1 percent of Vietnamese Americans were registered voters.[15] Don Nakanishi, an expert on the Asian American electorate, has noted that a fundamental reason for low rates of voter registration and the high proportion of independent voters among certain Asian Pacific groups may be "their political experiences in nation-states like Taiwan and the People's Republic of China, which have different voting procedures and where the connotation of political party as the Communists and Kuomintang is far different from what is normally associated with the Democratic and Republican parties."[16] Besides, Asian Americans are "pulled apart by their diverse nationalities, languages, religions, and historical animosities."[17] As a *New York Times* article pointed out, "there is not much common ground . . . between a fourth-generation Japanese American physicist and a recently arrived Cambodian refugee, between a Chinese-American from Hong Kong and one from the mainland, or between a Filipino supportive of Marcos and one aligned with Aquino."[18]

In recent years, however, Asian Americans have become restive and are asking better value for their money. In 1986, S. B. Woo and Anna Chennault founded the bipartisan Interim Coordinating Committee for Chinese Americans (ICCCA) to persuade 1988 presidential candidates to commit themselves to appointing at least three Chinese Americans to policymaking positions if they were elected to office. Pointing out that "Chinese Americans have made disproportionately large contributions of money . . . yet, no Chinese American citizen has ever been appointed to any policy-making federal government position,"[19] the ICCCA asked its many thousands of signatories to withhold future monetary contributions to any person who failed to honor his or her commitment to Chinese Americans. It managed to get the support of practically all well-known Chinese Americans in the country, including Nobel Laureates, members of the National Academy of Science, and others.

Apparently, the strategy worked: ICCCA succeeded in getting commitments from all six presidential candidates, beginning with Paul Simon and ending with George Bush. After Bush was elected, ICCCA promptly reminded him of his promise, and he did appoint quite a few Asian Americans, including some thirty Chinese Americans, to relatively high posts in the White House or at a subcabinet level—more than any previous administration had done.[20]

Asian Americans have also been more willing to make themselves felt in local, state, and national politics, showing considerable skill in mobilizing resources and talents to defend their interests. In 1987, they led a statewide movement to block the appointment of Congressman Daniel Lungren (Rep.–Long Beach) as state treasurer of California. As the vice-chair of the Commission on Wartime Relocation and Internment of Civilians, Lungren had been the only member to oppose reparations to Japanese Americans interned during World War II. He had committed a host of other political sins as well, voting against civil rights, environmental legislation, and other progressive social measures; indeed, his stands on a wide range of issues were so conservative that San Francisco attorney Don Tamaki, spokesperson for Californians for Responsible Government, a coalition formed to oppose the appointment, aptly referred to him as the "Jesse Helms of the House."[21] The coalition lobbied state lawmakers, especially those identified as "swing votes," inundating them with phone calls and letters, and the California Senate rejected Lungren, 21–19.

A year later, Asian Americans again demonstrated their political influence with the successful redress and reparations movement.[22] Ever since the camps were closed, there have been efforts to redress the injustices committed against the Japanese Americans during World War II. In 1948, the Japanese American Citizens League (JACL), a national organization of mostly *nisei*, lobbied for the Evacuation Claims Act, which was supposed to provide restitution but "in fact failed miserably, paying only for property losses, yielding on average a mere $340 per victim."[23] With the advent of the Asian American Movement, which radicalized many Japanese Americans, especially *sansei*, came a renewed interest in redress. In 1970 a general resolution was passed at the Seattle JACL convention urging the organization to pursue a redress bill in Congress, but without tangible results. In 1978 a resolution at the Salt Lake City JACL convention called on the organization to seek direct individual monetary compensation, a minimum of $25,000 per victim. As a result of the resolution, JACL established a National Committee for Redress. Two other organizations were formed to seek redress and reparations: In July 1978 a broad coalition of community groups and individuals founded the National Coalition for Redress/Reparations (NCRR), and in May 1979 William Hohri, a participant in the civil rights and peace movements, founded the National Council for Japanese American Redress. Among the founders of NCRR were the Little Tokyo People's Rights Organization, the Japanese American Community Progressive Association, and the Asian Pacific Student Union—progressive groups that sought to place the redress and reparation movement in a larger political context. In November 1980, in Los Angeles, the NCRR organized an interorganizational redress conference to mobilize the Asian American community for a protracted struggle.

In 1980, a study commission bill was approved and the following year, President Jimmy Carter's Federal Commission on Wartime Relocation and Internment of Civilians held public hearings to investigate belatedly the concentration camps and their effects on prisoners. Unexpectedly, many former prisoners came forth to testify about their ordeal, and even more came to listen to them. Equally important, the commission concluded that the internment had not been justified by military necessity. "It listed the 'historical causes' shaping the decision to relocate the Japanese Americans to be 'race prejudice, war hysteria and a failure of political leadership.' " [24]

After years of persistent effort, the redress and reparations movement was successful. On 10 August 1988, President Ronald Reagan signed the Civil Liberties Act, authorizing $1.25 billion in reparation payments to an estimated seventy thousand survivors of the concentration camps. Each internee was to receive $20,000 and a formal letter of apology from the president of the United States. When Attorney General Dick Thornburgh handed out the first payments to elderly Japanese American internees, he told the recipients that even when the American "system (of government) failed you, you never lost faith in it . . . by finally admitting a wrong, a nation does not destroy its integrity but, rather, reinforces the sincerity of its commitment to the constitution and hence to its people." [25]

Both the Lungren controversy and the redress and reparations movement proved that Asian Americans were becoming a political force to be reckoned with, that they could overcome their diversity and develop a common political agenda. The political power they displayed was, in part, the result of their previous decade of involvement in party politics.

Party Politics

The story of Asian Americans' involvement in party politics since the mid-1970s is principally the story of their participation in the Democratic party. Initially, Democrats worked harder than their Republican rivals to recruit Asian Americans. Democrats portrayed themselves as the party of the underdog, and "highlighted anti-Asian discrimination as an issue that bridges the political and cultural divisions among immigrants from different parts of the Far East."[26] This approach has been more effective with older Asian American groups such as the Chinese and Japanese, who have had to endure a long history of discrimination in the United States, than with newer immigrants who came with some money and those who have achieved economic success. Another exception has been Southeast Asian refugees: Because of their strident anticommunism, they may be considered the Cubans of the Asian American community and have gravitated toward the more conservative Republican party, with its emphasis on family, education, the work ethic, and an anticommunist foreign policy.[27]

The 1976 Jimmy Carter presidential campaign first stimulated significant Asian American interest in electoral politics. Carter waged a populist and moralist campaign, one that included a role for minorities. He deserves credit for being the first candidate to include Asian Americans in the making of a president. He was undoubtedly sincere when he sent *Bridge* magazine a letter saying, "Asian Pacific Americans have played a role in the development of our country, and we wish that their legitimate aspirations be recognized. Together with all people we can work for an America that is truly democratic."[28] In a more pragmatic vein, he appreciated the political potential of minority voters, especially since it was the support of his African American constituency that had made him governor of Georgia. The passage of the 1975 Voting Rights Act underscored that potential. It prohibited literacy tests and required bilingual elections in states and counties that had 5 percent or more single-language minority citizens of voting age. For the first time, election handbooks and ballots were printed in Chinese and other languages for the primary elections, and bilingual registration cards were used in the presidential election.

As a matter of personal conviction and practical politics, Carter offered Asian Americans a role in his presidential campaign. He reached out to the Asian American communities through the Asian/Pacific American Unit (A/PA Unit), which was officially established on 7 September 1976—the first time any presidential candidate had given Asian Americans an opportunity to work in a presidential campaign.[29] The A/PA Unit developed from the national Asian Pacific Caucus, an ad hoc group that had participated in the Democratic convention in New York City. After the convention, some of the caucus people and one of Carter's representatives discussed the needs of Asian Americans. The Carter staff subsequently invited the caucus to form the A/PA Unit, which served mainly as a fund-raising machine. It became a part of the party's Minority Affairs section, together with black and Hispanic units. Even though it was a marginal one, astute Asian Americans recognized that here was an unprecedented opportunity to enter the political arena, and they responded with alacrity.

Since then, Democrats, especially those in California, have sought Asian American support. A case in point is Senator David Roberti, the senior California senator, who in 1987 established the Office of Asian/Pacific Affairs to give Asian Americans a direct means of making their views known on legislation and policies that affect their political, economic, and social interests. Roberti did this in order to compensate for the absence of Asian American legislators; since the defeat of Floyd Mori in 1980, not one of California's eighty assemblymen and forty senators has been Asian American. Roberti's Democratic colleagues were also reaching out to their Asian American constituency through their staffs. In 1986, Democratic assemblymen and senators appointed 98 percent of all Asian American staff in the state legislature.

In the Democratic party, Asian American involvement reached its apex with the establishment of the Asian Pacific Caucus (APC) in the summer of 1983. According to its founding chair, Thomas Hsieh, the APC grew out of Asian Americans' "frustration at not winning influence within the Democratic Party despite their heavy volume of campaign contributions in the 1980 Presidential election."[30] With the APC, it seemed that Asian Americans had finally come of age in the world of electoral politics. Congressman Norman Mineta called it the "best vehicle to maximize [Asian Americans'] political role."[31] Considered the voice of Asian American Democrats, the APC wielded substantial influence; at the 1984 national convention, it provided the party with an Asian Pacific Caucus platform, and candidates actively sought its support.

The APC planned to develop a network of state chapters to support an Asian American agenda, encourage Asian Americans to participate in Democratic politics, and affect the direction of the party and presidential candidate in 1988.[32] Envious Asian American Republicans began to want their own APC. At the 1984 National Republican Convention in Dallas, Anna Chennault, vice-chair of the Reagan campaign's ethnic voter division, and other Asian Americans asked the Republican National Committee (RNC) to set up a similar Asian Pacific Caucus and to treat them with the same regard given to other minorities, especially African Americans and Latinos. But Frank Fahrenkopf, the chair of the RNC, argued that a Republican Asian Pacific Caucus was "not necessary because we are all Americans" and that the special caucuses for Jews, African Americans, and Latinos were a thing of the past and would eventually be eliminated.[33]

Meanwhile, the Democrats were drawing the same conclusion, though for different reasons. Paul G. Kirk, Jr., the chair of the Democratic National Committee (DNC), thought that the Asian Pacific Caucus was also unnecessary. On 17 May 1985, the executive committee of the Democratic party voted to end the official status of the APC. After losing the 1984 presidential election, Kirk and other party leaders decided that in order to get away from the perception of Democrats as the party of special interests, they would have to eliminate the caucus system. Consequently, the APC was terminated, along with the gay and lesbian, liberal and progressive, and business and professional caucuses of the DNC. Only the black, Hispanic, and women caucuses, protected by the party's charter and bylaws, were unaffected.

Asian American Democrats were outraged. Mabel Teng, Northern California chair of the California Democratic party's Asian Pacific Caucus, denounced it as scapegoatism: "The blame for the Democratic Party's failure was placed on minorities . . . but this perception is wrong, as the minority vote has always been the backbone of past Democratic victories."[34] Carol Ono of the West San Gabriel Asian Pacific Democratic Club said that the party's message to Asian Americans was that "our concerns are meaningless, our vote is useless and our financial contributions are worthless."[35] Sandy Mori of the Nihonmachi Political Association condemned it simply as another example of exclusion and astutely anticipated that the Republicans would exploit it to recruit Asian Americans into their party.

Asian American Democrats demanded the return of their caucus, but the best they could get was the National Democratic Council of Asian and Pacific Americans (NDCAPA), the first independent national organization of Asian American Democrats. Political pundits perceived this as a thinly disguised effort to tap the financial resources of the Asian American community without granting it any political power. But Ginger Lew, the interim chair of the NDCAPA's steering committee, defined its mission as building the political strength of Asian Americans throughout the country. Later, Maeley Tom, who co-chaired the organization, reaffirmed this, saying that its goal was "to help mobilize, empower and unite the Asian Pacific Democratic constituency in order to impact a political process that has taken our dollars and votes for granted." [36]

For the 1988 presidential campaign, the NDCAPA sponsored "Target '88— Margin of Victory" (16–18 October 1987), the first national convention of Asian American Democrats. The success of the event prompted Senator Daniel Inouye to note that Asian Americans "were finally growing up . . . our national political leaders have seen this and I'm certain they've felt the strength, commitment and dedication emanating from this crowd." [37] Asian American political clout was demonstrated by the large number of high-level political figures attending this unprecedented event. Several presidential candidates, seeking both money and endorsements, addressed the gathering. While Senator Paul Simon "outpromised" the others by pledging, if elected, to name an Asian American to his cabinet, among other high posts, it was Jesse Jackson who was received with the most enthusiasm.

The Rainbow Coalition

When Jesse Jackson entered the 1984 and 1988 presidential races, he dramatically raised the nation's awareness of ethnic concerns and minority politics. He based his bid for the Democratic party's presidential nomination on a Rainbow Coalition that welcomed people of every hue—a variant of the traditional Democratic party strategy of building political power on a coalition of ethnic groups, in this instance mainly racial minorities. As the only candidate to inject the interests of the poor and powerless into the campaign, he, more than anyone else, spoke for people of color. Even though the Rainbow Coalition was mainly dominated by African Americans, it promised greater involvement for Asian Americans and other disenfranchised members of society in national politics. Essentially, Jackson told Asian Americans and others who had been traditionally excluded from power that their time had come. On 26 May 1988, in a speech to Asian American supporters in San Francisco, he said: "We must remove all the barriers based upon ethnicity, sex or religion. We are fully American citizens [with] every right and every privilege appertaining thereto. It's not enough for you just to support me. . . . You must be so free in your spirit, expressing your Americanness to break out of any stereotype that will limit your growth or limit your participation." [38]

As a matter of principle, Jackson emphasized the singular importance of economic and social justice in a democratic society and stood for such classic liberal principles as individual equality, minority rights, and freedom of expression. On domestic issues, he called for a comprehensive national health program, subsidized child care, and a federal jobs program; on international issues, he advocated self-determination, human rights, and economic development. Jackson was convinced that Ronald Reagan had brought the government to the brink of economic and political crises with his excessive military spending and maldistribution of wealth. If elected, Jackson intended to change the government's priorities and allocate funds "to education, health care, job retraining, public works, and debt reduction." [39] Meanwhile, his party rivals followed popular political trends and moved to the right to counter the conservatism of the Republican party.

Jackson was the first presidential candidate to take Asian American concerns seriously. He went to Asian American communities to talk to people directly and to learn about their lives. On 31 March 1984, he went to New York's Chinatown, the first presidential candidate ever to do so.[40] He addressed Asian American issues, integrating them into larger campaign themes such as the demand for corporate responsibility to all the American people and the impact of Reaganomics on people of color. Speaking of the brutal beating of Vincent Chin on 19 June 1982 in Detroit by two European American auto workers who thought that he was Japanese and taking away their jobs, Jackson added that "perhaps, it would have been a fairer trial if all the politicians, all the corporate executives, the union leaders, and the journalists who have told the American people to 'blame it on the Japanese' had stood trial with those two auto workers." [41] In his stunning speech at the Democratic National Convention, Jackson said, "The Rainbow Coalition includes Asian-Americans, now being killed in our streets—scapegoats for the failures of corporate, industrial and economic policies." [42] For a group historically excluded from and abused by the political process, this was heady stuff.

Jackson remained consistent in his support of Asian American concerns throughout both campaigns. On 26 May 1988, in San Francisco, he spoke to those same issues: "In each instance [of racial violence], someone felt they had the right to eliminate another human being, because they didn't like the way they looked, or talked or what they stood for. That idea threatens us all. When they killed Vincent Chin, they said, "We're sorry. We thought he was Japanese." [43] Unlike Richard Gephardt, a Democratic rival who deliberately engaged in Asia-bashing to win votes, Jackson placed the blame squarely on the shoulders of American corporations: "The fact is that the largest computer company in Japan, that hires 18,000 employees, is IBM. Last year, America bought seven million bicycles from Taiwan. Taiwanese didn't take jobs away from us. Schwinn and other companies took jobs to Taiwan. Let's be fair." [44] He stated what should have been obvious to others—that Asian Americans were not responsible for America's troubles: "Asian Americans didn't make the decision to run up this budget deficit. Asian Americans didn't make the decision to run up the trade imbalance, to cut back on affordable housing, or arms for hostages." [45]

Jesse Jackson's core Asian American supporters were political activists, usually "progressive, or to the left on the political spectrum of liberals." [46] They were people who identified politically with the poor and working-class sectors of the Asian American communities and with Jackson's constituency of "the damned, disinherited, disrespected and the despised." [47] They saw his campaign as an opportunity to strengthen their ties to African Americans and other oppressed people. Initially, they participated in Jesse Jackson's Rainbow Coalition as a way to protest the Reagan administration's politics and policies. From their perspective, the Reagan era represented nothing less than a thermidorean period in which the bourgeoisie sought to recoup the profits and power it had lost earlier. It constituted a conservative assault that set the country back decades, and people of color bore the brunt of Reaganism. Among the casualties were the liberal reforms of the 1960s and 1970s. Affirmative action programs were rolled back; social and human services programs were dismantled. Asian Americans found their status as a protected group in jeopardy, with support for Asian American Studies, inclusion in college minority admissions and tutorial programs, and federal economic development programs eroding. They saw the

Jackson campaign as a legitimate way to advance their own political agenda. At the 1984 Democratic National Convention, for example, they worked with Latino delegates to organize a boycott of the convention as a way of expressing their dissatisfaction with immigration-reform legislation pending in Congress, though the boycott failed because of the opposition of Walter Mondale's supporters, who included the Asian American and Latino members of Congress.[48]

Asian American political activists rallied around Jesse Jackson because he was the only genuine liberal populist among the various presidential candidates, Democrat and Republican. They were attracted to him because he was leading a social movement as well as an electoral campaign. They readily identified with the charismatic civil rights leader and saw his political rallies as protest demonstrations reminiscent of an earlier era. As an editorial in *The Nation* aptly described it: "The [Jackson] campaign had became a new civil rights movement with an added dimension of economic justice deriving in spirit from the last campaigns of Martin Luther King Jr. with the black working poor."[49] They saw his campaign as a movement for political empowerment, one that did not end with the election of a president. For Asian American activists, political empowerment, broadly defined, meant on one level electing or appointing their own representatives to government positions; on another, it meant grassroots organizing. Or as "Butch" Wing, vice-chair of the Northern California Jackson for President Committee, put it, it involved "winning elections on the local level, running for the Board of Supervisors, running for the Board of Education, City Councils, Congress, Senate, . . . Presidency, but also . . . grassroots organizing, fighting for affirmative action, jobs for minority workers, anti-discrimination work."[50]

Jackson addressed issues to which many of them had devoted their political lives. From their perspective, his message was both left liberal and class militant; his agenda was for social change, income redistribution, and a noninterventionist foreign policy. This was reason enough to support him. They were undeterred by the fact that the public believed that he was unelectable. (According to polls taken in late 1987, even though Jackson had made enormous strides in gaining recognition as an able and attractive leader, one who was seen as caring about the needs of ordinary citizens, he was viewed unfavorably as a presidential candidate.[51]) Indeed, to these activists, the prediction that he would inevitably lose the race for the presidency may have made him even more appealing, since it protected them from accusations of "selling out" to the established political system. At most, they could be accused of joining a lost crusade.

Finally, Asian American political activists realized that Jackson appreciated them as no other candidate did. They were an integral part of his campaign, treated with respect, appointed to high-level positions in the national staff or in state campaign posts, not just token jobs.[52] Two of the most prominent were Mabel Teng and Eddie Wong, both of whom were and still are members of the Chinese Progressive Association. Teng was the highest vote-getter among the 5th Congressional District Jackson delegates in both 1984 and 1988 and had the singular honor of introducing Jackson to the 1984 Democratic National Convention and again in North Carolina when he announced the start of his 1988 campaign. Wong served as head of the California management team in 1984 and as national field director of the 1988 campaign. As field director, he built state organizations for the primaries and directed field operations in Virginia, Michigan, South Carolina, and other states. He and his staff identified congressional districts, analyzed past results, and designed voter-contact strategy, that is, the use of radio and television spots, telephone calling, and other methods of getting Jackson's message to Democrats voting in the primaries. During the election, Jackson singled out Wong for public praise: "Some of those victories in caucus states, where it was said we could not win, the guy who engineered those victories and thought through the details of that organization and how to win those states was Eddie Wong."[53]

An activist himself, Jackson recognized that Asian Americans such as Teng and Wong had valuable skills to contribute to his presidential campaign. He used their grassroots organizing experience and their network of community contacts to win primaries and caucuses throughout the country and to dumbfound his critics. With less money to finance a national campaign than his competitors, he had to decentralize his campaign. He allowed many important decisions to be made by "community organizers, tenant group leaders, unionists or local political figures who form the Jackson organization state by state."[54] Eddie Wong described the style of the campaign as "the equivalent of guerrilla warfare," one that relied "on the people who are our supporters to come up with whatever strategies they find are most appropriate."[55] This strategy allowed the Jackson campaign to win Alaska, even though the national campaign's investment was essentially a box of buttons mailed from the Chicago headquarters. Consequently, Jackson was able to gather his 1,300 delegates at an estimated cost of about $10,000 each, as against about $25,000 for Michael Dukakis, the biggest spender of the campaign. The Jackson campaign was American participatory democracy at its best.

Asian American political activists brought liabilities as well as assets to the Jackson campaign.[56] The most troublesome was the continuing rivalry between Asian Americans for Equality (AAFE) and the Chinese Progressive Association (CPA), both of which supported Jackson. Since they generally agreed on the issues Jackson should address, they had the basis for a rapprochement; instead, they saw the campaign as simply one more battleground to contest. The main struggle was over who would dominate the Asian American component of the Rainbow Coalition. Linda Peng, New York State Asian American coordinator for the Jesse Jackson 1984 campaign and adviser to AAFE, alleged that for political reasons CPA had tried to replace Bill Chong with Cindy Ng as head of the National Asian American Desk.[57] The CPA certainly considered Chong a distinct liability to the Jackson campaign and worked for his removal. Sasha Hohri, a member of the New York Asians for Jesse Jackson and a CPA supporter, noted in a letter to supporters of Jesse Jackson:

> The situation with the National Asian Desk (Bill Chong) is still not re-solved. We have been talking to the national campaign people both from New York and California. Washington recognizes that the situation is not good and has to be dealt with, although it is unclear exactly what they are going to do. We in New York and California feel that we have to pursue Chong's removal because he has been and continues to be damaging to the campaign.[58]

Given the presence of CPA members in high positions within the Jackson campaign and the paucity of AAFE members, it appears that the CPA wrested control of the campaign from AAFE. But, meanwhile, AAFE members continued to insinuate themselves into the Democratic party. For example, Bill Chong and Margaret Chin, both of whom are AAFE members, served on the National Democratic Council of Asian and Pacific Americans Board of Directors.

Before the 1984 and 1988 Jesse Jackson presidential campaigns, Asian American political activists had been living a frustrating life on the political fringe. The campaigns gave them an opportunity to work within the established political system without unduly compromising their ideals. They found it unnecessary to disavow their membership in left-wing organizations, since many of Jackson's staff had similar affiliations, convictions, and perspectives. Some of Jackson's key foreign policy advisers, for example, were from the Institute of Policy Studies, an organization that had "links to hard-left organizations all over the world." [59] The campaigns allowed them to expand their contacts with leftists as well as other political activists and to work with Democratic party regulars. They also gave them the opportunity to experience the electoral process firsthand. As Eddie Wong pointed out: "They picked up invaluable experience and training in putting together campaigns, registering voters, mobilizing support networks, and organizing political operations and fund-raisers, which will serve them well in future political efforts." [60]

Perhaps what is most significant, Asian American political activists who worked within the Rainbow Coalition have been inspired to continue working in electoral politics. Given the limited victories of the Jackson campaigns, it would have been understandable if they had abandoned electoral politics and retreated to radical politics. But they did not. Instead, they look forward to other races on the political horizon. As Eddie Wong noted, "We need to elect progressives. . . . We need to continue to find a way to broaden our base." [61] And Asian American political activists have been doing just that.

A New Generation of Politicians

As a result of their increased involvement in party politics, Asian Americans have been encouraged to seek public office. For most activists, the litmus test of political power will be their ability to elect their own to office. Beyond the matter of pride, Asian Americans feel that the time has finally come to reverse the historical trend of non- or underrepresentation in government. They feel that Asian American politicians will have a natural affinity for their needs and concerns and expect such politicians to be in the vanguard in authoring legislation and addressing issues that affect the community. They also believe that Asian American politicians will represent all Asian Americans, whether they are constituents or not. There are of course no guarantees, but the few Asian Americans elected to office have more or less met these expectations.

A recent case in point is these politicians' indispensable role in compelling the government to do a 100 percent tabulation of Asian Americans during the 1990 census. Originally, the Census Bureau had intended to abandon the 1980 census approach, which used a check-off system specifying nine Asian ethnic groups, in favor of one that lumped all Asian Americans into one category and asked respondents to write in their specific group. The check-off system was more accurate because, among other things, it would "enable many limited English proficient persons to understand and answer the race question accurately." [62] Political and community leaders realized that the bureau's alternative method would cost Asian Americans funding for social services and full representation in the redistricting process. Congressman Robert Matsui, for one, thought that the decision to collapse the categories into one was not simply a matter of economy but "an effort by the Office of Budget and Management to limit the count so that funds (to minorities) will be limited." [63] In 1988, both Matsui and Senator Spark Matsunaga sponsored bills that would require the bureau to use the check-off form of tabulation in the 1990 census. Even though Matsui's measure received unanimous support from both houses of Congress, President Reagan vetoed it, ostensibly because it would restrict all future forms regarding the race question and because the check-off method was less accurate. But the bureau finally bowed to continuous Asian American pressure.

Two kinds of Asian Americans have been elected to office on the mainland in recent years: those who worked their way up through conventional politics and those who made their way through the more circuitous route of radical politics. Mike Woo, who won a seat on the Los Angeles City Council in 1985, and Warren Furutani, who won a seat on the Los Angeles Board of Education in 1988, are representative types. Woo is an outstanding product of the orthodox political process. He believes that politics is an honorable profession and that public service is an obligation. Furutani is a radical par excellence, with a reputation for candor and charisma. He is the quintessential community organizer who has been associated with social justice issues most of his adult life. Both were the first Asian Americans ever to hold their respective elected offices, and both unseated incumbents who were out of touch with their constituencies. The key to their success was running as representatives of the entire community, rather than as Asian Americans. Their election to and continuation in office have reflected their ability to create coalitions by being sensitive to the many different ethnic groups in their districts, addressing broad issues, and gaining wide support. But the foundation of those coalitions has been Asian Americans.

In 1987, the *California Journal* selected Michael Woo as one of the seven most promising young politicians who would lead the state into the twenty-first century.[64] Two years earlier, Woo had defeated fourteen-year incumbent Peggy Stevenson and attained a place on the Los Angeles City Council. His journey to elected office was a relatively conventional one. It began at Alhambra High School, where he ran for president of the student body. Even though he lost, he retained his interest in the political process, particularly in how to build support among different groups. At the University of California at Santa Cruz (1969–1973), he participated in some local political campaigns. Except for taking some moral stances to protest the Vietnam War, he ignored campus protest politics. As a self-described moderate, he was not one for shutting down the campuses or joining the so-called Revolutionary Brigades. Instead of becoming alienated from government, like many of his generation, he developed a belief in "the ability of government to serve as a kind of equalizing force in society" and that "politics should provide the arena for debating and perhaps resolving disputes over our nation's commitment to military spending or the relative importance of social spending programs such as education."[65] In the summer of 1970, he served as an intern to state assemblyman David Roberti. When Roberti rose to senate majority leader six years later, he offered Woo a job as his aide. It was as Roberti's top aide that Woo learned his craft as a lawmaker.

Woo is the representative of the 13th District, an unusually diverse constituency of nearly a million people. He attributes his successful bid for office to a broad, multiethnic base of support that consisted of Asian Americans, Armenians, Latinos, gays and lesbians, political refugees from Central America, senior citizens, and 1960s' activists. But a significant portion of his funding came from the Asian American community. Approximately half of the $750,000 that Woo raised for his 1985 campaign came from Asian Americans, and they have supported him in other ways as well. When a court-mandated redistricting plan authored by his political opponent Richard Alatorre threatened to separate him from his political base in Hollywood and place him in a district designed for a Latino, a coalition of Asian American community groups rallied around him and went to City Hall to protest the plan. As one political pundit put it, the reason they came to his support was that since "Woo was the first and only Asian American ever elected to the Los Angeles City Council, his political survival became a community imperative."[66]

Instead of simply accepting an unfavorable reapportionment, Woo fought back with "a gusto and savvy that belied his relative newcomer status."[67] Labeling the plan as an attempt "to pit the city's two fastest-growing minorities against each other in the district,"[68] he angrily pointed out that it was designed to "make safer districts for the entrenched powers on the City Council who have stood in the way of representation for Hispanics for years."[69] Furthermore, he noted that it was unfair because "in addition to putting [him] in a district that's 65 percent Hispanic, they're creating a 50 percent white district in the center of the city to protect Councilman John Ferraro."[70] Probably as a result of Asian American pressure, Mayor Bradley immediately vetoed the Alatorre plan, saying, "My sense of justice and fairness simply will not permit me to redress an inequity to one ethnic protected class (Hispanics) at the expense of another ethnic protected class (Asian) which only a year ago achieved representation on the City Council for the first time in 205 years."[71] The plan that the City Council finally adopted preserved Woo's chances of retaining his seat. His successful fight against the original redistricting plan dispelled any images of him as a quiet Asian American who would not make waves, earning him the respect of political pundits.

Woo recognizes that he has a responsibility to all Asian Americans, who look to him as a spokesman for their community. He has appeared at reparations rallies in Little Tokyo and pushed for a senior citizens' center for Koreatown and a Chinese cultural center in Chinatown. He initiated negotiations with Frank Rothman, Metro-Goldwyn-Meyer/United Artists chairman and chief executive officer, that resulted in a disclaimer attached to the controversial movie *Year of the Dragon* which projected a negative image of Chinese and Chinatown.[72]

One of the dangers of speaking out on behalf of Asian Americans is being branded as a "special interest" candidate concerned only with Asian American issues. Woo believes that he had lost his 1981 campaign against Stevenson because he was perceived that way and that his ability to overcome this perception allowed him to win in 1985. He recognizes that his political future rests on his being taken seriously outside the Asian American community. As he told a group of Asian American Democrats, "We are faced with a very delicate balancing act: How to be as Asian as we need to be, in terms of developing a base of support, but at the same time not being so Asian that we offend or put off other people."[73]

Unlike Woo, Warren Furutani is a radical, though of the "individualist" sort.[74] When Furutani declared his candidacy for the Los Angeles Board of

Education, more than a few eyebrows were raised in the Asian American community. As the quintessential community activist with a history of involvement that goes back to the beginning of the Asian American Movement, he seemed like the last person to seek a position within the establishment, which he had regularly taken to task in his columns in *Gidra* and the *Pacific Citizen*. So it was with some satisfaction that older Japanese Americans thought that their prodigal son had finally grown up and returned to the fold. Others were of course disappointed; the Furutani they knew and respected was a dedicated activist who had spent the last twenty years of his life working on behalf of the Asian American community and speaking passionately about its concerns. It is little wonder that some were crying, at least metaphorically, "Say it ain't so, Warren."

Actually, Furutani remains essentially the same person with the same values; only his methods have changed with the times. Like many erstwhile leftists who witnessed the development and decline of the Asian American left, he suffered a crisis of faith and was forced to reconsider his involvement in radical politics. He realized that in order to be an effective community advocate in the 1980s, he had to move from radical politics, which was no longer a viable vehicle for bringing about social change, to the electoral politics arena. But his decision was not simply a matter of seeking political office for its own sake. If that had been the case, he could have run for a councilman's seat in Gardena, where he lived, rather than a seat on the Los Angeles Board of Education. Instead, he was convinced that education is the cornerstone of society and a vehicle for empowerment. He recognized that an excellent educational system is essential to the survival and success of Asian Americans and other minorities. For him, the school board is simply another venue for advancing the cause of Asian Americans and others. The difference is that now he had to come up with creative solutions to educational problems, rather than be concerned solely about the correctness of his position on an issue.

Against the advice of seasoned political observers, Furutani decided to challenge John Greenwood for the 7th District School Board seat. As a two-term incumbent, Greenwood appeared invulnerable and took his position for granted. Furutani observed that "he has been resting on whatever laurels he seems to think he has. His campaigning has been nominal. . . . We've been working extremely hard, and any advantage he has as an encumbent has been erased." [75] Only later in the campaign did Greenwood take Furutani's challenge seriously and began waging a mainly negative campaign against him. During a forum at the Ken Nakaoka Community Center, he accused Furutani of accepting campaign contributions from Japanese American businessmen implicated in a scheme to steal more than $100,000 worth of goods from the school district, trying to prove that he lacked the judgment necessary to make decisions involving the children in the district and the school district budget. While Furutani admitted receiving the donations, he had done so before the allegations against the businessmen were known. Meanwhile, Furutani had set the money aside and argued that the accused men were innocent until proven guilty. Because he took so much abuse for the crimes committed by fellow Japanese Americans and because he defended their right to a fair trial, Furutani won support from erstwhile opponents in the Japanese American community who had taken exception to his past activism.

Another tactic that backfired on Greenwood was his harping on Furutani's past activism and the "radical" statements Furutani had made as a *Pacific Citizen* columnist in the early 1970s, when he was a JACL staffer. Furutani turned this tactic to his advantage, for it allowed him to air the only skeleton in his closet: "Although attempts have been made to use what I've done in a negative way, we have said from the beginning that it's a strength. . . . We talked about it publicly because we're not ashamed of the activism, the willingness to stand up for justice, the willingness to take on the system when it was wrong—and now, the willingness to be a part of that system and make sure that it becomes right." [76] Indeed, Furutani's activism would hold him in good stead during the campaign, for his reputation as a long-time community activist attracted the support of hundreds of volunteers and the endorsements of well-known political figures and local organizations.

Furutani, the champion of the underdog, was now himself an underdog, albeit in an electoral campaign. He had become a cause célèbre, and Asian Americans rallied around him. They constituted a crucial part of his campaign, providing 70 percent of his volunteers and contributing 85 percent of his financial support. A small portion of his funding came from Asian Americans outside Los Angeles. He was invited to Asian American fund-raisers in San Francisco, New York, and Seattle, where he received support from such prominent people as Dale Minami, Don Tamaki, Kazu Iijima, and Yuri Kochiyama. While the amounts raised were modest—for example, $2,000 on his trip to Seattle—these trips gave his campaign a national character.

Unlike Michael Woo, Furutani was a novice in electoral politics and lacked the experience and resources to wage an effective campaign. He had to build a campaign organization from the ground up. As a veteran organizer who thought in political terms, however, he shrewdly decided to combine grassroots organizing with precinct organizing. He could count on hundreds of volunteers: Asian American as well as Latino and African American students from UCLA, European American teachers from the local union, and many others. They were the ones who went door to door to convince people to vote for him. Since the teachers had the most credibility with the people in the district, they were particularly effective. He recruited such political operatives as Sharon Maeda, who served as his campaign manager, and Carmen Perez, who served as the head of field operations, to assist him in mapping out campaign strategies and tactics. He focused on broad educational issues that concerned the different groups in the district, such as overcrowding in schools and bilingual education. He received widespread bipartisan, multiethnic support in the 7th District, which is 85 percent minority. Against all odds, Furutani managed to defeat the incumbent by a margin of 11,257 votes (51 percent) to 10,810 (48.9 percent), a mere 447 votes. Since then, he has been an effective advocate for his district, and in 1991 was reelected by 12,700 (or nearly 71 percent) of his constituents.

Other Asian American radicals have followed suit. The best known is Mabel Teng, founder of the Chinese Progressive Association in Boston and later cochair of the one in San Francisco. She sought a seat on the San Francisco Community College Governing Board, which has had such well-known Asian American members as Lillian Sing, Julie Tang, and Alan Wong. Because of Teng's high visibility in the Jackson campaigns and her platform to improve conditions for minorities in the city's community colleges, she received considerable support. Even the conservative Chinese Six Companies supported her "despite her pro-Communist China stands of the past . . . because (1) she's ethnic Chinese, and (2) she works for immigrant justice, an issue dear to their hearts." [77]

Teng was as good as her word. Upon assuming office in January 1991, she immediately worked to change the way the school worked with the minority community. The board passed two pro-minority resolutions calling for new hiring guidelines for the college and a plan to ensure the district's use of minority subcontractors. [78] The hiring guidelines were intended to increase the number of minority teachers: At present, City College has a faculty that is 73 percent European American and a student body that is 75 percent minority, including many Asian Americans. The second resolution enabled the district to develop a minority-enterprise program similar to the one used by the municipal government. Teng's only surprising stance was her opposition to a state assembly bill to encourage the election of minorities to community college boards by mandating elections by district rather than at-large. Her argument was that since Asian Americans were not concentrated in one area, they would be unable to elect one of their own people to college boards. She was probably correct and was simply looking after the interest of the Asian American community. Supporters of the bill thought that her position was based more on her desire to maintain the status quo in order to stay in office. If so, then Teng has learned the first rule of politics—survival. Her dilemma was hardly unique: It was a classic conflict between principle and politics, one that Asian American political activists will continue to face as they seek public office in the 1990s and beyond.

Asian Americans and Coalition Politics

One of the sobering realities of the 1980s was the demographic constraints on Asian American political power: The Asian American electorate was too small to win an election on its own. Asian Americans realized that the only possible way to acquire influence was to develop voting blocs and build political coalitions in major electoral districts. This was true in the April 1988 election of Judy Chu, a former activist, to the Monterey Park City Council.[79] According to an exit poll conducted by the Asian Pacific American Voters Coalition and the Southwest Voter Registration Institute of San Antonio, there was significant bloc voting for Chu, one of eight candidates for two City Council seats. Their data indicated that Chu received 88 percent of the Chinese vote and 75 percent of the Japanese American vote. But since Asian Americans make up only 35 percent of the city's electorate, success required significant support from others as well. And Chu got that support, receiving one in three European American and Latino votes. Altogether, she received a total of 3,594 votes, making her the highest vote-getter. In marked contrast, Victoria Wu, the other Chinese American council candidate, received only 22 percent of the Chinese American vote and had little appeal to the rest of the electorate. She finished last, with 530 votes. Don Nakanishi, one of the advisers to the exit-poll project, concluded that "Chu's success shows that Asians will give solid support to a strong candidate of their own race. At the same time . . . Wu's failure indicates that Asian voters do not automatically cast their votes along racial lines."[80]

What made the difference was Judy Chu's qualifications and an effective campaign organization. As a trained psychologist who counseled disabled students at Los Angeles City College and who had served on the Garvey School District Board of Education, she had the right credentials to run for the City Council seat. She organized a coalition that consisted of progressive elements of the slow-growth movement and the Citizens for Harmony in Monterey Park, and ran a model grassroots campaign involving extensive personal contact with voters and limiting contributions to $200 per person. Her platform emphasized ethnic harmony and controlled growth. If elected, she pledged to work toward bridging the gap that existed between various constituents in the city and to deal with its number one problem—development. Jose Calderon, president of the Latin United American Citizens of the San Gabriel Valley, characterized Chu this way:

> Unlike some individuals who are saying, "No growth, no development," she is saying we need to have the kind of development that will benefit the individuals in this community, that will allow for good quality schools and good quality living and people working together. She is not talking about any planned development at the expense of any group or individuals in this community. She works well with all people of all nationalities, and we decided that she's the type of person who can bring this community together.[81]

Since her election to the Monterey Park City Council, Chu has been embroiled in a number of controversies, usually on behalf of the Asian American community. Perhaps the most trying has been the one surrounding the firing of City Manager Mark Lewis for alleged incompetence and questionable conduct.[82] Chinese Americans protested the action because Lewis was known as one of their ardent supporters and were upset with Chu for casting the critical vote that led to his dismissal. But according to Chu, the protest against her was organized by Sam Kiang, the other Chinese American councilman, and former councilwoman Lily Chen. Their motives are uncertain, but presumably political and tinged with jealousy.

The first opportunity Asian American political activists have had to lay the foundation for viable voting blocs in selected districts around the country came with the 1990 census. In keeping with the law of the land, during 1991–1992 the government must reapportion and redistrict congressional seats according to the 1990 decennial census data. Under the 1965 Voting Rights Act and laws passed since then, it must also try to provide fair and effective representation for minority groups. In *Thornburgh* v. *Gingles* (1986), the Supreme Court ruled that, in effect, it was "illegal for a state or locality with racial bloc voting not to create a district in which minorities are in the majority if such a district can be created." [83]

During the 1981–1982 round of redistricting, officials had redrawn the district boundaries of Los Angeles County in such a way as to prevent the emergence of an Asian American voting bloc. Koreatown was split into three districts; Chinese Americans were divided between two council districts and Filipinos among four. [84] As a result, Asian Americans were reduced to no more than 5 percent in any one district, even though they make up 10 percent of the population and are the fastest-growing group in Los Angeles, one that will exceed the African American population within a decade. In a suit challenging the redistricting plan, Asian Americans criticized the City Council for ignoring the interest of the Asian American community. They alleged that the existing plan deprived them of an equal opportunity to participate fully in the political process, or to influence significantly the election of representatives of their choice, in violation of Section 2 of the Voting Rights Act; it also violated the Fourteenth (Equal Protection) and Fifteenth (Right to Vote) amendments.

The same pattern held true for New York City, where Chinatown was divided into two state assembly districts as well as two community board and school board districts, an action that Margaret Fung, executive director of the Asian American Legal and Education Fund, considered "almost the epitome of the doctrine of divide and conquer." [85] In her view, this gerrymandering made it "impossible for Asian Americans to have much impact on the electoral process, even if they voted in large numbers." [86] The reapportionment and redistricting that followed the 1990 census gave Asian Americans a chance to rectify this situation in both Los Angeles County and New York City.

The challenge for Asian Americans was to see that these two areas, as well as others in the country, were redistricted in a manner that maximized their political power. Their ultimate goal was to be able to elect Asian Americans to political office. As one political pundit noted, "advocating for politically advantageous district lines goes hand in hand with encouraging Asian Americans to run for political office." [87] Even though Asian Americans have been experiencing unprecedented population growth in the country in general and in California and New York in particular, there has not been a corresponding growth in Asian American elected officials. In California, they make up about 10 percent of the population, having increased by 127 percent during the 1980s; yet no Asian American held a seat in the state legislature during the decade, and currently they hold only 2 percent of all local, state, and federal elected offices in the state. New York State has the second-largest Asian American population in the country; yet no Asian American has held a seat in the state legislature or even the New York City Council.

Asian Americans in New York City have managed to obtain an "Asian-plurality" district as a result of the redistricting process. The New York City effort goes back to 1981 when it was determined that the Board of Estimate had discriminated against minority groups by violating the constitutional principle of one person, one vote. The board was eliminated and some of its authority was transferred to the City Council, making it a powerful part of the municipal government. Under a new city charter adopted in 1989, the City Districting Commission had the responsibility of transforming the thirty-five City Council districts into fifty-one and redrawing their boundaries to reflect the city's racial and ethnic diversity, creating "a historic opportunity to support candidates who reflect their philosophy." [88]

Since the Asian American population had grown from slightly more than 3 percent in 1980 to slightly more than 7 percent in 1990, activists had originally hoped to convince the commission to create at least two predominantly Asian American City Council districts: one based in New York's Chinatown, which is located on the lower east side of Manhattan, and the other in Queens, where a new Asian American community has emerged in recent years. But the demographic data showed that Asian Americans fell short of a majority in any one area; so, at most, they could carve out only one so-called Asian American district. Commission members were sympathetic to the idea of creating such a district, since they recognized the need for Asian Americans to protect themselves politically, a fact made painfully clear by the ongoing African American boycott of a Korean immigrant-owned grocery store in Brooklyn. The Asian American community proposed two conflicting redistricting plans. The central issue was, With whom should Asian Americans ally themselves—European Americans or Latinos?

Doris Koo, executive director of Asian Americans for Equality (AAFE), proposed plan A, which joined Chinatown to liberal European American areas.[89] She argued that because liberal European Americans had shown a past willingness to vote for Asian American candidates (an assertion supported by voting analyses from the 1987 judicial race), her plan gave the community a better chance of electing one of its own. Furthermore, she argued that combining minority groups into a single district, as her opponents had proposed, "not only runs the risk of blocking Asian representation but risks having all the minority groups defeated in favor of a white candidate." [90] But according to its opponents, plan A was really a thinly disguised attempt to facilitate the election of Margaret Chin, past president of AAFE, who had already announced her candidacy. It was at least true that the European American areas had overwhelmingly backed Chin in her race for the 1988 Democratic State Committee and reasonable to expect that they would support her bid for a seat on the City Council.

In contrast, a group known as the Lower East Siders proposed a multiracial district plan that joined Chinatown to neighboring Latino enclaves. They argued that their plan was in keeping with the spirit of the City Charter and would maximize minority representation. Their underlying belief was that "immigrant Chinese and Hispanic communities have common interests not shared by wealthier white voters, and together they can comprise a district that is 83 percent minority—enough to elect a minority candidate." [91] And that "AAFE sacrificed coalition-building among working-class people of color to advance its own political agenda: getting Chin elected." [92] According to Margaret Fung, "working-class Asians and Latinos in this area have successfully united in the past to win affordable housing, health care, immigrant services and bilingual education." [93] AAFE, however, noted that "its experience had shown Latino representatives on the Community Board would consistently vote down AAFE proposals for low-income housing because they perceived it as a threat to their own community." [94]

AAFE won. The City Redistricting Commission decided to create a district with the maximum Asian American population possible, rather than one in which the two groups would compete with each other. So, on 3 June 1991, it submitted a plan calling for an "Asian plurality" district. This district's voting-age population consists of about 41 percent European Americans and 38 percent Asian Americans, with the remainder mainly Chicanos–Latinos. Asian Americans will achieve a plurality if they can register the eligible voters. They will be able to exercise significant political influence if they can work with European Americans in the district, forming a coalition of such disparate elements as Chinatown garment workers and SoHo artists.

But AAFE's victory proved to be a hollow one. In the special September

1991 Democratic party primary election, its candidate, Margaret Chin, lost her bid for the District 1 seat on the City Council to Kathryn E. Freed, a party district leader and tenant lawyer. Chin was the favored candidate: She started campaigning early and outspent her opponent two to one, raising $80,000 and receiving $40,000 of public money.[95] (According to some political strategists, the "huge amount of publicity [surrounding] the bitter race compensated for . . . Chin's advertising.")[96] Yet she received only 31 percent of the vote, while Freed got 42 percent. Chin has charged that Asian American voters, presumably her supporters, were harassed and that "people were turned away from the polls, Chinese Americans were intimidated and called names."[97] Furthermore, she alleged that Freed supporters recruited another Asian American to run against her to split the Asian vote. In any event, she had decided to run as the Liberal party candidate. Since 70.7 percent of the voters were registered as Democrats, 10.4 percent as Republicans, and only .87 percent as Liberals, this was nothing more than a political gesture. Typically, winning the Democratic party's nomination was tantamount to winning the November general election; indeed, that is what happened.[98]

Chin's campaign was fraught with difficulties from beginning to end. She claimed with some justification that some people were trying to destroy her candidacy.[99] Asian American political activists who had opposed AAFE's redistricting plan also opposed her. They helped prevent her from receiving enough votes to obtain the endorsement of the Majority Coalition, which had been formed that summer to support "insurgent" City Council candidates. Later, they strongly protested the coalition's paying for her mailings and posters, arguing that only those candidates who received coalition endorsement were entitled to financial and organizational support. Another problem was the deceptive nature of her candidacy. The *New York Times* supported her opponent, in part, because Chin was "vague and misleading about her background and her positions on issues . . . [refusing] to clarify her past affiliations with the Communist Workers Party and other radical organizations."[100] It found this troubling because it reflected on her judgment and character. Evidently, so did the voters.

In their quest for empowerment, Asian Americans have explored two different political roads: radical and electoral. In the late 1960s, many of them took the radical road, which reached its apex in the mid-1970s. The antiwar movement had been the center of their political lives, keeping Asian Americans of different political persuasions together for the duration. When the Vietnam War ended in 1975, they were at a loss as to what to do next. Activists found themselves marooned in a political void and entered a period of reflection, reexamining strategies for bringing about fundamental change in American society and the Asian American community. Many concluded that the militant confrontational style of the late 1960s was no longer an effective tool for social change.

In the 1980s, the only viable option open to Asian American activists was electoral politics. By engaging in electoral politics they ended their political isolation and purely community role. The Jesse Jackson presidential campaigns made the transition from radical to electoral politics possible for many of them, especially those of a Maoist persuasion. These campaigns provided political activists with invaluable experience in conventional campaigning and contacts in the Democratic party, which they could transfer to other electoral efforts. In return, activists contributed organizational and communication skills honed over years of grassroots organizing and a commitment to changing society. Perhaps most important, the Jackson campaigns helped them overcome their ambivalence about a political system that had traditionally excluded Asian Americans and enabled them to enter mainstream politics without feeling that they had betrayed their ideals and abandoned their community. As more and more Asian American political activists become involved in electoral politics, the more likely it is that they will finally be able to achieve the Movement's goals of empowerment and equality, as well as progress toward the nation's goals of a democratic and ethnically pluralist society.

In anticipation that the 1990s would be a pivotal decade for empowerment, Asian Americans have been working to get more of their people involved in electoral politics. One of the earliest efforts in this direction was "Capturing the 1990s: The Decade of Asian Americans," a conference held on 24 March 1990 at the Clark Kerr Conference Center, the University of California at Berkeley. It was sponsored primarily by the League of Asian American Voters, which promoted it as the first national Asian American forum, with the mission of unifying, inspiring, educating, and encouraging Asian Americans to partici-pate more actively in the political process in the United States and share in their own governance. Only time will tell whether the 1990s will decisively empower Asian Americans, but it is at least certain that these years will be part of the slowly evolving but inexorable trend of Asian American involvement in the political process.[101]

Conclusion

The emergence of the Asian American Movement in the late 1960s was a watershed in the history of Asians in America. It was and remains a viable means to empower Asians in America by redefining them as Asian Americans and organizing them into an inter-Asian coalition to raise their sociopolitical status and improve their lives. As a reform movement, it sought to identify inequities in the existing system and tried to rectify them. At the same time, the Movement has given a national focus to previously separate and sporadic instances of resistance to racial oppression, linking diverse Asian ethnic groups and dispersed Asian ethnic communities in a common crusade for racial equality, social justice, and political empowerment. As such, it is in keeping with a fundamental tenet of American democracy, that group solidarity is a prerequiste for political power.

The Movement was born during a tumultous period in American history when the civil rights movement and other social movements challenged the country's definition of itself as a democratic pluralist society. It began when the antiwar movement made college-age Asian Americans aware that they suffered from a form of racial discrimination rooted in anti-Asian attitudes and could effectively oppose it through a pan-Asian movement based on a common history and culture. As members of a distinct racial minority, they realized that they shared a similar heritage and destiny in America. They learned to appreciate the political advantages to be gained from mutual cooperation and the pooling of resources. As their interests converged, they created a community that is a source of strength, capable of advancing those interests. At the same time, they actively organized others who agreed with their political goals, realizing that equal status and power could be attained only through collective action.

It is difficult to interpret the meaning and long-term significance of the Asian American Movement because those who participated in it have been divided in terms of their ideological outlook and practical relations with politics. The very nature and achievements of the Movement have become points of contention. Still, most would agree that its primary significance lies in its being a catalyst for change in individuals and their communities. At the center of the

Movement has been the emergence of an "Asian American" identity. Though this identity is still in the process of formation, it is clear that Asian Americans have transcended the communal and cultural limits of particular Asian ethnic groups to identity with the past experiences, present circumstances, and future aspirations of *all* Asians in America. By appealing to their shared experiences in America, a pan-Asian consciousness has evolved, overcoming the separate Asian ethnic nationalism that originally divided them. Simply by using the term *Asian American*, they helped make it part of society's vocabulary.

Equally important, the Asian American Movement created a generation of activists, individuals who were aware, astute, and willing to act for the collective benefit of the Asian American community. Not only did they become comfortable with their ethnicity, they also became knowledgeable about the problems confronting their people and adopted strategies, including militant demonstrations, to deal with them. In the course of participating in protest politics, they acquired invaluable organizational skills. Since most of them have been young adults, their involvement in Movement activities has proven to be the longest sustained voluntary effort of their lives, leaving an indelible imprint on them and a political legacy for those who follow to continue.

Whether reformers or revolutionaries, activists stand in direct contradiction to the derisive and dehumanizing stereotypes that depict Asians as a servile species—stereotypes created by the dominant society to keep Asian Americans in a subordinate place. Realizing this, Asian Americans have consistently challenged these crude caricatures and demanded portrayals that reflect their humanity and individuality. Through history, literature, art, and film, they have recovered old traditions, customs, and values and at the same time have developed new sensibilities, perspectives, and connections to serve as the basis for a new cultural synthesis that gives definition and depth to their ethnic identity. By developing an integrated identity and a coherent culture rooted in their experiences in America, they have begun to build the psychological–intellectual foundations for a pan-Asian solidarity that will enable them to approach mainstream American society on a more equal footing and participate more effectively in the ethnically pluralist society they are helping to build.

Activists also initiated other movements, none more important than the Asian American women's movement. As women activists grappled with the problem of racial inequality in American society, they became aware of the problem of gender inequality within the Movement. Almost from the beginning, they became conscious that Asian American women suffered from dual forms of oppression. Even if they successfully ended racism, they would still suffer from sexism. Like the larger Movement, theirs began with small, informal groups engaged in personal support and political study and evolved into large, formal organizations that addressed the status and concerns of Asian American women throughout the nation. This development has benefited the Movement in important ways: By actuating the potential of women activists, it has widened their participation in the Movement; and by politicizing formerly inactive women, it has moved them to participate in the common struggle for equality and empowerment. Even more important, it has empowered women to face inequalities in their lives and communities and to do something about those conditions.

The Asian American Movement further spawned a host of new institutions on campuses and in the communities that continue to serve as a basis for countervailing power in the wider society. One of the most influential has been Asian American Studies (AAS), a new field of inquiry in higher education. Throughout the country, AAS has introduced students to the Asian American experience, emphasizing a history of racial oppression and resistance, and has produced scholarship that offers a radical interpretation of that experience, challenging the glaring omissions and misrepresentations in existing texts and curricula. Among Asian American students, it has instilled the self-confidence and self-esteem that are essential for personal achievement and social activism.

While the struggle for AAS was being waged on college campuses, community activists founded, developed, and institutionalized equally important agencies in the Asian ethnic enclaves of America. They tried to make the existing social order more equitable and just by establishing two kinds of community-based organizations: social service organizations that provided services and resources mainly to working-class Asian immigrants and refugees, and alternative grassroots organizations that addressed such significant middle-class Asian American issues and concerns as discrimination in the workplace and the classroom. Of the two, the social service organizations have learned to adapt to the existing social system, making it possible to institutionalize themselves in the community and to serve their constituents over a longer period of time.

Both kinds of organizations, however, have contributed significantly to the social stability of the Asian American community by providing counseling services, welfare assistance, recreational facilities, and employment opportunities, thereby mitigating the deprivations of the ghetto, helping individuals to survive, families to remain intact, and communities to thrive. In the process, they have eclipsed the traditional organizations, which have failed to carry out their responsibility to provide for the welfare of the community. Furthermore, they have become a political force in their own right, challenging the control these conservative organizations had over the community and consequently democratizing its internal politics. And they have assumed the role of intermediaries to the dominant society as the traditional leaders and their organizations became increasingly irrelevant to the needs of the community. Perhaps most important, these community-based organizations have contributed to the Asian American community's cohesion, a necessary condition for collective action and advancement in a democratic pluralist society.

Though Asian American revolutionaries believed that these new campus and community institutions would have little lasting value and would eventually engender widespread frustration, they nevertheless tried to exploit them to obtain resources and influence in the Asian American community, as they prepared for the social *revolution* that was, to them, always looming over the political horizon. That revolution has not materialized—in part because the existing social order has been open and flexible enough to respond, albeit inadequately, to the needs of Asian Americans and other people of color. In the wake of sectarianism in the left community and the collapse of communism around the world, Asian American revolutionaries have deserted Marxist ideologies and Leninist organizations and have pursued their ideals through the electoral political system. Still, revolutionaries did bring a progressive political agenda to the Movement and helped policitize the community by raising important issues. And as experienced and disciplined cadres, they provided leadership and channeled resources to various social and political struggles. In the final analysis, their significance lies in having eroded the power of the conservative, traditional elite within the Asian American community and having served as a lighting rod for its malevolence. The chief beneficiaries of this development have been the reformers, whom the elite perceived as the lesser of two evils. Under such circumstances, reformers were able to tread their way between the revolutionaries and conservatives to effect social change in the community.

Finally, without necessarily intending to do so, the Asian American Movement has validated ethnic pluralism. Instead of increasing social fragmentation and tribalism, as some people feared might happen, it has enlarged the definition of who can be an American by serving as an effective means for Asian Americans to assert, on their own terms, their right to belong to this society and to be treated as respected and responsible members of it. Though American ethnic pluralism has hardly met its ideal specifications, it remains a viable concept to many and is certainly an idea worth pursuing. For that reason, a new generation of Asian American student activists has emerged to participate in the multicultural education movement, revitalizing the Movement on the eve of the twenty-first century. Multiculturalism traces its lineage to ethnic studies and is based on the belief that the country's common culture is the result of the interaction of its component cultures, of which Asian American culture is one. In other words, America's common culture is inherently multicultural. As such, multiculturalism is repudiating the older "melting pot" perspective, which predicted the eventual disappearance of ethnic differences in American society and the emergence of a homogeneous national culture, in favor of a "pluralist" perspective, which accepts and affirms ethnic pluralism as a positive phenomenon. According to the advocates of ethnic pluralism, being an ethnically pluralist society has been a major source of the nation's strength and a salient feature of its democratic tradition, protecting it from those who have advocated a social revolution as the solution to its problems. In a milieu where ethnic diversity is valued as a good—in itself or in its results—Asian Americans have done their share to oppose racial oppression, protest against social injustices, and participate in the political process, helping to build a stronger and more perfect union.

Abbreviations

AAFE	Asian Americans for Equality
AAFEE	Asian Americans for Equal Employment
AAFM	Asian Americans for a Fair Media
AAMHRC	Asian American Mental Health Research Center
AAPA	Asian American Political Alliance
AAS	Asian American Studies
AATFUA	Asian American Task Force on University Admissions
ACC	Asian Community Center
ACV	Asian Cinevision
AIWA	Asian Immigrant Women Advocates
APA	Asian Political Alliance
A/PA	Asian/Pacific Americans
APC	Asian Pacific Caucus
APSU	Asian Pacific Student Union
ASG	Asian Study Group
ASU	Asian Student Union
AWU-NY	Asian Women United–New York
AWU-SF	Asian Women United–San Francisco
CAA	Chinese for Affirmative Action
CAAAV	Committee Against Anti-Asian Violence
CADRA	Chinese American Democratic Rights Association
CCBA	Chinese Consolidated Benevolent Association (also known as Six Companies)
CCC	Campus Community Council
CHM	Chinatown History Museum
CLUW	Coalition of Labor Union Women
CPA	Chinese Progressive Association

CPC	Chinatown Planning Council (later, Chinese-American Planning Council)
CPUSA	Communist party–United States of America
CWP	Communist Workers party
DNC	Democratic National Committee
DPAA	Demonstration Project for Asian Americans
ECASU	East Coast Asian Student Union
EOP	Equal Opportunity Program
FANHS	Filipino American National Historical Society
GPA	Grade Point Average
ICCCA	Interim Coordinating Committee for Chinese Americans
ICLC	Intercollegiate-Liaison Committee
ICSA	Intercollegiate Chinese for Social Action
I-Hotel	International Hotel
IHTA	International Hotel Tenants Association
ILGWU	International Ladies Garment Workers Union
IWK	I Wor Kuen
IWY	International Women's Year
JACL	Japanese American Citizens League
JANM	Japanese American National Museum
KCCEB	Korean Community Center of the East Bay
KDP	Katipunan ng mga Demokratikong Pilipino (Union of Democratic Filipinos)
KMT	Nationalist party (Kuomintang)
Leway	Legitimate ways
LRS	League of Revolutionary Struggle
MAPASAN	Midwest Asian Pacific American Student Association Network
MLMTT	Marxism–Leninism–Mao Tse-tung Thought
NAACP	National Association for the Advancement of Colored People
NCRR	National Coalition for Redress/Reparations
NDCAPA	National Democratic Council of Asian and Pacific Americans

NLRB	National Labor Relations Board
NOW	National Organization for Women
NYC	New Youth Center
NYCHP	New York Chinatown History Project
OAW	Organization of Asian American Women
OCA	Organization of Chinese Americans
OCAW	Organization of Chinese American Women
PAAWWW	Pacific Asian American Women Writers-West
PACE	Philippine-American College Endeavor
Pan Asia	Organization of Pan Asian American Women
PCPA	Progressive Chinatown People's Association
PL	Progressive Labor party
PRC	People's Republic of China
RCP	Revolutionary Communist party (formerly Revolutionary Union—RU)
RNC	Republican National Committee
SCFA	Student Coalition for Fair Admissions
S/CP	Student/Community Projects
SDS	Students for a Democratic Society
SHE	Self-Help for the Elderly
Triple A	Asian Americans for Action
TWCC	Third World Coalition Council
TWLF	Third World Liberation Front
WEEA	Women's Educational Equity Act
WMS	Wei Min She
WVO	Workers Viewpoint Organization
YAASA	Yale Asian American Students Association

Notes

Introduction

1. Sucheng Chan, ed., *Entry Denied: Exclusion and the Chinese Community in America, 1882–1943* (Philadelphia: Temple University Press, 1991), discusses the Chinese exclusion laws, their implementation and significance.

2. Victor Low, *The Unimpressible Race: A Century of Educational Struggle by the Chinese in San Francisco* (San Francisco: East/West Publishing, 1982), discusses the struggle of Chinese Americans to gain access to a public school education in San Francisco. In that city, formal de jure segregation ended after World War II, though de facto segregation persisted for some years.

3. According to U.S. Department of Commerce, Bureau of the Census, *Subject Reports: Japanese, Chinese, and Filipinos in the United States* (1970), there were 51,256 Chinese Americans, 12,738 Filipino Americans, 38,329 Japanese Americans, and 5,043 Korean Americans enrolled in college. Why so many Asian Americans wanted to attend college is uncertain. Perhaps they realized that even though their chances of moving up in American society were slim, they would have no chance at all without an advanced education. Betty Lee Sung, *A Survey of Chinese-American Manpower and Employment* (New York: Praeger, 1976), argues that for Chinese Americans, the reason was the "high esteem accorded men of learning within the Chinese system of cultural values" (pp. 59 and 60).

4. Except for a few Asian Americans who received their political baptism in the earlier civil rights movement, most of the Asian American activists interviewed for this study recalled being involved in or influenced by the antiwar movement.

5. According to Peter Lyon, "The Emergence of the Third World," in *The Expansion of International Society*, ed. Hedley Bull and Adam Watson (Oxford, England: Oxford University Press, 1984), pp. 229–237, the name " 'the Third World' was first coined in France in the early 1950s" (p. 229). In this study the Third World refers to U.S. racial minorities (African Americans, Asian Americans, Latinos, and Native Americans). Apparently, during the 1960s, political activists appropriated the term from the international arena, where it was used to refer to the technologically less advanced nations of Asia, Africa, and Latin America, as a way of identifying with the formerly colonized nations of the world and to protest the domination by whites in American society. In the 1990s, it has been superseded by the expression "people of color."

6. On 21 January 1974, the U.S. Supreme Court unanimously decided in favor of the Asian Americans, agreeing that the San Francisco Board of Education had violated the Civil Rights Act of 1964 and the Department of Health, Education and

Welfare guidelines when it failed to provide adequate English instruction to 1,800 children of Chinese ancestry. L. Ling-chi Wang, *"Lau* v. *Nichols*: The Right of Limited-English-Speaking Students," *Amerasia* 2, no. 2 (Fall 1974): 16–45.

7. Samuel R. Cacas, "Asian Pacific Leaders Protest to Civil Rights Act," *Asian Week*, 13 December 1991.

8. Dennis Hayashi, "1991 Civil Rights Bill Has Roots in Anti-Asian Bias," *Asian Week*, 7 June 1991.

9. U.S. Department of Health, Education, and Welfare, Office of Special Concerns, *A Study of Selected Socio-Economic Characteristics of Ethnic Minorities Based on the 1970 Census, Volume II: Asian Americans* (July 1974), p. 10.

10. As with other social movements of the 1960s, there is no accurate way to determine how many Asian American activists there were in the beginning. Reports indicate that hundreds of Asian Americans participated in antiwar demonstrations and attended the early Asian American conferences. In addition, some joined the numerous campus and community organizations that emerged during the late 1960s and early 1970s.

11. James L. Wood and Maurice Jackson, *Social Movements: Development, Participation, and Dynamics* (Belmont, Calif.: Wadsworth Publishing, 1982), p. 3.

12. One of the reasons for its absence from the social movement literature is timing. Since the Asian American movement emerged only in the late 1960s, it would have been too late to be included in Anthony Oberschall, *Social Conflict and Social Movements* (Englewood Cliffs, N.J.: Prentice-Hall, 1973), the first systematic account of social movements to be published in the early 1970s; or in Barry McLaughlin, *Studies in Social Movements: A Social Psychological Perspective* (New York: Free Press, 1969), an anthology of essays on social movements from a social-psychological perspective. Conversely, the Asian American Movement emerged too early to have been of interest to Carl Boggs, *Social Movements and Political Power: Emerging Forms of Radicalism in the West* (Philadelphia: Temple University Press, 1986), since he focused on the social movements of the 1980s. Less understandable is the omission in James L. Wood and Maurice Jackson, *Social Movements* (Belmont, Calif.: Wadsworth, 1982) which could have included an essay about some aspect of it in their "Social Movement Dynamics" section. In the case of Stewart Burns, *Social Movements of the 1960s: Searching for Democracy* (Boston: Twayne, 1990), the omission resulted from a decision to focus on only the major mass movements. Fair enough. But Burns goes on to say that the "others that emerged toward the end of this period, notably for Hispanic and Indian rights, gay liberation, and ecology, call for separate treatment" (p. xiii). Presumably, he would have included Asian American rights and called for equal treatment if he had known about the Asian American Movement. Therein lies the central problem, the Asian American Movement is simply not known.

13. Burns, *Social Movements of the 1960s*, p. 102.

14. David Caute, *The Year of the Barricades: A Journey through 1968* (New York: Harper & Row, 1988), p. 420. Incidentally, Asian Americans consider "Ori-

ental" to be a pejorative term because "the Orient was conceived by whites as someplace exotic and east of London." In contrast, the term Asian American "captures the notion that Americans of Asian ancestry are asserting their rights as full-fledged citizens." Dexter Waugh, "Ethnic Groups Change Names with the Times," *San Francisco Examiner*, 2 September 1991. Edward W. Said, in *Orientalism* (New York: Vintage Books, 1979), explains the way the idea of "orientalism" was created and transmitted.

15. Sucheng Chan, *Asian Americans: An Interpretative History* (Boston: Twayne, 1991); and Diane Mei Lin Mark and Ginger Chih, *A Place Called Chinese America* (Dubuque, Iowa: Kendall/Hunt, 1982). Also see "Radicals and the New Vision," in *Longtime Californ': A Documentary Study of an American Chinatown*, ed. Victor G. and Brett de Bary Nee (New York: Pantheon Books, 1973), pp. 355–396; "Grass-roots Organizing and Coalition Building" in Peter Kwong, *The New Chinatown* (New York: Hill and Wang, 1987), pp. 160–173; and "Red Guard versus Old Guards" in Shih-shan Henry Tsai, *The Chinese Experience in America* (Bloomington: Indiana University Press, 1986), pp. 167–171.

16. Ronald Takaki, *Strangers from a Different Shore: A History of Asian Americans* (Boston: Little, Brown, 1989); and Roger Daniels, *Asian America: Chinese and Japanese Since 1850* (Seattle: University of Washington Press, 1988).

17. L. Ling-chi Wang, "A Critique of *Strangers from a Different Shore*," *Amerasia* 16, no. 2 (1990): 71–80.

18. Ronald Takaki, "A Response to Ling-chi Wang, Elaine Kim, and Sucheng Chan," *Amerasia* 16, no. 2 (1990): 113–131.

19. Besides the four essays and *Amerasia* issue mentioned here, miscellaneous works that deal with aspects of the Asian American Movement include Grace Lee Boggs, "Asian-Americans and the U.S. Movement," an address given at the Asian American Reality Conference, Pace College, 5–6 December 1970 (reprinted by Asian Americans for Action in 1973); Steve Louie, "The Asian American Student Movement" (typewritten, 1972); and "The Asian American Movement (Greater Los Angeles)," a chronology and summary of the Asian American movement that focuses on the critical role that students have played in its development.

20. Paul Wong, "The Emergence of the Asian-American Movement," *Bridge* 2, no. 1 (September/October 1972): 33–39; and Amy Uyematsu, "The Emergence of Yellow Power in America," in *Roots: An Asian American Reader*, ed. Amy Tachiki et al. (Los Angeles: Asian American Studies Center, University of California, 1971), pp. 9–13.

21. Uyematsu, "The Emergence of Yellow Power in America," p. 13.

22. Ibid.

23. Ron Tanaka, "Culture, Communication and the Asian Movement in Perspective," *Journal of Ethnic Studies* 4, no. 1 (1976): 37–52.

24. Stephen S. Fugita and David J. O'Brien, *Japanese American Ethnicity: The Persistence of Community* (Seattle: University of Washington Press, 1991), discusses patterns of Japanese American economic development and intermarriage

and disputes the assertion that Japanese Americans are becoming an extinct Asian ethnic group.

25. Richard J. Jensen and Cara J. Abeyta, "The Minority in the Middle: Asian-American Dissent in the 1960s and 1970s," *Western Journal of Speech Communication* 51 (Fall 1987): 404–416.

Chapter 1: Origins of the Movement

1. Bob Blauner, *Black Lives, White Lies: Three Decades of Race Relations in America* (Berkeley: University of California Press, 1989); Henry Hampton and Steve Fayer, *Voices of Freedom: An Oral History of the Civil Rights Movement from the 1950s through 1980s* (New York: Bantam Books, 1990); Manning Marable, *Race, Reform and Rebellion: The Second Reconstruction in Black America, 1945–1982* (Jackson, Miss.: University Press of Mississippi, 1984); Aldon D. Morris, *The Origins of the Civil Rights Movement: Black Communities Organizing for Change* (New York: Free Press, 1984); Harvard Sitkoff, *The Struggle for Black Equality, 1954–1980* (New York: Hill and Wang, 1981); and Juan Williams, *Eyes on the Prize: America's Civil Rights Years, 1954–65* (New York: Viking, 1987), are informative studies on the African American struggle for civil rights.

2. Alan Wong, telephone interview, 22 November 1988. There are different versions of the convocation. L. Ling-chi Wang claimed that he organized it, while Heykmara credited the Intercollegiate Chinese for Social Action. Wang's assertion is corroborated by George Woo, who was a member of ICSA. It is certain that both Wang and the students were involved in the convocation and the demonstration that followed it. Interview with L. Ling-chi Wang, 15 October 1985, provided by Gary Kawaguchi; Kuregiy Hekymara, "The Third World Movement and Its History in the San Francisco College Strike of 1968–69," Ph.D. dissertation, University of California at Berkeley, 1972, pp. 77–79; and George Woo, interview, San Francisco, 27 March 1986.

3. "I.C.S.A." (Intercollegiate Chinese for Social Action, San Francisco, 1968; mimeographed), p. 1, cited in Heykmara, "San Francisco State College Strike," p. 76.

4. Interview with L. Ling-chi Wang, 15 October 1985.

5. Unless otherwise noted, the discussion on Leway is based on Alex Hing and Mae Ngai, interview, New York City, 24 August 1985; Ray Hing, interview, San Francisco, 26 March 1986; and Stanford M. Lyman, "Red Guard on Grant Avenue: The Rise of Youthful Rebellion in Chinatown," in Stanford M. Lyman, *The Asian in North America* (Santa Barbara: ABC-Clio, 1977), pp. 177–199; and the following articles from *Getting Together*: "A History of the Red Guard Party," vol. 4, no. 4 (16 February–1 March 1973); "Activities of the Red Guard Party, Part II," vol. 4, no. 5 (2–15 March 1973); "Concluding History of the Red Guard Party," vol. 4, no. 6 (16–29 March 1973).

6. Lyman, "Red Guard on Grant Avenue," p. 183.

7. Rita Himes, "The Limitations of Third World Struggle in the Confines of the White University: The Third World Liberation Strike at U.C. Berkeley, 1969." Typewritten.

8. Steve Louie, "The Asian American Student Movement" (typewritten, 1972).

9. Anonymous A and B, interview, Los Angeles, 27 June 1988.

10. Jeannie Look, "Remembering the S.F. State Strike," *East/West*, 20 October 1988; and idem, "After the S.F. Strike: EOP and the School of Ethnic Studies," *East/West*, 27 October 1988.

11. Unless otherwise noted, the discussion of the ICSA is based on George Woo, interview, San Francisco, 27 March 1986; Hekymara, "San Francisco State College Strike"; and William Barlow and Peter Shapiro, *An End to Silence: The San Francisco State College Student Movement in the '60s* (New York: Pegasus, 1971).

12. Lyman, "Red Guard on Grant Avenue," p. 188.

13. The discussion on the Free University is based on Tom Wolfe, "The New Yellow Peril," *Esquire*, December 1969, pp. 190–199, 322; George Woo, interview, San Francisco, 27 March 1986; and Ray Hing, interview, San Francisco, 26 March 1986.

14. Look, "Remembering the S.F. State Strike."

15. Heykmara, "San Francisco State College Strike," pp. 110–111.

16. Dan Gonzales, interview, San Francisco, 4 June 1987.

17. Barlow and Shapiro, *An End to Silence*; Heykmara, "San Francisco State College Strike"; and Robert Smith, Richard Axen, and DeVere Pentony, *By Any Means Necessary: The Revolutionary Struggle at San Francisco State* (San Francisco: Jossey-Bass, 1970) are examples of such studies. According to anonymous A, interview, Los Angeles, 27 June 1988, a former member of AAPA, most members of the group were active in the strike.

18. Anonymous A, telephone interview, 18 November 1988. Wolfe, "New Yellow Peril," describes Woo as "good and fierce . . . Kwang Kung-style!"

19. Unless otherwise noted, the discussion of San Francisco State's Asian American Political Alliance is based on Anonymous A and B, interview; and Penny Nakatsu, telephone interview, 27 November 1988.

20. Lyman, "Red Guard on Grant Avenue," p. 188.

21. Unless otherwise noted, the discussion of the Berkeley AAPA is based on ibid.; "Understanding AAPA," *Asian-American Alliance Newsletter* 1, no. 5 (1969); interview with Richard Aoki (undated), provided by Gary Kawaguchi; and George Woo, interview, San Francisco, 27 March 1986.

22. Interview with Richard Aoki (undated).

23. Ibid.

24. George Woo, interview, San Francisco, 27 March 1986.

25. Ibid.

26. Amy Tachiki et al., eds., *Roots: An Asian American Reader* (Los Angeles: Asian American Studies Center, University of California, 1971), pp. 273–274.

27. Unless otherwise noted, the discussion of the Asian Community Center is based on Steve Yip, interview, New York City, 21 and 24 August 1985.

28. Ibid.

29. Him Mark Lai, "The Kuomintang in Chinese American Communities," in *Entry Denied: Exclusion and the Chinese Community in America, 1882–1943*, ed. Sucheng Chan (Philadelphia: Temple University Press, 1991), pp. 170–212; Peter Kwong, *The New Chinatown* (New York: Hill and Wang, 1987), pp. 100–106; Victor Nee, "The Kuomintang in Chinatown," *Bridge* 1, no. 5 (May/June 1972): 20–24; Shih-shan Henry Tsai, *The Chinese Experience in America* (Bloomington: Indiana University Press, 1986), pp. 132–139; they discuss the relationship between the KMT and the Chinese Six Companies/Chinese Consolidated Benevolent Association.

30. Dan Gonzales, interview, San Francisco, 4 June 1987.

31. Floyd Huen, interview, San Francisco, 27 March 1986; and Steve Yip, interview, New York City, 21 and 24 August 1985.

32. Don Nakanishi, "Eastern Movement," *Gidra*, November 1969.

33. Ibid.

34. Louie, "The Asian American Student Movement."

35. Unless otherwise noted, the discussion of Asian Americans for Action is based on Kazu Iijima, interview, New York City, 24 June 1986; Glenn Omatsu, "Always a Rebel: An Interview with Kazu Iijima," *Amerasia* 13, no. 2 (1986–1987): 83–98; "Roots Interview with Asian Americans for Action" (typewritten, 1974); articles in *Asian American for Action Newsletter*, particularly "Editorial," vol. 1, no. 5 (December 1969); "Editorial," vol. 2, no. 2 (October 1970); "Early History of A.A.A.: Birth of a Movement in New York City," vol. 5, no. 1 (December 1972–January 1973); and Merrilynne Hamano, "The New York Asian Movement," *Gidra*, July 1973.

36. Letter from Kazu Iijima to the author, 14 August 1991.

37. Kazu Iijima, interview, New York City, 24 June 1986.

38. Triple A was a member of the Asian Coalition, a group of independent Asian American individuals and groups opposed to the Vietnam War. "Asian Coalition: Position Paper and Statement of Beliefs," *Asian Americans for Action* 4, no. 1 (February–March 1972).

39. This was a recurring theme in Triple A's newsletter. During its first year, Triple A issued a special edition on "U.S. Imperialism and the Pacific Rim," *Asian Americans for Action* 1, no. 4 (n.d.).

40. Smith, Axen, and Petony, *By Any Means Necessary*, p. 305.

41. Louie, "The Asian American Student Movement," pp. 1–30.

42. It has been suggested that the internal split may have resulted from racial reasons. It is doubtful that past animosity between Chinese and Japanese stemming from World War II was the cause. Yet there may be some truth to the assertion that Japanese Americans tended to be more interested in anti-imperialist issues and

Chinese Americans tended to be more community oriented, presumably because there were still Chinatowns.

43. Louie, "The Asian American Movement."

44. "Roots interview with Asian Americans for Action."

45. Ibid.

46. Unless otherwise noted, the discussion of the Asian Community Center is based on "Rally 'Round the Projected Asian Community Center!" *Asian Americans for Action Newsletter* 4, no. 2 (April–May–June 1972); Bill Kochiyama, "Accent Is on Harmony at Official Opening of Asian Center," *Asian Americans for Action Newsletter* 5, no. 1 (December 1972–January 1973); and "New York Asian Movement," *Gidra*, July 1973.

47. Rice Paper Collective, Madison Asian Union, "Rice Paper," *Rice Paper* 1, no. 1 (Summer 1974): 3.

48. For perspectives on the Chicago conference, see *Rice Paper* 1, no. 1 (Summer 1974); for position papers on the Madison conference, see *Rice Paper* 1, no. 2 (Winter 1975); and for a report on the mental health conference, see Madison Asian Union, "Asian American Health, Education and Welfare, Chicago Conference," *Rice Paper* 1, no. 1 (Summer 1974): 29–30.

49. Some of the more active groups were the Ann Arbor Asian Political Alliance (later called Yisho Yigung and succeeded by East Wind), Chicago New Youth Center, Detroit Asian Political Alliance, Madison Asian Union, Minneapolis Asian American Political Alliance, Oberlin Asian-American Alliance, and University of Illinois Asian American Alliance. For brief histories of the Oberlin Asian-American Alliance, Madison Asian Union, and Chicago New Youth, see *Rice Paper* 1, no. 1 (Summer 1974): 4–7.

50. Minneapolis Asian American Alliance, untitled handbill, 12 April 1974. Mimeographed.

51. University of Illinois Asian American Alliance, untitled and undated handbill. Mimeographed.

52. Oberlin Asian-American Alliance, "Asian-American Program at Oberlin," handbill, 9 April 1974. Mimeographed.

53. Unless otherwise noted, the discussion on the Ann Arbor Asian Political Alliance, Yisho Yigung, and East Wind is based on the author's observations while a graduate student at the University of Michigan in Ann Arbor from spring 1970 to summer 1978.

54. Ann Arbor Asian Political Alliance handbill announcing that it will hold a caucus during the Peace Treaty Conference to unite all Asian Americans against the war in Indochina, spring 1972. Mimeographed.

55. Told to the author by a former Asian Political Alliance member, who is currently working as an attorney in California.

56. During the Second Midwest Asian American Conference at Madison, there was a workshop on human sexuality. This prompted participants to write short

essays on the issue of homosexuality among Asian Americans. See Don Kao, "Sexuality: Highlighted at Midwest Conference," and Daniel Tsang Chun-tuen, "Asian Sexuality: An Asian-American Male Gay," *Rice Paper* 1, no. 2 (Winter 1975).

57. Mao Tse-tung, *Quotations from Chairman Mao Tse-tung* (Peking: Foreign Language Press, 1967), p. 80.

58. Philip L. Hays, "Teaching the Asian American Experience," 21 December 1973. Typewritten.

59. East Wind pamphlet, n.d.

60. Paul Terwilliger, "Minority Conference: 'Unity among All People,'" *Michigan Daily*, 1 March 1974.

61. Articles from the *Michigan Daily*: Gordon Atcheson, "Tranquil Mood Pervades Takeover," 19 February 1975; Rob Meachum, "Minorities Still Hold Ad. Bldg., 150 Vow to Remain Unless 'U' Complies," 20 February 1975; Rob Meachum, "Students End Ad. Bldg. Sit-In, Talks on Demands to Continue on Monday," 21 February 1975.

62. David Weinberg, "Sit-in '75: Ain't the Old Days," *Michigan Daily*, 27 February 1975.

63. Ibid.

64. One of the better-known supporters was Senator Daniel Inouye, who sent a special note to University President Robben Fleming to support the Asian American advocate demand. Editorial, "Asian-Americans Neglected," and Letters to the Editor, *Michigan Daily*, 21 February 1975; Editorial, "TWCC Demands Mixed Bag," *Michigan Daily*, 21 February 1975; and Cheryl Pilate, "Students Ask for Asian Advocate," *Michigan Daily*, 6 August 1974.

65. Editorial, "Asian-Americans Neglected," *Michigan Daily*, 21 February 1975.

66. The failure of the University of Michigan and other institutions of higher learning to address adequately the needs and concerns of their minority members would result in a return of racism to the campuses in the 1980s. Charles S. Farrell, "Black Students Seen Facing 'New Racism' on Many Campuses," *Chronicle of Higher Education* 34, no. 2 (27 January 1988); Susan Skorupa, "At Michigan Campus: Racial Tension Rises," *Colorado Daily*, 14 April 1987; "Campus Uniting Against Racism," *Michigan Today*, February 1988.

67. "Chronology of East Wind Locomotion: March 1975–May 1976." Typewritten.

68. Margaret Yao, "Asian Group's Activism Cools: East Wind Refocuses," *Michigan Daily*, 17 April 1976.

69. Unless otherwise noted, the discussion of the New Youth Center is based on Ted Liu, interviews, New York City, 18 and 24 August 1985; and "What Is the New Youth Center?" *Chinatown Newsletter*, no. 25 (October–November 1974).

70. A communication from Special Agent in Charge, Chicago, to Acting Director, FBI (marked secret), 23 June 1972.

71. Memorandum from Special Agent in Charge, Chicago, to Acting Director, FBI, 24 April 1973. After following the activities of the New Youth Center over a two-year period, the Chicago office finally concluded that "there is no indication that the objective of the New Youth Center (NYC) is to overthrow the United States Government by force or violence." Airtel communications from Special Agent in Charge, Chicago, to Director, FBI (marked secret), 12 March 1974.

72. "What Is the New Youth Center?" *Chinatown Newsletter*, no. 25 (October–November 1974).

73. "Teach-in at Pekin," *Chinatown Newsletter*, no. 25 (October–November 1974). The description is erroneous. According to Mrs. Vi Brajkovich, secretary to the principal of the east campus, Pekin High School, telephone conversation, 17 October 1989, there were two mascots called "Chink" and "Chinklette."

74. "Daycare Center's Progress," *Chinatown News* 2, no. 1 (May 1975); and "Pilsen's Day Care Fight," *Chinatown News* 2, no. 2 (June/July 1975).

75. Charles DeBenedetti and Charles Chatfield, assisting author, *An American Ordeal: The Antiwar Movement of the Vietnam Era* (Syracuse, N.Y.: Syracuse University Press, 1990) have probably written the best study on the antiwar movement, tracing its roots to the earlier peace movement. Other useful works are Lawrence M. Baskir and William A. Strauss, *Change and Circumstance: The Draft, the War and the Vietnam Generation* (New York: Knopf, 1978); Michael Ferber and Staughton Lynd, *The Resistance* (Boston: Beacon Press, 1971); Irving Louis Horowitz, *The Struggle Is the Message: The Organization and Ideology of the Anti-War Movement* (Berkeley, Calif.: Glendessary Press, 1970); and Nancy Zaroulis and Gerald Sullivan, *Who Spoke Up?: American Protest Against the War in Vietnam, 1963–1975* (New York: Holt, Rinehart and Winston, 1985).

76. Amy Tachiki, "Introduction" to the section on "Identity," in Tachiki et al., *Roots: An Asian American Reader*, pp. 1–5; in the same volume, Norman Nakamura, "The Nature of G.I. Racism," pp. 24–26, and Evelyn Yoshimura, "G.I.'s and Asian Women," pp. 27–29, discuss the problem of racism in the American armed forces.

77. Dave Roediger, "*Gook*: The Short History of an Americanism," *Monthly Review* 43, no. 10 (March 1992): 50–54. I am grateful to Dean Toji for bringing this article to my attention.

78. Roediger, "*Gook*," observed that according to the 1989 *Oxford English Dictionary*, the word refers to "a foreigner," but the editors failed to appreciate the irony of Americans using it to refer to natives in lands where *they* were the "foreigners."

79. Vietnam Veterans Against the War, *The Winter Soldier Investigation: Inquiry into American War Crimes* (Boston: Beacon Press, 1972), p. 152. The subhead, "You've Gotta Go to Vietnam, You've Gotta Kill the Gooks," captures the essence of the problem of "gookism" in the American military.

80. Ibid., p. 153. Also see Editorial, "Asians in the Anti-War Movement," *Getting Together*, 22 June–6 July 1973, pp. 2, 6.

81. In his 1969 report "The G.I.s and the Gooks," war correspondent Robert Kaiser reported the pervasive use of this expression, a variation of "the only good Indian is a dead Indian," on U.S. bases throughout Vietnam. Roediger, "*Gook*," p. 53.

82. Vietnam Veterans Against the War, *The Winter Soldier Investigation*, p. xiii.

83. Michael Bilton and Kevin Sim, *Four Hours in My Lai* (New York: Viking Press, 1992), have reconstructed in detail this horrific incident.

84. Eugene Franklin Wong, *On Visual Media Racism: Asians in the American Motion Pictures* (New York: Arno Press, 1978), p. 35.

85. Vietnam Veterans Against the War, *The Winter Soldier Investigation*, p. xiii.

86. *Asian Americans for Action Newsletter* 1, no. 5 (December 1969): 6; and Paul Wong, "The Emergence of the Asian-American Movement," *Bridge* 2, no. 1 (September/October 1972): 33–39.

87. "Bay Area Asian Coalition Against the War," *New Dawn*, June 1972.

88. Editorial, "Asians in the Anti-War Movement," *Getting Together*, 22 June–6 July 1973, p. 3. In the same issue, "Bay Area Asian Coalition Against the War Dissolves" discusses the history of the Bay Area Asian Coalition Against the War, which was probably the largest of the Asian American antiwar organizations. It was founded in May 1972 and ended a year later.

89. Stokely Carmichael and Charles V. Hamilton, *Black Power: The Politics of Liberation in America* (New York: Vintage, 1967), is the standard work on the subject of Black Power. Other useful works are Claybourne Carson, *In Struggle: SNCC and the Black Awakening of the 1960s* (Cambridge, Mass.: Harvard University Press, 1981); and Malcolm X, *The Autobiography of Malcolm X* (New York: Grove Press, 1965).

90. John Liu, "Towards an Understanding of the Internal Colonial Model," in *Counterpoint: Perspectives on Asian America*, ed. Emma Gee (Los Angeles: Asian American Studies Center, University of California, 1976), pp. 160–168. Michael Omi and Howard Winant, *Racial Formation in the United States, from the 1960s to the 1980s* (New York: Routledge, 1986), provide explanations and critiques of the internal colonial paradigm. Critics note that the model overlooks the relationships among race, gender, and class, or that the analogy with colonies has certain limitations.

91. L. Ling-Chi Wang, "Student Throng Jams 'Yellow Identity' Meet," *East/West*, 15 January 1969.

92. Jennifer Jordan, "Cultural Nationalism in the 1960s," in *Race, Politics, and Culture: Critical Essays on the Radicalism of the 1960s*, ed. Adolph Reed, Jr. (Westport, Conn.: Greenwood Press, 1986), pp. 29–60, provides a critique of African American cultural nationalism that can be selectively applied to its Asian American counterpart.

93. Edward Iwata, "Race without Face," *San Francisco Focus*, May 1991, pp. 50–53, 128–132.

94. Amy Uyematsu, "The Emergence of Yellow Power in America," in *Roots* (Los Angeles: Asian American Studies Center, University of California, 1971), p. 9.

Chapter 2: Who Am I?

1. For many young militants, Herbert Marcuse, *One-Dimensional Man: Studies in the Ideology of Advanced Industrial Society* (Boston: Beacon Press, 1964), provided one of the most comprehensive critique of these institutions.

2. L. Ling-Chi Wang, "Student Throng Jams 'Yellow Identity' Meet," *East/ West*, 15 January 1969.

3. Ibid.

4. Ibid.

5. Amy Tan, "Mother Tongue," lecture given at the University of Colorado at Boulder, 30 April 1991.

6. Edward Iwata, "Race without Face," *San Francisco Focus*, May 1991, pp. 50–53, 128–132.

7. Stanley Sue and Derald Wing Sue, "Chinese-American Personality and Mental Health," in *Asian-Americans: Psychological Perspectives*, ed. Stanley Sue and Nathaniel N. Wagner (Palo Alto, Calif.: Science and Behavior Books, 1973), pp. 111–124.

8. Akira Iriye, *Across the Pacific: An Inner History of American-East Asian Relations* (New York: Harcourt, Brace and World, 1967); Harold Isaacs, *Scratches on Our Mind: American Views of China and India* (Armonk, N.Y.: M.E. Sharpe, 1980), and Edward W. Said, *Orientalism* (New York: Vintage, 1978), provide insightful analyses of how Westerners, including Americans, perceive Asia and Asian people.

9. Being caught between two worlds is a perennial theme among Asian American writers. See, for example, Misha Berson, ed., *Between Worlds: Contemporary Asian-American Plays* (New York: Theatre Communications Group, 1990); and Amy Ling, *Between Worlds: Women Writers of Chinese Ancestry* (Elmsford, N.Y.: Pergamon Press, 1990).

10. Frank Chin et al., "An Introduction to Chinese- and Japanese-American Literature," in Frank Chin et al., *Aiiieeeee! An Anthology of Asian-American Writers* (Garden City, N.Y.: Doubleday Anchor, 1975), pp. 3–36; Frank Chin, interview, San Francisco, 18 August 1989.

11. Richard A. Oehling, "The Yellow Menace: Asian Images in American Film," in *The Kaleidoscopic Lens: How Hollywood Views Ethnic Groups*, ed. Randall M. Miller (Englewood, N.J.: Jerome S. Ozer, 1980), pp. 182–206.

12. Elmer C. Sandmeyer, *The Anti-Chinese Movement in California* (Urbana: University of Illinois Press, 1973); Alexander Saxton, *The Indispensable Enemy:*

Labor and the Anti-Chinese Movement in California (Berkeley: University of California Press, 1971); Roger Daniels, *The Politics of Prejudice: The Anti-Japanese Movement in California and the Struggle for Japanese Exclusion* (New York: Atheneum, 1974); Gary Y. Okihiro, *Cane Fires: The Anti-Japanese Movement in Hawaii, 1865–1945* (Philadelphia: Temple University Press, 1991); Howard DeWitt, *Anti-Filipino Movements in California: History, Bibliography and Study Guide* (San Francisco: R & E Research Associates, 1976); and Bruno Lasker, *Filipino Immigration to the Continental United States and to Hawaii* (New York: Arno Press, 1969) are some of the major studies of the anti-Asian movements in the United States. On the phenomenon of nativism, see John Higham, *Stranger in the Land: Patterns of American Nativism, 1860–1925* (New York: Atheneum, 1978).

13. Roger Daniels, *The Politics of Prejudice: The Anti-Japanese Movement in California and the Struggle for Japanese Exclusion* (Berkeley: University of California Press, 1962), chap. 5, "The Yellow Peril," pp. 65–78; Robert McClellan, *The Heathen Chinee: A Study of American Attitudes towards China, 1890–1905* (Columbus: Ohio State University Press, 1971); and William F. Wu, *The Yellow Peril: Chinese Americans in American Fiction, 1850–1940* (Hamden, Conn.: Archon Press, 1982) discusses the historical development of the "Yellow Peril" phenomenon.

14. Michio Kaku, "Media: Racism in the Comics," *Bridge* 3, no. 1 (February 1974): 25–29.

15. Richard Sorich, "A Discussion of the Asian Image in American Schools and Public Media," *Bridge* 1, no. 4 (March/April 1972): 10–17.

16. "How Children's Books Distort the Asian American Image," *Bridge* 4, no. 3 (July 1976): 5–7.

17. Ibid.

18. Carlos E. Cortés, "The Societal Curriculum and the School Curriculum: Allies or Antagonists?" *Educational Leadership* 36, no. 7 (April 1979): 475–479.

19. Grace Wai-tse Siao, "Yellowface Makeup 'Psychological Violence,' Protesters Charge at 'Mikado' Performance," *Asian Week*, 9 November 1990.

20. Kaku, "Media: Racism in the Comics," pp. 25–29. Also see "Asian Images—A Message to the Media," *Bridge* 3 no. 2 (April 1974): 25–30; and Carla B. Zimmerman, "From Chop-Chop to Wu Cheng: The Evolution of the Chinese Character in *Blackhawk* Comic Books," in *Ethnic Images in the Comics*, ed. Charles Hardy and Gail F. Stern (Philadelphia: Balch Institute for Ethnic Studies, 1986), pp. 37–42.

21. Ronald Tanaka, "I Hate My Wife for Her Flat Yellow Face," in *Roots*, ed. Amy Tachiki et al. (Los Angeles: Asian American Studies Center, University of California, 1971), pp. 46–47.

22. Siao, "Yellowface Makeup 'Psychological Violence.' "

23. Chin et al., *Aiiieeeee!* p. 11.

24. Unless otherwise noted, the discussion of Asian Americans for a Fair Media is based on Michio Kaku, "Media: Asian Americans for a Fair Media," *Bridge* 2,

no. 6 (August 1973): 40–42. Another organized effort was mounted by Chinese for Affirmative Action, which had a Chinese Media Committee that monitored the media for stereotypes. Kathy Fong, "A Chinaman's Chance Revisited," *Bridge* 2, no. 6 (August 1973): 19–22.

25. "Asian Images—A Message to the Media," 25–30, is a copy of the handbook. Since then, there have been other works conveying the same message: Bill Sing, ed., *Asian Pacific Americans: A Handbook on How to Cover and Portray Our Nation's Fastest Growing Minority Group* (Los Angeles: National Conference of Christians and Jews, Asian American Journalist Association, and Association of Asian Pacific American Artists, 1989); and Asian American Journalists Association, *Project Zinger: The Good, the Bad and the Ugly* (Seattle: Center for Integration and Improvement of Journalism, 1991).

26. Kaku, "Asian Americans for a Fair Media," p. 42.

27. "News Notes," *Bridge* 7, no. 3 (Spring/Summer 1980): 45. Also see Forrest Gok, "The Canning of Charlie Chan," *Bridge* 7, no. 4 (Winter 1981–1982): 32–41.

28. Dorothy Ritsuko McDonald, "Introduction," Frank Chin, *The Chickencoop Chinaman and The Year of the Dragon* (Seattle: University of Washington Press, 1981), p. xxii.

29. Arthur Hu, "Miss Yellowface?" *Asian Week*, 24 August 1990.

30. Unless noted otherwise, the discussion of the *Miss Saigon* controversy is based on articles in *Asian Week*, 10 August to 14 December 1990, and the *New York Times*, 26 July 1990 to 21 January 1991.

31. Mervyn Rothstein, "Union Bars White in Asian Role; Broadway May Lose *Miss Saigon*," *New York Times*, 8 August 1990.

32. Mervyn Rothstein, "Producer Cancels *Miss Saigon*; Actors Challenge Union Ruling," *New York Times*, 9 August 1990.

33. Mervyn Rothstein, "Panel Criticizes *Saigon* Producer," *New York Times*, 16 August 1990.

34. Alex Witchel, "Actors' Equity Attacks Casting for *Miss Saigon*," *New York Times*, 26 July 1990.

35. Keiko Ohnuma, "Asians Blast Actors Equity over *Miss Saigon* Issue," *Asian Week*, 28 September 1990.

36. William Wong's column, *Asian Week*, 24 August 1990.

37. "Actors' Equity Had to Fight over *Miss Saigon*," Letters to the Editor, *New York Times*, 10 August 1990. Some minority actors have criticized Equity for being unsupportive of their efforts to acquire more and better roles. Keiko Ohnuma, "*Miss Saigon* Casting Blasted at New York City Hearing," *Asian Week*, 14 December 1990.

38. Him Mark Lai et al., *Island: Poetry and History of Chinese Immigrants on Angel Island, 1910–40* (San Francisco: HOC DOI Project, Chinese Culture Foundation of San Francisco, 1980).

39. Fred Wei-han Houn, "Revolutionary Asian American Art: Tradition and Change, Inheritance and Innovation, Not Imitation!" *East Wind* 5, no. 1 (Spring/Summer 1986): 4–8.

40. Frances Leventhal, "Loni Ding Spent Five Years Making *Color of Honor*," *Asian Week*, 13 January 1989. Several other documentaries on the internment of Japanese Americans have been produced recently, such as *Nisei Soldier*, *Unfinished Business*, *Family Gathering*, and *Days of Waiting*. Steven Okazaki's *Days of Waiting*, the story of Estelle Ishigo, a Caucasian woman who was voluntarily incarcerated with her *nisei* husband, is the best known, having won an Oscar for short documentary in 1991. There are even feature-length movies on the subject, such as *Farewell to Manzanar* and, most recently, *Come See the Paradise*. According to Keiko Ohnuma, " 'Paradise'—History But Not Art," *Asian Week*, 4 January 1991, the latter film is "destined to become part of the emerging canon of persecution pornography depicting the internment of Japanese Americans during World War II."

41. National Asian American Telecommunications Association, "CrossCurrent Media: 1990–91 Asian American Audiovisual Catalog," p. 7.

42. Unless otherwise noted, the discussion of *Forbidden City, U.S.A.* is based on Arthur Dong, interview, Los Angeles, 26 October 1989, and Gerrye Wong, "First Person: *Forbidden City* from Pen to Silver Screen," *Asian Week*, 24 November 1989.

43. William Wong's column, *Asian Week*, 26 January 1990.

44. Mervyn Rothstein, "Survival vs. Dignity in an Asian-American Play," *New York Times*, 7 June 1989.

45. Ibid.

46. The term "cultural rescue mission" was first used by J. Tevere MacFadyen, "Recording Chinatown's Past While It's Still There," *Smithsonian* 13, no. 10 (January 1983): 70–79, to describe the New York Chinatown History Project.

47. Him Mark Lai, "Chinese American Studies: A Historical Survey," *Chinese America: History and Perspectives, 1988*, provides information on other Chinese American historical societies, the earliest of which was the Chinese Historical Society of America, which was founded in San Francisco in January 1963.

48. Unless otherwise noted, the discussion of the New York Chinese History Project is based on: MacFadyen, "Recording Chinatown's Past"; Candace Floyd, "Chinatown," *History News* 39, no. 6 (June 1984): 6–11; John Kuo Wei Tchen, interview, New York City, 9 January 1990; and *Bu Gao Ban*, Summer 1984 to Winter 1991.

49. MacFayden, "Recording Chinatown's Past."

50. Ibid.

51. Joyce Yu, "Looking Backwards into the Future," *Bu Gao Ban* 7, no. 1 (Summer 1990).

52. Ibid.

53. John Kuo Wei Tchen, "Creating a Dialogic Museum: The Chinatown History Museum Experiment," in *Museums and Communities: The Politics of Public Culture*, ed. Ivan Karp et al. (Washington, D.C.: Smithsonian Institution Press, 1992), pp. 285–326.

54. Ibid.

55. Yu, "Looking Backwards into the Future."

56. Letter from John Wei Kuo Tchen to the author, 26 July 1991.

57. " 'Remembering New York Chinatown': Implementing Vehicles of Dialogue" (n.d.), pp. 1–22. Typewritten.

58. Unless otherwise noted, the discussion of the Japanese American National Museum is based on the *Japanese American National Museum Bulletin* 1, no. 2 (Fall 1986) to 6, no. 1 (Winter 1991); and "Japanese American National Museum Benefit Program," 1985.

59. Unless otherwise noted, the discussion of the Filipino American National Historical Society is based on Dorothy Laigo Cordova, telephone interview, 22 and 24 May 1991; and materials (newsletters, reports, conference programs, etc.) she sent to the author.

60. Bob Shimabukuro, "Dorothy Cordova," *International Examiner*, 19 June 1991, is an interview with Cordova, who won the newspaper's Community Voice Award.

61. Filipino American National Historical Society brochure.

62. Fred Cordova, "The Filipino American: There's Always an Identity Crisis," in Sue and Wagner, eds., *Asian-Americans: Psychological Perspectives*, pp. 136–139.

63. Nathaniel N. Wagner, "Filipinos: A Minority within a Minority," in Sue and Wagner, *Asian-Americans: Psychological Perspectives*, pp. 295–298.

64. Fred Cordova, *Filipinos: Forgotten Asian Americans* (Dubuque, Iowa: Kendall/Hunt, 1983).

65. Edward Iwata, "Hot Properties: More Asian Americans Suddenly Are Winning Mainstream Literary Acclaim," View section, *Los Angeles Times*, 11 September 1989.

66. Houn, "Revolutionary Asian American Art."

67. Ibid.

68. Teri Lee, "An Interview with Janice Mirikitani," *Asian American Review*, Asian American Studies, Department of Ethnic Studies, University of California, Berkeley, 1976, pp. 34–44.

69. "Editorial," *Aion* 1, no. 1 (1970).

70. Unless otherwise noted, the discussion of A Grain of Sand and its individual members is based on "Charlie" Chin, interview, New York City, 31 May 1989; and Nobuko Miyamoto, interview, Los Angeles, 24 October 1989; and on Diane Mark, "Nobuko Miyamoto: The 'Mountain Moving Days' Continue," *Bridge* 10, no. 1 (Spring 1985): 15–19, 28, 29.

71. Fred Wei-Han Houn, "An ABC from NYC: 'Charlie' Chin, Asian American Singer and Songwriter," *East Wind* 5, no. 1 (Spring/Summer 1986): 4–8.

72. Chris Kando Iijima, Joanne Nobuko Miyamoto, and "Charlie" Chin, "Statement," *A Grain of Sand*, Paredon Records, 1973.

73. Nobuko Miyamoto, interview, Los Angeles, 24 October 1989.

74. "Statement," *A Grain of Sand*.

75. Chris Iijima and "Charlie" Chin, *Back to Back*, East/Wind Records, 1982, album cover.

76. Jon Woodhouse, "Bridging East and West: 'Talk Story' Shares Stories of New, Old Immigrants," *Maui News*, 15 November 1987.

77. Though less prominent, Asian Americans have been increasingly influential in film, video, and radio. From a variety of creative and critical perspectives, *Moving the Image: Independent Asian Pacific American Media Arts*, ed. and intro. Russell Leong (Los Angeles: Asian American Studies Center, University of California at Los Angeles, and Visual Communications, 1991), explores their contribution over the last twenty years.

78. Fred Wei-Han Houn, "A Voice Is a Voice, But What Is It Saying," an unpublished review of Elaine Kim's *Asian American Literature*, 1984.

79. McDonald, "Introduction," p. xxviii.

80. Ibid., p. ix.

81. Chin et al., "Introduction to Chinese- and Japanese-American Literature," p. 35.

82. McDonald, "Introduction," p. xviii.

83. Lawson Fusao Inada, "Introduction," in John Okada, *No-No Boy* (Seattle: University of Washington Press, 1976).

84. Stephen Talbot, "Talking Story: Maxine Hong Kingston Rewrites the American Dream," Image section, *San Francisco Examiner*, 24 June 1990, p. 8.

85. Bobby Fong, "Maxine Hong Kingston's Autobiographical Strategy in *The Woman Warrior*," *Biography* 12 (Spring 1989): 116–125.

86. Letter from Fred Ho (formerly Houn) to the author, 17 July 1991.

87. Chin et al., "An Introduction to Chinese- and Japanese-American Literature," p. 14.

88. Talbot, "Talking Story."

89. Edward Iwata, "Word Warriors," *Los Angeles Times*, 24 June 1990.

90. Talbot, "Talking Story."

91. Frank Chin, *The Chinamen Pacific & Frisco R.R. Co.* (Minneapolis: Coffee House Press, 1988); Maxine Hong Kingston, *Tripmaster Monkey: His Fake Book* (New York: Vintage, 1990). Kingston has publicly denied that Wittman Ah Sing is modeled on Frank Chin. During her visit to the University of Colorado at Boulder, she told the author that he was a composite of several people and that various individuals have thought they were the model, including her husband, Earl, who has been known to mimic a monkey just for the fun of it. Chin, however, is certain that Wittman Ah Sing is himself.

92. Iwata, "Hot Properties." Janice C. Simpson, "Fresh Voices above the Din," *Newsweek*, 3 June 1991, discusses new works by four writers who "splendidly illustrate the frustrations, humor and eternal wonder of the immigrant's life." The "Pacific Reader," Literary Supplement, *International Examiner*, 19 July 1989, provides critical reviews of some of the more recent books by Asian Americans.

93. Iwata, "Hot Properties."

94. Ibid.

95. Ibid.

Chapter 3: Race versus Gender

1. The European American women's liberation movement began with the founding of the National Organization for Women (NOW, 29 October 1966) and when women activists began meeting in separate caucuses in the mid-1960s to discuss the problem of sexism in the New Left. Its participants are usually classified as either liberal, socialist, or radical feminists. Liberal feminists belonging to NOW and other women's organizations are mainly middle-class professional women concerned with equal rights and opportunities. Though they failed to get the Equal Rights Amendment passed, they continue to be involved in legislative politics. Their younger socialist feminist sisters have been involved in left politics and are committed to a revolution that will solve the problem of sexism through a fundamental reordering of social values and reshaping of human behavior. Because of the adverse circumstances of the left in the United States and internationally, their numbers have declined during the 1970s and 1980s. Meanwhile, during the 1980s, as lesbians and gays "came out of the closet," increasing numbers of radical feminists became involved in the women's liberation movement. They are concerned about gender discrimination, with the goal of ending homophobia, and the development of a women's culture. Though all three types of feminists can be found in the Asian American women's movement, it is dominated by liberal feminists concerned with social and political reform. They are the most numerous and shape the discourse on women's issues. Esther Ngan-Ling Chow, "The Feminist Movement: Where Are All the Asian American Women?" in *Making Waves: An Anthology of Writings by and about Asian American Women*, ed. Asian Women United of California (Boston: Beacon Press, 1989), pp. 362–377; Judy Lam, "Asian Women and the Women's Movement," *International Examiner*, January/February 1978, p. 5; April West and Rita Elway, "Asian and Pacific Women: A Cohesive Force in Women's Movement," *International Examiner*, December 1977, p. 6; and Liang Ho, "Asian-American Women: Identity and Role in the Women's Movement," "Asian Women '80" issue, *Feminist International*, no. 2 (1980): 55–57, discuss the participation of Asian American women in the mainstream women's liberation movement.

2. Letter from Colleen Fong to the author, 3 November 1987.

3. Gayle Graham Yates, *What Women Want: The Ideas of the Movement* (Cambridge: Harvard University Press, 1975), p. 4.

4. Rita Kramer, "The Third Wave," *Wilson Quarterly* 10, no. 4 (Autumn 1986): 110–129.

5. Patricia Hill Collins, *Black Feminist Thought: Knowledge, Consciousness, and the Politics of Empowerment* (New York: Routledge, 1991), p. 7. There is a significant body of literature on the mainstream women's liberation movement, which divides its history into three distinct waves, with the last being the one to emerge in the 1960s. Sara Evans, *Personal Politics: The Roots of Women's Liberation in the Civil Rights Movement and the New Left* (New York: Knopf, 1979); Jo Freeman, *The Politics of Women's Liberation: A Case Study of an Emerging Social Movement and Its Relation to the Policy Process* (New York: McKay, 1975); and Gayle Graham Yates, *What Women Want: The Ideas of the Movement* (Cambridge: Harvard University Press, 1975) are three of the standard works on the women's liberation movement. John D'Emilio, *Sexual Politics and Sexual Communities: The Making of a Homosexual Minority in the United States, 1940–1970* (Chicago: University of Chicago Press, 1983), provides a sympathetic history of homosexual political struggles. Usually, the literature on the mainstream women's liberation movement ignores women of color, in part because the mainstream assumes, incorrectly, that white women and women of color have the same concerns, issues, and priorities. But as Elizabeth V. Spelman, *Inessential Woman: Problems of Exclusion in Feminist Thought* (Boston: Beacon Press, 1988), suggests, the distinctions between any two racial groups may be more significant than those between women and men within any such group (p. 148). If women of color are discussed, it is usually African American women because of their relatively higher proportion of the population and their significant role in the civil rights movement. If Asian American women are discussed, it is usually in passing, such as in Chapter 6, "Woman: The One and the Many," in *Inessential Women*, where they constitute one of Spelman's schematic categories, or in Maren Lockwood Carden, *The New Feminist Movement* (New York: Russell Sage Foundation, 1974), which mentions the existence of "organized clinics for Asian women" (p. 77).

6. Letter from Becky Hom to the author, 26 October 1987.

7. Ibid. She pointed out that "very visible exceptions in NYC were the women leaders of I Wor Kuen . . . and they have maintained their visibility today in the League of Revolutionary Struggle."

8. Colin Watanabe, telephone interview, 16 July 1985. Killer Fawn [Linda Iwataki], "In the Movement Office," *Gidra*, January 1971, provided one woman's view of what a sexist atmosphere was like. Though it referred to the JACS-AI office, Mike Murase, letter to the author, 20 October 1986, noted that it was "surely relevant to the *Gidra* office as well." For a general discussion of the problem of male chauvinism, see Wilma Chan, "Movement Contradiction," in the same issue.

9. Evelyn Yoshimura, interview, Los Angeles, 7 January 1987.

10. Anonymous source E, interview, Monterey Park, 9 January 1987.

11. Evelyn Yoshimura, interview, Los Angeles, 7 January 1987.

12. Miya Iwataki, "The Asian Women's Movement: A Retrospective," *Spe-*

cial Feature: Essays on Asian American Women's Liberation, *East Wind* 2, no. 1 (Spring/Summer 1983): 35–41.

13. Letter from Becky Hom to the author, 26 October 1987.

14. Anonymous source E, interview, Monterey Park, 9 January 1987.

15. Berkeley Asian Women's Study Group, *Asian Women* (Berkeley: Asian American Studies Program, University of California, 1971), p. 4.

16. Ibid.

17. Alice Ito, "Women's Studies: A Collective Approach to Education," *Winds*, Special Section on Asian American Women, November 1977, p. 10. Judy Chu, "Asian American Women's Studies Courses: A Look at the Beginning," *Frontiers* 8, no. 3 (1986): 96–101; and May Ying Chen, "Teaching a Course on Asian American Women," in *Counterpoint*, ed. Emma Gee (Los Angeles: Asian American Studies Center, University of California, 1976), pp. 234–239, are other essays on Asian American Women's studies.

18. Berkeley Asian Women's Study Group, *Asian Women*, p. 4. Usually, Asian American women's writings appeared in special issues of Asian American publications such as *Gidra* (January 1971), *Amerasia Journal* 4, no. 1 (1977); *Bridge* 6, no. 4 (Winter 1978–1979), 7, no. 1 (Spring 1979), and 8, no. 3 (Summer 1983); and *East Wind* 2, no. 1 (Spring/Summer 1983).

19. Berkeley Asian Women's Study Group, *Asian Women*, p. 6.

20. Iwataki, "The Asian Women's Movement," p. 40. Unless otherwise noted, the discussion of the Asian Women's Center is based on Miya Iwataki, interview, Los Angeles, 7 January 1987; and Irene Hirano, interview, Los Angeles, 9 January 1987.

21. Iwataki, "The Asian Women's Movement," p. 41. According to Iwataki, interview, Los Angeles, 7 January 1987, activists were influenced by Ramsey Liew, "The Money Tree Bears Strange Fruit: Federal Funds in the Asian Community," *Gidra*, May 1973, pp. 18–19.

22. Pat Eng, interview, New York City, 28 October 1986, and telephone interview, 2 October 1991; and Barbara Chang, interview, New York City, 24 October 1986.

23. Young Hai Shin, interview, Oakland, 9 December 1986.

24. Katie Quan, interview, New York City, 24 October 1986.

25. Peter Kwong, *The New Chinatown* (New York: Hill and Wang, 1987).

26. Letter from Kazu I. Iijima to the author, 16 October 1987.

27. Letter from Juanita Tamayo Lott to the author, 15 October 1987.

28. Unless otherwise noted, the discussion of Asian Women United–San Francisco is based on Elaine Kim, interview, Berkeley, 11 December 1986; and Judy Yung, interview, San Francisco, 6 December 1986.

29. Unless otherwise noted, the discussion of the Organization of Asian Women is based on Becky Hom, interview, New York City, 26 October 1986; and Kazu I. Iijima, interview, New York City, 28 October 1986.

30. Letter from Becky Hom to the author, 26 October 1987.

31. Unless otherwise noted, the discussion of the Organization of Pan Asian Women is based on *Pan Asian Women: A Vital Force* (Washington, D.C.: Organization of Pan Asian Women, 1985); Juanita Tamayo Lott and Canta Pian, *Beyond Stereotypes and Statistics: Emergence of Asian and Pacific American Women* (Washington, D.C.: Organization of Pan Asian Women, 1979); Marguerite Gee, interview, Oakland, 6 December 1986; and Juanita Tamayo Lott, telephone interview, 4 October 1991.

32. Unless otherwise noted, the discussion of the Pacific Asian American Women Writers–West is based on Momoko Iko, interview, Los Angeles, 26 October 1989; Joyce Nako, interview, Los Angeles, 26 October 1989; PAAWWW "Statement of Purpose," 1989; and Miko Kunitaki, "PAAWWW: Caught in the Act of Living," *Pacific Citizen*, 3 October 1980.

33. PAAWWW "Fact Sheet," 1989.

34. "Pac. Asian Women Writers Call for Submissions," *Rafu Shimpo*, 7 May 1987.

35. Susan Smith, "The Creativity of Asian-Americans," *Los Angeles Times*, 5 July 1980.

36. Kunitaki, "PAAWWW: Caught in the Act of Living."

37. Ibid.

38. Manuscript comments accompanying letter from Momoko Iko to the author, 31 October 1991.

39. Unless otherwise noted, the discussion of Unbound Feet is based on Genny Lim, interview, San Francisco, 15 August 1989; and Nancy Hom and Bob Hsiang, interview, San Francisco, 14 August 1989.

40. Genny Lim, interview, San Francisco, 15 August 1989.

41. Anonymous source F, San Francisco, 16 August 1989.

42. Freedom Socialist Party, "Special Edition: Merle Woo's Case against the University of California," issued by the National Office and Seattle Local, 3 August 1983. Woo eventually sued the University of California to regain her teaching position and reached a settlement.

43. Elaine Kim, *Asian American Literature: An Introduction to the Writings and Their Social Context* (Philadelphia: Temple University Press, 1982), and Amy Ling, *Between Worlds: Women Writers of Chinese Ancestry* (Elmsford, N.Y.: Pergamon, 1990), provide background information and insightful analysis of the works of Maxine Hong Kingston and Amy Tan.

44. Edward Iwata, "Hot Properties: More Asian Americans Suddenly Are Winning Mainstream Literary Acclaim," View section, *Los Angeles Times*, 11 September 1989.

45. Ling, *Between Worlds*, p. 194.

46. John B. Breslin, "A Prize Book," *America*, 26 February 1977, pp. 175–176.

47. Ibid.

48. Kim, *Asian American Literature*, p. 199.

49. Ling, *Between Worlds*, p. 156.

50. Amy Tan, *The Joy Luck Club* (New York: Putnam's, 1989), p. 254.

51. Carole Angier, "Chinese Customs," *New Stateman and Society*, 30 June 1989, p. 35.

52. David Gates, "A Game of Show Not Tell," *Newsweek*, 17 April 1989.

53. Christopher Lehmann-Haupt, "Mother and Daughter, Each with Her Secret," *New York Times*, 20 June 1991.

54. For a statement on the differences between the Asian American women's movement and the mainstream women's liberation movement, see Asian Women's Collective, "Our Perspective," *As Asian Women* 2, no. 4 (May 1975): 7. Feelie Lee, interview, Los Angeles, 8 January 1987.

55. Evelyn Yoshimura, interview, Los Angeles, 7 January 1987.

56. Letter from Becky Hom to the author, 26 October 1987.

57. Iwataki, "The Asian Women's Movement," p. 38.

58. Katheryn M. Fong, "Feminism Is Fine, but What's It Done for Asian America?" *Bridge* 6, no. 4 (Winter 1978–1979): 21–22.

59. Esther Ngan-Ling Chow, "The Development of Feminist Consciousness among Asian American Women," *Gender and Society* 1, no. 5 (September 1987): 284–299.

60. Pauline Tsui, interview, Washington, D.C., 8 July 1987.

61. Helen Chang, "Organization of Chinese Americans Split over Maverick Women's Group," *East/West*, 3 September 1987.

62. Letter from Pauline Tsui to the author, 7 December 1987.

63. "Asian American Women's Caucus: An Interview with Esther Kee," *Bridge* 6, no. 1 (1978): 51–52.

64. Ibid.

65. Unless otherwise noted, the discussion of AWU–NY is based on Jackie Huey, interview, New York City, 26 June 1986; and Ruby Tsang, "Another Point of View," *Bridge* 6, no. 1 (1978): 53–55.

66. Becky Hom, interview, New York City, 26 October 1986.

67. "National Women's Conference: Esther Kee, 'Asian/Pacific American Women Delegates to the International Women's Year Conference-Houston, Texas, November, 1977' and Linda Lee, 'Back From Houston . . . A Point of View,' " *Bridge* 5, no. 4 (Winter 1977): 30–32.

68. Judy Yung, *Chinese Women of American: A Pictorial History* (Seattle: Chinese Culture Foundation of San Francisco and University of Washington Press, 1986), p. 98.

69. "Substitute Minority Women Resolution," *Bridge* 5, no. 4 (Winter 1977): 33.

70. National Network of Asian and Pacific Women pamphlet.

71. Figure from the "Asian Pacific American Women's Education Seminar.

Second Revised Budget. Negotiated July 1980." Appended to a letter from Tin Myaing Thein to Emma Gee, Mitsuye Yamada, and Irene Hirano, 11 October 1979.

72. Letter from Emma Gee to Tin Myaing Thein, 25 October 1979.

73. Letter from May Ying Chen, Sue Embrey, Lillian Fabros, and Miya Iwataki to Members of the Los Angeles Coordinating Committee of Asian/Pacific Women on the Move: Strategies in Educational Equity, and the National Coordinator, 8 November 1979.

74. Ibid.

75. Feelie Lee, interview, Los Angeles, 8 January 1987; and Irene Hirano, interview, Los Angeles, 9 January 1987.

76. Irene Hirano, interview, Los Angeles, 9 January 1987.

77. "AP Women to Meet in D.C.," *In Touch: Newsletter of Asian Women United (NYC)* 3, no. 6 (June 1980).

78. "AP Conference Wrap Up," *In Touch* 3, no. 7 (September 1980).

79. Feelie Lee, interview, Los Angeles, 8 January 1987.

80. Pat Luce, interview, San Francisco, 11 December 1986.

81. Feelie Lee, interview, Los Angeles, 8 January 1987.

82. Pat Luce, interview, San Francisco, 11 December 1987.

83. *In Touch* 7, no. 7 (April–May 1985).

84. National Network of Asian and Pacific Network newsletter, Summer 1985.

85. Pat Luce, interview, San Francisco, 11 December 1986.

86. Caryl Ito, interview, San Francisco, 10 December 1986.

Chapter 4: Speaking Out

1. There were of course exceptions, such as the *Rodo Shimbun* and other labor or socialist periodicals that promoted a particular political perspective.

2. James T. Lee, "A Hundred Flowers Bloom: A Study of Chinese Publications in New York," *Bridge* 2, no. 2 (December 1972): 35–42. This problem continues to the present. See Editorial, "Is Taiwan Keeping Tabs on Chinese Americans through U.S. Chinese Press?" *East/West*, 21 July 1988.

3. Many of the periodicals produced by the Asian American Movement are listed in Maureen E. Hady and James P. Dansky, comps., *Asian American Periodicals and Newspapers: A Union List of Holdings in the Library of the State Historical Society of Wisconsin and the Libraries of the University of Wisconsin-Madison* (Madison: Wisconsin State Historical Society, 1979); and Rockwell Chin, "Getting Beyond Vol. 1, No. 1: Asian American Periodicals," *Bridge* 1, no. 2 (September/October 1971): 29–32. For works on the "dissident" press of America, see, for example, Robert Glessing, *The Underground Press in America* (Bloomington: Indiana University Press, 1970); Michael Johnson, *The New Journalism* (Lawrence: University of Kansas Press, 1971); Laurence Leamer, *The Paper Revolutionaries: The Rise of the Underground Press* (New York: Simon and Schuster, 1972); Lauren Kessler,

The Dissident Press: Alternative Journalism in American History (Beverly Hills: Sage, 1984); and Sally Miller, ed., *The Ethnic Press in the United States*, (Westport, Conn.: Greenwood Press, 1987). (Both Kessler and Miller contain some material on the Asian ethnic press.) An exception to the neglect of the Asian American alternative press is Roger Lewis, *Outlaws of America: The Underground Press and Its Context* (Harmondsworth, England: Penguin Books, 1972), who briefly mentions *Gidra* in his chapter "The Alliance of the Oppressed: Minority Groups and Other Allies."

4. "Editorial," *Gidra*, October 1969.

5. Bill J. Gee, "*Bridge* Suspends Publication Due to Financial Pressure," *East/West*, 18 December 1985.

6. Chin, "Getting Beyond Vol. 1, No. 1," pp. 29–32.

7. Memorandum from Special Agent in Charge, Los Angeles field office, to Director, Federal Bureau of Investigation, 6 November 1969. After monitoring *Gidra* for two years, the FBI's Special Agent in Charge of its Los Angeles field office concluded that "to date, no articles have been noted which specifically advise or advocate civil disobedience or violence." He decided that its value was as an intelligence source, since it showed "the trends among the more radical type of Asian Americans as well as their identities," but that an investigation was unnecessary and "could result in embarrassment." Memorandum from Special Agent in Charge, Los Angeles Investigation, 29 June 1971.

8. They filed incorporation papers on 6 June 1969. The directors were listed as Tracy Okida, Seigo Hayashi, and Colin Watanabe. Its stated purpose was "to engage exclusively in charitable and educational activities in order to develop initiative and leadership in Asian American youths and to inform Asian American youths of current matters affecting themselves and other minority groups, including but not limited to the providing of educational, welfare, vocational training and medical services as are permitted to be carried on by a corporation exempt from Federal income tax." Federal Bureau of Investigation, Los Angeles field office report, "*Gidra*," office file #105-27572, pp. 2–3. Unless otherwise noted, the discussion of *Gidra* is based on Mike Murase, Evelyn Yoshimura, and Bruce Iwasaki, interview, Los Angeles, 2 November 1985; David Monkawa, interview, Los Angeles, 5 November 1985; Colin Watanabe, telephone interview, 16 July 1985; and *Gidra*, April 1969 to March 1974.

9. Jeffrey Matsui, *Pacific Citizen*, 11 April 1969.

10. Letter from Dean Toji to the author, 5 December 1986.

11. These "fine print" messages began appearing with the November 1971 issue. Bruce Iwasaki noted that these messages reflected staff concerns and growth, rather than serve merely as an outlet for frustrations. Mike Murase, Evelyn Yoshimura, and Bruce Iwasaki, interview, Los Angeles, 2 November 1985.

12. Colin Watanabe, telephone interview, 16 July 1985.

13. Letter from Dean Toji to the author, 5 December 1986.

14. Two of these articles were Name Withheld, "White Male Qualities!" *Gidra*, January 1970; and Violet Rabaya, "I Am Curious [Yellow?]," *Gidra*, October 1969.

15. Amy Tachiki et al., ed., *Roots: An Asian American Reader* (Los Angeles: Asian American Studies Center, University of California, 1971); and Emma Gee, ed., *Counterpoint: Perspectives on Asian America* (Los Angeles: Asian American Studies Center, University of California, 1976).

16. Larry Kubota, "Necessary but Not Sufficient: Yellow Power!" *Gidra*, April 1969.

17. Amy Uyematsu, "The Emergence of Yellow Power in America," *Gidra*, December 1969.

18. David Ota, "We Are Americans," *Gidra*, November 1969; and idem, "A Time to Choose," *Gidra*, January 1970.

19. Steve Tatsukawa, "No Time to Play," *Gidra*, December 1969.

20. Frank Kofsky, "The Nature of Racism," *Gidra*, March 1970.

21. During *Gidra*'s first year, one of its major themes was to disabuse readers of the belief in the so-called quietness of *nisei*. Much of this effort centered on Bill Hosokawa's *Nisei: The Quiet Americans*. Mary Tani in particular took exception to the title and its implications. Mary Tani, "SHHH! A Nisei Is Speaking," *Gidra*, October 1969; "Nisei: The Traumatized Americans," *Gidra*, November 1969; "Quiet Americans," *Gidra*, December 1969. Also see Yuji Ichioka's review of *Nisei*, *Gidra*, January 1970.

22. Pat Sumi, "U.S. War Crimes in the Philippines," *Gidra*, July 1971.

23. Bruce Iwasaki, "Woodstock/Third World Nation," *Gidra*, October 1970.

24. *Bridge* did better than most. It had three issues that featured Asian women: *Bridge* 6, no. 4; 7, no. 1; and 8, no. 3. *Amerasia*'s 1977 issue was more or less a women's issue, with three of its five major articles on Asian American women. It included "Selected Statistics on the Status of Asian-American Women," which documented the discrimination that Asian American women faced. According to Denise Imura, interview, San Francisco, 24 March 1986, one of the earliest themes of *East Wind* was Asian American women. *East Wind* 2, no. 1 (Spring/Summer 1983) was a very popular number and was completely sold out.

25. *Gidra*, March 1971.

26. *Gidra*, August 1971.

27. Mike Murase, "Towards Barefoot Journalism," *Gidra*, April 1974.

28. For example, Tracy Okida, "Okinawa Kaiho!" *Gidra*, May 1972.

29. "JACL and the U.S.–Japan Security Pact," *Gidra*, June/July 1970; "Ampo Fusai," *Gidra*, February 1972.

30. For example (reprinted from *New Dawn*), "Japanese Militarism," *Gidra*, July 1972.

31. Mike Murase, Evelyn Yoshimura, and Bruce Iwasaki, interview, 2 November 1985.

32. Letter from Mike Murase to the author, 20 October 1986.

33. Naomi Hirahana et al., eds., *Gidra 1990: Twentieth Anniversary Edition*.

34. *Bridge* 3, no. 1 (February 1974).

35. Editorial, "A Reaffirmation," *Bridge* 3, no. 1 (February 1974).

36. Unless otherwise noted, the discussion of *Bridge* is based on Diane Mark, interview, New York City, 22 August 1985; Peter Chow, interview, New York City, 10 June 1986; Chuck Lee, interview, New York City, 17 June 1986; Odoric Wou, interview, New York City, 22 June 1986; David Oyama, interview, New York City, 23 June 1986; and *Bridge* 1, no. 1 (July–August 1971) to 10, no. 1 (Spring 1985).

37. Robin Wu, "New York's Chinatown: An Overview," *Bridge* 1, no. 1 (July–August 1971): 13–15.

38. Fay Chiang, "Looking Back," *Basement Yearbook 1986* (New York: Basement Workshop, 1986), p. 3.

39. Letter from Frank Ching to the author, 18 February 1986.

40. Peter Chow, interview, New York City, 10 June 1986.

41. Ibid.

42. *Bridge* 1, no. 1 (July–August 1971): 4.

43. "Who's Afraid of Frank Chin, or Is It Ching?" *Bridge* 2, no. 2 (December 1972): 29–34.

44. Ibid.

45. Betty Lee Sung and Diana Chang joined the fray to defend themselves against Chin's passing accusation that they were "white supremacists." Chang had the added distinction of being referred to as "one with brain damage." They noted Chin's self-serving remarks and his iconoclastic assaults on one and all. "Chin vs. Ching, Part II," *Bridge* 2, no. 3 (February 1973): 34–37.

46. "Who's Afraid of Frank Chin, or Is It Ching?"

47. Letters, *Bridge* 2, no. 4 (April 1973): 49–51.

48. Letter from Frank Ching to the author, 18 February 1986.

49. The most common topics concerned Chinatowns (21 percent), followed by those that dealt with the People's Republic of China (11 percent).

50. Editorial, "An American in Disguise," *Bridge* 1, no. 2 (September/October 1971): 4–5.

51. "Editorial," *Bridge* 2, no. 2 (December 1972): 49–50.

52. "Editor's Note," *Bridge* 3, no. 4 (February 1975): back cover.

53. *Bridge* articles in the last issue of the first volume were Leighton Dingley, "A Wartime Odyssey: Recollections of a Relocation Officer in an Internment Camp," pp. 10–12; Pamela Eguchi, "Childhood," p. 31; Rockwell Chin, "Gold Watch and Ghosts: Asian Reality in America," pp. 13–14; and Bill Wong, "A Review of Executive Order 9066," pp. 18–23. A decade later, *Bridge* 7, no. 4 (Winter 1981–1982) focused on the redress and reparations movement.

54. *Bridge* 6, no. 4 (Winter 1978–79) and 7, no. 1 (Spring 1979). In 1983, Asian American women were once again a *Bridge* cover feature.

55. Editorial, "Asian American Women Today," *Bridge* 6, no. 4 (Winter 1978–1979): 5.

56. Editorial, "What Price 'Peace With Honor,'" *Bridge* 2, no. 4 (April 1973): 3.

57. "Editorial," *Bridge* 2, no. 1 (September/October 1972): 3.

58. "Editorial," *Bridge* 5, no. 4 (Winter 1977): 3.

59. Guest Editorial, "Asians for Asian Roles," *Bridge* 2, no. 3 (February 1973): 3.

60. David Oyama, "Introduction: Asian American Poetry—'A Culture Discovering Itself,'" *Bridge* 4, no. 4 (October 1976): 5–6.

61. Ibid.

62. Letter from Diane Mark to the author, 7 October 1988.

63. David Oyama, interview, New York City, 23 June 1986.

64. Letter from Diane Mark to the author, 7 October 1988.

65. "To Our Readers," *Bridge* 4, no. 4 (October 1976): 2.

66. Letter from Frank Ching to the author, 18 February 1986.

67. Ibid.

68. Editorial, "A Reaffirmation," *Bridge* 3, no. 1 (February 1974): 3.

69. Nack Young An, "To the Readers of Bridge," *Bridge* 5, no. 3 (Fall 1977): 29–30.

70. "Editor's Note," *Bridge* 5, no. 3 (Fall 1977): back cover.

71. William T. Liu and Alice K. Murata, "The Resettlement of the Refugees," part 5, *Bridge* 6, no. 4 (Winter 1978): 55–60, 64. The other parts are of "The Vietnamese in America" published in *Bridge*: part 1, "Refugees or Immigrants?" 5, no. 3 (Fall 1977): 31–39; part 2, "Perilous Flights, Uncertain Future," 5, no. 4 (Winter 1977): 42–50; part 3, "Life in the Refugee Camps," 6, no. 1 (Spring 1978): 36–46; part 4, "Life in the Refugee Camps (continued)," 6, no. 2 (Summer 1978): 44–49.

72. *Bridge* 6, nos. 2–3.

73. Unless otherwise noted, the discussion of *Amerasia* is based on Russell Leong, interviews, 30 October and 1 November 1985; Don Nakanishi, interview, Los Angeles, 6 November 1985; Glenn Omatsu, interview, Los Angeles, interview, 12 September 1986; and *Amerasia* 1, no. 1 (March 1971) to 17. no. 3 (1991).

74. "A Message to Our Readers," *Amerasia* 1, no. 1 (March 1971).

75. Stanley and Derald Sue, "Chinese-American Personality and Mental Health," *Amerasia* 1, no. 2 (July 1971): 36–49. The journal has published commentaries on some of its other articles, but none have had the force of the Sue/Tong exchange. See, for example, Paul Takagi's "The Myth of Assimilation in American Life," *Amerasia* 2 (Fall 1973): 149–158; and George Kagiwada's "Confessions of a Misguided Sociologist," *Amerasia* 2 (Fall 1973): 159–164, which mainly critiqued the use of "assimilation" as a "scientific category" and only implicitly rebutted the thesis presented by Joe R. Feagin and Nancy Fujitaki in "On the Assimilation of Japanese Americans," *Amerasia* 1, no. 4 (February 1972): 13–30.

76. Ben Tong, "The Ghetto of the Mind: Notes on the Historical Psychology of Chinese America," *Amerasia* 1, no. 3 (November 1971): 1–31. Further commentary can be found in *Amerasia* 2, no. 2 (Fall 1974): Jerry Surh, "Asian American Identity and Politics," pp. 158–172; Stanley Sue, "Personality and Mental Health: A Clarification," pp. 173–177; and Ben Tong, "A Living Death Defended as the Legacy of a Superior Culture," pp. 178–202.

77. Apparently there is one area that *Amerasia* is reluctant to explore—the internal politics of Asian American communities. Because of their sensitivity, the journal has shied away from essays on New Left organizations and the postwar influence of the KMT in American Chinatowns. Russell Leong, interview, Los Angeles, 7 January 1985. Presumably such essays would only serve to divide and alienate the community.

78. Letter from Russell Leong to the Association for Asian American Studies, 1986.

79. Ibid.

80. All three articles were published in *Amerasia* 6, no. 2 (Fall 1979).

81. Gary Y. Okihiro, "Japanese Resistance in America's Concentration Camps: A Reevaluation," *Amerasia* 2 (Fall 1973): 20–34; and Arthur A. Hansen and David A. Hacker, "The Manzanar Riot: An Ethnic Perspective," *Amerasia* 2, no. 2 (Fall 1974): 112–157.

82. Okihiro, "Japanese Resistance," p. 21.

83. "Preface," *Amerasia* 7, no. 2 (1980): ix–xi.

84. "A Message to Our Readers," *Amerasia* 1, no. 1 (March 1971).

85. Amerasia Editors, "Moving the Image," *Amerasia* 17, no. 2 (1991): v–vi. Special Edition, "Burning Cane," *Amerasia* 17, no. 2 (1991), may also be a response to Anson Gong, "A Half-Empty Cup of Tea," *Amerasia* 16, no. 1 (1990), which criticized *Amerasia* for failing "to live up to its original campus roots and mission of supporting student writers by encouraging student submissions, reviewing student publications regularly, hiring younger staff and reviving its defunct writing contest to give students incentive and opportunity to pursue writing as a sideline occupation or as a career."

86. See the introduction to "Part I: Critical Perspectives," in Gee, *Counterpoint*, pp. 4–12.

87. Letter from Russell Leong to the author, 2 November 1988.

88. *Amerasia* 14, no. 1 (1988).

89. Editors, "To Our Readers," *Amerasia* 16, no. 2 (1990) iii–v.

90. "War and Asian Americans" issue, *Amerasia* 17, no. 1 (1991).

91. Alexander Saxton, "The New World Order and the Rambo Syndrome," *Amerasia* 17, no. 1 (1991): ix–xvi.

92. Editorial, "The Mainstream Press and the Asian American Communities," *East/West*, 4 August 1988.

93. Letter from Russell Leong to the author, 2 November 1988.

94. Philip, "*Rice Magazine* Aims to Become a Staple for Asian Americans."

Similar criticism was leveled at *Jade*, a glossy quarterly that came out in 1974. Ironically, it had as its purpose the defining of Asian American identity. See Joan Shigekawa, "Through Jaded Eyes," *Bridge* 3, no. 2 (April 1974): 31, for a critical review.

Chapter 5: Activists and the Development of Asian American Studies

1. Chalsa Loo, "The 'Middle-Aging' of Asian American Studies" in *Reflections on Shattered Windows*, ed. Gary Y. Okihiro et al. (Pullman: Washington State University Press, 1988), pp. 16–23.

2. Originally, the Ethnic Studies Department was supposed to evolve into a College of Third World Studies, and each of the four programs—African American, Asian American, Chicano, and Native American—was to become a department within it. This plan came to a sudden halt when the African American Studies program moved into the College of Letters and Sciences. According to Ronald Takaki, interview, Berkeley, 20 March 1985, it apparently left out of concern for its future survival as a unit, since the Ethnic Studies Department was considered too unstable. Jere Takahashi, interview, Berkeley, 18 March 1985, observed that at the time Asian Americans viewed the defection as an effort to become part of the mainstream but predicted that it would result in a loss of autonomy for African American Studies.

3. Unless otherwise noted, the discussion of the AAS program at CCNY is based on interviews with Betty Lee Sung, 19 and 21 November 1984, and T. K. Tong, 19 and 20 November 1984; Betty Lee Sung, letter to the author, 11 December 1984; T. K. Tong, letter to the author, 27 January 1985; and R. Takashi Yanagida, "Asian Students vs. University Control: The Confrontation at C.C.N.Y.," *Bridge* 1, no. 5 (May/June 1972): 11–12.

4. Sucheng Chan, "On the Ethnic Studies Requirement, Part I: Pedagogical Implications," *Amerasia* 15, no. 1 (1989): 267–280; and "Report of the Committee Appointed to Review the Department of Ethnic Studies" (July 1973).

5. Mike Murase, "Ethnic Studies and Higher Education for Asian Americans," in *Counterpoint: Perspectives on Asian America*, ed. Emma Gee (Los Angeles: Asian American Studies Center, University of California, 1976), pp. 205–223.

6. Raymond Lou, " 'Unknown Jerome': Asian American Studies in the California State University System," in Okihiro, *Reflections on Shattered Windows*, pp. 24–30.

7. Jeffrey Chan, interview, San Francisco, 18–20 March 1985.

8. Manuscript comments accompanying letter from Malcolm Collier to the author, 14 December 1990.

9. Manuscript comments accompanying letter from Betty Lee Sung to the

author, 1 December 1990. Incidentally, community workers frequently cite her work in their proposals. As she notes in "The Thrust of Asian American Studies," *American Asian Review* 2, no. 2 (Summer 1984): 108–121, "informed decisions based upon sound research can help communities like Chinatown sustain their growth and vitality instead of degenerating into slums and ghettos."

10. For a cogent discussion of this phenomenon, see the commentaries by Chalsa Loo and Don Mar, "Research and Asian Americans: Social Change or Empty Prize?" *Amerasia* 12, no. 2 (1985–1986): 85–93; and Maurice Lim Miller, "Whom Should Academic Researchers Serve?" *Amerasia* 12, no. 2 (1985–1986): 95–99.

11. For example, AAS programs have helped promote many community programs with direct funding: Berkeley financed Everybody's Bookstore and programs in the Asian Community Center; UCLA financed *Gidra*; CCNY financed the Asian Children Underground and Asian American Resource Center. Spring Wang, "A Tool of Control or a Tool of Change: The Second Asian American Conference," *Bridge* 3, no. 1 (February 1974): 31–33.

12. Manuscript comments accompanying letter from Malcolm Collier to the author, 14 December 1990.

13. Asian Students Committee of the City College of New York, "Declaration of Asian American Studies at City College of New York," *Bridge* 3, no. 2 (April 1974): 36–38.

14. Manuscript comments accompanying letter from Malcolm Collier to the author, 14 December 1990.

15. Karen Umemoto, "Student/Community Projects Unit Summation and Evaluation, 1989–90 Academic Year," 21 June 1990. Unless otherwise noted, the discussion of the Student/Community Projects unit is based on Karen Umemoto, interview, Los Angeles, 11 July 1990; and Warren Furutani, "S/CP Then . . . and Now," *Cross Currents* 11, no. 1 (Fall and Winter 1987): 6–9.

16. Furutani, "S/CP Then . . . and Now."

17. Umemoto, "Student/Community Projects Unit Summation and Evaluation."

18. Ibid.

19. Unless otherwise noted, the discussion on the AAS program at San Francisco State is based on interviews in San Francisco with George Woo, Jeffrey Chan, Danillo Begonia, Jim Okutsu, Lane Hirabayashi, Marilyn Alquizola, and Malcolm Collier, conducted 18–20 March 1985; and Neil Gotanda, interview, Fullerton, California, 10 July 1990.

20. Manuscript comments accompanying letter from Malcolm Collier to the author, 14 December 1990.

21. Letter from Lane R. Hirabayshi to the author, 15 December 1990, suggested another explanation: "As older, more experienced, and well-linked leaders, both George [Woo] and Mason [Wong] knew, from the very beginning, who the

leaders of politically oriented groups were in the San Francisco Bay area. On this basis, in conjunction with the Filipinos and the Koreans, they carefully controlled the linkages between the AAS program and the plethora of AA community groups. They kept an ad-hoc stance, operationally, that allowed coalitions, but kept the identity and the interests of the program, distinct. Thus, with the exception of the JTC case, which was resolved fairly quickly and definitively, State has been able to avoid sectarian political battles."

22. Unless otherwise noted, the discussion of Berkeley's AAS program is based on "An Analysis of the Historical Development of Asian American Studies," 28 August 1975, typewritten; Asian Students Marxism Study Group, "Asian American Studies and the Fight Against Racism," Winter 1974, typewritten; History and Goals Subcommittee of the Asian American Studies program in "An Analysis of the Historical Development of the Asian American Studies Program"; Ray Collins et al., "Report of the Committee Appointed to Review the Department of Ethnic Studies," July 1973; Jere Takahashi, interview, Berkeley, 18 March 1985; Elaine Kim, interview, Berkeley, 19 March 1985; L. Ling-chi Wang, interview, Berkeley, 20 March 1985; Ronald Takaki, interview, Berkeley, 20 March 1985; Patrick Hayashi, telephone interview, 4 June 1985; and anonymous source C, telephone interview, 4 June 1985. Incidentally, according to a letter from Betty Lee Sung to the author, 1 December 1990, "a few Marxists tried to co-opt the AAS program at CCNY . . . they tried to radicalize the movement, but after 1975, they had withdrawn."

23. Appendix B.2, Historical Documents: "Position of '8' on the Take-over," in "Analysis of the Historical Development of Asian American Studies," 28 August 1989, typewritten.

24. Ibid.

25. Asian American Studies, "Asian American Report," no. 1 (August 1977), University of California, Berkeley.

26. Ibid.

27. Political Education Meeting Minutes, 10 May 1972, in "Introduction to the Analysis of the Historical Development of Asian American Studies."

28. According to Sucheng Chan, in a personal communication to the author, 10 March 1992, the Academic Senate's Committee on Courses constantly rejected courses submitted by the program until Chan offered to serve on the committee and worked to have the curriculum approved.

29. Personal communication from Sucheng Chan to the author, 10 March 1992.

30. Steve Yip, interview, New York City, 21 and 24 August 1985. Another Marxist group was the KDP, which exercised control over the Filipino courses. Interview with Elaine Kim (undated), provided by Gary Kawaguchi.

31. "Pilipino National Anti-Imperialist Organization Formed," *Getting Together*, 1–15 September 1973; "Getting Together Interview with Katipunan ng mga Demokratikong Pilipino," *Getting Together*, 14 September–4 October 1973; and "Part II, Katipunan ng mga Demokratikong Pilipino," *Getting Together*, 18–

31 October 1973; provide information about the origins, programs, and goals of KDP.

32. "Asian American Report," no. 1 (August 1977) and no. 2 (December 1977).

33. Personal communication from Sucheng Chan to the author, 10 March 1992, notes that "although the threat of closing down the program was there, the Berkeley administration could never have succeeded because the militant reformers would have strenuously resisted such a move."

34. Unless otherwise noted, the discussion of the Association for Asian American Studies is based on Gary Okihiro, telephone interview, 28 June 1990.

35. During this period, the association's most exciting event was unquestionably the uproar surrounding Ronald Takaki's *Strangers from a Different Shore*, which won its 1990 book award. "Amerasia Forum—*Strangers from a Different Shore*," *Amerasia* 16, no. 2 (1990): 63–145, contains an editorial on the acrimonious debate, commentaries on the book, viewpoints on various aspects of the controversy, and Takaki's response to his critics.

36. Jon Wiener, "Reagan's Children: Racial Hatred on Campus," *The Nation*, 27 February 1989, 260–264.

37. Dennis Kelly, "Report: Quality of College Life Declines," *Colorado Daily*, 2 May 1990.

38. Nancy Gibbs, "Bigots in the Ivory Tower," *Time*, 7 May 1990.

39. Asian Week, *Asians in America: 1990 Census, Classification by States* (San Francisco: Grant Printing House, 1991). There is a slight discrepancy in census data. Usually, the 1980 figure cited is 3.5 million, rather than 3.8 million, because it is based only on the "nine specific Asian or Pacific Islander groups listed separately in the 1980 race item" (see *Asians in America*, p. 4n). The larger figure is from the sample tabulations and comparable to the 1990 count. Asian American population growth is keenly felt in certain states like California. See Paul Ong, "Asians in California in the Year 2000: A Project Summary," in *Cross Currents* 13, no. 1 (Summer/Fall 1989): 3–4.

40. Peter Nien-chu Kiang, "Bringing It All Back Home: New Views of Asian American Studies and the Community," in *Frontiers of Asian-American Studies: Writing, Research, and Commentary*, ed. Gail M. Nomura et al. (Pullman, Wash.: Washington State University Press, 1989), pp. 305–314.

41. Laird Harrison, "Ethnic Studies on the Rise, Part I: Asian American Studies Joins the Ivy League," *Asian Week*, 15 May 1987.

42. MidAtlantic/ECASU, "Draft Sum-up of ECASU Split," 16 March 1979. According to this document, IWK usurped the conference's thrust to discuss the Bakke issue. Suzanne Pan and Ellen Lam, "ECASU: Education for Action," *East Wind* 6, no. 1 (Spring/Summer 1987): 27–28, provide useful information on ECASU.

43. MIT Asian American Caucus, *A Call for Asian American Studies*, Spring 1989. Pamphlet.

44. James Dao, "Passing Grades: A Progress Report on Twenty Years of Asian American Studies," *Asian Times* 1, no. 6 (June–July 1989): 5–6.

45. Lee C. Lee, "Director's Message," *Connections: Asian American Studies Program Newsletter*, Fall 1988.

46. Chan, "On the Ethnic Studies Requirement, Part I: Pedagogical Implications."

47. W. S. Simmons, "Proposal for an American Cultures Breadth Requirement," Report by the Special Committee on Education and Ethnicity, University of California at Berkeley, 28 March 1989; and L. Ling-chi Wang, "The Ethnic Studies Requirement: Its Impact on Asian American Studies," plenary session, Association for Asian American Studies Meeting at the University of California, Santa Barbara, 18–20 May 1990. Both provide background on this requirement.

48. David Ho and Margaret Chin, "Admissions: Impossible," *Bridge* 8, no. 3 (Summer 1983): 7, 8, 51. Also see John H. Bunzel and Jeffrey K. D. Au, "Diversity or Discrimination? Asian Americans in College," *Asian Week*, 22 May 1987; and L. Ling-chi Wang, "Meritocracy and Diversity in Higher Education: Discrimination Against Asian Americans in the Post-*Bakke* Era," *Urban Review* 20, no. 3 (1988): 189–209.

49. Sucheng Chan and Ling-chi Wang, "Racism and the Model Minority: Asian-Americans in Higher Education," in *The Racial Crisis in American Higher Education*, ed. Philip G. Altbach and Kofi Lomotey (Albany, N.Y.: SUNY Press, 1991), pp. 43–67.

50. Ying Yuen Chan, "Admissions Quotas Debated," *Asian Times*, December 1988.

51. Unless otherwise noted, the discussion of quotas at Berkeley is based on Associated Students of the University of California Presidential Commission on Admissions and Affirmative Action, "A Student Perspective on Admissions," Spring 1989; W. A. Shack et al., "Report of the Special Committee on Asian American Admissions of the Berkeley Division of the Academic Senate, University of California, Berkeley," February 1989; Jerome B. Karabel et al., "Freshman Admissions at Berkeley: A Policy for the 1990s and Beyond," 19 May 1989; Judith A. Lyons, "Asians Blast UC Berkeley Report," *Asian Week*, 3 March 1989; Joy Morimoto, "Students Charge Whitewash in Berkeley Admissions Report," *Asian Week*, 10 March 1989; Patrick Anderson, "University of California Showdown: Berkeley Chancellor Apologizes for Bias," *Asian Week*, 17 March 1989; and "Roberti Calls for Probe of UC Admissions of Asians," *Asian Week*, 20 March 1987.

52. Shack, "Report of the Special Committee on Asian American Admissions," p. 4.

53. Ibid., p. 10.

54. Lyons, "Asians Blast UC Berkeley Report."

55. Morimoto, "Students Charge Whitewash"; and Andersen, "University of California Showdown."

56. Arthur Hu, "Commentary: Time to Rethink Quotas for Minority Admis-

sions," *Asian Week*, 10 February 1989; "Voices: Average Is Hard to Define," *Asian Week*, 14 April 1989; "Hu's on First," *Asian Week*, 28 April 1989; "Hu's on First: 'Part II: Affirmative Action After Asian Quotas,' " *Asian Week*, 23 June 1989; "Hu's on First," *Asian Week*, 1 September 1989; "Hu's on First: 'Berkeley, Me, and the Asian American Movement,' " *Asian Week*, 9 February 1990.

57. Asian American Task Force on University Admissions, "Help? Or Attacks on Affirmative Action," *Asian Week*, 3 November 1989.

58. Judith A. Lyons, "Berkeley Students Call for More Minority Faculty," *Asian Week*, 5 May 1989.

59. Judith A. Lyons, "Asian Profs Least Likely to Win Tenure," and idem, "Long Path to Tenure," *Asian Week*, 10 February 1989.

60. "Affirmative Action Reports to the Regents," Memorandum from Emily Calhoun to President E. Gordon Gee, 29 April 1986; and Memorandum on Affirmative Action Report from William Baughn, Chancellor, to E. Gordon Gee, President, 30 April 1986.

61. William Wei, "Asian/Pacific American Faculty at the University of Colorado," Boulder, 12 May 1986. Typewritten. The rest of the Asians held special faculty titles, usually research associate. Another characteristic of the Asian American faculty members was that most of them were foreign born, which conformed to national trends, and were concentrated in the science and technology fields.

62. Takaki, *Strangers from a Different Shore*, p. 476.

63. Deborah Clark, "Students: Tenure Denial Unfair," *Daily Californian*, 22 February 1990.

64. Grace Wai-tse Siao, "Nakanishi Wins Tenure at UCLA: Battle Symbolized 'Glass Ceiling,' " *Asian Week*, 2 June 1989. Glenn Omatsu, comp. and ed., " 'Power to the People!' The Don Nakanishi Case at UCLA," *Amerasia* 16, no. 1 (1990): 61–169, contains eight articles on aspects of the Nakanishi case, plus a chronology of events.

65. Dan Ashby, "Professor Discusses Tenure Denial: Cites Numerous Procedural Irregularities," *Berkeley Graduate* 4, no. 2 (December 1989): 15, 26–28; Marcy Wang Tenure Task Force and Asian American Political Alliance, "Discrimination against Asian Pacific Americans?" (packet concerning the tenure case of Marcy Li Wang), 5 October 1989.

66. William Wong, "Sexism, Racial Bias and Academic Tenure," *The Tribune*, 5 March 1990.

Chapter 6: "To Serve the People"

1. Fox Butterfield, "Asians Spread across a Land, and Help Change It," *New York Times*, 24 February 1991. For detailed discussions and statistics of the 1980 census, see Robert W. Gardner et al., "Asian Americans: Growth, Change, and Diversity," *Population Bulletin* 40, no. 4 (October 1985); and Bureau of the Census, U.S. Department of Commerce, *We, the Asian and Pacific Islander Americans*

(Washington, D.C.: Government Printing Office, n. d.). For statistics on the 1990 census, see Asian Week, *Asians in America, 1990 Census, Classification by States* (San Francisco: Grant Printing House, 1991).

2. According to Samuel Yette, "the Community Action Program, a billion dollar con game about 'involvement,' pledged 'maximum feasible participation' of the black and poor in local decision-making but actually became a name-taking web that helped to identify and isolate the natural leaders of every black community in America, each leader's name ultimately fixed to a massive pick-up list at the Pentagon awaiting the moment when the order is given." Ramsey Liem, "The Golden Apple or a Real Lemon?" *Gidra*, May 1973, pp. 18–19.

3. Garrett Spector-Leech, "Ethnic Community Mobilization within an Urban Environment: An Analysis of Asian/Pacific Community and Advocacy Organizations in Los Angeles County," Master's thesis, University of Southern California, 1988, cited in Yen Le Espiritu, "Cooperation and Conflict: Panethnicity among Asian-Americans," Ph.D. dissertation, University of California at Los Angeles, 1990.

4. Alan Wong, telephone interview, 22 November 1988; and George Woo, interview, San Francisco, 27 March 1986; "Larry J. Wong Resigns as EOC Deputy Chief," *East/West*, 2 December 1970. It should be noted that Larry J. Wong was instrumental in organizing the San Francisco Economic Opportunity Council in 1964. He was credited with being the principal social architect of the EOC's growth to a $14 million social institution that tried to help the 150,000 San Franciscans living in poverty.

5. Jeannie Look, "Remembering the S.F. State Strikes," *East/West*, 20 October 1988; and idem, "After the S.F. State Strike: EOP and the School of Ethnic Studies," *East/West*, 27 October 1988.

6. "Success Story of One Minority Group in U.S.," *U.S. News & World Report*, 26 December 1966, reprinted in Amy Tachiki et al., eds., *Roots: An Asian American Reader* (Los Angeles: Asian American Studies Center, University of California, 1971).

7. William Barlow and Peter Shapiro, *An End to Silence: The San Francisco State College Student Movement in the '60s* (New York: Pegasus, 1971).

8. Kuregiy Hekymara, "The Third World Movement and Its History in the San Francisco State College Strike of 1968–69," Ph.D. dissertation, University of California at Berkeley, 1972, p. 82.

9. Unless otherwise noted, the description of San Francisco's Chinatown is based on Victor G. and Brett de Bary Nee, *Longtime Californ': A Documentary Study of an American Chinatown* (New York: Pantheon Books, 1973); and Barlow and Shapiro, *An End to Silence*. The description of New York's Chinatown is based on Robin Wu, "New York's Chinatown: An Overview," *Bridge* 1, no. 1 (July–August 1971): 13–15.

10. "Chinatown TB Rate on Decline," *East/West*, 19 August 1970.

11. William H. Orrick, Jr., *College in Crisis: A Report to the National Commis-*

sion on the Causes and Prevention of Violence (Nashville: Aurora Publishers, 1970), p. 110.

12. Unless otherwise noted, the discussion of the CPC is based on Charles Pei Wong, interview, New York City, 11 January 1990; Allen B. Cohen, "Developing Comprehensive Services for the Chinese American Community," *Bridge* 6, no. 3 (Fall 1978): 51–52; and Peter Kwong, *The New Chinatown* (New York: Hill and Wang, 1987). The discussion on SHE is based on Anni Chung, interview, San Francisco, 29 March 1990; Self-Help for the Elderly, *Annual Report: 1966–1986* (San Francisco: Public Media Center, 1986); Richard Springer, "Self-Help for the Elderly Celebrates Its 20th Anniversary!" *East/West*, 28 August 1986. The discussion on CAA is based on Henry Der, interview, San Francisco, 30 March 1990; Kathy Owyang Turner, telephone interview, 6 December 1990; Kathy Fong, "A Chinaman's Chance Revisited," *Bridge* 2, no. 6 (August 1973): 19–22; and Chinese for Affirmative Action, *Annual Report: 1988–1989*. There are of course counterparts to these three Chinese American agencies in other Asian American communities—For example, the Little Tokyo Service Center in Los Angeles, Kimochi and Filipinos for Affirmative Action in San Francisco.

13. Springer, "Self-Help for the Elderly." According to Richard Springer, "Give 'Em Hell, J.K.," *East/West*, 20 April 1989, J. K. Choy was a feisty community leader in San Francisco's Chinatown.

14. Henry Der, interview, San Francisco, 30 March 1990.

15. Stuart H. Cattell, *Health, Welfare, and Social Organization in Chinatown, New York* (New York: Community Service Society, 1962), p. ii.

16. Cohen, "Developing Comprehensive Services," p. 50.

17. Cattell, *Health, Welfare and Social Organization*, p. 89.

18. "NY Chinatown Agency Accused of Unfair Labor Practices," *East/West*, 26 January 1989.

19. Springer, "Self-Help for the Elderly."

20. Susan Herbert, "Anni Chung—Helping the Elderly," *San Francisco Independent*, 27 March 1990.

21. "Asian/Pacific Islander Elderly Show Four-Fold Increase from 1965–1975," *East/West*, 14 August 1986. Also see Grace Wai-tse Siao, "Asian American Elderly to Number One Million by Year 2000," *Asian Week*, 23 November 1990.

22. Eunice Chen, "Full Board to Consider Pineview/Georo," *East/West*, 7 August 1985.

23. Carol Wong, "Pineview Housing Atop B'Way Tunnel Still Hanging," *East/West*, 23 October 1985.

24. Johnny Ng, "Senior Housing Project Opens in S.F. Chinatown," *Asian Week*, 26 October 1990.

25. Robert Lee, "From the Beginning: The CAA Story," Chinese for Affirmative Action, *Annual Report, 1988–1989*, p. 10; and Kathy Fong, "A Chinaman's Chance Revisited," *Bridge* 2, no. 6 (August 1973): 19–22.

26. Lee, "From the Beginning," p. 10. Also see "FEPC to Hear Asian Com-

munity Comments," *East/West*, 2 December 1970; and "Chinese List History of Job Discrimination," *East/West*, 16 December 1970.

27. L. Ling-chi Wang, "One and One and One is Three," *East/West*, 27 May 1970.

28. Ibid.

29. Ibid.

30. L. Ling-chi Wang, "Holiday Inn, Community in Harmony," *East/West*, 2 September 1970.

31. Ibid.

32. According to Kathy Owyang Turner, telephone interview, 11 December 1990, while the organization's primary interest remains the civil rights of Chinese Americans, that is part and parcel of its Asian American advocacy efforts. Occasionally, the staff does consider changing its name to reflect this broader concern but never gets around to doing anything about it. This may reflect bureaucratic inertia and the tenacity of tradition more than anything else.

33. *Chinese for Affirmative Action Newsletter*, Spring 1990.

34. The argument that federal programs were part of a counterinsurgency strategy can be found in "The Money Tree Bears Strange Fruit: Federal Funds in the Asian Community," *Gidra*, May 1973, pp. 18–19. This article consists of two readings: Ramsey Liem, "The Golden Apple or a Real Lemon?" and Shin'ya Ono, "Dancing to a Sour Tune."

35. Liem, "The Golden Apple or a Real Lemon?"

36. Ono, "Dancing to a Sour Tune."

37. Mini Liu and Monona Yin, Committee Against Anti-Asian Violence, Letter to Friends, 7 November 1990.

38. Unless otherwise noted, the discussion of Basement Workshop is based on Fay Chiang, "Looking Back," in *Basement Yearbook 1986* (New York: Basement Workshop, 1986); and Fay Chiang, interview, New York City, 15 and 21 August 1985.

39. Chiang, "Looking Back," p. 3.

40. Ibid., p. 6.

41. Ibid.

42. They wanted it to serve as a political-front organization to support the work of Asian Americans for Equal Employment. Conflicts arose over the use of Basement resources. For example, people were angry that even though a former director was paid a salary to manage Basement, he spent his time traveling around the country promoting the activities of Asian Americans for Equal Employment. Fay Chiang, interview, New York City, 15 and 21 August 1985.

43. Chiang, "Looking Back," p. 7.

44. Ibid.

45. Ibid., p. 10.

46. The fees were modest indeed. For example, poets received $75 to $100 for

a reading, artists $250 for exhibiting their paintings, and performers $75 to $200 for doing a show. Given the severe reduction in financial support for the arts during the Reagan administration, however, these token sums were welcomed for their symbolic as well as monetary value. Fay Chiang, interview, New York City, 15 and 21 August 1985.

47. Anonymous source D, interview, Boulder, 18 March 1990.

48. Ibid.

49. Fay Chiang, interview, New York City, 15 and 21 August 1985.

50. Letter from anonymous source D to the author, 17 July 1991.

51. There was some discussion within Basement about increasing its earned income through the production of media that could be sold or rented. But that never amounted to anything, perhaps because there were already several well-established organizations—Asian Cine-Vision, Visual Communications, and the National Asian American Telecommunications Association—engaged in media production.

52. Unless otherwise noted, the discussion of the Asian Law Caucus is based on Dale Minami, "Asian Law Caucus: Experiment in an Alternative," *Amerasia* 3, no. 1 (Summer 1975): 28–39; Peggy Saika, interview, San Francisco, 28 March 1990; Max Millard, "Community Profile: Asian Law Caucus," *East/West*, 23 October 1986; Asian Law Caucus annual benefit programs: "10th Anniversary Celebration" (21 May 1982), "In Defense of Civil Rights" (3 June 1983), "In Defense of Civil Rights: Contributions of Asian Women" (1 June 1984), "Immigrant Rights: Civil Rights Issue of the 80's" (31 May 1985), "In Defense of Civil Rights: Strengthening Our Movement" (7 June 1986), "15th Anniversary Celebration: In Defense of Civil Rights" (4 April 1987), "Working for Economic Justice" (30 April 1988), and "In Defense of Civil Rights: Justice, Equality, Empowerment" (20 May 1989). Besides the Asian Law Caucus, other legal organizations served the Asian American community, such as Asian Pacific American Legal Center of Southern California in Los Angeles (APALC) and the Asian American Legal Defense and Education Fund (AALDEF) in New York City.

53. "Networking: Asian Law Caucus Founders Recall Activist Beginnings," *East/West*, 19 March 1987.

54. Ibid. Dale Minami, "Asian Law Caucus," discusses the origins and development of this suit.

55. "Immigrant Rights: Civil Rights Issue of the 80's," 31 May 1985.

56. "Community Profile: Asian Law Caucus," *East/West*, 23 October 1986.

57. Carol Wong, "Asian Law Caucus Trend: Cases Becoming More Political in Character," *East/West*, 2 January 1986.

58. Peter Irons, *Justice at War: The Story of the Japanese American Internment Cases* (New York: Oxford University Press, 1983), p. viii.

59. Serena Chen, "Don Tamaki Wins State Bar Award," *East/West*, 27 August 1987.

60. *Korematsu* v. *United States*, *United States Reports*, vol. 323, October Term 1944 (Washington, D.C.: Government Printing Office, 1945), pp. 225–248, contains the three dissenting opinions.

61. Ibid., pp. 233, 242.

62. David Margolick, "Legal Legend Urges Victims to Speak Out," *New York Times*, 24 November 1984.

63. "Justice Overdue: The Coram Nobis Cases," in "In Defense of Civil Rights," 3 June 1983. A more recent example of the failure of the judicial system was the Filipina Narciso and Leonara Perez case. In July 1977, these two Filipino nurses were convicted of poisoning patients at the Ann Arbor Veterans Administration Hospital. But on 1 February 1978 all charges against them were dropped after Judge Philip Pratt, the presiding judge in the case, granted the defense motion for a new trial, citing the "insidious accretion of prosecutorial misconduct," which "polluted the waters of justice." News section, *Bridge* 6, no. 1 (Spring 1978): 58. Also see James S. Burris, "Innocent Until Proven Guilty, and That Beyond a Reasonable Doubt! Personal View of the Narciso–Perez Case," *Bridge* 5, no. 3 (Fall 1977): 40–47, for a critical review of the judicial proceedings. Burris notes that for many people, including Asian Americans, the case represented the "need for a 'scapegoat' to 'explain' the breathing failures in a government hospital; the focus on 'foreigners' (in this case of a different race) as the likely suspects, to the exclusion of serious and complete investigation of others."

64. "Justice Overdue: The Coram Nobis Cases."

65. Dale Minami, "*Coram Nobis* and Redress," in *Japanese Americans: From Relocation to Redress*, ed. Roger Daniels et al. (Salt Lake City: University of Utah Press, 1986), p. 202. Though Justice Patel was referring specifically to the Korematsu case, her remarks are applicable to the other internment cases as well.

66. U.S. Commission on Civil Rights, *Recent Activities Against Citizens of Residents of Asian Descent* (Washington, D.C.: Government Printing Office), p. iii. See pp. 43 and 44 for a summary of the Vincent Chin case. Christine Choy and Renee Tajima have made a documentary on the tragedy entitled *Who Killed Vincent Chin?* which has been shown on public television. The report concluded that "anti-Asian activity exists in numerous and demographically different communities across the Nation" (p. 5). Since its publication, anti-Asian violence has continued to rise at an alarming rate. No incident has been more senseless than the "Stockton Massacre": On 17 January 1989 Patrick Purdy's hatred for Vietnamese sent him on a bloody rampage at an elementary school in Stockton, California, where he killed or wounded 36 children. Purdy specifically targeted Asian students. Of the 5 killed, Rathanar Or, Oeun Lim, Sokhim An, and Ram Chun were Cambodian; Tran Thanh Thuy was Vietnamese. Of the 31 wounded, 22 were of Southeast Asian descent. Serena Chen, "Stockton Bids Farewell to Massacre Victims," *East/West*, 26 January 1989.

67. Unless otherwise noted, the discussion of the Committee Against Anti-

Asian Violence is based on Mini Liu and Monona Yin, interview, New York City, 8 January 1990; letter from Mini Liu and Monona Yin to the author, 1 January 1992; and *The CAAAV Voice: Newsletter of the Committee Against Anti-Asian Violence*, Fall 1988–Winter 1991.

68. "Anti-Asian Violence: Forum Spurs Community Action," *New York Nichibei*, 23 October 1986. At that time, the Coalition Against Anti-Asian Violence consisted of the Asian American Legal Defense and Education Fund; the New York chapters of the Coalition of Labor Union Women; Japanese American Citizens League; and Organization of Chinese Americans; Khmer Association in the United States; Korean American Women for Action; and Young Korean American Service and Education Center.

69. Ibid.

70. Sara Miles, "Mini Liu: Stopping Cops and Fighting Racial Violence," in "Special Section: Heroes and Heroines," *Mother Jones*, January 1990, pp. 35–36, contains an essay on Mini Liu, who was included in its fourth annual honor roll of "ordinary folks who rise up shining and fight the power."

71. Coalition Against Anti-Asian Violence pamphlet. "Wong/Woo Family Support Committee—Conveys Community Demands to DA Morgenthau's Office," *New York Nichibei*, 2 April 1987; "CAAAV—Civil Suit Filed for Wong/Woo Family and 'Indictment' Delivered to 5th Precinct," *New York Nichibei*, 6 August 1987; Barbara Lippman, "Chinatown Bruhaha: Family Claims Brutality, Sues Police," *Daily News*, 29 July 1987; and Helen Thorpe, "Chinese Family's Suit Alleging Police Brutality Ends in $90,000 Settlement," *New York Observer*, 14 August 1989.

72. Cohen, "Developing Comprehensive Services," p. 51.

73. Grace Wai-tse Siao, "L.A. Study: $2.42 Billion in Foundation Grants, but Only 0.17% Goes to Asians," *Asian Week*, 6 April 1990.

74. Kathy Owyang Turner, telephone interview, 11 December 1990.

75. Judith A. Lyons, "Chinese Are Generous, USF Researcher Finds," *Asian Week*, 2 February 1990. This is a controversial subject. In an earlier article, "Study: Asians Wink," *Asian Week*, 26 January 1990, Lyons reported that in a study compiled by Cathie Witty, Asians ranked lowest as contributors to workplace charitable campaigns compared to whites and other minority groups.

76. Lyons, "Chinese Are Generous."

77. Kwang-woo Han, interview, Oakland, California, 27 March 1990; Korean Community Development Corporation, Korean Community Center of the East Bay, "Tenth Anniversary Program," 30 April 1988; *Koryo Village Center: Investment and Project Summary* (n.p., n.d.); "Korean Community Center of the East Bay News" (July 1987); Wanda Soon, "Profile: East Bay's Korean Comm'ty Center Plans $1.5 Million Koryo Village Project," *East/West*, 21 May 1987. Although the KCCEB was established to provide services for Korean immigrants, half of its clients are non-Korean immigrants, including refugees.

78. Soon, "Profile: East Bay's Korean Comm'ty Center."

79. "CAAAV Expansion—Preparing for the Challenges to Come," *CAAAV Voice*, Winter 1991.

Chapter 7: The Emergence and Eclipse of Maoist Organizations

1. Edward J. Bacciocco, *The New Left in America: Reform to Revolution, 1956–1970* (Stanford, Calif.: Hoover Institution Press, 1974); George R. Vickers, *The Formation of the New Left: The Early Years* (Lexington, Mass.: Lexington Books, 1975); Irwin Unger, *The Movement: A History of the American New Left, 1959–1972* (New York: Dodd, Mead, 1974); and Wini Breins, *The Great Refusal: Community and Organization in the New Left, 1962–1969* (New York: Praeger, 1982); these are some of the standard works on the history of the New Left. Milton Cantor, *The Divided Left: American Radicalism, 1900–1975* (New York: Hill and Wang, 1978); Richard Flacks, *Making History: The American Left and the American Mind* (New York: Columbia University Press, 1988); and Maurice Isserman, *If I Had a Hammer . . .: The Death of the Old Left and the Birth of the New Left* (New York: Basic Books, 1987); these place the New Left in historical context.

2. Kirkpatrick Sale, *SDS* (New York: Random House, 1973) is considered the definitive study of the Students for a Democratic Society. Other pertinent works are Judith C. Albert and Stewart E. Albert, *The Sixties Papers: Documents of a Rebellious Decade* (New York: Praeger, 1984); Todd Gitlin, *The Sixties: Years of Hope, Days of Rage* (New York: Bantam Books, 1987); Harvey Klehr, *Far Left of Center: The American Radical Left Today* (New Brunswick, N.J.: Transaction, 1988); and James Miller, *"Democracy Is in the Streets": From Port Huron to the Siege of Chicago* (New York: Simon and Schuster, 1987).

3. Gitlin, *The Sixties*, p. 3.

4. David Lane, *Leninism: A Sociological Interpretation* (Cambridge, England: Cambridge University Press, 1981), p. 48.

5. Charles DeBenedetti and Charles Chatfield, assisting author, *An American Ordeal: The Antiwar Movement of the Vietnam Era* (Syracuse, N.Y.: Syracuse University Press, 1990), p. 225, points out that in May 1969 the FBI "launched a new Counterintelligence Program (Cointelpro) intended to 'expose, disrupt, and otherwise neutralize' the New Left and its allies." For a discussion of the phenomenon of U.S. security forces and radical organizations, see Frank J. Donner, "Hoover's Legacy," *The Nation*, 1 June 1974; and Ross K. Baker, "The False Connection: Police and the Violent Left," *The Nation* 15 June 1974.

6. Bobby Seale, *Seize the Time: The Story of the Black Panther Party and Huey P. Newton* (New York: Random House, 1968), pp. 79–85, recalled purchasing the popular "Red Books," as the *Quotations From Chairman Mao Tse-tung* were called because of their red plastic covers, at thirty cents apiece and reselling them to "leftist radicals at Berkeley" for a dollar, making enough to buy two shotguns.

7. Roy Nakano, "Marxist–Leninist Organizing in the Asian American Community: Los Angeles, 1969–79," essay written for "Asian Americans and Politics," Asian American Studies course 297, University of California at Los Angeles, March 1984.

8. Unless otherwise noted, the discussion of the Red Guard party is based on Alex Hing, interview, New York City, 24 August 1985; Ray Hing, interview, San Francisco, 26 March 1986; and the following articles from *Getting Together*: "A History of the Red Guard," vol. 4, no. 4 (16 February–1 March 1973); "Part II: Activities of the Red Guard Party," vol. 4, no. 5 (2–15 March 1973); "Concluding History of the Red Guard Party," vol. 4, no. 6 (16–29 March 1973). See also Stanford M. Lyman, "Red Guards on Grant Avenue," *The Asian in North America* (Santa Barbara: ABC-Clio, 1977), pp. 177–199.

9. Tom Wolfe, "The New Yellow Peril," *Esquire*, December 1969, 190–199, 322.

10. Nakano, "Marxist–Leninist Organizing."

11. Eldridge Cleaver, *Soul on Ice* (New York: Dell, 1968), is a powerful work that captures the ethos of the Black Panthers. Cleaver served as their minister of information. Gene Marine, *The Black Panthers* (New York: New American Library, 1969); Don A. Schanche, *The Panther Paradox: A Liberal's Dilemma* (New York: McKay, 1970); and Seale, *Seize the Time*, are other books about the Black Panther organization and its members.

12. Lyman, "Red Guards on Grant Avenue," p. 185.

13. "Rally," *Red Guard Community News*, 9 April 1969; and "Red Guard Rally," *Asian-American Political Alliance Newspaper* 1, no. 4 (n.d.). Wolfe, "The New Yellow Peril," p. 198, has provided a unique description of one of those rallies: But they had to go the stone total way and call it the Red Guard . . . and then take over a Sunday program in Portsmouth Square that was supposed to star Chou Tung-hua, the consul-general from Formosa. They bumped him and everybody else off the program, even a liberal and popular guy like Franklin Chow of the E.O.C., and stood out there under portraits of Mao with their Black Panther-Raoul-Che berets on and field jackets and red armbands that said "Red Guard" in Chinese. They lined up holding Red flag staffs out at stiff-arm attention and announced: "We want the freedom to make our own destiny! Chiang Kai-shek is ruling us through the Six Companies!"

14. "What Is Wei Min?" *Wei Min*, April–May 1975.

15. Unless otherwise noted, the discussion of Wei Min She is based on Steve Yip, interview, New York City, 21 and 24 August 1985. Within the organization, there may have been some confusion about its history. According to a memorandum from Special Agent in Charge to Acting Director, FBI, 31 October 1972, a WMS leaflet stated that it had "existed for three years whose purpose is to strive for the unity of the Chinese people and to struggle for racial and economical equality." This would make the year of origin 1969. Perhaps WMS members sought to give their organization a longer political history by tracing its date of origin to ACC.

According to "Opportunism in the Asian Movement-Wei Min She/Revolutionary Union," *I.W.K. Journal: The Political Organ of I Wor Kuen*, no. 2 (May 1975): 1–30, Wei Min She was "an organization the [Revolutionary Union] helped to build from its beginning" and is "the most developed of the Revolutionary Union's so-called anti-imperialist organizations within a national movement."

16. This interpretation is different from the FBI's. According to a confidential memorandum from the San Francisco office, 7 August 1973, an FBI informant said that "the ACC serves as a front for the WMS which is strongly pro-Chinese Communist. The WMS in order to reach a large portion of the Chinese community and extend its influence, created the ACC and its publicly oriented program." Also see Memorandum from the Special Agent in Charge, San Francisco, to Acting Director, FBI, 21 May 1973.

17. Steve Yip, interview, New York City, 21 and 24 August 1985.

18. "Trouble at a Chinatown Electronics Plant," *Getting Together* 5, no. 14 (15–31 July 1974). The discussion of the Jung Sai garment workers' strike is based on articles in *Getting Together* and *The Worker*; and "IV. Political Summation of the Jung Sai Strike," in *I.W.K. Journal: The Political Organ of I Wor Kuen*, no. 2 (May 1975): 49–72.

19. *Getting Together* 5, no. 17 (1–15 September 1974).

20. Confidential letter captioned "Revolutionary Union (RU)" originally from FBI, Chicago, Illinois, 10 November 1972, forwarded by Special Agent in Charge, San Francisco, to Acting Director, FBI.

21. Klehr, *Far Left of Center*, p. 95.

22. Simon Strong, "Where the Shining Path Leads," *New York Times Magazine*, 24 May 1992, pp. 12–17, 35.

23. Unless otherwise noted, the discussion on I Wor Kuen is based on Rocky Chin, "New York Chinatown Today: Community in Crisis," *Amerasia Journal* 1, no. 1 (March 1971): 1–24; Carmen Chow, "I Wor Kuen in Chinatown New York," *Hawaii Pono Journal: Special Issue, "Ethnic Studies Interim Conference, 1971 Report,"* vol. 1, Issue No. Conference Special (April 1971): 58–71; Carmen Chow, "I Wor Kuen: Righteous Harmonious Fist," *Gidra*, June 1971; and Virgo Lee, interview, New York City, 23 August 1985.

24. According to FBI memorandum on domestic pro-Chinese Communist organizations to E. S. Miller, 21 March 1973, I Wor Kuen, along with the Revolutionary Union, Venceremos Organization, Communist League, American Communist Workers Movement, and October League, was sufficiently "revolutionary" to be selected for investigation by the Committee on Internal Security, U.S. House of Representatives.

25. Chin, "New York Chinatown Today," p. 10.

26. Memorandum from Special Agent in Charge, New York City, to Director, FBI, 23 April 1970.

27. Chin, "New York Chinatown Today," p. 11.

28. Nakano, "Marxist-Leninist Organizing."

29. *New Dawn*, October 1971.

30. Unless otherwise noted, the discussion of the CPA is based on Wilma Chan, "Chinese Progressive Association: Looking Back on a Decade of Work, Looking Ahead to the Future," *Chinese Progressive Association: 10th Anniversary Book* (1982), pp. 19–22, and anonymous source G, San Francisco, 23 March 1986.

31. Harry Chen and Pam Tau, "From CPA's Co-Chairs," *Chinese Progressive Association: 10th Anniversary Book*, p. 18.

32. Confidential Memorandum from Special Agent in Charge, San Francisco to Acting Director, FBI, 21 June 1973, and Confidential Memorandum from Special Agent in Charge, San Francisco to Director, FBI, 29 August 1973.

33. Letter from anonymous source G to the author, 15 December 1990. Letter from Alex Hing to the author, 3 January 1991, raises the legitimate question: "Why does the fact that some CPA members also belong to IWK (or the League) make CPA a 'front' "? The answer is that membership alone does not, but IWK members' manipulation of CPA and its members for external political purposes does. Letter from Mae Ngai to the author, 8 January 1991, also raises an important question: "If individual members or leaders of community organizations are communists, does this make their contribution to the community, or the contributions of these organizations, less worthy?" Not at all. Regardless of political persuasion, a person or an organization that makes a contribution to the community should be commended. Conversely, a person or an organization that detracts from a community should be condemned.

34. According to the FBI, the Steering Committee members and major activists of the U.S.–China Friendship Association, San Francisco, were secret members of the Revolutionary Union. Confidential Memorandum from Special Agent in Charge, San Francisco, to Director, FBI, 29 August 1973.

35. Chan, "Chinese Progressive Association," p. 21.

36. "About the Author" in Jerry Tung, *The Socialist Road: Character of Revolution in the U.S. and Problems of Socialism in the Soviet Union and China* (New York: Csear Cauce Publishers & Distributors, 1981).

37. According to Yochi Shimatsu, interview, San Francisco, 28 March 1986, there was at least one instance in which Jerry Tung tried to commit suicide but was talked out of it by a close friend.

38. "Forged in Five-Years of Glorious Struggle, CWP Charges Forward to Break the Bourgeoisie," *Workers Viewpoint*, Supplement, 5 November 1979.

39. Nakano, "Marxist-Leninist Organizing."

40. Ibid.

41. For a discussion of the concept of revolutionary cadre core, see Tung, *The Socialist Road*, pp. 246–255.

42. Gitlin, *The Sixties*, p. 382, was referring to the Progressive Labor party, but his description seems to fit its descendant, the Workers Viewpoint Organization, as well.

43. Unless otherwise noted, the discussion of AAFEE is based on Doris Koo,

interview, New York City, 21 August 1985; Asian Americans for Equality, *Toward the Dream of Equality*, A Special Publication, 1986; and the following two newspaper clippings provided by Asian Americans for Equality (formerly Asian Americans for Equal Employment): Sybil Baker, "Seven Seized at Chinatown Site as 200 Charge Hiring Bias," *Daily News*, 1 June 1974; and Paul L. Montgomery, "Asians Picket Building Site, Charging Bias," *New York Times*, 1 June 1974. Also the following *East/West* articles: "N.Y. Chinese Demand Construction Jobs," 22 May 1974; David Tong, "Confucius Plaza: N.Y. Asians Continue to Demand Construction Jobs," 26 June 1974; "Confucius Plaza Struggle Reaps 24 Jobs for Chinese," August 14, 1974. According to Peter Kwong, *The New Chinatown* (New York: Hill and Wang, 1987), p. 164, in the mid-1970s, Workers Viewpoint Organization (WVO), which had evolved from the Asian Study Group, and I Wor Kuen realized that they had to "tone down their 'revolutionary' rhetoric" and to improve their relationship with the community, so they established community groups. WVO created Asian Americans for Equality to serve as a front organization.

44. *Towards the Dream of Equality*, p. 18.

45. "N.Y. Asians Continue Demands for Construction Jobs," *East/West*, 5 June 1974.

46. Paul L. Montgomery, "Asians Picket Building Site, Charging Bias," *New York Times*, 1 June 1974.

47. Tong, "N.Y. Asians Continue to Demand Construction Jobs."

48. Montgomery, "Asians Picket Building Site."

49. "Confucius Plaza Struggle Reaps 24 Jobs for Chinese."

50. Edmund Newton, "Chinatown Enters the Age of Protest," *New York Post*, 20 May 1975. The demonstrations against police brutality attracted the attention of the FBI's New York City office. See Teletype from Special Agent in Charge, New York Office, to Director, FBI: 17, 19, 20 May 1975, for detailed descriptions of AAFEE's role in these demonstrations.

51. Teletype from Special Agent in Charge, New York office, to Director, FBI, 19 May 1975.

52. Nakano, "Marxist–Leninist Organizing."

53. CADRA is also known as "Mun Yick Wui" (People's Benefit Association). Chen Kai-tai, "New York Groups Attack Each Other," *San Francisco Journal*, 6 June 1979.

54. Ted Liu, interview, New York City, 18 and 24 August 1985.

55. Chen, "New York Groups Attack Each Other." Threatening the press has been a recurring AAFE tactic. On two separate occasions, the Chinese Language Journalists Association has felt the need to rebuke AAFE for its treatment of reporters: in 1985, when Chinese reporters tried to question AAFE about its support of the scandal-ridden Golden Pacific National Bank, and in 1991, when they tried to cover former AAFE president Margaret Chin's campaign for the First Council District seat. According to "Statement by Chinese Language Journalists Association, Inc. Regarding Attempts to Hinder Coverage of First District City Council

Campaign," 29 August 1991, an official of Chin's campaign had threatened legal action and anonymous persons had made threatening phone calls.

56. Chen, "New York Groups Attack Each Other."

57. Editorial, "Internal Fighting—No Winners," *San Francisco Journal*, 6 June 1979.

58. "Forged in Five-Years of Glorious Struggle, CWP Charges Forward to Break the Bourgeosie." "Shootout in Greensboro," *Time*, 12 November 1979, notes that CWP had perhaps 200 members, most of them in Los Angeles and New York City. That figure seems much too high.

59. "The Old South," *Newsweek*, 12 November 1979; and "Shootout in Greensboro."

60. According to Margaret Chin, a CWP member and spokesperson, "the FBI hired paid assassins involved in the shooting." Fredric Dicker, "State-Funded Asian Group Led by Ex-Red," *New York Post*, 24 November 1986.

61. Harvey Klehr, "Comrades in the Takeover Wars," *Wall Street Journal*, 9 January 1986.

62. Ibid.

63. *Towards the Dream of Equality*, p. 21. For a review of AAFE's arguments challenging the Special Manhattan Bridge District, see Steve Dobkin et al., "Zoning for the General Welfare: A Constitutional Weapon for Lower-Income Tenants," *Review of Law and Social Change* 13, no. 4 (1984–1985).

64. See the State of New York Court of Appeals, no. 199 opinion, *Asian Americans for Equality et al.* v. *Edward Koch, Mayor of the City of New York, et al.* for the decision. The Special Manhattan Bridge District zoning variance was never passed because of the Asian American Legal Defense and Education Fund's successful suit, *Chinese Staff and Workers Association* v. *City of New York*, to block the construction of Henry Street Tower. According to Margaret Fung, telephone interview, 18 November 1991, AALDEF adopted a different strategy from AAFE and argued that the proposed rezoning would have an environmental impact under the State Environmental Quality Review Act by displacing low-income residents and businesses and changing the character of the neighborhood.

65. Klehr, "Comrades in the Takeover Wars."

66. Nees, *Longtime Californ'*, p. 28.

67. Chow, "I Wor Kuen in New York Chinatown," p. 66.

68. Virgo Lee, interview, New York City, 23 August 1985.

69. "Statement by East Wind on its Unity with the League," April 1979. Unless otherwise noted, the discussion of the Asian nation line is based on "Asian Nation," *Gidra*, October 1971; "Preliminary Draft on the Asian National Question in America: Part I. The Chinese National Question," July 1973; and "Revolution, the National Question and Asian Americans," speech presented by IWK at a forum on the National Question at the Asian Center in New York City (March 1974).

70. "Statement by East Wind on its Unity with the League" (April 1979).

71. "Preliminary Draft on the Asian National Question in America."

72. Ibid.

73. Anonymous, "Split" (n.p., n.d.).

74. Unless otherwise noted, the discussion of the ECASU split is based on Pat Eng, interview, New York City, 26 October 1986; Mary Li Hsu, interview, New York City, 28 October 1986; MidAtlantic ECASU, "Draft Sum-Up of ECASU Split," 16 March 1979; and the minutes of the following meetings: Intercollegiate Communications–Liaison Committee meetings on 9 July 1977, 24 September 1977, and 28 January 1978; ECASU Coordinating Committee meetings on 3 June 1978, 20 August 1978, 22 October 1978, and 9 December 1978; MidAtlantic Regional/ ECASU meetings on 1 July 1978, 22 July 1978, 27 August 1978, 30 September 1978, 25 February 1979, and 7 April 1979.

75. Ibid. In a 21 May 1981 letter to the MidAtlantic/ECASU, Virgo Lee, Chairman of the Progressive Chinatown People's Association, repudiated the allegations in the "Draft Sum-up of ECASU Split."

76. Lynn Yokoe, "ECASU: Strength Through Collective Action," *East Wind* 2, no. 2 (Fall/Winter 1983): 25–28.

77. Mary Li Hsu, interview, New York City, 28 October 1986.

78. Unless otherwise noted, the discussion on the League of Revolutionary Struggle is based on *Peace, Justice, Equality and Socialism: Program of the U.S. League of Revolutionary Struggle (Marxist–Leninist)* (Oakland: Getting Together Publications, 1984); and the following articles by Michael Friedly in the *Stanford Daily*: "Nationwide Organization Active Here, Students Say," 18 May 1990, "League Has Played Little-known Role in Campus Politics," 23 May 1990; and "League Recruitment Deterred Many," 30 May 1990. See also Daryl Joseffer, "The League of Revolutionary Struggle: A Self-Proclaimed Revolutionary Vanguard," *Stanford Review*, 12 February 1990.

79. *Peace, Justice, Equality*, p. 90.

80. Carlos Muñoz, Jr., *Youth, Identity, Power: The Chicano Movement* (London: Verso, 1989), pp. 6, 119, 185–186. According to MidAtlantic Regional/ ECASU meeting minutes, 25 February 1979, "the Asian Pacific Student Union (West Coast) is now controlled by I Wor Kuen (IWK) (a group affiliated with the PCPA) and has been kicking out people who didn't follow the IWK line."

81. Wilson Chen, Helen Choi, Robert Liu, Viet Nguyen, and Eileen Voon, interviews, Berkeley, 25 March 1990. According to anonymous source C, interview, 4 June 1985, the Asian Student Union was an IWK front organization in the late 1970s.

82. Letter from Wilson Chen to the author, 17 December 1990.

83. For example, some activists in the Chicano community at Stanford University recalled that league members who had attained leadership positions in MEChA would "physically encircle, verbally harass and generally intimidate students who opposed their political views." Those who questioned such tactics were called "disrupters," "community destroyers," and "sellouts." When meetings were held

to create an alternative Chicano organization, they were crashed. Miguel Canales et al., "League's Tactics Include Threats," *Stanford Daily*, 30 May 1990. Also see Delia Ibarra, "League's Tactics Have Damaged MEChA, Community," *Stanford Daily*, 29 May 1990. According to Juan Yniguez, "League Critics Have Endured Harassment by Peers," *Stanford Daily*, 7 June 1990. League opponents were subjected to degrading and menacing phone calls and had their places of work repeatedly vandalized; in one case, an opponent's four-year-old daughter encountered decapitated birds on her doorstep at home.

84. Daryl Joseffer, "Gordan Chang Connected to Maoist Cult," *Stanford Review* 4, no. 16 (12 February 1990) and Joseffer, "The League of Revolutionary Struggle."

85. Joseffer, "League of Revolutionary Struggle."

86. Letter from Michael Friedly to the author, 15 December 1990.

87. Unless otherwise noted, the discussion of the league's activity at Stanford University is based on the following articles by Friedly in the *Stanford Daily*: "Nationwide Organization Active Here," "League Has Played Little-Known Role," "League Recruitment Deterred Many," and "Administrators Had Hands-off Concern about League," 24 May 1990.

88. Michael Friedly, "Poster Attacks Alleged Political Ties of Chang," *Stanford Daily*, 18 May 1990. Also see his "Creator of Chang Flier Comes Forward in Letter," *Stanford Daily*, 25 May 1990; and Tom Terrell, "An Open Letter to the Stanford Community."

89. Judith A. Lyons, "Stanford Students Took Their Demands Straight to the President," *Asian Week*, 19 May 1989; and idem, "Asians among Students Arrested at Stanford," *Asian Week*, 9 June 1989.

90. Letter from Michael Friedly to the author, 15 December 1990. Also see Richard Suh, "League Information Given Out of Concern for Multiculturalism," *Stanford Daily*, 30 May 1990; and Friedly, "League Has Played Little-Known Role."

91. Stephen Ostrander, "League Members, Unwilling to Share Power, Malign Opponents," *Stanford Daily*, 7 June 1990.

92. Ibid.

93. Friedly, "League Has Played Little-Known Role." Also see Richard Suh, "League Information Was Given out of Concern for Multiculturalism," *Stanford Daily*, 30 May 1990.

94. Anonymous source D, telephone interview, 8 September 1990.

95. Michael Friedly, telephone interview, 20 September 1990. Apparently, the group seeking to create a new political organization is associated with *Unity* newspaper, which had earlier dissociated itself from the League.

96. "Statement on the Dissolution of the League of Revolutionary Struggle" (n.d.). Typewritten.

97. Editorial, "A Tragedy of Immense Proportions for the Chinese People,"

Unity, 6 June 1989. John Trinkl, "Left Condemns Chinese Massacre of Students," *The Guardian*, 21 June 1989, reports on the reaction of the American left community to the Tiananmen massacre.

98. Strong, "Where the Shining Path Leads," p. 12.

99. Fred Wei-han Ho, "Marxism and Asian Americans: Needed Now More than Ever!" (1992, typewritten). "A Call to Build an Organization for the 1990s and Beyond" (typewritten), provides the rationale for the establishment of a new organization.

Chapter 8: From Radical to Electoral Politics

1. See "Citizenship: *United States* v. *Wong Kim Ark*" section of Charles J. McClain and Laurene Wu McClain, "The Chinese Contribution to the Development of American Law," in *Entry Denied: Exclusion and the Chinese Community in America, 1882–1943*, ed. Sucheng Chan (Philadelphia: Temple University Press, 1991), pp. 3–24; and William L. Tung, *The Chinese in America, 1820–1973: A Chronology and Fact Book* (Dobbs Ferry, N.Y.: Oceana Publishers, 1974), pp. 104–105; for a discussion of the *Wong Kim Ark* case (1898), which affirmed the constitutional right of American citizenship to a person born on American soil.

2. Succinct summaries of the most important immigration acts as well as judicial decisions can be found in Hyung-chan Kim, ed., *Dictionary of Asian American History* (Westport, Conn.: Greenwood Press, 1986).

3. Susan C. Lee, "Your Vote Is Essential," *Asian Week*, 24 October 1986.

4. For example, Alexander Saxton, *The Indispensable Enemy: Labor and the Anti-Chinese Movement in California* (Berkeley: University of California Press, 1971), analyzes how the Democratic party in California was able to rehabilitate itself during the post–Civil War period by exploiting anti-Chinese sentiment. After the Democrats swept California in the election of 1867, they made the "Chinese Question" a national issue. And as John Higham, *Strangers in the Land: Patterns of American Nativism, 1860–1825* (New York: Atheneum, 1974), has noted, the Republican party was the "main vehicle for restriction sentiment" (p. 98), which ultimately led to the 1924 Immigration Act and the prohibition of Japanese immigration.

5. Yung-hwan Jo, ed., *Political Participation of Asian Americans: Problems and Strategies* (Chicago: Pacific/Asian American Mental Health Research Center, 1980); and Alfred H. Song, "Politics and Policies of the Oriental Community," in *California Politics and Policies*, ed. Eugene P. Dvorin and Arthur J. Misner (Reading, Mass.: Addison-Wesley, 1966), pp. 386–411; both discuss various aspects of Asian American political participation.

6. Bruce E. Cain and D. Roderick Kiewiet, *Minorities in California* (Pasadena:

Division of Humanities and Social Sciences, California Institute of Technology, 1986), p. I-22 and table I-4, p. I-34.

7. Julie Lew, "Asian Americans More Willingly Stuff Campaign Warchests Than Ballot Boxes," *East/West*, 27 August 1987; and Judy Tachibana, "California's Asians: Power from a Growing Population," *California Journal*, November 1986, 535–543.

8. David Takami, comp., "National News," *International Examiner*, 4 November 1987.

9. Tachibana, "California's Asians"; and Lew, "Asian Americans More Willingly Stuff Campaign Warchests Than Ballot Boxes."

10. Campaign letter from Bill Chong, National Asian American Coordinator, Jesse Jackson for President Committee, to supporters, 12 January 1984.

11. David Takami, "Can Asian Americans Influence the Election?" *AsiAm*, January 1988, pp. 23–26, 45.

12. Scott Armstrong and John Dillin, "Ethnic Votes Are Vital in California Primary," *Christian Science Monitor*, 24 May 1988.

13. William Wong, "Asian Americans and Political Power," *East/West*, 3 September 1987.

14. Cain and Kiewiet, *Minorities in California*, p. I-21.

15. Don T. Nakanishi, "Low Registration, Independence Weaken Asian Pacific Vote," *Public Affairs Report* 32, no. 5 (September 1991).

16. Ibid.

17. Jane Gross, "Diversity Hinders Asians' Influence," *New York Times*, 25 June 1989.

18. Ibid.

19. Interim Coordinating Committee for Chinese Americans, "The Chinese American Declaration Concerning the 1988 Presidential Election" (n.p., n.d.). Tan Shih-ying, interview, Monterey, California, 27 June 1988. One of the positions that the ICCCA requested be filled by a Chinese American was a seat on the Civil Rights Commission. During the Republican National Convention, the White House announced the appointment of Sherwin T. Chan, an aerospace engineer and active Republican, to this post. His appointment was not met with universal approval. William Wong, "Is Sherwin T. Chan Up to the Task of U.S. Civil Rights Commissioner?" *East/West*, 1 September 1988.

20. "ICCCA Reminds Bush of Appointment Vow," *Asian Week*, 16 December 1988. Other Asian American groups had also lobbied Bush for high-level appointments. Grace Wai-Tse Siao, "Asian Voter Group Pressures Bush for High Appointments," *Asian Week*, 16 December 1988.

21. John Ota, "Asian American Political Clout: A Look at the Defeat of Redress Foe Rep. Dan Lungren," *East Wind* 7, no. 1 (Spring/Summer 1989): 4–6; Laird Harrison, "Statewide Asian Coalition Decries Lungren Appointment," *Asian Week*, 25 December 1987; William Wong, "A New Statewide Role for Asian Ameri-

cans," *East/West*, 21 January 1988; "Lungren Defeat Signifies Political Maturation of Asian Americans," *East/West*, 30 June 1988.

22. Unless otherwise noted, the discussion of the redress and reparations movement is based on Rockwell Chin with Sasha Hohri, Bill and Yuri Kochiyama, Marsha Tajima, and Eddie Wong, "The Long Road: Japanese Americans Move on Redress," *Bridge*, Winter 1981–1982, pp. 11–16; Brian T. Niiya, "Redress and Reparations: The New Movement," a paper presented to Dr. Rick Tsujimoto, May 1982; and William Minoru Hohri, *Repairing America: An Account of the Movement for Japanese-American Redress* (Pullman: Washington State University Press, 1988).

23. Hohri, *Repairing America*, p. 34.

24. John Tateishi, "The Japanese American Citizens League and the Struggle for Redress," in *Japanese Americans: From Relocation to Redress*, ed. Roger Daniels et al. (Salt Lake City: University of Utah Press, 1986), p. 194. Also see the Commission on the Wartime Relocation and Internment of Civilians, *Personal Justice Denied: Report of the Commission on the Wartime Relocation and Internment of Civilians* (Washington, D.C.: Government Printing Office, 1982).

25. Ronald J. Ostrow, "Thornburgh Kneels to Apologize to Those Interned in WWII," *Daily Camera*, 10 October 1990.

26. Paul Pringle, "Los Angeles Asians Seeking Political Clout," *Dallas Morning News*, 11 June 1987.

27. Cain and Kiewiet, *Minorities in California*; Don T. Nakanishi, "The UCLA Asian Pacific American Voter Registration Study," Asian Pacific Legal Center, 1986; Tachibana, "California's Asians"; Grant Din, "An Analysis of Asian/Pacific American Registration and Voting Patterns in San Francisco," Master's thesis, Claremont College, 1984; Patrick Andersen, "Nearly One-Third of S.F. Chinese Voters Uncommitted," *Asian Week*, 20 September 1985; all indicate that Asian Americans in California (and perhaps the nation) do not represent a solid bloc of voters for either the Democrats or Republicans. First, Asian Americans have relatively weak party loyalties and tend to engage in crossover voting; second, a large number of Asian Americans expressed no party preference.

28. Letter from Jimmy Carter to *Bridge* magazine, 23 September 1976, *Bridge* 4, no. 5 (November 1976): 12.

29. Comments on the Asian/Pacific American Unit are based on C. N. Lee, "A View from the Campaign Headquarters," *Bridge* 4, no. 5 (November 1976): 18–21; and Robin Wu, "Profile: Joji Konoshima, Asian Americans in the Democratic National Committee," *Bridge* 6, no. 1 (Spring 1978): 61–63. The Republican party did not have anything comparable to the A/PA Unit working in its campaign. Apparently, the Republicans tried to form a similar unit but were too late. What they did have was the Heritage Group, which was conceived by Richard Nixon in 1968 to recognize small minority groups. In 1976, the Heritage Group had thirty minority organizations, including the Chinese American National Federation.

30. "First National Convention of the National Democratic Council of Asian Pacific Americans," *Asian Week*, 16 October 1987.

31. Mark J. Jue, "Caucus Warns Demo Party Leaders to Pay Heed to Asian Pacific Issues," *East/West*, 18 July 1984.

32. Bob Kiyota et al., "Proposed National Strategy, Asian Pacific Caucus of the Democratic National Committee, 1985–1988," study commissioned by the Democratic National Committee—Asian Pacific Caucus, 25 January 1985. Typewritten.

33. "Chennault Tells OCA of Frustrations in Dallas," *Asian Week*, 31 August 1984.

34. Ernestine Tayabas, "Demo Drops Asian Caucus," *East/West*, 22 May 1985.

35. "Asians Appointed to DNC; Caucus Status in Doubt," *Pacific Citizen*, 12 July 1985.

36. "First National Convention of the National Democratic Council of Asian Pacific Americans."

37. "Major Political Figures Attend Asian Demo Conference in LA," *East/West*, 22 October 1987.

38. Grande Lum, "Jesse Jackson to Asian Americans: Empower Yourselves!" *East/West*, 2 June 1988.

39. Morton M. Kondracke, "Jesse's World: President Jackson's Foreign Policy," *New Republic*, 25 April 1988, pp. 11, 12, and 14. Barbara Ehrenreich, "Why I Back Jackson," *New Republic*, 21 March 1988, pp. 16–19, discusses Jackson's domestic agenda.

40. New York Asians for Jesse Jackson, "Jackson Visits Chinatown/Asian Network Coordinator Addresses Harlem Rally." News release. This was in marked contrast with the earlier Carter campaign, when vice-presidential candidate Walter Mondale visited New York's Chinatown only after the Asian Pacific/American Unit asked that he do so after his scheduled visit to the Italian Festival in nearby Little Italy. Lee, "A View from the Campaign Headquarters."

41. Jesse Jackson, "The Rainbow Coalition: An End to Racial Division," *East Wind* 3, no. 1 (Spring/Summer 1984): 21–22.

42. "Jesse Jackson's Speech to Democratic Convention," *Congressional Quarterly Weekly Report* 42, no. 29 (21 July 1984): 1785–1789.

43. Lum, "Jesse Jackson to Asian Americans."

44. Ibid.

45. Ibid.

46. William Wong, "Jesse Jackson and the Campaign That Sizzles in the Asian American Community," *East/West*, 14 April 1988.

47. "Jesse Jackson's Speech to Democratic Convention."

48. Rob Gurwitt and Nadine Cohodas, "Hispanic-Asian Boycott: A Gesture Fizzles," *Congressional Quarterly Weekly Report* 42, no. 29 (21 July 1984): 1733.

49. Editorial, "For Jesse Jackson and His Campaign," *The Nation* 246, no. 15 (16 April 1988): 517, 519.

50. "Butch" Wing, interview, San Francisco, 25 March 1986.

51. Everett C. Ladd, "Political Paradox of Jesse Jackson: Public Calls Him a Front-Runner but Says He's Unelectable," *Christian Science Monitor*, 21 December 1987.

52. For example, in 1984, Mike Murase was deputy field coordinator and Asian American coordinator (California); Irene Hirano served on the California steering committee; "Butch" Wing and Ying Lee Kelley were vice-chairs of the Northern California Jackson for President committee; and May Joan Louie was the Massachusetts constitutency coordinator. Ranko Yamada, "After Reagan's Storm Comes the Rainbow," *East Wind* 3, no. 1 (Spring/Summer 1984): 18–20. Many of them would return to work for Jackson in 1988. Mike Murase was his California campaign director, May Louie was his New England campaign director, and "Butch" Wing was his Northern California field coordinator. Laird Harrison, "Democratic Presidential Candidates: Jackson Articulates Strongest Positions on Asian Issues," *Asian Week*, 25 March 1988. Mabel Teng served as his special adviser. Laird Harrison, "Mabel Teng Rises to the Top with Jackson Campaign," *Asian Week*, 17 June 1988.

53. Lum, "Jesse Jackson to Asian Americans: Empower Yourselves!" and Jerry Adler and Sylvester Monroe, "Jackson's White Organizers," *Newsweek*, February 8, 1988.

54. Michael Oreskes, "Jackson Campaign, Up from Chaos, Gets the Most Out of Fewest Dollars," *New York Times*, 27 March 1988.

55. Ibid.

56. As an astute politician, Jesse Jackson was probably aware of the rivalry between AAFE and CPA, but allowed it to persist as long as it did not adversely affect his campaign. Perhaps he thought that his leadership was sufficient to keep the two groups, as well as the other factions in his campaign, in line.

57. Linda Peng, interview, New York City, 15 and 20 August 1985.

58. Sasha [Hohri], Letter from the New York Asians for Jesse Jackson to Supporters and Friends, 22 May 1984.

59. Kondracke, "Jesse's World." For example, Eqbal Ahmad, an Asian Indian who had contributed to the 1984 "Briefing and Recommendations for an Asian Pacific American Platform for the Rev. Jesse Jackson" was a member of the Institute for Policy Studies.

60. Eddie Wong, "Asian Empowerment and Jackson: Moving from the Background to the Political Foreground," *East Wind* 7, no. 1 (Spring/Summer 1989): 7–11.

61. Sasha Hohri and Penny Fujiko Willgerodt, "Asian Delegates Assess Post-Convention Future," *East/West*, 28 July 1988.

62. Judith A. Lyons, "Census Bill Passes Senate," *Asian Week*, 21 October 1988.

63. Serena Chen, "Matsui Charges 1990 Census Shortchanges Asians," *East/West*, 17 March 1988.

64. Unless otherwise noted, comments on Michael Woo are based on A. G. Block, "Politicians on the Rise," *California Journal*, November 1987, pp. 534–542; Tachibana, "California's Asians"; John Takasugi, "L.A. Councilman, Michael K. Woo," *AsiAm*, April 1987, pp. 12–15, 51, 54, 62; J. Derek Nakashima, "The New Leaders," *AsiAm*, January 1987, pp. 38–43; and Michael Woo, "Biographical Information," August 1987, provided by Bill Chandler, press deputy.

65. Takasugi, "L.A. Councilman, Michael K. Woo."

66. Block, "Politicians on the Rise."

67. Ibid.

68. Max Millard, "Asians Rally Behind Mike Woo at City Hall Press Conference," *East/West*, 10 July 1986.

69. Ibid.

70. Ibid.

71. J. K. Yamamoto, "Woo to Run in New Council District," *Pacific Citizen*, 1 August 1986.

72. John Horn, " 'Dragon' to Get a Disclaimer," *Los Angeles Times*, 30 August 1985.

73. Block, "Politicians on the Rise."

74. Unless otherwise noted, comments on Furutani are based on Warren Furutani, interview, Los Angeles, 28 June 1988. Since Furutani was a well-known community activist and speaker, he was much sought after by Marxist–Leninist organizations. When he refused to align himself with either the League of Revolutionary Struggle or the Communist Workers party, he was branded an "individualist," which in the Marxist lexicon is a politically suspect person.

75. J. K. Yamamoto, "Incumbent Tries to Tie Furutani with Scandal," *Pacific Citizen*, 3 April 1987.

76. J. K. Yamamoto, "Furutani Wins in Close School Board Race," *Pacific Citizen*, 24 April 1987.

77. William Wong's column, *Asian Week*, 28 June 1991.

78. Keiko Ohnuma, "Minorities Win a Few at S.F. Community College," *Asian Week*, 14 June 1991.

79. Unless otherwise noted, comments on Judy Chu are based on Judy Chu, interview, Monterey Park, 25 June 1988, and press statement of Judy Chu, candidate, Monterey Park City Council, 4 January 1988.

80. Mike Ward, "Asian Voter Poll Shows Chinese Tilting to GOP," *Los Angeles Times*, 28 July 1988; and Stewart Kwoh, "How Do Asian Pacific Americans Vote?" *Rice*, October 1988, p. 57.

81. Karen Lew, "Chu Elected in Monterey Park," *Asian Week*, 15 April 1988.

82. Edward Cheng, "Councilwoman Judy Chu Draws Ire of the Chinese American Community," *Asian Week*, 2 August 1991; and Howard Hong, "Chinese Split Signals Power Play in Monterey Park," *Asian Week*, 2 August 1991.

83. Frank R. Parker, "Changing Standards in Voting Rights Law," in *Redistrict-*

ing in the 1990s: A Guide for Minority Groups, ed. William P. O'Hare (Washington, D.C.: Population Reference Bureau, 1989), p. 60.

84. Alvina Lew, "Chinese, Koreans, Filipinos, Join Against Remap Plan," *Asian Week*, 22 August 1986; "Concerns about Asian Representation," *Pacific Citizen*, 16 May 1986; Grace Wai-Tse Siao, "L.A. Asians Warned Against Gerrymandering in Reapportionment," *Asian Week*, 26 October 1990; and Tania Azores and Paul M. Ong, "Reapportionment and Redistricting in a Nutshell," Public Policy Project, Asian American Studies Center, University of California, Los Angeles, 1991.

85. Asian American Legal Defense and Education Fund, "Asian American on City Council in 1991?" *Outlook*, Winter 1991.

86. Ibid.

87. Keiko Ohnuma, "Expert Says State Not Likely to Get Asian-Majority District in 1991 Remap," *Asian Week*, 14 December 1990.

88. Felicia R. Lee, "Coalition That Backed Dinkins Is Pressing for Council Seats," *New York Times*, 3 June 1991.

89. Felicia R. Lee, "Minority Blocs Claim a Chinatown Seat," *New York Times*, 30 April 1991; and Keiko Ohnuma, "Asian Camps Split on District Lines for Lower Manhattan," *Asian Week*, 26 April 1991.

90. Ohnuma, "Asian Camps Split." Antonio Pagan, an executive committee member of the Puerto Rican–Hispanic Political Council, implicitly supported this contention: "The Multiracial distrcit proposal would force Latinos and Asians to fight for a single council seat." Letter to the Editor, *New York Times*, 2 May 1991.

91. Ohnuma, "Asian Camps Split."

92. Valerie Chow Bush, "Division Street," *Village Voice*, 23 July 1991.

93. Ibid.

94. Ibid.

95. James C. McKinley, Jr., "Money Talked in Race but So Did Volunteers," *New York Times*, 15 September 1991. According to Lucette Lagnado, "Friends in High Places: Margaret Chin's Ties to the Chinatown Elite," *Village Voice*, 17 September 1991, part of Chin's financial support comes from the most conservative business interests in Chinatown.

96. Ibid.

97. Sheila Muto, "Two Asians Lose in NYC Demo Primary," *Asian Week*, 20 September 1991.

98. Not only did Chin lose the November election, she failed "to win even the majority of Chinatown voters, who supported Republican candidate Fred Teng by a narrow margin." Letter from Margaret Fung to the author, 13 November 1991. Also see Jere Hester, "Freed Romps," *Downtown Express*, 11 November 1991, for an analysis of the election.

99. Muto, "Two Asians Lose"; and Kevin Sack, "New Coalition, Organized to Support Insurgents, Is Divided as Council Race Nears," *New York Times*, 10 September 1991.

100. Editorial, "For City Council from Manhattan," *New York Times*, 6 September 1991.

101. This is a paraphrase of William Wong's observation that "Asian American involvement in American politics is a slowly evolving but inexorable trend." William Wong's column, *Asian Week*, 2 November 1990.

Index